CHINESE BUDDHISM

Copyright © 2008 BiblioBazaar
All rights reserved

Original copyright: 1893

Joseph Edkins
Author of "Religion in China,"
"Introduction to the Study of the Chinese Characters,"
"A Mandarin Grammar," etc.

CHINESE BUDDHISM

A Volume of Sketches,
HISTORICAL, DESCRIPTIVE,
AND CRITICAL.

BIBLIOBAZAAR

CHINESE BUDDHISM

PREFACE TO SECOND EDITION.

THE number of Buddhists in the world has been much exaggerated. Formerly it was stated to be four hundred millions; and this incredibly large estimate led to careful consideration. Dr. Happer, resident for more than forty years in Canton, thinks that in China the tonsured Buddhist priests are twenty millions in number, and he declines to allow that the rest of the Chinese can be rightly called Buddhists. Dr. Gordon, of Japan, a good authority who has carefully studied Japanese Buddhism, considers that it would not be fair to represent only the tonsured Buddhists as followers of the Buddhist religion in Japan; yet it is a fact that few of the laity in China and Japan make and keep Buddhist vows. The same is true of Tauism. The most of the population of China claim to be Confucianists, and conform occasionally to Buddhist and Tauist ceremonies. The rich Chinaman calls himself a Confucianist, and therefore he must count as such. But he subscribes to the rebuilding of Buddhist temples and pagodas, because he thinks the act will bring him prosperity. He worships Tauist idols more than those in Buddhist temples; but he adores the Buddhist images also on certain occasions. He conforms to three religions, but on the whole he is made by ancestral worship properly speaking a Confucianist. His religious faith is a sad jumble of inconsistent dogmas. As to becoming a tonsured priest, he never thinks of it, unless he grows weary of the world and aspires to monastic life as a relief from social cares and domestic sorrow. Let us include lay Buddhists who keep their vows at home, and rate the whole number of those Chinese who take Buddhist vows, monastic or lay, at forty millions. The Tauists may be roughly estimated at fifteen millions, and the Confucianists at 320 millions. It is ancestral worship that gives the Confucianists so large a preponderance.

The schoolmasters are all Confucianists. None of the books used in education are Buddhist or Tauist. Of newly published works, ten per cent. may be Buddhist and ten per cent. Tauist. These include exhortations to virtue, and treatises urging to charity. There is no demand for Buddhist or Tauist books. Eighty per cent. of all books newly published count as Confucianist, or as belonging to general literature. Booksellers, as a rule, keep no Buddhist or Tauist books. On the whole, it seems better to allow the Chinese claim, and class 320 millions of them as Confucianists. To go to school is to become a Confucianist, and even those who have no book-learning worship their ancestors.

Yet Buddhism is powerful in China by its doctrines. It has made the Chinese idolaters, and besides this it has taught them the wind and water superstition which has proved to be an effective barrier against civilised improvements and a most thorough hindrance to true enlightenment. For these two reasons, after all that can be said, still it is a Buddhist country, and the people are idolaters and the victims of Hindoo superstition. The art too is Buddhist. The favourite subjects of artists are Buddhist or Tauist. Here the ascetic element prevails, and that familiarity with nature which marks the true Buddhist. The lion, a Persian animal, is the symbol of victory, and is a common ornament in temples as symbolical of Buddha's success in argument. The lotus also is symbolical of Buddha's appearance as saviour. He rises suddenly from the sea of misery, an object of beauty to thousands who are rescued by his powerful teaching from their hopeless delusions. The lovely flower, the *padme*, is an indispensable ornament to Buddha's throne. Buddhism taught the Chinese and Japanese artists to paint animal and vegetable forms and carve them in temples. Through this medium ideas of Assyrian and Greek art found their way to these Eastern races, and elevated them. Buddhism, by introducing to China notions of Western art, has conferred a positive benefit, and she has also inspired multitudes with a sort of hope of deliverance from suffering. Since the first edition of this book was published, several thousands belonging to

Buddhist and Tauist sects in North China, having already an undefined longing for redemption stirring within them through Buddhist teaching, have found that redemption in the doctrines of the Bible and accepted the Christian faith. Buddhism alone could only awaken aspirations after belief. Christianity coming after it satisfies those aspirations.

The Karma and the twelve *Nidanas* or causes unveil to view the chain of a twelve-fold necessity which controls human life, an impersonal fate made up of causes and inevitable effects. This idea of destiny is suggested by events such as sudden death, sickness, and old age. In Isa. lxv. 12 (revised version) human destiny is said to be in the hands of the goddess Meni, as the Babylonians thought. But Meni means the "divider." The Greeks believed in the three Moirai, the Fates or the Dividers. The idea of destiny in Babylon and Greece preceded the fact of personifying. So was it in Buddhism. First the twelve causes were taught under the control of Karma; afterwards, in Northern Buddhism, Yama, god of death, divided out, as it was said, human destiny and fixed the hour of death for every one. Since it is not a Vedic doctrine, this belief in an impersonal destiny is Babylonian, and is astrological, but the keen Indian intellect separated the astrological element from it carefully and made it purely metaphysical. There are five causes at work—existence, grasping firmly, love, activity, ignorance. There are seven consequences—bodily decay, birth, sensation, touch, the senses, colour, consciousness. Buddhist logic not believing in the outer world is here seen busying itself with the senses and the sensations which are the constituent elements of our phenomenal life. This is destiny stated in the language of Hindoo metaphysics, and when it proceeds to detail, all we can take hold of is our sensations, our consciousness, our emotions, and our activity. It would certainly be clearer if put in the language of Cousin or of Sir William Hamilton. It is truly a misfortune for the Buddhists that they have not had their philosophical dogmas expounded as our Western philosophers would expound them. In describing our environment Buddhism is pessimistic. Nothing could be worse than our delusions and our condition. In promising a cure, Buddhism adopts a most triumphant tone. Buddha discovered the remedy, and God had nothing to do with it. It is in every man's power to save himself. In this system the assertion that an impersonal fate, morally retributive, rules all men's destiny, and is the basis of the metempsychosis, is Babylonian. The transmigration of souls is foreign, and the moral basis of necessary law on which it rests is, in fact, both native and foreign. Buddha found his countrymen believing in the new doctrine of transmigration, and he himself believed it and shaped it into the twelve causes and effects. He did not resist or deny the Mesopotamian fate. He gave it logical form, and undertook to set men free from it by treating it as a delusion.

Science and philosophy on arriving in India originated science and philosophy in that country under new forms. Buddhism forsook the Veda religion so far as to omit all mention of the gods Varuna, Agni, and the Maruts. Buddha did not cite the Vedas as authorities. He built his system on the ideas he found current in Central India. For himself, he claimed to have discovered the highest truth. The cause of his atheism was the polytheism of the time. Its extreme anthropomorphism provoked a reaction in his mind against the idea of deity. The gods, thought he, are unequal to the task of saving men from delusion. There is a wisdom that can do it, and I have discovered it. To this confidence in his own insight he was led in part by the national love for argument, and for that variety of illustration in conducting argument which the collision between foreign and native thought had awakened. To this was to be added the effect of lonely meditation. The youthful thinker was thrown on his own resources in his chosen retirement. Shutting off all avenues by which other thoughts than his own could reach him, he waited for light till it came. He had a compassionate heart, and thus his natural disposition found its way into his system and marked his whole life-work as a national teacher. It is this enthusiastic sympathy for humanity which drew to him so many millions of adherents. That this is the real explanation of Buddhism as a phenomenon in the history of mankind, can be shown in many ways.

Southern Buddhism is in its development of thought very decidedly more Hindoo than Northern Buddhism. The impact from Western philosophy produced a slighter effect in Southern India, communication being entirely by sea. Northern Buddhism branched out in a striking manner from the old root of Buddhist ideas, and the cause should be sought in its close conflict with Persian and Babylonian thought. The Persians, when they came down from the north, charged with Aryan conceptions and beliefs, to conquer their country, were powerfully influenced by Babylonian civilisation. The Zoroastrian religion was the result. They became earnest believers in their new faith, and this access of national zeal reacted on the Buddhists in North-Western India. A characteristically new, original, and popular modification of Buddhist thinking was soon produced.

Amitabha, the Buddha who leads to the paradise of the west, is a new Ormuzd, god of light, believed in by the Persians as the supreme deity, and promising his followers eternal joy in the paradise where he dwells. Buddhism, when it proclaimed general scepticism, opened the way for free speculation. The Buddhists found the Persians as earnest as themselves, and they incorporated the Persian view of a supreme god and a future life of happiness in their own system. Buddhism, by adopting the principle of contemplation and inward light, became mystical. The Paradise of the Western heaven was evolved by Northern Buddhists in hours of contemplation. The new teaching soon attained a widespread popularity. Continued studies in ancient Chinese philosophy have convinced me that the three religions of the Chinese have all been greatly influenced by Persian ideas. First, the ancient Chinese learned dualism from Persia, and adopted it in the Book of Changes. They also adopted the worship of the sun and stars with astrology. Then they accepted the belief in a future life in early Tauism. Finally, Buddhism brought them a later form of the future life as developed in the worship of Amitabha. Mr. De Groot, in his comprehensive work on the religion of the Chinese, agrees with me in these views, and conversation with him in China led me to expand them still more. Tibetan Buddhism lays great stress on astrology, and by so doing points plainly to Babylon.

The same is true of the Hindoos. Their cosmogonies are Babylonian. Their triad of gods, Brahma, Vishnu, and Siva, is based on a Babylonian model, just as the Chaldean triad of the higher gods is derived from the Accadian. Hindu sculpture is based on that of Greece. Hindoo arithmetic is Babylonian in origin. Babylonian thought was adopted by the Hindoos, because it was more refined and profound than their own. In the history of philosophy it is as true in Asia as in Europe that every new philosophy rests on its predecessors. The origin of each new philosophy can only be satisfactorily explained when attention has been adequately given to those systems of thought which, by their influence, tended to produce it.

Chinese Buddhism is Northern Buddhism, and it can only be suitably accounted for in this way. How necessary it is to make plain from what source the variations found in Northern Buddhism from the primitive standard have sprung, is clear from what one of my critics, Dr. Rhys Davids, has stated. In the *Academy* of October 2, 1880, he says that to speak of Buddha as "entering into Nirvana" is an expression which absolutely contradicts the doctrines of the early Buddhists. My author says there are three Nirvanas—1, a pure nature, that of heretics; 2, purity gained by practising the methods of the greater or lesser vehicle; 3, the purity of Buddha's death. This I take from *Kiau chêng fa shu*, one of my best Chinese authorities. The reason is in the change which came over Buddhism through contact with Persia. Dr. Rhys Davids also assumes that the Chinese have only one date for Buddha's birth. I have carefully pointed out that they have at least two, one among them being B.C. 623, given in the Imperial dynastic histories. In fact, Northern Buddhism is undervalued by Pali scholars. It has gone through the purifying process of a thousand fights with Brahmins and other sects in India, with Parsees, Manichæans, and Christians abroad, and with Confucianists in China. The Chinese author thinks much of style, and possesses an immense répertoire of elegant phrases. The original Sanskrit is changed into these phrases, and comes to mean something much nearer to men's business and bosoms, and more polished in expression, than it did in the Indian form. The Chinese translator accepts no new idioms which can be avoided. Foreign lingo must be modified to suit Confucianist taste. It would be well if Dr. Rhys Davids would allow for the influence on Northern Buddhism of foreign systems of thought, and also take into consideration the qualities of the Chinese translators. He says Brahmajala does not mean "net of Brahma." The Chinese author says it does. I prefer to follow my authority, and leave my critic to prove that he is wrong. When the Sanskrit bears two or three meanings, the Chinese translator sometimes gives them all, wishing to get all he can out of his text. Dr. Rhys Davids, on the contrary, selects one and denies the others. He also expects me to follow the Pali as translated by Gogerly, vouched for by Dr. Rhys Davids himself as accurate. I think, however, it is better for me to follow my Chinese guides. Native Buddhist works by Chinese are, I believe, more entertaining and interesting than those written in Pali by Hindoos. In saying this, I fear I shall not get Dr. Rhys Davids to agree with me. But however this may be, what I give is taken from Chinese authorities, except where European writers are cited expressly. I began studying Chinese Buddhism more than forty years ago. Dr. Eitel, Rev. Samuel Beal, and Mr. Consul Watters followed me, and have done well. Before they began publishing, I had already pointed out that the Chinese Buddhist schools of authorship all spread to Japan many centuries ago, and were firmly planted in that country. It is surely worth the earnest thought of Pali students that Buddhism was developed powerfully in North-Western India under Persian and Christian influence so far as to allow of the teaching of a future life, and to treat the Nirvana practically as a euphemism for death. In this state Buddhism entered China. No sooner had it arrived than controversy commenced on immortality. The Chinese Buddhists contended vigorously for the immortality of the soul against the followers of Confucius. Pali Buddhism, if it had been propagated in China, would not, probably, have originated such a controversy. It was the Northern doctrines invigorated by faith in the immortality of the soul which gave Chinese Buddhism sufficient energy to found new schools.

JOSEPH EDKINS.

PREFACE.

WHEN the first Hindoo missionaries arrived at the capital of China and were admitted to see the emperor, it was, the Buddhists tell us, in the last month of the year A.D. 68, and the 30th day of that month. By imperial command they were entertained in a building called *Pe-ma sï*, "Office of the white horses;" so named because they had ridden on white horses on their way from Cabul. The two Brahmans enjoyed the imperial favour, and one of the books they translated has remained popular to the present time.

Thirteen years before these men reached China, the first missionaries of Christianity crossed the Ægean Sea and entered Europe. Instead of being received, however, with the smiles of those in power and enjoying imperial hospitality, they were publicly whipped and imprisoned by the magistrates of a Roman colony, and ignominiously dismissed.

Buddhism covered China with monasteries and images; Christianity covered Europe with churches and charitable institutions. A hundred authors have written on the history of the spread of Christianity in the various countries of Europe. Very few have ever studied the history of Buddhism as it has spread through China, and taught its doctrines in every part of that empire. There is room for new information on the entrance, progress, and characteristics of Chinese belief in the religion founded by Shakyamuni.

Especially is there a need for facts on the history of Buddhism, because it is that one among the world's religions which has acquired the greatest multitude of adherents, and has also above any other carried out most systematically the monastic institute.

Isaac Taylor drew attention in his *Ancient Christianity* to the knowledge of Hindoo monasticism possessed by Clement of Alexandria, and traced the origin of the monasticism of Christianity to that of India.

Buddhism never became the State religion of China. It has grown side by side with the State religion, and obtained only the partial faith of the people. In this it differed from Christianity, which in Europe took the place of the old State religions of the various countries, after first vanquishing them all.

One of the titles of Buddha is "the Lion;" another is "the Great hero;" another is "Honoured one of the world;" another is "King of the Law." His followers love to represent him as completely victorious over metaphysical opponents by argument, and as gaining a thorough and final conquest over temptation impersonated by demons. He is also spoken of as victorious in saving from their unbelief all sorts of heretics, of men sunk in pleasure, and every class of adversaries. He has infinite pity, as well as infinite wisdom.

Such is the ideal of Buddha. Let it be compared with that of the Christian Saviour. Let the result of the teaching of Shakyamuni on the Chinese be compared with that of the teaching of Christ on Europe. Is China as much better for Buddhism as Europe is for Christianity? If the beginnings of the world's religions are very interesting and important subjects of inquiry, their progress and development are not less so. The various causes which operated to aid the spread of Buddhism, if carefully investigated, will be a valuable contribution to the history of humanity. Koeppen has said that, at the time of Alexander's conquests, while there was a tendency imparted by him to the races he conquered, which led to the breaking up of a restrictive nationalism, and to the welding of various peoples, formerly separated by blood, customs, religions, and culture, into a higher unity in the consciousness of a common humanity, so also India was, by the propagators of Buddhism, putting forth vigorous efforts in the same cause. Alexander sought to make all mankind one. So did Buddhism. The Greek spirit and the spirit of Buddhism sympathised with each other and helped each other. In this way he finds an explanation of the rapid spread of the Buddhist religion in the Punjab, Afghanistan, Bactria, and the countries near. He then proceeds to compare Buddhism with Christianity, which he speaks of as cosmopolitan Judaism to which had been added Alexandrian and Essene elements. Just as Christianity conquered the Western world, so Buddhism the Eastern; and this it was able to do because it rejected caste and taught the brotherhood of humanity.

It must ever be regarded as a noble instinct of the Hindoo race, which prompted them to throw off the yoke of caste. But it should not be supposed that the yoke of caste was so strong then as it now is. It was easier then than now for a Hindoo to visit foreign countries. The social tyranny of caste was then less powerful.

What gave the first Buddhists their popularity? In part, doubtless, the doctrine of the common brotherhood of men; but there were several other principles in their teaching which rapidly won adherents, and must also be taken into account.

They taught the universal misery of man, and offered a remedy. They met the yearning of humanity for a redemption by giving instruction, which they said came from the Buddhas and Bodhisattwas, each of whom was a powerful saviour to the devotee.

These saviours, instead of being members of the Hindoo hierarchy of popular gods, like those of Olympus, were either human beings or incarnations of ideas, and combining wisdom with mercy in their acts and teaching.

The early Buddhists surrounded death with a halo of lofty spiritual glory, and called it the Nirvâna. Death became synonymous with absolute peace, and so was looked on with less dread and dislike.

When the Buddhists began to teach races to whom the subtle Hindoo metaphysics were a riddle beyond their comprehension, they taught, for the Nirvâna, a Western Heaven ruled by a newly-invented Buddha, and additional to the paradises of the Devas. This is a new doctrine of a future life which is commonly accepted by the Northern Buddhists, from the Himalayas to the Altai mountains, and from Thibet to Japan.

Another popular element was communism joined with the monastic institute. The monastery is a refuge for the unhappy, for those who have not succeeded in trade, for sickly children, for all who feel a call to enter on a monastic life. In the monastery they subsist on the common fund supplied by the gifts of the charitable. A home, a quiet life, and very little to do, was the prospect held out to those whom society can very well spare, and is not unwilling to part with. Another popular element was the charm of nobleness attached to the monastic life. Self-denial becomes attractive, and not at all difficult to those who are sensible of this charm. The renunciation of the world, and the absorbing occupation of a religious life, seem to many who enter the gates of the monastery a pleasant dream, and very desirable.

Another attractive element in Buddhism has been the social character of the worship. The monks meet for morning and evening prayers in the presence of the images. To this should be added the agreeableness to the eye of dressed altars, lofty gilt images, and the encouraged belief that they are representative of powerful beings, who will afford substantial protection to the devotee who faithfully discharges his duty as a disciple.

Then there is the doctrine of the *Karma*. Every act of worship, every Buddhist ceremony, every book of devotion read, every gift to a monastery or a begging priest, every mass for the dead, every invocation of a Buddha or Bodhisattwa, every wish for the good of others, infallibly causes great good, through the necessary operation of the law of cause and effect in the moral sphere.

How far these and other causes have helped to spread Buddhism through the many countries where it now prevails deserves the careful thought of the European student of the history of religions. Next to India itself, China has done more for the development of Buddhist thought than any other Buddhist country. This is a remarkable fact and very useful; showing, as it does, that, judging from the past, the Chinese are susceptible to a very considerable degree of a foreign religion. They will also use intellectual energy in teaching and expanding it. Let any one who doubts this look over Kæmpfer's account of Japanese Buddhism. He will there find nearly all the Chinese sects described in this volume occurring again. They have been transplanted entire with their books and discipline into that island empire,—a striking proof of the vigour of Chinese Buddhism.

Why should they not accept Christianity with the same zeal, and apply to the task of teaching it as much mental force?

Dr. Draper says, [1] "From this we may also infer how unphilosophical and vain is the expectation of those who would attempt to restore the aged populations of Asia to our state. Their intellectual condition has passed onward never more to return."

My own conviction is, that so far as this theory of despair affects China, it is not warranted. The eras of intellectual expansion in that country may be briefly enumerated in the following way:—After the Chow period, the most famous of all, came that of Han, when classical studies, history, and Tauist philosophy flourished together. Then followed a Buddhist age. Then came an age of poetry and elegant literature, that of the T'ang dynasty. After this came the time of the Sung philosophers, who were most prolific in moral and critical writings tinctured with a peculiarly bad philosophy of nature. The present is an age of classical criticism, a reaction from that of the Sung writers.

We have six distinct periods of intellectual vigour, covering nearly three thousand years, and what do we now see? The intellectual vigour connected with Buddhism and Tauism dead, past any hope of a resurrection. Confucianism is still living, but it is not very strong. The people have an excellent physique, adapting them for various climates. They emigrate extensively. They have at home an autonomous empire of immense dimensions, administered by printed codes of laws, and such a mode of governing as to enable them to keep that empire from falling to pieces in a time of foreign wars and rebellions.

They are not then to be despaired of intellectually. What they need is to be educated in the mass, to be elevated by the diffusion of a living Christianity, to have improvements in the physical condition of the poor, with a system of scientific instruction in every province, and a development of the mineral and manufacturing resources of the country.

No one need despair of the intellectual progress of the people, or of their susceptibility of spiritual development. Christianity fosters mental growth, and the science of the West is eminently stimulating to thought. The descendants of the men whose mariners sailed with the compass seven hundred years ago, and whose schoolmasters were at the same time making use of printed books in education, will not fail to respond to these powerful influences.

That Buddhism has affected Chinese literature and thought to a considerable extent, is shown in the following pages. It taught them charity, but it did not impart a healthy stimulus to the national mind. It made them indeed more sceptical and materialistic than they were before, and weakened their morality.

But since Buddhism has had among the Chinese its age of faith, prompting them to metaphysical authorship, and the formation of schools of religious thought, and also impelling them to undertake distant and perilous journeys, to visit the spots where Shakyamuni passed his life, it must be admitted that there is a very promising prospect for Christianity, and that the beneficial effect on the people must be in proportion to the excellence of the Christian religion.

Perhaps Dr. Draper, in view of the facts contained in this book, would not be unwilling to modify his theory of the necessary decline of nations so far as it appertains to China, or at least allow the people of that country a further tenure of national life, till Christianity and education have had a trial.

The present volume is the fruit of many years' studies. Some parts of it were written nearly twenty-five years ago; nearly all is the fruit of Chinese reading.

Dr. Eitel of Hongkong and Mr. Thomas Watters have since written ably and extensively on the same subject. But my mode of treatment differs from theirs, and in my revision it has been an advantage to have the results of their researches before me. My own collection of native books on Buddhism has increased, while my acquaintance with the actual form of this religion in its popular development at the present time has been considerably enlarged.

The facts here collected on the esoteric sects are adapted to throw light on the history of Buddhism in India, and will help, it may be, to define the position of the Jains.

In the section on *Feng-shui*, I ask attention to the view there given on the influence of Buddhism in producing the modern Chinese doctrine of the physical influences of nature, and the part that, through the Buddhists, India and Greece have both had in producing the superstitious materialism of the Chinese in its modern shape.

PEKING, *October* 1879.

Footnotes

1. *Draper's Intellectual Development of Europe*, vol. i. p. 57.

CONTENTS

INTRODUCTION. 35

A LIFE OF BUDDHA IN FOUR CHAPTERS.

CHAPTER I.—LIFE OF SHAKYAMUNI TILL HIS APPEARANCE AT BENARES AS A TEACHER. 45
    Previous lives—Chronology—The seventh Buddha—Birth—Early life—Becomes a hermit—Becomes Buddha—Legendary stories of his early preaching—Hwa-yen-king—Extramundane teaching—Appearance at Benares

CHAPTER II.—LIFE OF BUDDHA FROM HIS APPEARANCE AS A TEACHER AT BENARES TO THE CONVERSION OF RAHULA... 60
    The four truths—Godinia and his four companions—The first monastic community—The first lay brother—Conversion of five hundred fire-worshippers in the kingdom of Magadha—Buddha at Rajagriha—At Shravasti, Shravasti in Jeta's garden—Appoints punishments garden—Appoints punishments for crimes of monks—Goes to see his father after twelve years' absence—Story of his son Rahula

CHAPTER III.—FROM THE COMMENCEMENT OF RAHULA'S RELIGIOUS LIFE TILL THE NEAR APPROACH OF THE NIRVANA. 67
    Buddha sends for Rahula—Arrangements for instructing Rahula and other boys—Tutors—Boys admitted to the vows—Nuns—Rapid spread of monasticism—Disciplinary rules—Education

in metaphysics—Ananda and the Leng-yen-king—Buddha in these works like Socrates in Plato—Buddha said to have gone to Ceylon—Also to the paradise of desire—Offer of Devas to protect Buddhism—Protectors of China—Relation of Buddhism to Hindoo polytheism—Prajna-paramita—King Prasenajit—Sutra of the Benevolent King—Daily liturgy—Ananda becomes Buddha's attendant disciple—Intrusted with the Sutras in twelve divisions—Buddha teaches his esoteric system—Virtually contained in the "Lotus Sutra"—In this the sun of Buddha culminated—His father's approaching death announced—Buddha reaches the forty-ninth year of his public preaching

CHAPTER IV.—LAST DISCOURSES AND DEATH OF BUDDHA..79

Buddha's immortality in his teaching—Death real and final—Object of Nirvâna teaching—Buddha visits the Tau-li heaven—Descends again by Indra's staircase—The first images—Death of Buddha's aunt—Death of Shariputra—Buddha at Kushinagara—Between the Sala trees—Last instructions—Kashiapa made patriarch—Flesh prohibited—Relieves the king of Magadha—Sends for Ananda—Answers to four questions—Brahma comes—Buddha's last words—Death—Gold coffin—Maya comes—Cremation—His relics—Pagodas

CHAPTER V.—THE PATRIARCHS OF THE NORTHERN BUDDHISTS..92

Features of Asiatic life in the time of the patriarchs—Character, powers, and intellectual qualities of the patriarchs—Series of thirty-three patriarchs—Appointment of Kashiapa by Shakyamuni—The Svastika—Council of Rajagriha, for writing out the books of Buddha, and settling what should be received as canonical—The part taken by Ananda in the authorship of the Buddhist books—Ananda, second patriarch—The third was Shangnavasu—Remarks on samadhi and reverie—Fourth,

Upagupta—Conversion of a wicked woman when dying—Fifth, sixth, and seventh patriarchs—Buddha's prophecy regarding Buddhanandi, the seventh—Struggle between filial love and Buddhist conviction in Buddhamitra—The way in which he subdued an unbelieving king—Maming given to the king of the Getæ to induce him to raise the siege of Pataliputra—Kapimara, the thirteenth—Nagarjuna, the fourteenth—Converts ten thousand Brahmans—Writes the Ta-chï-tu-lun—Vigorous defence of Buddhism by Kanadeva—Assassination of Kanadeva—Sanghanandi, precocious as a boy—Prophecy respecting him—Rahulata ascends to heaven—Sangkayasheta's discussion on the nature of sound—Converts five hundred hermits—Kumarada's views on the inequality of present retribution—Difficulties met with by Manura in teaching Buddhism in Southern and Western India—A patriarch's power over birds—Haklena converts Singhalaputra, who succeeded him as patriarch (the twenty-fourth), but was killed by the king of Candahar—The orthodox school has only twenty-four patriarchs—The contemplative school has twenty-eight—Pradjnyatara, the twenty-seventh, converts Bodhidharma, the twenty-eighth, who proceeds to China—Hindoo knowledge of the Roman empire

CHAPTER VI.—SKETCH OF THE HISTORY OF BUDDHISM IN CHINA..................118

The emperor Ming-ti sends an embassy to India for images, A.D. 61—Kashiapmadanga arrives in China—Spread of Buddhism, A.D. 335—Buddojanga—A pagoda at Nanking, A.D. 381—The translator Kumarajiva, A.D. 405—The Chinese traveller, Fa-hien, visits India—His book—Persecution, A.D. 426—Buddhism prosperous, 455—Indian embassies to China in the Sung dynasty—Opposition of the Confucianists to Buddhism—Discussions on doctrine—Buddhist prosperity in the Northern Wei kingdom and the Liang kingdom—Bodhidharma—Sun-yün sent to India—Bodhidharma leaves Liang Wu-ti and goes to Northern

China—His latter years and death—Embassies from Buddhist countries in the south—Relics—The Liang emperor Wu-ti becomes a monk—Embassies from India and Ceylon—Influence of Sanscrit writing in giving the Chinese the knowledge of an alphabet—Syllabic spelling—Confucian opposition to Buddhism in the T'ang dynasty—The five successors of Bodhidharma—Hiuen-tsang's travels in India—Work as a translator—Persecution, A.D. 714—Hindoo calendar in China—Amogha introduces the festival for hungry ghosts—Opposition of Han Yü to Buddhism—Persecution of 845—Teaching of Ma-tsu—Triumph of the Mahayana—Bodhiruchi—Persecution by the Cheu dynasty—Extensive erection of pagodas in the Sung dynasty—Encouragement of Sanscrit studies—Places of pilgrimage—P'u-to—Regulations for receiving the vows—Hindoo Buddhists in China in the Sung dynasty—The Mongol dynasty favoured Buddhism—The last Chinese Buddhist who visited India—The Ming dynasty limits the right of accumulating land—Roman Catholic controversy with Buddhists—Kano hi of the Manchu dynasty opposes Buddhism—The literati still condemn Buddhism

CHAPTER VII.—THE SCHOOLS OF CHINESE BUDDHISM...... 183

The growth of esoteric sects in India—The Jains—Their series of twenty-four patriarchs—Bodhidharma headed a new school in Southern India, and was heretical as viewed from the Jams standpoint—He founded the contemplative school in China—Nagarjuna, the author of the most revered hooks of this school—Tsung-men—Kiau-men—Divisions of Tsung-men—The Tsung-men sects are heretical in the view of the old orthodoxy-Specimen of the teaching of the Tsung-men—Lin-tsi school—Professes strict discipline—Its founder died A.D. 868—His monument on the bank of the Hu-to river in Chi-li—Resemblance to European speculation on the absolute—Is Buddhism pantheistic?—Exoteric sects—Lü-men (Vinaya)—Yogachara—Fa-siang—Madhyamika—Fa-sing—Tsing-tu, or sect of the "Pure land" or "Western heaven"—T'ien-t'ai—Poetry of the Tsing-tu school

CHAPTER VIII.—ON CHI-K'AI AND THE T'IEN-T'AI SCHOOL OF BUDDHISM. 203

T'ien-t'ai, a place of great note in Chinese Buddhism—Chï-k'ai resided there in the sixth century—His cloak and rice bowl—Fu-lung feng—Fang-kwang sï and the rock bridge—Legend of the Lo-hans—Twelve monasteries founded—He taught the Fa-hwa-king—System of threefold contemplation—Six connectives—Eight modes of characterising Buddhism—Ten steps in progress—Derived much from Nagarjuna—T'ien-t'ai, a middle system-Regulations

CHAPTER IX.—THE BUDDHIST MORAL SYSTEM. 215

The Ten virtues and Ten vices—The cause of human stupidity is in the passions—The Five prohibitions—The Ten prohibitions—Klaproth's praise of Buddhism—But it is atheistic, and therefore this praise should be qualified—Kindness to animals based on the fiction of transmigration—Buddhism teaches compassion for suffering without inculcating obedience to Divine law—Story of Shakyamuni—Sin not distinguished from misery—Buddhists teach that the moral sense is innate—They assign a moral nature to animals—The Six paths of the metempsychosis—Hindoo notions of heaven and hell—Countless ages of joy and suffering—Examples—Exemption from punishment gained by meritorious actions—Ten kings of future judgment—Fate or Karma—Buddhism depreciates heaven and the gods—Buddha not God, but a Saviour—Moral influence of the Paradise of the Western heaven—Figurative interpretation of this legend—The contemplative school identifies good and evil—No moral distinctions in the Nirvâna—Buddhism has failed to produce high morality—The Confucianist condemnation of the Buddhists—Mr. P. Hordern's praise of Buddhism in Birmah—The Birmese intellectually inferior to the Chinese—Kindness to animals known to the Chinese before they received Buddhism—Buddha's reasons for not eating flesh

CHAPTER X.—THE BUDDHIST CALENDAR....................231
National festivals—Festivals in honour of celestial beings—In honour of the Buddhas and Bodhisattwas—In honour of characters in Chinese Buddhist history—Supplemental anniversaries—Singhalese Buddhists keep a different day for Buddha's birthday—In the T'ang dynasty Hindoo astronomers reformed the calendar—Gaudamsiddha—The week of India and Babylon known to the Chinese—Word mit for Sunday—Peacock Sutra—The Hindoo Rahu and Ketu

CHAPTER XI.—RELATION OF BUDDHISM TO THE OLDER HINDOO MYTHOLOGY. 239
Buddhism accepted the Hindoo mythology, with the sacred books of the Brahmans, so far as it agreed with its own dogmas—The gods Indra, Brahma, and Ishwara listen as disciples to Buddha—Eight classes of Devas—Four kings of Devas—Yakshas—Mahoragas—Pretas—Maras—Mama, king of the dead—Creation is denied to the Hindoo gods in the Chung-lun and other works

CHAPTER XII.—THE BUDDHIST UNIVERSE. 247
The universe passes through incessant changes—Kalpas of various lengths—Kalpas of establishment, of destruction, &c.—Saha world—Sumeru mountain—The Southern continent is Jambudvipa—Heaven of the thirty-three—Tushita paradise—Upper tier of paradises—Heavens of form and of desire—Heavens without form—Brahma's paradise—No wise man is born there, because Brahma says he created the universe—The bells—Story from the "Ti-tsang Sutra,"

CHAPTER XIII.—THE EXTENDED UNIVERSE OF THE NORTHERN BUDDHISTS. 254
Primitive Buddhism aimed at moral improvement and the Nirvâna—Its mythology was of popular growth—The Mahayana

mythology was introduced by the metaphysicians of Buddhism itself—Nagarjuna the chief inventor—Hwa-yen-king—An extended universe invented to illustrate dogma—Ten worlds beyond the Saha world in ten different directions—New divinities to worship—Amitabha—His world in the West—Kwan-yin and Ta-shï-chï—The world of Ach'obhya Buddha in the East—World of Yo-shï Fo, the healing teacher—Mercy, wisdom, &c., are symbolised in the Bodhisattwas—Wu-t'ai shan in China is introduced in the Hwa-yen-king

CHAPTER XIV.—BUDDHIST IMAGES AND IMAGE WORSHIP..264

Temples—Entering hall, Sï-to-t'ien-wang—These four kings described—The laughing Buddha, Mi-li Fo—Behind him, Wei-to—Chief hall, Ta-hiung-pau-tien—Shakyamuni—Ananda—Kashiapa—Kwan-yin, Wen-shu, and other Bodhisattwas—Buddha represented as teaching—Buddha of the past, present, and future—Chapels to O-mi-to Fo, Ti-tsang, and the Ten kings—Representation of the eight miseries from which Kwan-yin delivers—Temples in Ceylon—Images in temples near Peking—Tan-cho sï snake—Pi-yün sï—Hall of Lo-hans—Diamond throne of Buddha—Colossal images of Maitreya—Musical instruments—Reflections

CHAPTER XV.—MONASTERIES AT P'U-TO. 283

This establishment more modern than T'ien-t'ai and Wu-t'ai—Many Thibetan inscriptions—Frequent visits of Peking lamas—Dedicated to Kwan-yin—Gifts by Kang-hi—Images—Caves—Pagodas—Inscriptions—Resident defenders of Buddhism—The Potala of Jehol in Mongolia—It is also the name of the palace—Temple of the Dalai Lama—In China an island was preferred to be the tau-ch'ang of Kwan-yin

CHAPTER XVI.—BUDDHIST PROCESSIONS, ASSOCIATIONS, PILGRIMAGES, AND CEREMONIES FOR THE DEAD......292

Yü-lan-hwei, "Association for giving food to the dead"—Worship of ancestors—Liturgical services in the houses of the rich, for the liberation of the souls of the dead from hell—Village processions—Based on the old rural processions of classical times—Masquerades—Plays—Pilgrimages to Miau-feng shah—Pilgrims wearing iron chains—Supposed efficacy of the prayers of the priests—Zeal of the laity in promoting pilgrimages to celebrated shrines

CHAPTER XVII.—BUDDHIST LITERATURE 297

Buddhist libraries presented to monasteries by emperors—Ch'eng-tsu, of the Ming dynasty, was the first to print the entire series of the Buddhist accepted books—Prajna-paramita, eighty times as large as our New Testament—The Pei-tsang, or second printed edition, dates from the sixteenth century—The Kia-hing edition of the Pei-tsang—Division into King, Lü, Lun—First Council—Work of Ananda—The Mahayana of Northern Buddhism—Council of Cashmere—Authors of the Mahayana—Lung-shu wrote the Hwa-yen-king—Contrasts between the primitive and Mahayana books—List of translators, A.D. 70 to A.D. 705—Sixteen hundred works are classified, inclusive of those by Chinese authors—On the councils for settling the canon—Translations by Burnouf and others—Lotus—Book of Forty-two Sections—Character of this and other early works—Stories illustrative of ancient life—Fan-wang-king—Chan-tsï-king translated by Beal—Pratimoksha

CHAPTER XVIII.—THE LENG-YEN-KING.—FIRST CHAPTER 313

The Sutra of firm establishment in all doctrine, describing clearly the secret merit and attainments in the religious life of Tathagata, who appears as Buddha in his great and unsurpassed stature; also the many acts of the Bodhisattwas

CHAPTER XIX.—THE EKASHLOKA SHASTRA. 326

The "Ekashloka Shastra," translated from the Chinese, with an analysis and notes

CHAPTER XX.—EFFECT OF BUDDHISM ON THE PHILOSOPHY OF THE SUNG DYNASTY..................342

The Sung philosophers differ from Confucius—Five periods of Chinese intellectual development—The Sung writers changed the old cosmogony—The Han writers had already done so—Diagram of the Great Extreme—Other pictorial illustrations—Avoidance of the doctrine of a personal God—Materialistic philosophy of nature—New view of divination

CHAPTER XXI.—FENG-SHUI; OR, THE WIND AND WATER SUPERSTITION OF THE CHINESE. 351

An obstacle to civilisation—Meaning of Feng, "Wind"—Of Shui, "Water"—Use of cyclic characters—Meaning of Lung, "Dragon"—Names of the geomancers—Hindoo nomenclature—Sha-ch'i, "Destructive vapour"—Dark arrow—Chen-wu, or "Protecting shield"—Feng-shui professedly based on the "Book of Changes"—Modern Feng-shui is based on the Han-lung-king—Buddhist element in Feng-shui—The four elements of the Greeks—The Hindoo "Air and water" is Feng-shui—Earth, water, fire, and air are creative forces, existing in successive kalpas, and forming successive worlds—Resemblance to the theories of the Ionian philosophers—Geomancy in the T'ang dynasty—Rahu and Ketu—The Feng-shui system grew out of Buddhism—Native element in Feng-shui—Nine fancied stars—Causes of the contour of hills and plains—Stars of the six houses—Feng-shui inconsistent with genuine Confucianism

CHAPTER XXII.—BUDDHIST PHRASEOLOGY IN RELATION TO CHRISTIAN TEACHING............................376

Use of Buddhist terms in the Nestorian inscription, A.D. 781—Mo, "demon;" in Sanscrit, mara—Ti-yü, "hell," is naraka—Ten judges of hell—Among them Pau Cheng, the famous judge of the Sung dynasty—The Sung philosophers encouraged the popular belief in future retribution—This prepares for Christianity—T'ien-t'ang, "heaven"—Defects of this term—Ming-kung, &c., as names for "heaven"—Buddhist paradises possibly borrowed from Western Asia or some other country farther west—Redemption—Ti-tsang and Kwan-yin—Pity—Instruction—Effect of sin—Decreed forgiveness to penitents—Secret merit—Happiness and merit confounded—Sin and misery confounded—Illustration from the narrative of a Christian convert

CHAPTER XXIII.—NOTICE OF THE WU-WEI-KIAU, A REFORMED BUDDHIST SECT...393

Originated two hundred and seventy years ago by a native of Shantung—No showy ceremonial—No images—Sacred books six in number—Interview of the founder with the emperor of the period, Cheng-te—Discussion with opponents—Victory—One of their leaders was crucified

CHAPTER XXIV.—BUDDHISM AND TAUISM IN THEIR POPULAR ASPECTS...402

The popularity of Buddhism rests on its doctrine of retribution, and not on its ethics—Magical claims of the Tauists—Swan-yin, since the twelfth century, usually a female—Powers and claims of Swan-yin—Popular Buddhism loves to have prayers said for the dead—Hopes for paradise hereafter—Popular Tauism believes in haunted houses, in charms, and in the efficacy of the wizard in controlling demons—The present head of the Tauists and chief magician—Went from Western China to Kiang-si, where he has ever since resided as hereditary Pope—The Tauist divinity Yü-hwang shang-ti has incarnations assigned to him—Chang Sien the bowman, a physician—Tail-cutting delusion—Tauist prayers for the dead—The Buddhist Yen-lo-wang, "God of death"—The eight genii—The eighteen Lo-hans—The Tauist delusions dangerous politically—T'ien-tsin massacre—Need of the light of education—The effect of the assault of Christianity on these religions

CHAPTER XXV.—ON THE USE OF SANSCRIT BY THE CHINESE BUDDHISTS. 419

    Changes in Chinese sounds since the time of the Buddhist transliteration of Indian words—Examples of Sanscrit words in old and new Chinese—The importance of translations made in A.D. 60 to A.D. 76 for reading the Four Books—The Hindoo translators did not speak pure Sanscrit—Sanscrit was the language of the books—No Pali books in China—The translators spoke Pracrit—The term po-li, "glass"—Use of Sanscrit words in magic—Dharani—Inscription in six languages at Kü-yung kwan

CHAPTER XXVI.—BOOKS AND PAPERS THAT MAY BE CONSULTED FOR THE STUDY OF CHINESE BUDDHISM. 429

    Foĕ kouĕ ki by Remusat—Works of Julien—Interesting passage from Fa-hien—Translations by Beal—Schott, Ueber den Buddhaismus in Hoch Asien und in China—Writings of Palladius—Eitel's Handbook for the Student of Chinese Buddhism—Watters' account of Chinese Buddhism—Eitel's Three Lectures, and article on Nirvâna

INTRODUCTION.

Buddhism deserves examination—Researches of Remusat, Burnouf, Koeppen, and St. Hilaire—Sanscrit manuscripts from Nepaul—Buddhist books reveal to view the ancient Hindoo world—The opening scene of the *Kin-kang-king.*

AT the present time, when foreign intercourse with China is increasing every year, and our knowledge of that country is extending in proportion, an account of the history and literature of Buddhism in that land will perhaps find more readers than at any former period. The traveller will not fail to inquire why this Indian religion has sunk into such helplessness and decay as he observes. The philosophical historian naturally will wish to know the causes of the vast extension of Buddhism, and of its present decline. The Christian missionary would willingly learn the amount and nature of the religious feeling possessed by the monks, and the strength of the opposition which the religion of Christ has to expect during its propagation, from them and from the Buddhist laity. Especially the statesman needs to be informed how far the Chinese people are likely to be offended by the introduction of Christianity, and whether the opposition to idolatry which it excites will strike at any of their most dearly-cherished prejudices and beliefs.

A religion that has extended its sway over so many Eastern nations, and whose converts far outnumber those of any other sect in the world, deserves minute investigation. The present sketch will be necessarily too brief to do justice to the subject, but it is hoped some results will be brought forward that may assist the foreign observer to explain the great and long-continued success of the Buddhistic system, the causes of its growing weakness, and the many indications of its hopeless decay.

Among European scholars Remusat and his successors in the study of Chinese literature have bestowed considerable attention on Buddhism, and their labours have been rewarded with many interesting and valuable results. Especially is the world indebted to Burnouf and St. Hilaire for their work in this field of Buddhist inquiry, and lucid exposition of their results. The aid to be derived from their investigations has not been neglected in the account now given to the reader. Further, the most direct means of gaining information is to study some parts of the voluminous works extant in Chinese on this subject. The numerous Indian priests who came to China early in the Christian era were indefatigable translators, as is shown by what they have bequeathed to their disciples. These monuments of the highly civilised race that spoke the Sanscrit language, give to the inquiry a special literary interest. They were till lately inaccessible in their original form. The European students of Sanscrit for a long period sought in vain for an account of Buddhist doctrines and traditions, except in the writings of their adversaries. The orthodox Indians destroyed the sacred books of their heretical brethren with assiduous care. The representations they give of the views of their opponents are necessarily partial, and it may be expected that what Colebrooke and others have done in elucidating Buddhism from the polemical writings of the Brahmans, would receive useful corrections and additions as well from Chinese sources as from the Sanscrit manuscripts of Buddhist books obtained by Hodgson. [1] An extended critique of the Buddhist literature of China and the other countries professing Buddhism, such as Burnouf planned and partly accomplished for India, would be a valuable contribution to the history of the Hindoo race. The power of this religion to chain the human mind, the peculiar principles of its philosophy, its mythological characteristics, its mode of viewing human life, its monastic and ascetic usages, all result from the early intellectual development of the nation whose home is south of the Himalayas. In the Buddhist classics it is not the life of China that is depicted, but that of Hindostan, and that not as it is now, but as it was two thousand years ago. The words and grammatical forms that occur in their perusal, when deciphered from the hieroglyphic Chinese form that they have been made to assume, remind the reader that they spring from the same stem of which the classical languages of Europe are branches. Much of their native literature the Buddhist missionaries left untouched—for example, the highly-wrought epic poems and dramas that have recently attracted the admiring notice of Europeans; but a large number of fables and tales with a moral are found in Chinese Buddhist books. Many specimens of this peculiar mode of composition, which, originating in Greece, was adopted by the Hindoos, and spread into the various literatures of modern Europe and Asia, have long since been made to wear a Chinese garb. [2] Further, the elements of grammar and the knowledge of the alphabet, with some important contributions from mathematical science, have reached China through the same medium. Several openings are thus presented into the old Hindoo world. The country where speculative philosophy, with grammatical and arithmetical science, attained greater perfection than anywhere else in ancient times, is seen spreading its civilisation into the neighbouring countries, and producing remarkable and permanent changes in the national life of China. To witness this, as may be done in the Buddhist books, cannot be regarded as devoid of attraction. The very existence of Buddhism is sufficient evidence of the energy of the Indian race as it was long ago. The Mongols, Thibetans, and Singhalese, with the inhabitants of the Indo-Chinese peninsula, combine with the Chinese and Japanese to prove by the faith they still maintain in Buddhism the enthusiasm of its first missionaries, and their power to influence mankind. Buddhism was not always that decrepit and worn-out superstition that it now appears.

Having said thus much by way of preface, it is time to introduce to the reader's attention the founder of the religion. No way of doing this suggests itself as more suitable than to translate from the opening scene of a popular Buddhist work called the "Diamond Classic" a few passages, where he appears in the midst of his disciples, instructing them in some of the principles of his system. The time, according to the Singhalese chronology, was in the sixth century before Christ. The place is Sha-wei,[3] a city in Central India. The hero is Shakyamuni himself, *i.e.*, Buddha or Julai. The subordinate characters are the Bikshu[4] or religious mendicants, who are so denominated because they beg instruction for the mind and food for the body. They consist of two classes, says the editor of the Diamond Classic. Those who have abandoned vice and are aiming at virtue are the small Bikshu. Those who are released from both alike are great Bikshu. Among the latter, who have gone deeper than the others into the profundities of Buddhist doctrine, are included those called Bosat and Lahan, or, as these characters are now pronounced by the Chinese, Pusa and Lohan.

The chief minister of the king having at Rajagriha heard Buddha's instructions, and been deeply impressed by them, wished to invite him to some suitable dwelling. Jeta, the king's son, had a garden. The minister offered to buy it. The prince said by way of jest that he was willing if he would cover it with gold. The minister, who was childless, obtained gold-leaf and spread it over the garden. The prince then gave it him free of cost. According to another account the minister ordered eighty elephants loaded with gold to come immediately. The prince, admiring the doctrine which had so affected the minister as to make him willing to give all this gold for a hall to teach it, gave it for nothing. In a house "in this garden, which lay outside the city Sha-wei, Buddha with his disciples, 1250 in number, assembled. It was the time of taking food. Buddha put on the robe" called *seng-gha-li*, and with his *pat*[5] or "mendicant's rice bowl" in his hand, entered the city to beg for food. When having gone from door to door he had finished his task, he returned to his lodging-place. "His meal being ended, he put his robe and rice vessel aside, and washed his feet," for it was the practice of this religious reformer to walk with naked feet.

"He then sat cross-legged on a raised platform," remaining some time in meditation before he began to teach.

"At that time the aged Subhûti, who was sitting among the crowd of disciples, arose. With his right shoulder uncovered, and kneeling on his right knee, he raised his joined hands respectfully, and addressed Buddha in the following words:—"Rare is it to meet with the world's honoured one, [6] Julai, [7] who in the best manner protects his disciples (Bosat), keeps them in his thoughts, and gives them his instructions. World-honoured sage! (*Shï-tsun*) if good men and good women exhibit *the unsurpassed just and enlightened heart*, how should they place it firmly, and how should the evil risings of the heart be suppressed and subdued?" The words in italics, corresponding to the Sanscrit *anutara samyaksambuddhi*, [8] are written with Chinese characters in the text, and are explained by the commentator as consisting of *an*, "not," *utara*, "superior," *samya*, "right and equal," *sambodi*, "rightly knowing." Buddha replied, "The question is a good one, and you have truly described my disposition. It is thus that a resting-place can be found and the heart controlled." The words *ju-shï*, "thus," says the commentator, refer not to what precedes, as in Chinese syntax, but to what follows, according to the usage of Sanscrit grammar. Subhûti then expresses his anxious desire to hear the instructions of the sage, who consequently addresses his disciples called Bosat and Great Bosat (*Ma-ha-sat*). "All men, whether they resemble in their nature oviparous animals," that are light and fly, or imitate the moral dispositions and reflecting habits of "the mammalia, or are like the fish," sprung from spawn, instinctively following the multitude in the path of evil, "or are of the same class with animals born by transformation," and pass through remarkable changes, should enter that state which is final and unchangeable [9]—the Nirvâna, [10] "Whether they still think" on the phenomena of the sensuous world "or have ceased to think," *i.e.*, become so far enlightened as to pay no attention to passing scenes, "or are neither with thought nor without thought," that is, have become entirely indifferent to life or death, appetite or aversion, love or hatred, "they should thus seek salvation in destruction." Why do not all living men obtain this immeasurably great release? "If the Bodhisattwa (Bosat, *he who knows and feels*) has for his aim self, or man, or the world of living things, or old age, he is not a true Bodhisattwa." Buddha now bade Subhûti resume his seat, and went on to inform him concerning the fixed place of rest for which he had inquired. "The Bodhisattwa in action should have no fixed resting-place for his thoughts. In what he does he should not rest on colour, sound, smell, taste, collision, or any particular action. He should not rest in forms of things, that is, allow himself to attend to any special sensational phenomena. If he thus acts, his happiness and virtue will be boundless." Buddha is asked by his disciple for a further explanation of this doctrine. He replies by inquiring if the four quarters of space can be measured by thought. Receiving a negative answer, he says that the same is true of the doctrine that the Bodhisattwa in acting without regard to particular objects obtains great happiness and virtue. He then asks if with the material body and its senses Julai or Buddha can be truly perceived. No, says the disciple, for body and form are not truly body and form. Buddha himself replies by denying the existence of all matter in the words "whatever has form is an empty delusion. If any one sees that all things having forms are not forms, *i.e.*, nothing, he then truly perceives Julai" in his formless and matterless reality; that is, has attained to a profound understanding of Buddhist doctrines.

In these few passages from the *Kin-kang-king* or "Diamond Sutra," some of the most prominent doctrines of Buddhism are brought to view, viz.:—(I.) The happiness of the Nirvâna or state of unconsciousness which frees him who attains it from the miseries of existence. (2.) The mischievous influence of human life, with its struggles after particular forms of happiness, and of the sensuous world with its deceptive phenomena. (3.) The non-existence of matter, to be convinced of which is to take the first grand step on the road to enlightenment.

This introduction into the Buddhist sphere of thought makes the system appear to be based rather on philosophy than on any religious principle. More will subsequently occur to confirm the correctness of this opinion. With regard to the real character of Buddhism, piety towards the Ruler of the world does not form either its foundation or the result to which it aims to elevate its votaries. It will be seen that, while striving to escape from the evils incident to life, and from every selfish aim, it is nothing but selfishness in an abstract philosophical form, stripped of the grosser qualities which are manifested in the common course of human history.

In enumerating the various kinds of sensations conveyed to our minds by the senses, a verb "to strike or pierce," ch'u, is employed in place of "touch," the familiar term of our own popular philosophy. All these sensations are said by the Buddhists to be produced by the respective organs with which they are connected. They are called the six kinds of "dust" or "worldly things"—the unwelcome accretions that attach themselves to our garments as we walk through the world. "Action," *fa*, said to emanate from the "will," *yi*, is classed with them as the sixth mode assumed by worldly phenomena.

The preceding specimen of Buddha's teaching, surrounded by his disciples in a city of ancient India, is sufficient to introduce the subject. The principal facts in the life of that sage will now be detailed. Buddha will be here represented as he appears in the Chinese biographies. They describe him as a sort of divine man, possessed unbounded magical power, and visiting the most distant spots, as, for example, the paradises of the gods, in an instant of time.

In giving an account of Chinese Buddhism, I feel the importance of exhibiting Shakyamuni in the form which is familiar to the Chinese devotee. It is well, in our picture, to retain the details of a marvellous nature which have been so abundantly added by the Northern Buddhists to the simplicity of the first narrative. Man cannot live without God. This was an effort to recover the divine. When God, through the absurdities of polytheism, was pushed out of view, the substitute was Buddha, the perfect sage, the model ascetic, the patient and loving teacher, the wonder-working magician, the acknowledged superior of gods and men. Such was the conception worked out by the Hindoo mind to take the place of the old polytheism of India, and accepted by all the Buddhist nations north of Shakyamuni's birthplace. In the history of religions it is of extreme importance that this fact should be recognised and appreciated.

Footnotes

1. During his residence in Nepaul. Of these works, the *Lotus of the Good Law*, in Chinese *Miau-fa-lien-hwa-king*, has been translated by Burnouf, Paris, 1852. The Rev. S. Beal, Professor of Chinese in University College, London, has translated from Chinese *A Catena of Buddhist Scriptures*, and *The Romantic Legend of Sâkya Buddha*.
2. Of these works Stanislas Julien has translated *Les Avadanas*, consisting of tales and apologues. 1859.
3. Sha-wei was on the north of the Ganges, about 200 miles above Benares. It is also written Shravasti. All the upper part of the valley of the Ganges was embraced in what was known as Central India.
4. This Sanscrit word is pronounced according to K'ang-hi *Bi-k'u*. The orthography here adopted for Chinese and Sanscrit words, agrees nearly with that of Sir T. Wade and of the French writers on kindred subjects. For *ou*, the *oo* of Morrison, u is here written.
5. In modern Chinese the *t* is dropped and the *a* (a in father) changed to *o*. In Sanscrit the word is *pâtra*.
6. A title of Buddha—*Shï-tsun* in Sanscrit, *Lokês'vararâja* (Eitel's *Handbook of Chinese Buddhism*), or *Lokadjyesht'a*, v. Remusat's *Mélanges Asiatiques*, vol. i. p. 164.
7. *Julai* is the Chinese translation of Tathagata. It means literally "thus come," and is explained, "bringing human nature as it truly is, with perfect knowledge and high intelligence, he comes and manifests himself."
8. These words are pronounced in old Chinese *a nu-ta-la sam-mia sam-bo-di*, and in Mandarin *a neu-to-lo san-miau san-p'u-t'i*.
9. Without remainder, *Wu-yü*.

10. *Nit* is translated by the commentator "go out if," and *ban*, "harassment." By the French Sinologues it is identified with Nirvâna, the happy condition of perfect rest at which the Hindoos aim. The dictionary *Ching-tsz-t'ung*, says, that "the Chinese equivalent of this Sanscrit term is, to announce that he is at rest, and that it is applied to describe the death of Buddha, because his is not a true death like that of other men, whose *tsing-shin* (soul) does not die." The sound *ban* was selected, it may be, by a Hindoo who pronounced the word Nirbana. It is called in some translations Nirwan. The Hindoo translator would pronounce Nirwana. The Chinese character used for *ni* was called *nit* in some parts of China, and *nir* in others.

A LIFE OF BUDDHA IN FOUR CHAPTERS.

CHAPTER I.

LIFE OF SHAKYAMUNI TILL HIS APPEARANCE AT BENARES AS A TEACHER.

Previous lives—Chronology—The seventh Buddha—Birth—Early life—Becomes a hermit—Becomes Buddha—Legendary stories of his early preaching—*Hwa-yen-king*—Extramundane teaching—Appearance at Benares.

IN examining the Buddhist writings, the reader is at once reminded that he has entered a field where he is deprived of the trustworthy guidance and careful adherence to facts and dates of native Chinese authors. Not only is this true of works that contain the wilder extravagances of Indian mythology, and introduce the wondering disciple to the scenery and inhabitants of numberless other worlds, even those that wear an historical look, and yield the most information, do not fail thus to betray their foreign origin. The doctrine of transmigrations, and an eternal succession of kalpas past and future, is tempting to the biographer who wishes for variety of incident. He can place his hero wherever he pleases, in the universe boundless in space and time of the Indian imagination.

The founder of Buddhism, Shakyamuni, or the "Sage of the house of Shakya," is a case in point. It is said of him that before his birth more than two thousand years since in the present *kalpa*, he had during many previous ones taken religious vows, and honoured the Buddhas who then instructed the world. His name is associated particularly with Dipankara, in Chinese, Janteng, a fictitious Buddha, who received him as his disciple, and foretold that he would in a subsequent kalpa become Buddha, and bear the name by which he is now known. The time when this happened was too long ago to be expressed by common Chinese numerals. It was at a distance of numberless kalpas.[1] In modern Chinese temples, an image behind that of Julai sometimes represents Janteng. In the kalpa immediately preceding the present, Shakya is said to have risen to the rank of Bodhisattwa. He was then born in the heaven called Tushita,[2] and when the time was come his soul descended to our world. He came on a white elephant having six tusks. The date of Shakya's birth is very variously given. The Siamese, Peguans, and Singhalese, all using the Pali versions of the Buddhist classics, differ among themselves. The numbers as stated by them are B.C. 744, 638, and 624.[3] The Chinese historian, Ma Twan-lin, mentions two dates as assigned by various authorities to this event, viz., 1027 and 668. The former is what is commonly given in Chinese books. Burnouf rightly prefers the chronology of the Southern Buddhists. Their discrepancies between themselves form an objection, but not at all a fatal one, to such a conclusion. The uncertainty that involves this question is an instance of the difficulty attending researches in Indian chronology and history, as contrasted with the fulness and accuracy of Chinese writers. What was the original language of Buddhism is another point not yet fully determined. The settlement of it would throw light on the chronology. Only one of the dates can be right, for there is no doubt as to Buddha's identity. If Sanscrit was the language in which he taught his disciples, it must have been just dying out at the time, for the old Buddhist inscriptions, in the countries watered by the Ganges, are in a dialect derived from the Sanscrit and differing little from Pali. The mother-tongue of the Hindoos must then have been already supplanted by a derived dialect in the time of Ashôka, king of Central India, who reigned near Patna, as both the Northern and Southern Buddhists inform us, about 150 or 200 years after Buddha's death. It is to his age that those monuments are ascribed. Perhaps a discussion as to whether the Sanscrit or Pali versions of the sacred books were the earlier, may have led to a designed altering of dates by the Northern or Southern school of Buddhism. The deception was an elaborate one, by whichever party it was practised, for the interval from the death of Buddha until modern times is in the writings of both schools filled up by a series of events and dates. [4] The lives of some of the patriarchs, as given in Chinese books, appear too long. Ananda, a favourite disciple of Buddha, is made to die eighty-three years after him. Of his successors in the office of patriarch, the first two held it for sixty-two and sixty-six years respectively. The average of the first fourteen patriarchs is more than fifty-two years to each. Without forgetting the simple and abstemious habits of these ancient ascetics, their lives must be regarded as prolonged beyond probability. Perhaps the most convincing argument for the claim of the Pali to be that which was spoken by Buddha himself, is that the ascertained interval between him and Ashôka is too short for the formation of a new language.

The work called *San-kiau-yi-su* [5] places the Buddha called Shakyamuni in the seventh place among those whom it commemorates as having, on account of their perfect enlightenment, received that title. The list begins with the ninety-eighth Buddha of a preceding *kalpa*. He is called the Biba Buddha. The two next, who are supposed to live toward the close of the same vast period of time, are called Shï-chï and Baishevu. The three first Buddhas of the present kalpa are said to have been named Kulusan, Kunashemuni, and Kashiapa. In Ward's *Mythology of the Hindoos*, it is said, "The Buddhists assign to their hero ten incarnations, and designate the histories of these incarnations by the names of ten Hindoo sages." But the true history of the religion begins with Shakyamuni.

Where all is fictitious, it matters not very much whether the preceding six Buddhas were incarnations of Shakyamuni Buddha, or were separate in their personality. There appears to be no ground for believing in any Buddhism before Buddha. Given a hero, it is easy to invent for him six preliminary lives, or six predecessors in the same dignity. One would like to know whether the Mohammedan series of seven sages, selected out of the Jewish and Christian Scriptures, from Adam to Christ, is imitated from this Hindoo series of seven sages.

The effects of the teaching of each of the past Buddhas are recorded. The most ancient of the seven is said to have saved 34,800 men. The figures diminish, step by step, to 20,000, the number attributed to the immediate predecessor of the historical Buddha.

The names of the most faithful, and also the two proficient disciples, are given in the case of each Buddha. The city in which they lived is also mentioned, and the tree under which they were fond of delivering instruction. The favourite city of Shakyamuni was Shravasti, and his tree, the Bodhi tree. His disciples were too many to number. His faithful disciple was Rahula, his son, and his two most proficient pupils were Shariputra and Maudgalyayana.

The true history of the Buddhist religion begins with Shakyamuni. He was the son of Suddhodana, king of the city Kapilavastu, near the boundary of Nepaul. The king of Kapilavastu was subject to the king of Magadha, a country in Southern Bahar, to which the Ganges provinces were then tributary. Suddhodana is called in Chinese Tsing-*fan*—"He who eats food freed from impurities."

Buddha was born B.C. 623, and attained the rank of Buddha at thirty-five years of age, in B.C. 588, the sixteenth year of the reign of Bimbisara. He died at seventy-nine, in the eighth year of the reign of Ajatashatru, B.C. 543. These are Ceylonese dates, and are, says Turnour, too late by sixty-five years. According to the Siamese and Birmese chronology, the birth and death of Buddha are assigned to the years B.C. 653 and B.C. 628. Koeppen prefers the former dates, on the ground that they are usually accepted by the Southern Buddhists, and the date of the Nirvâna is sanctioned by a very extended official use. He suggests that the Buddhists of China and other northern countries were influenced by the prophecy uttered by Shakyamuni, which stated that his doctrines would spread in China a thousand years after his death. It was in A.D. 64 that Buddhism entered China. The Nirvâna, therefore, should have its date a thousand years earlier. From this we may understand why the Chinese Buddhists place the life of Buddha so much earlier than do their brother believers in the south. Koeppen also remarks that Ceylon was converted to Buddhism much earlier than countries north of India, and that historical events are, therefore, more likely to be correctly recorded in Ceylon. The events in Buddha's life were fresher in remembrance when the early Buddhist literature of Ceylon was compiled, than when Buddhism spread in China and other northern countries.

The accepted date in China for Buddha's birth is B.C. 1027. His name was Siddharta, and that of his mother was Maya. She died ten days after his birth. The question in regard to this date is thus treated by the author of *Fo-tsu-t'ung-ki*. He first gives six grounds for accepting the older chronology. 1. A portent in the year B.C. 1027. According to a work called *Cheu-shu-yi-ki*, a bright light of five colours was seen to pierce the constellation Tai-wei, and pass over the whole west. On seeing it, the historian Su Yeu remarked that a great sage was born in the west. Seventy-nine years later, a white rainbow was seen, having twelve stripes stretching from south to north. The historian Hu To, seeing it, said, "It is the sign of the death of a great sage in the west." 2. Kashiapmadanga said to the Han emperor, Ming-ti, who introduced Buddhism into China, that it was in the year B.C. 1027, on the eighth day of the fourth month, that Buddha was born. 3. The statement of the third Chinese patriarch in the sixth century, that it was in the fifty-first year of the cycle, on the fourth month and eighth day. 4. Another early work of a Chinese

Buddhist gives the year B.C. 1027, the month and day agreeing. 5. The same is true of a statement by a Buddhist in the *History of the Wei*, an imperial work. 6. Early in the seventh century, the emperor T'ai-tsung ordered an investigation into the date of Buddha's birth. Lieu Te-wei, a minister of State, inquired of a famous Buddhist named Fa-lin the reason of the discrepancy in the current accounts. The consequence was that Fa-lin settled it to be B.C. 1027.

The same author proceeds to give several other epochs, believed in by as many authorities. 1. Inscription on a stone pillar. This gives B.C. 718. 2. The statement of the pilgrim Fa-hien, B.C. 1197. 3. The statement of the work *Siang-cheng-ki*, B.C. 753. 4. Another statement places it in the time of Hia-kie, B.C. 1800. The fifth authority, *Chung-sheng-tien-ki*, gives the date B.C. 457. The sixth states that B.C. 687 was the year in question, and that then, according to the *Tso-chwen*, there was a shower of falling stars. This phenomenon is supposed to indicate Buddha's birth. A learned Buddhist, Ku-shan, argues that the birth must have taken place in the second month of the modern Chinese calendar, because in the Cheu dynasty the year began two months later. To this the defenders of the orthodox Chinese view say in reply, that in three Sutras the birth of Buddha is said to have taken place in the fourth month, and as they were all translated since the modern calendar was adopted, a century before the Christian era, it is not open to us to say that it took place in the second month.

At fifteen years of age he was, in an assembly of nobles and Brahmans, formally invested with the rank of heir-apparent. The nobles presented to his royal father basins filled with water from the four seas, and ornamented with the seven precious things. They also sprinkled water on the prince's head, and gave him the seal of the seven precious things.

At seventeen he was married to a Brahman maiden of the Shakya family called Yashodara. He was taught in his youth every possible accomplishment, and was supplied with all the delights that high position and riches could afford, but he soon learned to despise them.

At eighteen years of age he left the palace to visit certain pleasure gardens and groves. Passing the east gate of the city he saw there a Deva who had assumed the form of an old man, with white hairs and crooked back. He thought sadly on the rapidity with which men grow old. They become aged like lightning, and yet are not afraid. Going out again, the same divinity presented himself at the south gate in the disguise of a sick man, with languid features and swelled paunch. At the west gate he saw a dead man, and the members of his family laughing as they followed him to the grave. He went out once more, and saw at the north gate a begging priest, a Bikshu in fact. He wore the garb of an ascetic, and carried a bowl. A staff was in his hand. The prince asked him who he was. He replied, "I am a Bikshu, practising sacred duties, and always obtaining the reward of freedom from action." As he finished these words he rose into the air, and was soon out of sight. The prince thought, "I fear lest I may be pressed down by old age, sickness, death, the miseries I have witnessed. This Bikshu has arrived at the perception of my feelings. He shows me the path of deliverance." From this time the prince began to desire the ascetic life.

At twenty-five years old he sought an interview with his father, and said, "Kindness and affection, multiplied as they may be, lead but to partings. Allow me to enter on the ascetic life, that I may learn what wisdom is." His father tried in vain to detain him. On the seventh day of the second month the prince, while reflecting on the life of the recluse, emitted from his body a light which shone to all the palaces of the Devas. These beings then knew that Siddharta had become a recluse, and came to congratulate him. He asked their aid, and left his father's palace in the night-time under their escort, resolved to be a hermit, and saying, "If the eight miseries"—viz., birth, death, sickness, love, hatred, &c.—"be not abandoned, wisdom cannot be attained." He refused to return to his father's palace, and lived on the Himalaya Mountains in solitary spots, trying various methods to attain mental satisfaction, but in vain. He lived on hemp and barley, and assuaged his thirst with snow, till at thirty years of age he came to the perception of the true condition and wants of mankind. "He sighed, and said, 'It is strange that all men while they have within them *Julai* (the capacity of perceiving the true nature of life and worldly phenomena), and possess knowledge and virtue as the original property of their nature, should be entangled by deceptive thoughts and remain in ignorance of these things.' After this he lived forty-nine years, and delivered thirty-five discourses of special importance."

There were, during Buddha's life, five principal periods of instruction.

I. The time of delivering the *Hwa-yen-king*.—The scene was mostly in the paradises of the Devas, and the audience was composed of mythological personages. This was the first grand outburst of Buddhist thought, and it belongs to the "Greater development."

II. The deer garden period.—Buddha now becomes historical. His teaching and his audience are human. This is the period of instruction in the four miseries, examples of which we have in the *Sutra of Forty-two Sections*, and other works.

III. The teaching of squareness and equality;—where all the principles of Shakyamuni's philosophy appear in symmetry, as in the *Leng-yen-king*.

IV. The period of the Prajna.—Here Shakyamuni becomes most coldly metaphysical, and expounds the doctrine of salvation for man and all living beings in the triumphant tone of an icy logic. The miseries of society are to be terminated by minute hair-splitting and belief in certain profound abstractions, which, after all that may be said for them, are simply impossibilities.

V. The closing period of Buddha's public life included the announcement of the Lotus of the Good Law, and the doctrine of Nirvâna. Here, in prospect of death, the warmth of human feeling returns. Shakyamuni becomes sympathetic and touching, as in the days of youth when he founded the Hindoo monastic societies, and when, as an enthusiastic preacher, he visited one after another the great cities of Oude and Bahar.

At first Buddha appeared like the sun in the east illuminating the tops of the western hills. Bodhisattwas from immense distances were attracted, and came to recognise him as the teacher whose instructions would guide mankind to the highest truth. This was the Hwa-yen period. Next the sun shone on the valleys, and then upon the wide plains. After the Bodhisattwas had been taught, the first disciples of the human race, the *Shramanas*, or "listeners," were instructed in the valleys, and then all mankind in the plains. The changes of milk are referred to in illustration. The first teaching was like milk fresh from the cow. There are four subsequent stages, cream, ordinary butter, rich butter, and the oil which appears on the surface in the last boiling process. In Mongolia and North China milk is boiled to make butter.

The Hwa-yen doctrine is described also as *tun*, "an abrupt outburst." The teaching of the Bikshus is "gradual and elementary" (*tsien*), proceeding step by step from the *Book of the Forty-two Sections* to the *Leng-yen*, or "Square and equal," and from thence to the *Prajna paramita*. Beyond that, in the later years of his life, Buddha unfolded the "secret" (*pi-mi*) and "unfixed" (*pu-ting*) aspects of his doctrine.

The scene of the delivery of the *Hwa-yen* Sutra was laid in nine places. The first was under the *Bodhi* tree of *Aranya* in the kingdom of Magadha. This is different from the *Bodhi* tree of the *Agama* Sutras of the Small Development school. *Aranya* is "wild," "a quiet place," "belonging to the woods;" and *Aranyakah* "a forester," "a hermit," "living in seclusion" (see Eitel). The addition of *ka* marks an agent. Before Buddha's time, and during his youth, the hermit life had already become a fashion in India. He would, when a young and enthusiastic hermit, find himself more at home with men of this class than any other. In some green glade of the forests that skirt the mighty Himalayas, Shakyamuni is pictured by his northern followers with numberless mythological personages assembled before him. P'u-hien, or, as he is called in Sanscrit, *Samantabhadra*, is the principal speaker. He is one of the fabulous Bodhisattwas. Manjusiri, another, follows hit.

The scene is then suddenly changed to the paradises of the Devas. Indra receives Buddha in one of his palaces [6] on the Sumeru Mountain, and utters an encomium upon him in a speech in which he states that Kashiapa Buddha had discoursed on the same spot. He is followed by ten Bodhisattwas, who all speak in praise of Buddha's wisdom.

Buddha is next found in the heaven of Yama, the Indian Pluto, and after this in that called Tushita, literally "the happy," where his mother Maya resides. After this, the scene of the instructions and encomiums of the Bodhisattwas in the presence of Buddha is transferred to other Deva paradises, where Indra and other gods of the Brahmanical mythology hold conference with them.

Last of all, at the close of this long Sutra, the scene is laid in the garden of Jeta as in the "Sutra of the Diamond," *Kin-kang-king*. Shariputra and other disciples are there by anticipation, but do not see Buddha, nor the magnificent assemblage of Bodhisattwas. Before the assembly breaks up, Manjusiri takes his farewell of Buddha, and sets forth on a southward journey among mankind. Shariputra and 6000 Bikshus went to him for instruction. He exhorted them to practise the duties of the Bodhisattwas, that they might obtain the *samadhi* of faultless vision, and see the Buddha regions and all the Buddhas. Manjusiri then proceeded to the "city of happiness," on the east of which he met the youth familiarly known among the Northern Buddhists as Shan-ts'ai-t'ung-tsi, who became his disciple and learned from him the knowledge of Bodhi. He also traversed Southern India, where he taught in 110 cities.

Shakyamuni himself says very little in the course of this Sutra. It is intended rather for developing the mythology of the great Bodhisattwas. As such, it is highly valued in China, where the images of Wen-shu (Manjusiri) and P'u-hien are common in the temples. P'u-hien in one speech mentions China under the name Chen-tan,[7] as a region where many Bodhisattwas have been engaged in past times in instructing the people.

But the time had arrived when Shakyamuni must become a teacher of mankind, and we now find him suddenly making his appearance at Benares.

Legend having resolved to exalt Shakyamuni to the utmost extent of her resources, busied herself particularly with the year when he attained that perfect vision of truth which is called the state of Buddha.

He had passed six years in the exercises of severe abstinence and meditation. One day he thought, "I had better eat, lest the heretics should say that Nirvâna is attained in famishing the body. Let me eat, and then attain to perfect knowledge." He went to the Nairanjana river to bathe. Here a shepherdess gave him food which suddenly grew on a lotus-flower at her feet. He took it, and felt his strength return. He went to sit under a banyan tree (Pippala), or tree of Bodhi. The god Indra brought him a straw seat. He sat here, resolved not to move till the transformation he was about to undergo should be completed.

The king of the Maras, perceiving that the walls and foundations of his palace were shaking, thought in himself, "Gautama is now attaining perfect knowledge. Before he has reached the height of wisdom, I will go and trouble him." He went with bow and arrows, and attendant demons, to the tree where the object of his attack was sitting. He then addressed him—"Bodhisattwa! give up the monastic principle (*c'hu-kia fa*), and become a 'wheel king.' [8] If you rise not, I will shoot my darts at you." The Bodhisattwa was unmoved. The darts, as they fell, became lotus flowers. The king of the Maras then offered him his three daughters to attend on him. Shakyamuni said, "You attained, by a small act of virtue, the body of a Deva. You think not on the perishing, but seek to tempt me. You may leave me; I need you not." The king of the Maras again said, "I will resign to you my throne as a Deva, with the instruments of all the five pleasures." "No," replied the Bodhisattwa, "you attained the rank of Ishwara by some charitable deed. But this happiness has an end. I wish it not."

An army of spirits now issued from the ground and rebuked the tempter, who, as his last device, summoned a host of demons to assault the unconquerable youth. The air was filled with grim faces, gnashing teeth, and bristling spears. The Bodhisattwa looked on this scene as if it were child's play. A spirit in the air was now suddenly heard to say, "The Bodhisattwa attains this day, under the Bodhi tree, the perfection of knowledge. Here stands the diamond throne of many past Buddhas. It is not for you to disturb him. Cease your hostility, and wait upon him with respect." The king of the Maras then returned to his palace.

It was on the seventh day of the second month that Shakyamuni, after this victory, attained the rank of Buddha. This is described as entering into a state of reverie, emitting a bright light, and reflecting on the four modes of truth. [9] It is added, that he comes to the complete knowledge of the unreality of all he once knew as good and evil acting, long and short life, and the five paths of the metempsychosis, leading all living beings into a perpetual interchange of sorrow and joy. As the morning star of the eighth day of the month appeared, he suddenly awoke to this consciousness, and attained the perfect view of the highest truth.

As soon as Shakyamuni had risen from the state of P'usa to that of Fo, the assembly of the forty-one great teachers embodying the law, and of innumerable Devas, Nagas, and other supernatural beings, gathered round him, as the clouds gather round the moon.

To them he discoursed, as already described, in the *Hwa-yen-king*.

While he was meditating on the hopelessness of attempting the instruction of mankind, none but a Buddha being able to comprehend what Buddha knew, it first appeared better that he should enter at once into the Nirvâna. But from this wish he was dissuaded by Brahma and Indra, who came to intercede for mortals, and induce Buddha to become a public teacher. During seven days he received in silence Brahma's entreaties. In the second week he reflected on the sufferings and sorrows of man. In the third week, he said, "I ought to open the gate of the sweet law. Who should first hear it? The hermit Arara, who desired the perfect knowledge of truth? Let me first save him." A voice in the air said, "He died yesterday." Again he thought, "Then let the hermit Nalana be the first." The voice again said, "He died last night." He thought once more, "The five messengers sent by the minister of state had a like wish. Let them first hear the law." Buddha accordingly set out for Benares.

On the way, he sat by a pool in a state of *samadhi* for seven days. A blind Naga (snake or dragon) that lay in the pool felt the light that shone from Buddha restore his vision. He came out of the water, was transformed into a youth, and received the vows as a disciple.

On the seventh day of the third month, the spirit of the tree under which Buddha had for seven days been in a state of *samadhi*, took notice of Buddha's long abstinence from food. Five hundred travelling merchants passed at the moment, and the oxen that drew their waggons proved unable to pull the vehicles over the obstacles that lay in the road. Two of the merchants came to the tree to ask the spirit's aid. The spirit advised them of the presence of Buddha near the pool, and said they should offer him food. They gave him barley mixed with honey. The four kings of the Devas (who are seen in the front hall of Buddhist temples) took from the mountain stones four sweet-smelling bowls, which they found there by a happy chance. In these they offered the food. Buddha took all the bowls, for fear of giving offence to any of the kings. He then piled them up on his left hand, and, with his right (by magical manipulation), formed them into one, holding it so that all present might see it. Then, after uttering a charm, he ate the food, and proceeded at once to administer the vows to the two merchants, who, with their companions, all attained high grades in Buddhist knowledge.

Buddha, in this instance, imposed on the neophytes the ordinary five prohibitions suited for men and Devas. This must be regarded, therefore, as *exoteric* teaching. But as the grade attained was high in proportion to the amount of training, it belongs so far to the unfixed or arbitrary division of the exoteric doctrine *Hien-lu-chï-pu-ting-kiau*, "manifested, and not fixed teaching."

It is at this point in Shakya's biography that a new section begins.

Mankind were not at this time in a state to receive the doctrine of the Greater development, and Buddha must be content to leave the brilliantly-illuminated regions of the great Bodhisattwas and shine upon the retired valleys, where he will, by a gradual process of teaching, reform and make happy such groups as he may meet of ordinary mortals in their wretchedness and desolation. He will, for the time, postpone his more elevated discourses, and proceed to Benares to teach the rudiments of his system. The shining robes of the recognised Buddha must be exchanged for the tattered garb of the ascetic. This is to him a temporary disguise.

The Northern school, with all the looseness of its chronology, professes great exactness in dates.

Month.	Day.	Event.
2	8	Shakyamuni becomes Buddha.
,,	29	Teaches the Hwa-yen doctrine.
3	6	In reverie by the pool.
,,	7	Receives food from the merchants.
,,	8	In the garden at Benares.

In these dates, says the biographer, intervals of three, four, and five weeks may be observed.

Footnotes

1. *A-send-gi-kap.* The Sanscrit word *Asankhyâ* means "innumerable." *Kalpa* is applied to periods of time varying from a few hundreds to many thousand years.
2. Tushita now pronounced *Tushïto.*
3. See Klaproth's *Life of Buddha*, and Turnour's *Examination of the Pali Buddhistical Annals.*
4. The suggestion of Turnour to account for the sixty-five years discrepancy of the Singhalese and Greek dates is, that dates were altered to reconcile

5. *San-kiau-yi-su*, "Supplementary account of the three religions."
6. The *Tau-li-t'ien*, or "Heaven of the number 33;" in Sanscrit, *Triyastrimsas*. Sumeru is probably Elburz, an isolated mountain of the Caucasus range, 18,000 feet in height, and surrounded by low ground. The syllable *su*, like *el*, is a prefix. If this supposition be correct, the Hindoo race, when forming its legends of the Deva worlds in their first form, must have lived in the vicinity of the Caucasus. $Su = El; Me = Bu; Ru = r$.

Buddha's prophecies with facto. This throws light on the design of the Northern Buddhists in antedating Buddha's birth by 447 years.

7. *Hwa-yen-king*, chap. xxvi. *Tan* means "country," as in Hindostan, Afghanistan.
8. A king who rules the world, and causes the wheel of doctrine everywhere to revolve. The great Ashôka was a wheel king. The word is *Chakravarti* in Sanscrit, from *Chakra*, "wheel," the symbol of activity, whether of Buddha in preaching, or of kings like Ashôka in ruling.
9. These are, *Ku*, "misery," *Tsi*, "assembling," *Mie*, "destruction," and *Tau*, "the path," consisting in knowledge of misery, truth, and oppressive restraints, the need of separation from the ties of passion, the possibility of destroying the desires, and the path of salvation as regards the practical Buddhist life.

CHAPTER II.

LIFE OF BUDDHA FROM HIS APPEARANCE AS A TEACHER AT BENARES TO THE CONVERSION OF RAHULA.

The four truths—Godinia and his four companions—The first monastic community—The first lay brother—Conversion of five hundred fire worshippers in the kingdom of Magadha—Buddha at Rajagriha—At Shravasti, in Jeta's garden—Appoints punishments for crimes of monks—Goes to see his father after twelve years' absence—Story of his son Rahula.

IT was exactly thirty-five days after his arriving at perfect wisdom that Buddha opened his public life at Benares, by discoursing to Godinia and others on the four truths. "You should know," he said to his auditors, "the fact of misery (DUK'A), and the need of becoming separated from the accumulation of entanglements caused by the passions (SAMUDAYA). These two truths belong to the world from which you are now exhorted to take your departure. You should also experience the extinction of these miseries and entanglements (NIRODA), and the path of reformation (MARGA). These two truths belong to the monastic life on which you should now enter."

Having these subjects to discourse on, Buddha went forth to appeal to the youth of India, the hermits, the followers of the Zoroastrian fire-worship, the Brahman who studied the Vedas, and to men of every class.

The wheel of doctrine revolved thrice. There was first didactic statement, then exhortation, and lastly appeal to evidence and personal experience. The image is that of grinding. The chaff and refuse are forced from the good flour by repeated revolutions of the wheel. The statement of facts, the urgent appeal, and the proof are repeated in the inculcation of each of the "four truths." The wheel of Buddhist preaching was thus made to perform twelve revolutions. [1]

Having once launched the subject under these four heads, it was natural that the Hindoo minds of the time, fond as they were of dialectical hair-splitting, should ramify them into numberless subdivisions. They talked of the eighty-one states of misery, the eighty-eight varieties of deception, the thirty-seven methods of reformation, &c.

One of Buddha's earliest converts was Godinia, who was attracted by his teaching upon the four truths, and attained the first grade of clear vision. It was at Benares, the ancient Varanasi, in the Mrigadava garden (*Lu-ye-yuen*), that this conversion and that of four others took place. Thus began the revolving of the wheel of the Buddhist law, which was destined to spread the new doctrine over so wide a portion of Asia, and to continue for so many centuries. These new disciples asked to be permitted to commence the monkish life. This Shakya allowed, saying, "Bikshus! it is for you to take off your hair, wear the kasha, and become Shramanas." He discoursed of the non-permanence of human actions, of the emptiness of the external world, the non-existence of the *Ego*, the deliverance of the mind from thraldom by the cessation of faults, and the consequent attainment of the moral and intellectual rank of Arhan.

"Thus," adds the delighted Buddhist historian, "the world for the first time had six Arhans, and (including the new doctrine) the *Three Precious Ones* (*San Pau*). The first was Buddha, the second was the revolving of the wheel of the doctrine of the four truths (*Dharma*), and the third was the company of the five Arhans (*Sanga*). Well might that garden be regarded as the happy land of men and Devas (*T'ien*)." This was the foundation of the spiritual communities of Buddhism. The *Sanga*, or assembly of believers, distinguished by common vows of abstinence from marriage, from animal food, and the occupations of social life, now commenced. The Sangarama and Vihara, [2] or *monastery*, was soon rendered necessary for the residence of the voluntary cœnobites, who daily grew in numbers, and the greatest social revolution that ever took place in India was fairly begun.

Soon afterwards, a youth of great intelligence saw in the night-time a light. He opened the door of the house, and went out in search of the light. He soon reached Buddha's garden, was taught, became an Arhan, and requested permission to take the vows, to which Buddha at once consented. The father of this youth came in search of him, and was also taught by Buddha. He became a convert; with purged vision took the vows of adherence to the Three Precious Ones, and returned home to become the first Upâsaka, or lay brother, keeping the rules, but living at his own house. It was permitted to the neophyte, if he preferred it, to continue in the position which he held in social life, and not to join the monastic community.

As soon as the number had increased to fifty-six, another great step was taken by Shakyamuni. He broke up the community, and dismissed all its members to travel everywhere, giving instruction in the doctrine of the four miseries to all persons with whom they met. This occupation was connected with begging for food. At this time the Buddhist community had no property. It was supported by the liberality of the new members, or by the gifts of rich persons. Whether the monks were in the monastery or upon their travels, the normal mode of gaining support was by the charity of neighbours, of passersby, of kings and nobles, and all the kindly disposed. The system was thus gradually, in the early years of Shakyamuni's teaching, assuming the form it has taken in all Buddhist countries. Monastic vows, living in spiritual communities, voluntary poverty, and universal preaching—these formed the basis on which the great Buddhist structure was erected. We cannot but admire the wonderful practical genius of the man who conceived the system, and carried it out with such triumphant success. In a few years India was covered, through the labours of the Buddhist preachers, with flourishing communities of monks, and in the cool season of the year the Bikshus, or religious mendicants, were everywhere seen on the roads and in the cities teaching the true path to the Nirvâna.

As Shakyamuni was the first in time of the founders of monastic communities, so he surpassed them all in the originality of his conceptions, in the success of his system, and in the force of his influence.

The Buddhist preachers left their master, who proceeded from Benares to Magadha. At evening he slept in the house of Uluvilva Kashiapa. He there subdued a fiery snake, and administered to him the vows of adherence to Buddha, the Law, and the Priesthood. To produce an impression on Kashiapa's mind, he enclosed the snake in a rice bowl. Kashiapa was still deficient in knowledge, but from this time he ripened and progressed visibly.

On the banks of the Nairanjana river, Shakyamuni had an interview, says the legend, with his old enemy, the king of the Maras (the Chinese *mo* in *mo-kwei*, "devil"), who wished to enter the Nirvâna. But Buddha refused his thrice repeated request, on the ground that he was not *mentally prepared* for the change. Thus, legend—which was never more active in inventing wonderful stories about any one than about Shakyamuni—makes him sovereign over the most powerful supernatural beings. He did not, however, always refuse applicants for salvation from other worlds. He is said to have gone up to the Tushita paradise to instruct his mother Maya in the new law. On the banks of the same river, five hundred fire-worshippers, after hearing his discourse on the four miseries, became Arhans, and threw their implements of worship into the river. Their religion—frequently mentioned in early Buddhist history—was, as it would appear, propagated from Persia to India not long before the time of Cyrus. In Persia, fire-worship had been added to the old Magian worship of the heavenly bodies. But while it had triumphed through Zoroaster's influence in Persia, it was destined to be expelled from India by Buddhism. With these new converts, Buddha went to the city of Rajagriha, and was received there with perfect confidence and admiration. The king Vimbasâra, Ajatashatru's father, [3] and all the principal persons in the city, Brahmans, officers, and people, became his disciples.

The ruins of this city are still visited by the Jains, at a spot sixteen miles south-west of Bahar. [4] It was the metropolis of the Magadha princes till the era of Ashôka, the Buddhist monarch who ruled all India about two hundred years after the time of Shakyamuni. Here Buddha taught for many years, and received some of his most celebrated disciples, such as Shariputra, Maudgalyayana, and Kashiapa. At this time Buddha began to appoint the wearing of the *shangati*, or upper robe, reaching to the knees. It is worn outside the *kasha*, or long robe, which was in use from the commencement of the monastic institute.

Three years later, Shakya was invited to Shravasti, to occupy a house and garden expressly provided for him by the king's eldest son and a rich noble, as already described. It was the Jetavana Vihara, or Monastery of Jeta's Garden. Here he was in the kingdom of Kosala, then ruled by Prasenajita; who, with the chief. persons of influence, were all in favour of the new doctrine.

Buddha was obliged to become a legislator. As thefts, assassination, and evil-speaking occurred in his community, he made special rules for the punishment of such crimes (*Fo-tsu-t'ung-ki*, iii. 30).

His father sent a messenger to him, after he had been absent from home for twelve years, to inform him that he wished to see him, and to invite him to come for a visit. The messenger was a Brahmachâri (a religious student or observer of Brahmanical rules of purity), named Udaya. On hearing Buddha discourse, Udaya at once attained to the state of Arhan (Lohan). Buddha now resolved to go to see his father, and attempt, by teaching, to save both him and his mother. He sent forward Udaya to inform the king, and perform before him the eighteen changes—a series of magical effects. The king was delighted, and went out of the city thirteen miles, accompanied with an escort of ten thousand persons, to welcome Shakyamuni, who was conspicuous for his stature—being sixteen feet in height—and his brilliant golden colour. He appeared like the moon among the clouds. Around him were many Brahmachâri who had long been in the woods and mountains, and whose bodies were black. They seemed like those black-winged birds that fly round the purple-golden mountain. The king then ordered five hundred youths of distinguished families to become monks and attend on Buddha, like phoenixes round Mount Sumeru.

The hermit life in India preceded the monastic life. Buddha himself was at first a hermit, like the Brahmachâri of the time. But while they aimed at the old Brahmanical purity, his mind swelled with new thoughts and aims. They were content to avoid the stains of a secular life. He was bent on saving multitudes by teaching.

When Buddha was come to see his father after twelve years' absence, his wife brought his little son, Rahula, to see him. The boy was just six years old, and the courtiers doubted if Buddha was his father. Buddha said to the doubters, "Yashodara has been true to her duty. I will give proof of it." He then, by his magical power, caused the monks present all to become Buddhas in appearance. Yashodara then took a signet ring and gave it to the boy, saying to him, "This is your father's; give it to him." Rahula took it and gave it at once to Buddha. The king and all the courtiers said, "Good! this boy is truly the son of Buddha." [5]

Footnotes

1. *Shï-er-hing-fa-lun.*
2. *Sanga*, "assembly;" *arâma*, "garden;" *Vihâra*, "a place for walking about in."
3. From *Vimba*, "shadow;" *sâra*, "strength." In old Chinese, *Bimbasala.*
4. Eitel's *Handbook of Chinese Buddhism.*
5. Other stories take the place of this in Mr. Beal's translation of *The Romantic Legend of Sâkya Buddha.*

CHAPTER III.

FROM THE COMMENCEMENT OF RAHULA'S RELIGIOUS LIFE TILL THE NEAR APPROACH OF THE NIRVANA.

Buddha sends for Rahula—Arrangements for instructing Rahula and other boys—Tutors—Boys admitted to the vows—Nuns—Rapid spread of monasticism—Disciplinary rules—Education in metaphysics—Ananda and the Leng-yen-king—Buddha in these works like Socrates in Plato—Buddha said to have gone to Ceylon—Also to the paradise of desire—Offer of Devas to protect Buddhism—Protectors of China—Relation of Buddhism to Hindoo polytheism—Pradjna Paramita—King Prasenajit—Sutra of the Benevolent King—Daily liturgy—Ananda becomes Buddha's attendant disciple—Intrusted with the Sutras in twelve divisions—Buddha teaches his esoteric system—Virtually contained in the "Lotus Sutra"—In this the sun of Buddha culminated—His father's approaching death announced—Buddha reaches the forty-ninth year of his public preaching.

WHEN Buddha was forty-four years old he sent a messenger to his father and wife to say that his son Rahula was now nine years of age, and ought to commence the religious life. Maudgalyayana was the messenger. The mother replied, "When *Julai* (Tathâgata) was a prince he married me, and before we had been married three years he went away to lead a mountain life. Having after six years become Buddha, and returned to visit his country, he now wishes me to give him my son. What misery can be so great as this?" She was, however, persuaded to consent to this sacrifice, and committed him to the care of the messenger. With him the king sent fifty sons of noble families to be his companions in taking the vows and receiving instruction.

They were placed, says the legend, under the care of Shariputra and Maudgalyayana as their tutors—*Ho-shang* (*Upâsaka*), and *A-che-li* (*Acharya*). [1] The original meaning of the ordinary Chinese term for Buddhist priest thus appears to be "tutor." The primary duty of the Ho-shang was to be the guide of young monks. The term was afterwards extended in Eastern Turkestan to all monks. From that country it was introduced into China, where it is still used in the wider sense, all monks being called *Ho-Shang*.

It was now arranged by Buddha that while boys might be received into the community, if the parents were willing, when still of tender years, as from twelve to seventeen, they should not receive the full vows till they were twenty. He also ordered the erection of an altar for administering the vows. It is called *Kiai-t'an*, "Vow altar." It is ascended by three flights of steps. On the top sit the officiating priest and his assessors. The flights of steps are so arranged that the neophyte passes three times round the altar on his way up, to indicate his triple submission to Buddha, the Law, and the Priesthood.

Women began to ask and received permission to take the vows. They were called in India *Bikshuni*, and in China *Niku*. *Ni* is the Sanscrit feminine termination of *Bikshu*, and *ku* is a common respectful term used of aunts, young girls, &c.

In twelve years from the commencement of his public teaching Buddha's doctrines had spread over sixteen Indian kingdoms, the monastic system was founded, and the outline of the regulations for the monks and nuns was already drawn.

Shakyamuni taught morality by rules. He hedged round his community with the strictest regulations, but he made metaphysics the staple article of his oral instructions. He tried first to bring his disciples out of danger from the world's temptations by introducing them to the spiritual association of the Bikshus. Here there was community of goods, brotherhood, the absence of secular cares, strict moral discipline, and regular instruction. The only respite was when the whole community went out into the streets of the city to receive the alms of the householders in the form of money or food. The instruction consisted of high metaphysics and a morality which speaks chiefly of mercy, and only looks at duty on its human side. Obedience to the law of God is in Shakyamuni's morality kept assiduously out of view. Instead of theology he taught metaphysics, and instead of a history of God's dealings with mankind, such as the Bible is to the Christian, he supplied them with an unlimited series of the benevolent actions of the Buddhas and Bodhisattwas.

This is true of Northern and Southern Buddhism, but the system prevailing in Ceylon and Siam has perhaps somewhat less of the metaphysical and more of the moral element than that found in China and Mongolia.

One of the most striking examples of the use of metaphysics as a cure for moral weakness, is found in the *Leng-yen-king*. The incident, which is of course legendary, is placed by Buddha's biographers in the forty-fifth year of his age and in the city Shravasti. Ananda, the favourite disciple, lingered one evening in the streets, where he proceeded alone from door to door begging. He accidentally met a wicked woman named Matenga. The god Brahma had already resolved to injure Ananda, and now drew him by a spell into the house of Matenga. Buddha, knowing of the spell, after the evening meal returned from the house of the rich man who entertained him, sent forth a bright lotus light from his head and received a charm. He then directed Manjusiri to take the charm with which he had thus been miraculously furnished, and go to save Ananda. By means of it he was told to bring Ananda and Matenga for instruction. Ananda on arriving made his bow and wept, blaming himself that he had not come before, and that after much teaching his "strength" (*tau-li*) was so far from perfect. Earnestly he asked the aid of the Buddhas of the ten regions that he might obtain the first benefits of knowledge (Bodhi). Buddha in agreeing to his desire announced to him the doctrine of the *Leng-yen-king*. The attempt is made to strengthen the disciple against temptation by a grand display of metaphysical skill. The man who founded the monastic institute as a cure for worldliness, might consistently teach philosophical negations as a remedy against bad morality. But it is for ever to be regretted that Shakyamuni failed to see the true foundations of morality. Confucius was able to uncover the secret of the origin of virtue and duty so far as to trace it to conscience and natural light. Judaism found it in the revealed law of God. Christianity combined the law written on the heart with the revealed law of the Divine Ruler. But Shakyamuni failed to express rightly the relation of morality to God or to human nature. Here is the most grievous failure of his system. He knew the longing of humanity for deliverance from misery, and the struggle which takes place perpetually in the heart of mankind between good and evil; but he misunderstood them because he was destitute not only of Christian and Jewish, but even of Confucian light. Fortunately, however, all the imperfect teaching in the world cannot destroy the witness which conscience in every land bears to the distinctions of eternal and immutable morality, or Buddha's teaching would have been still more harmful.

The occurrence of the *Leng-yen-king* early in Buddha's public life constitutes a difficulty to the Buddhist commentators. Buddha is perfect. He commences with the superficial, and finishes with the profound. How was it that this most polished specimen of his acumen, acknowledged to be so by noted Chinese Confucianists like Chu-fu-tsï, should equal the Sutras which were delivered at the end of his life? They therefore deny its equality with the *Fa-hwa-king*, "The Lotus of the Good Law," delivered, so they say, when Shakyamuni was an old man.

It has cost much labour to reduce the Sutras into a self-consistent chronological order. The Northern Buddhists when they added the literature of the Mahayana to that which was composed by Shakyamuni's immediate disciples, felt obliged to show in a harmonious scheme of his long life, to what years the various Sutras of the *Hinayana* and *Mahayana*, or "Smaller" and "Greater Development," should be assigned.

Imagine a life of Socrates composed by a modern author on the hypothesis that he really spoke all that Xenophon and Plato said in his name. Each or these authors imparted his own colouring to his account, and introduced his own thoughts in various proportion; and Plato's works certainly constitute the record of his own intellectual life rather than that of Socrates. His rambles in the world of thought have ever since his time been regarded as his own much more than they were those of his revered teacher. How foolish and useless would be the endeavour to construct a biography of Socrates on the principle that he wrote Plato, that the Platonic dialogues were all the products of his mind, that the incidents real or fictitious they record were all capable of arrangement in a self-consistent scheme, and that the philosophical principles they contain were all developed in a symmetrical succession, and at definite epochs in the life of Socrates! Such is the hopeless task undertaken by Buddha's Northern biographers.

Buddha, in the eighteenth year of his public teaching, is said to have gone to Ceylon, called in the Sutras Lenga island. He went to the top of Adam's Peak, and here delivered the *Lenga Sutra*. A Bodhisattwa said to him, "Heretics prohibit the eating of flesh. How much more should Buddha enforce abstinence from flesh!" Buddha assented, and gave several reasons why Bodhisattwas and others should conform to this rule. Lenga Island is described as inhabited by Yakshas, and as unapproachable by men except by those who are endowed with magical power.

During the next year Buddha is said to have visited one of the heavenly paradises, in the middle of the second range of the heaven of colour and desire, where an assemblage of Buddhas and Bodhisattwas from the ten regions gathered before him. Here he delivered the *Ta-tsi-king*. Each P'usa appeared in the form of the element he governed, whether it were "air" (*k'ung*), water, or any other. The Devas and Nagas now came forward, and said, "We will henceforth protect correct doctrine. If any kings scourge members of the monkish community, we will not protect their kingdoms. The disciples of Buddha will abandon their inhospitable territories, which will then remain unblessed. Not having the religious establishments which bring happiness on a country, pestilence, famine, and war will commence, while wind, and rain, and drought will bring ruin on the agriculture."

After the gods and dragons had finished this speech, Buddha addressed himself to a son of a Deva called Vishvakarma, the patron of artisans, [2] the Yaksha Kapila, and fifteen daughters of Devas, having eyes with two pupils, and directed them to become the patrons of China. Each of them was told to take 5000 followers and wherever there was strife, litigation, war, or pestilence, to put a stop to those evils, so that the eye of Buddha's law might long remain in that land.

The mythology of India appears in this description in its true light. The aboriginal inhabitants of a distant island like Ceylon were thought of as a race of demons. The beings called Devas, the *Theoi* of Greece, and the *Dei* of the Latins, were a class subordinate to Buddha, the self-elevated sage. For want of a better word, the Chinese term for "Heaven," *T'ien*, is applied to them. The "dragons," or *nagas*,—with which the Hebrew *nahash* [3] and English snake may be compared,—are here viewed as a class of celestial beings.

All these beings, however exalted, are regarded by the Buddhists as subject to the commands of their sage. Continuing to rule the world, they do so in the interest of the new law which Shakyamuni has introduced. Hence in Buddhist temples they are placed at the door, and are worshipped as invisible protectors of all faithful Buddhists.

When the legend says that "gods" (Devas) and "dragons" (Nagas) agreed to protect Buddhism, the meaning is, that at this period in

Buddha's life the Indian kings began to favour his religion in a more public and extended manner than before.

Shakyamuni next delivered—according to the Chinese account of him—the Prajna Paramita (*Pat-no-pa-la-mit-ta*). *Prajna* is "wisdom." *Para* is "the farther side" of a river. *Mita* is "known," "measured," "arrived at." There are six means of arriving at the farther shore of the sea of misery. They constitute the six Paramitas. Of these, that called the Prajna is the highest. The original works containing this system were thought too voluminous to be translated in full by Kumarajiva. It was not till the seventh century that Hiuen-tsang the traveller, after his return from India, undertook the laborious task of translating one of these works, which extended to six hundred chapters, and one hundred and twenty volumes. Nagarjuna, the most noted writer among the twenty-eight patriarchs, founded on some of these works the Shastra of the "Measure of Wisdom." [4] The Chinese Chï-k'ai, the sage of T'ien-t'ai, made much use of the Prajna in constructing his system. He had only Kumarajiva's fragmentary translations, such as the "Diamond Classic."

The "Benevolent King" (*Jen-wang*), here takes his place in the Chinese narrative of Shakyamuni's life. This of t-mentioned personage was Prasenajita, king of Shravasti. It was to him that Buddha is said to have delivered one of the Prajna discourses, and to have given the advice that he should, for the avoidance of national calamities, invite a hundred priests to recite this Sutra upon a hundred elevated seats twice in one day. Thus he would be able to prevent rebellion, the invasion of hostile armies, portents in the sun, moon, and stars, great fires, inundations, dearth, destructive winds, and drought. The king, when travelling, should have the Sutra placed upon a table ornamented with the Seven Precious Things, viz., articles of gold, silver, crystal, glass, cornelian, coral, and pearls, and it should be fully a hundred paces in advance of himself. When at home, it should be kept on an elevated throne, over which hang curtains ornamented with the same precious things. It should be honoured daily with reverential bows, as a man would honour his father and mother.

Here is the first mention of the daily service, and of the superstitious reverence for the sacred books called Sutras common among the Buddhists of all countries. The possession of a "Sutra" or *nom* among the Mongols, and a *king* among the Chinese, is believed to bring good luck to the family and the state. They are often written in gilt letters, and occupy an honourable position near the domestic idol. The rulers of nature will protect those who honour Buddha's true words. Such is the Asiatic fetishism. Buddha himself, and the books containing his teaching, become worshipped objects; and the grand liturgical services performed by large companies of priests at the call of emperors and rich men in times of drought, sickness, death, and other calamities, are believed by the people to be beneficial on the ground of such passages as that just given.

When the same Sutra—the *Prajna Paramita*—was heard by the kings of sixteen Indian States, they were, says the enthusiastic but evidently not truthful narrator, so delighted, that they gave over the affairs of their governments to their brothers, adopted the monastic life, and became devoted seekers after Buddhist perfection. The names of the countries or cities they ruled were—Shravasti, Magadha, Paranai or Benares, Vaishali the seat of the second synod, Kapilavastu Buddha's birthplace, Kushinara the city where he died, Kosala the modern Oude and Berar, Cophen the modern Cabul, Kulu, Gatakana, Kucha, &c.—(*Fo-tsu-t'ung-ki*).

In the sixtieth year of his age, Ananda was selected to be the personal attendant of Shakyamuni, and in his care were deposited the Sutras in twelve great divisions. This statement means that Ananda was the most active of the disciples in preserving the sayings of his teacher, and perhaps in composing the older Sutras. Godinia's offer of service was declined on account of his age. Maudgalyayana, in a state of reverie, saw that Shakyamuni's thoughts were on Ananda. He told Godinia, who persuaded Ananda to accept the duty.

In temples Ananda is placed on the right hand of Buddha, for, says the legend, Shakyamuni set his heart upon him, as the sun at his rising sheds his light straight on the western wall. In Singhalese temples Ananda's image is not placed in that close proximity to Buddha which is common in China. [5] This circumstance suggests that he does not, among the Southern Buddhists, occupy so prominent a position as keeper of the Sutras and personal attendant on Shakyamuni as he is entitled to in the opinion of their Northern brethren. In the sentence "Thus have I heard," which opens all the Sutras, the person who speaks is Ananda.

At seventy-one years of age, Buddha gave instruction in his esoteric or mystic doctrine. It was in answer to thirty-six questions propounded to him by Kashiapa. Nagarjuna lays it down as a rule that "every Buddha has both a revealed and a mystic doctrine." The exoteric is for the multitude of new disciples. The esoteric is for the Bodhisattwas and advanced pupils, such as Kashiapa. It is not communicated in the form of definite language, and could not, therefore, be transmitted by Ananda as definite doctrine among the Sutras. Yet it is virtually contained in the Sutras. For example, the *Fa-hwa-king*, or "Sutra of the Lotus of the Good Law," which is regarded as containing the cream of the revealed doctrine, is to be viewed as a sort of original document of the esoteric teaching, while it is in form exoteric.

This work, the *Saddharma Pundarika*, or "Great Lotus of the Good Law," takes its name from the illustrations employed in it. The good law is made plain by flowers of rhetoric. For example, in the fifth chapter, Maitreya rises in the assembly and addresses Buddha, reminding him of the time, forty and more years before, when he became an ascetic, left the palace of the Shakya clan, and lived near the city of Gaya as a hermit. He then points to the multitude of immeasurably exalted

Bodhisattwas, the fruit of his teaching. "The wonderful result is," he says, "to men incredible. It is as if a man of beautiful countenance and black hair, about twenty-five years of age, should say, pointing to an old man of a hundred, 'This is my son;' and the old man should point to the young man and say, 'This is my father.' Their words would be hard to believe, but it is not less so to credit the fact of the marvellous results of Buddha's exertions in so short a space of time. How is it, too," he asks, "that these innumerable disciples have, during past periods of boundless time, been practising Buddha's law, exercising magical powers, studying the doctrines of the Bodhisattwas escaping the stains of the world, emerging, like the lotus from its miry bed, and now appear here with reverence in the presence of the World's Honoured one?"

This Sutra marks the time when, say the biographers, Buddha's sun reached the zenith and cast no shadow. They take the opportunity to remark here that Central India, where Buddha lived, is in fact the Middle kingdom, as shown by the gnomon, which, at the summer solstice, in that latitude casts no shadow. China, they say, cannot so well be called the Central kingdom, because there is a shadow there on the day mentioned.

When Buddha's father was an old man, and was seized with a threatening sickness, the son sent him a comforting message by Ananda. Having, by attending to the prohibitions of purity, caused the removal of pollution from his heart, he should rejoice and meditate on the doctrine of the Sutras. The messenger was directed first to leap in the air, so as to produce a supernatural light, which should shine upon the sick king, causing relief from pain. Then he was to put his hand upon his forehead, and state the message. Immediately afterwards, the king, placing his hand on his heart in an attitude of worship, suddenly took his departure preparatory to his next transmigration. Members of the Shakya clan placed him in his coffin, and set him upon the throne ornamented with lions. At the funeral, the four kings of the Devas, at their own request, officiated as coffin-bearers, having for this purpose assumed the human form. Buddha himself went in front carrying an incense-holder. The coffin was burnt, with sandal-wood for fuel, and the bones were collected in gold caskets by various kings, who afterwards erected Dagobas and Stupas over them. Buddha informed his followers that the deceased, on account of his purity of life, had been born into one of the higher paradises above the Sumeru mountain.

Early Buddhism favoured no castes. Persons of all castes were equal in the eyes of Buddha. This circumstance made the new religion very popular with men of humble origin. This, perhaps, was the cause of the preservation of Buddha and Ananda when the clan of Shakya, to which they belonged, was massacred. Prasenajita had a son by a woman of low caste. This boy, when eight years old, had been insulted by the Shakya clan. He was learning archery in the house of a tutor. A new house for Buddha to discourse in had just been completed, and the sage had been invited with his followers. Ruli, the young prince, mounted the lion throne, when he was sarcastically reviled by members of the Shakya clan for presuming to sit on the throne, he being of ignoble birth. On succeeding to the kingdom, he went to make war on the Shakyas, and had an immense number of them trodden to death by elephants in pits. His brother, Jeta, giver of the garden of that name, was also killed by him for refusing to take part in this cruel act.

Buddha told his followers that Jeta was born anew in the *Paradise of Indra*, usually called in Chinese "The thirty-three heavens." He also foretold the early destruction of Ruli and his soldiers in a thunder-storm, which took place, it is said, according to the prediction, when they all went to the hell called Avichi. Buddha also said that the unhappy fate of the Shakyas was due to their mode of life. They were fishermen, and, as they had been destroyers of life, so were they destroyed.

In the view of Shakyamuni, a moral fate rules the world. Innumerable causes are constantly working out their retributive effects. These are the *yin-yuen* of which we hear the Chinese Buddhists say so much. This moral fate is impersonal, but it operates with rigid justice. Every good action is a good *yin-yuen*, securing at some future time an infallible reward. All virtuous and wise persons are supposed to be so, as the result of good actions accumulated in former lives.

Buddha was now approaching the last year of his life. In the eleventh month he said to the Bikshus gathered round him in the city Vaishali, "I shall enter the Nirvâna in the third month of next year."

Footnotes

1. Eitel's *Handbook*. The word Ho-shang is translated from *Upâsaka* into the former language of Khoten. From Turkestan it was introduced into China.—(*Fan-yi-ming-i*).
2. Eitel's *Handbook*.
3. Nahash in Hebrew, "serpent," is said to be named from the hissing sound of the animal. To "utter incantations" is *nahash* or *lahash*.
4. *Chi-tu-lun*. See *Fo-tsu-t'ung-ki*, xxx. 13.
5. When at Galle in 1858 I noticed this.

CHAPTER IV.

LAST DISCOURSES AND DEATH OF BUDDHA.

Buddha's immortality in his teaching—Death real and final—Object of Nirvâna teaching—Buddha visits the Tau-li heaven—Descends again by Indra's staircase—The first images—Death of Buddha's aunt—Death of Shariputra—Buddha at Kushinagara—Between the Sala trees—Last instructions—Kashiapa made patriarch—Flesh prohibited—Relieves the king of Magadha—Sends for Ananda—Answers to four questions—Brahma comes—Buddha's last words—Death—Gold coffin—Maya comes—Cremation—His relics—Pagodas.

THE fifth period of development in the discourses of Buddha embraces those books which belong to the "Lotus of the Good Law," and the "Nirvâna." They close his public life as a teacher, and are regarded as the mellowest and richest of his productions. They were adapted to excite the longing of his disciples for higher attainments. This was his meaning when he said, "I am not to be destroyed, but shall be constantly on the 'mountain of instruction' (*ling-shan*, 'efficacious mountain')." This, says the writer, is what is intended by Buddha entering the Nirvâna, where there is neither life nor death. He is not dead, because he lives in his teaching.

Thus interpreted, the claim of the Northern Buddhists on behalf of their sage amounts to an immortality in the results of his instructions.

This is the Buddhist *non omnis moriar*. It is consistent with much scepticism, and may amount by implication to a denial of the future life, and the continued existence of the soul in any form.

We must not forget that the enthusiastic Buddhists who wrote the treatises we are now examining belonged to the same actual waking, moving world with ourselves. They fell back, not seldom, from a state of metaphysical reverie into the condition of common men under the dominion of the senses. Then they took a firm grasp of the world. Metaphysics vanished. Death they looked on as a real death. The destruction of the material organisation is real. As for the soul, it lives in its actions. A great hero like Buddha lives only in the results of his life work. Perhaps our Sung dynasty author of six centuries ago felt satisfaction occasionally in resting the truth of his philosophy, as an expounder of the Mahayana, on the reality of visible things. In this case he finds the Nirvâna of Shakyamuni in the unbroken continuance of the results of his teaching.

The same tendency to look out on the actual world accounts for the view here taken of the Nirvâna as a system of ultimate doctrine adapted to correct the faults of negligent and misguided monks and others. After the earlier instructions had been delivered, down to the period of the "Lotus of the Good Law," there were still some men who failed to comprehend the full sense of Buddha's teaching. To them it was necessary still to discourse on the true nature of Buddha, that they might learn what is "really permanent" (*chen-c'hang*), and so enter the Nirvâna, As the farmer has the early and the late harvest, so Buddha, when the first sowing of instruction had been followed by the ripening and the harvest, proceeded to a later sowing and harvest. It was then that a multitude of disciples, high and low in attainment, came to see, as never before, the true nature of Tathâgata, and to bear the fruit of a ripe experience. After their autumn harvesting and winter garnering, there was no more for them to do. Among them were those who advanced from the *Prajna Paramita* to the *Fa-hwa* (lotus), and others who, their perceptions still blunted, found the *Fa-hwa* beyond their reach, and were only capable of being reduced to a state of mental and moral submission by the *Nirvâna*. They find in the Nirvâna doctrine that which enables them to see Buddha's nature.

The historian has his eye upon those monks of later times who like to read other books than those of Buddha himself, and cease to use the books of Buddha for their instruction. They learn to encourage injurious and destructive thoughts, even when under the control of Buddha's law. They shorten wisdom's life, and let go completely from their possession the "embodiment of the law" (*fa-shen*). It is for such backsliders that the doctrine of permanence was introduced. Its fulness and reality were to furnish them with a firm support. This was why, near the close of his life, Shakyamuni discoursed specially on the Nirvâna before himself entering into that state of blissful extinction. By this means he is stated to have strengthened the authority of the monkish system of rules, and with it that of the three divisions of the Buddhist library.

We see the teaching of the Nirvâna to be the doctrine of Buddha in his old age, when his experience was ripe. It was the result of his observation of the needs of the Buddhist community. It was the completing process in the development of doctrine, and was adapted to affect minds which remained unmoved under earlier and simpler forms of teaching.

In the year 947 B.C., according to the chronology of the Northern school, Buddha went to the Tau-li heaven, and remained three months. He sent Manjusiri to his mother to ask her for a time to bend before the Three Precious Things. She came. Immediately milk flowed from her and reached Buddha's mouth. She came with Manjusiri to the place where Buddha was, who instructed her. She attained the Su-da-wan fruit. In the third month, when Buddha was about to enter Nirvâna, Indra made three flights of steps. By these Buddha, after saying farewell to his mother, descended to the world, led by a multitude of disciples, and went to the Jetavana garden in the city of Shravasti. The king Udayana, of Kaushambi, felt for Buddha a loving admiration, and made a golden image. Hearing that Buddha was about to descend by the steps Indra had made, he came with the image and bowed before Buddha. The image was of "sandal-wood" (*chan-tan*), and five feet high. When the king Prasenajita heard of it, he also caused an image to be made of purple gold. It was five feet high. These were the first two images of Buddha known to have been made in the world of Jambudvipa. These images radiated light while the sky rained flowers.

Buddha joined his hands, and said to the image, "After my entrance into the state of extinction and salvation, I give into your charge my disciples."

Buddha's aunt, Mahâprajâpatî, could not bear the thought of seeing Buddha enter the state of extinction and salvation that would hide him from mortal view for ever. She took with her five hundred women and girls under vows of fasting, and made obeisance to Buddha. They then returned to the house, where they resided according to their rules, and each then exhibited the eighteen movements, attitudes, and marvellous performances. Some walked on the water as on dry land; others, leaving the ground, walked in the air, or sat, or lay down, or stood still, all in the same element. Fire and water were seen flowing from the right side of some, and from the left side of others. In others it was seen issuing from their mouths. They then all together entered the Nirvâna.

Buddha now ordered Ananda to go into the city, and announce to all the resident Buddhist householders, that it would be proper for them to make five hundred coffins. When the burning of the bodies with the coffins was completed, the relics were gathered and placed in temples erected for the purpose, where they might be continually honoured with worship.

Shariputra and Maudgalyayana were also grieved at the prospect of witnessing the entrance of their master into the Nirvâna, and themselves died first. At the same time 79,000 Lohans also entered the state of extinction. Buddha, seeing that his disciples of all four classes were also exceedingly disturbed in mind, made use of his magical power, and changed the two proficient ones into the form of two attendant disciples, one on his right and the other on his left. All living beings rejoiced when they saw this, and were at once liberated from every anxiety and vexation.

On the fifteenth day of the second month, Buddha was at the city Kushinagara. He went to a spot between two Sala trees, and here in a short time entered Nirvâna. A great voice was heard proclaiming to all the assembly, "Today the World's Honoured One is about to enter the Nirvâna. Whoever has any doubts, now let him come forward and ask for a solution of them. It is the last opportunity of asking Buddha for instruction."

At this time the great Bodhisattwas, the various kings of the Jambudvipa continent, the kings of the Devas, the kings of the mountains and rivers, and of the birds and beasts, with the personal disciples of Buddha, all arrived with offerings, wishing to administer to the wants of the World's Honoured One. In silence he firmly declined to receive anything. Chunda, a "lay disciple" (*Upâsaka*), addressed him in the words, "We look to Julai for food in the future. Now we desire to receive sorrowfully the vows of the obedient, and to make our small offering." Buddha replied, "I accept your offering, for it is the last offering you will present to me."

Chunda said in reply, "Though I know the benefit that is derived to mankind from Buddha entering the Nirvâna in a public manner, yet I cannot but grieve." For this Buddha commended him.

At this time the kings of the Devas and Nagas urged Shakyamuni, but in vain, not to enter the Nirvâna at present. In reply, the World's Honoured One discoursed on the symbol "I," written with three dots (∵) , arranged as a triangle resting on its base. This he used as a symbol of the embodied form of Tathâgata when released from the three methods of the Prajna. All the assembly of Bikshus then invited him to discourse on the cessation of permanence, on misery, on emptiness, and on the negation of self. Buddha, in consequence, gave them instruction in the four antitheses, viz., the permanence which is not permanent, the joy that involves sorrow, the I that is not I, and the purity that contains impurity.

The vast audience of Bikshus said, "Julai being without these four contradictions, why will he not remain with us for a *kalpa* or half a *kalpa*, that we may be informed how to escape from the four contradictions?"

Buddha said in answer, "I have already committed to Maha Kashiapa the complete and unsurpassed doctrine, to keep in trust, that you may all have a form of teaching on which you can rely. It will be the same as if you had Buddha himself." He then added, "I also intrust to you, kings of countries and leaders of supernatural armies, the deposit of sound doctrine that you may defend it by punishments and lawful force, in case of want of diligence, negligence, or wilful breaking of monkish rules."

The prohibition of animal food is referred by the Great Development school to this period. The compiler takes the opportunity here to throw blame on the Lesser Development school, because it allows fish and flesh to be eaten on certain occasions. This refers to the teaching of Shakyamuni in the Deer garden at Benares, where the *Agama Sutras* of the Lesser Development school were delivered.

In the first Sutras, those of the *Hwa-yen* and *Fan-wang* class, the Bodhisattwas could not eat animal food. This was the state of the question also at the time of the teaching in Benares. It occurs again in the *Lenga Sutra*, as a restriction on the Bodhisattwa. In the work called *Shih tsien*, "Tallies of the Shakya communities," it is said, that the restriction on the entire Buddhist community began subsequent to the Agama period. In the Nirvâna teaching of Buddha it was that the law was first made binding on all disciples of the Buddhist religion. Thus the Nirvâna teaching made an important addition to the Buddhist code of discipline.

Ajatashatru, king of Magadha, had killed his father, and in consequence, by natural retribution, suffered from a painful ulcer. He had six ministers of depraved minds who counselled him, in their deceptive way, to apply for relief to the six heretical teachers, Purana Kashiapa, &c., who taught that there is no need to honour prince or parents, and that happiness and misery do not depend on the moral character of actions, but come by chance.

Another adviser informed the king that Buddha could cure him. While the king was lamenting that Buddha was about to enter the Nirvâna, Shakyamuni himself went into a remarkable state of *samadhi*, by which he was enabled to radiate pure and cool light as far as to the body of the king, whose ulcer was at once healed. The king, with the queen and 580,000 of his subjects, then proceeded to Kushinagara to see the sage, who there taught them. In consequence, the heavy crime of Ajatashatru became much lightened. He, his wife and daughters, made high attainments in the Bodhi wisdom, and then bade farewell to the sage, and returned to their palace.

Buddha now said to Godinia, "Where is Ananda?" Godinia replied, that he was beyond Salaribhu, involved in the delusions of sixty-four thousand millions of demons. These demons had transformed themselves into so many Buddhas, discoursing on the law and displaying marvellous powers. Ananda was led to think himself receiving instruction from true Buddhas, while he was at the same time entangled in a demon thrall. Consequently he did not come, and remained in this state of great unhappiness. Buddha then addressed Manjusiri in the words, "Ananda has been my disciple and has served me for more than twenty years. My teaching of the law has been heard by him in its entireness. As water flows into a vessel, so he received my instructions. Therefore, I ask, Where is he? I wish him to hear from me the *Nirvâna Sutra*. He is now vexed with demons. Take in your hand this 'charm' (*dharani*) of mighty power, and go and save him." Manjusiri took it and went. The kings of the Maras, on hearing the charm recited, at once began to feel "wise thoughts" (*Bodhi*) stirring within them. They immediately abandoned the devices of Maras, and released Ananda, who returned to Buddha.

Buddha now informed Ananda that Subhadra, an "ascetic" (*Brahmachâri*) of a hundred and twenty years old, who lived beyond the Salaribhu kingdom, although he had acquired the eyesight and hearing of a Deva, and the power to search into other persons' minds and purposes, had not been able to put away his pride. He directed Ananda to go to him and say that Buddha, who came into the world like the "Udumbara tree" (*Ficus glomerata*),[1] would tonight enter the Nirvâna. If he would do anything he should do it quickly.

Ananda went as commanded. Subhadra came with him to see Buddha, who discoursed to him so effectively that he attained the rank of Arhan, and immediately used his endeavours to induce Buddha to delay entering the Nirvâna. The sage made silent signs that his resolution was unchanged, and Subhadra, not able to bear the pain of witnessing the entrance into the Nirvâna, himself first entered the state of destruction. On this, Buddha said to the assembled multitude, "From the time that I attained wisdom I have been engaged in saving men. The first was Godinia, the last was Subhadra. I have now nothing more to do."

Ananda, at the instance of Anuruddha, asked him four questions:—"With whom should we live? Whom shall we take as our teacher? Where shall we live? What words shall we use as a sign?" Buddha replied, "In regard to your first question, my judgment is that, after my death (entrance into the Nirvâna), such men as Chandaka, belonging to the six classes of unreformed Bikshus, must come under the yoke, and put away their evil dispositions.

"As to the question, Whom after Buddha's death you should take as your teacher? I reply that your teacher will be the *Shipara* system of discipline.

"As to the question, Where shall you reside? I reply, In the four places of meditation. 1. Meditation on the body. The body and the moral nature are identical in vacancy. 2. Meditation on receptiveness. Reception is not inside; nor is it outside; nor is it in the middle. 3. Meditation on the heart. It is only a name. The name differs from the nature. 4. Meditation on 'the Law' (*Dharma*). The good Dharma cannot be attained; nor can the evil Dharma be attained.

"As to the words you should regard as a sign, there should be in all Sutras, at the beginning, the sentence *Ju-shi-wo-wen*—'Thus have I heard.'

This should be followed by an announcement of the place where Buddha was teaching, and of whom his audience was composed."

Ananda again asked, "After Julai has entered the Nirvâna, how should the burial be conducted?" Answer, "Like that of the wheel kings. The body should be wrapped in fine white hair-cloth, [2] and coated with a pulp of odoriferous dust. The inner coffin should be of gold, the outer of iron. When the body of the king is placed in it, it should be sprinkled with melted butter and burned with fragrant wood. When the burning is completed, let the remaining fragments of bone be taken up and placed under a pagoda, tower, or other monumental building. Those who see it will both rejoice and grieve as they think of the king who ruled his country justly. In this our land the multitudes of men still to live will continue to bury with washing, and with burning, and construct tombs and pagodas with a great variety of customary practices."

"Within the Jambu continent is the kingdom of China. I will send three sages to renovate and instruct the people there, so that in pity and sympathy, and in the institution of all needful ceremonies, there may be completeness."

This passage is founded on statements in the Sutra *Tsung-mu-yin-yuen-king*, "Sutra of Tombs in connection with sympathetically operating causes." The three sages are Confucius, Laou-tsï, and Yen Hwei. They are called the Bodhisattwa of light and purity, the Kashiapa Bodhisattwa and the Bodhisattwa of moonlight.

Northern Buddhism gives its approval to the morality of Confucius, the ascetic philosophy of Li Laou-tan, and the high purpose of Yen Hwei. It also looks benevolently on the funeral customs of the Chinese.

Brahma not appearing in the assembly when Buddha was about to enter the Nirvâna, was sent for by the angry multitude, who appointed the immortal man of a hundred thousand charms to go on this mission. Brahma's city was found to be in a filthy condition. Filthy things filled the moat, and the hermit died.

Buddha created a diamond king by the exercise of his magical power, who went to Brahma's abode, and pointing to the filth, transformed the moat into good land. He then pointed to Brahma, and made use of a small portion of his adamantine and indestructible strength. This had its effect in inducing Brahma to come to the place where Buddha was.

Buddha then proceeded to tell his disciples that they must follow the instructions of the book of discipline called *Pratimoksha Sutra*. This work details the laws by which the priests are to conduct their lives. They must not trade, or tell fortunes, or make profit by land, or train slaves and serving girls for families. They must not cultivate plantations for gain, or concoct medicines, or study astrology. The rules he ordered them to maintain were of this kind. This treatise was to be their teacher in place of himself.

The last words ascribed to Buddha by the author of *Fo-tsu-t'ung-ki* (iv. 12) are, "While I have been in this continent of Jambudvipa, I have appeared several times; and though I have entered the Nirvâna, it has not been a complete Nirvâna. Therefore you ought to know the 'Law' (*Dharma*) that constantly remains, the unchanging law."

Buddha then, as he lay on the couch of the Seven Precious Things, reclined on his right side, with his head to the north, his feet to the south, his face to the west, and his back to the east. At midnight, without a sound, he entered the *Paranirvâna*. He lay between eight Sala trees, arranged in four pairs. When he had entered the Nirvâna, the two pairs that lay east and west became one tree, as did also the two pairs that lay north and south. They united to spread their shade over Buddha, and through extreme grief changed to a storklike whiteness.

The grief of the multitude, manifested in loud cries, now filled the universe with sadness. A large number going into the city made a gold coffin, ornamented with the Seven Precious Things. They also prepared banners and canopies of sandal-wood, aloes, and other fragrant substances. They came to where Buddha was, and presented them respectfully. With sincere grief the multitude raised Buddha and placed him in the coffin of gold. Four strong men were appointed to invite the coffin to enter the city. They could not raise it. Then sixteen strong men tried to lift it, but failed.

Anuruddha now said, "If all the people in the city were to try to lift it, they would be unable. The Devas must be appealed to, for they can do it." Before he had finished speaking, Indra Shakra appeared in the air carrying a magnificent canopy. A host of Devas of the visible heavens came with Shakra offering service. Buddha was moved with pity. He himself lifted the coffin into the air to the height of a Sala tree. The coffin of itself entered the west gate, and came out by the east. It then entered the south gate, and came out by the north. In this way Buddha went the round of the city gates seven times, and arrived at last slowly at the place of cremation.

When the coffin reached the grove of the Seven Precious Things, the four kings of the Devas arrived carrying branches of sandal-wood and aloes.

On the twenty-second of the second month, Buddha, having entered the Nirvâna seven days, wished to leave his coffin. His disciples carried him weeping to the grove of the Seven Precious Things. They then took odoriferous water and sprinkled him with it, and wrapped him from head to foot in silk and fine hair-cloth. After this they lifted him into the coffin, and placed him as he lay in the coffin upon a high framework constructed of fragrant wood. Each of them then took a torch of fragrant wood, proceeded to the wooden structure, and all was consumed.

Anuruddha went up to the Tushita heaven to announce these events to Maya, the mother of Buddha. Maya at once came down, and the coffin opened of itself. The Honoured One of the world rose up, joined his hands, and said, "You have condescended to come down here from your abode far away." Then he said to Ananda, "You should know that it is for an example to the unfilial of after ages that I have risen from my coffin to address inquiries to my mother."

Kashiapa was instructing five hundred disciples at the Gridhrakuta mountain when an earthquake occurred, from which he knew that Buddha had entered the Nirvâna. At once he set out with his disciples to go to the spot where the coffin was. Buddha compassionated him. The coffin opened of itself, and presented to view the golden and purple body of Buddha, strong and beautiful. Kashiapa, weeping, sprinkled it with fragrant water, and wrapped it again with the hair-cloth.

The coffin again closed, and a *Gatha* was chanted by Kashiapa, when the feet of Buddha became again visible, and the representations of the wheel of a thousand spokes (on which Buddha sits) appeared outside of the coffin. Kashiapa performed reverent salutations to the feet indestructible as the diamond, and saw them return within the coffin. Another wonder was added. Flame from the heart and bones of Buddha was seen extending out of the coffin. The process of cremation went gradually on till the seventh day, when the entire frame of fragrant wood on which the coffin rested was consumed.

According to another account, Kashiapa took fire and lit the pile of fragrant wood. The Sung dynasty author, Chï-p'an, prefers the statement that the cremation was caused by a flame issuing from Buddha's own body.

Seven days had passed after the death (literally destruction and extrication) of Buddha, when Kashiapa announced to 500 Arhans that they should go to all worlds and gather Arhans who possess the six powers of penetration. [3] No fewer than 808,000 came and received instruction in Dharma near the two trees.

On the twenty-ninth of the second month, seven days after the cremation of Buddha, Indra Shakra opened the coffin and took out a right tooth of Buddha. He caused two pagodas to be erected in his paradise. A Raksha also took two teeth. The people of the city came and filled eight golden pots with relics. They took them into the city, and made offerings to them for seven days in succession.

There was much contention among those who desired a share in the relics. Those who struggled were the kings of the Devas, the kings of the Nagas, and eight kings of India. To end the strife, Upakutta proposed a division into three parts for the Devas, the dragon kings, and the Indian kings respectively. His advice was followed.

King Ashôka obtained 84,000 relics, and also the moustaches of Buddha. On his way home he met Nanda, a king of the Nagas, who begged relics from him, threatening to destroy his kingdom if he refused. Ashôka gave him a hair of Buddha's moustaches, which he took to the Sumeru mountain. He there erected a pagoda of rock-crystal for its safe keeping. In various parts of the Jambudvipa continent ten pagodas were soon erected with a similar object in view.

Footnotes

1. This tree, a fig-bearing fruit without distinct flowers, is said to bloom once in three thousand years.
2. *Tie*, 8, *dip*, "Fine hair-cloth," *cf. tapis*, tapestry.
3. These are such as the power of distinguishing all sounds, the feelings and aims of all persons, varieties of form, life, death, and retribution, &c.

CHAPTER V.

THE PATRIARCHS OF THE NORTHERN BUDDHISTS.

Features of Asiatic life in the time of the patriarchs—Character, powers, and intellectual qualities of the patriarchs—Series of thirty-three patriarchs—Appointment of Kashiapa by Shakyamuni—The Svastika council of Rajagriha, for writing out the books of Buddha, and settling what should be received as canonical—The part taken by Ananda in the authorship of the Buddhist books—Ananda, second patriarch—The third was Shangnavasu—Remarks on samadhi and reverie—Fourth, Upagupta—Conversion of a wicked woman when dying—Fifth, sixth, and seventh patriarchs—Buddha's prophecy regarding Buddhanandi, the seventh—Struggle between filial love and Buddhist conviction in Buddhamitra—The way in which he subdued an unbelieving king—Maming given to the king of the Getæ to induce him to raise the siege of Pataliputra—Kapimara, the thirteenth—Nagarjuna, the fourteenth—Converts ten thousand Brahmans—Writes the Ta-chï-tu-lun—Vigorous defence of Buddhism by Kanadeva—Assassination of Kanadeva—Sanghanandi, precocious as a boy—Prophecy respecting him—Rahulata ascends to heaven—Sangkayasheta's discussion on the nature of sound—Converts five hundred hermits—Kumarada's views on the inequality of present retribution—Difficulties met with by Manura in teaching Buddhism in Southern and Western India—A patriarch's power over birds—Haklena converts Singhalaputra, who succeeded him as patriarch (the twenty-fourth), but was killed by the king of Candahar—The orthodox school has only twenty-four patriarchs—The contemplative school has twenty-eight—Pradjnyatara, the twenty-seventh converts Bodhidharma, the twenty-eighth, who proceeds to China—Hindoo knowledge of the Roman empire.

WE are now in the midst of the Asiatic world of two thousand and sixteen hundred years ago. In India, in Afghanistan, and in Turkestan, Buddhist priests had entered actively on that pilgrim life to which monasticism inevitably gives origin. With the object either of instructing, or of worshipping at some celebrated shrine, travellers were constantly seen on each foot-worn mountain path proceeding to some distant monastery. Such scenes as the following, illustrating the beliefs of the time and locality, would not seldom occur. A wayfarer in the country of the Getæ (Jats) (Afghanistan) knocks at the door of a Brahman family. A young man within answers, "There is no one in this house." The traveller was too well taught in Buddhism not to know the meaning of this philosophical nihilism, and at once answered, "Who is no one?" The young man, when he heard this, felt that he was understood. A kindred spirit was outside. Hurriedly he opened the door, and invited the stranger to enter. The visitor was the patriarch of the time (seventeenth), with staff and rice bowl, travelling to teach and make new disciples. On his entrance, he at once proceeded to utter a statement that this young man was the object of a long foretold destiny. A thousand years after Buddha's death, a distinguished teacher would appear in the country of the Getæ, who would reform his contemporaries, and follow up the work of illustrious predecessors. This meant that he was to become patriarch. He is eighteenth in the series.

A patriarch is represented as one who does not look at evil and dislike it; nor does he, when he sees that which is good, make a strong effort to attain it. He does not put wisdom aside and approach folly;

nor does he fling away delusion and aim at comprehending truth. Yet he has an acquaintance with great truths which is beyond being measured, and he penetrates into Buddha's mind to a depth that cannot be fathomed. His lodging is not with the sage, nor with the common class. Because he is above every one else in his attainments, he is called a patriarch.

A patriarch has magical powers. He can fly through the air, cross rivers on a boat of leaves, rain milk [1] at will from the air, and enter into a very great variety of trances or *samadhi*.

A patriarch has the keenest intellectual perception. He can dive into men's thoughts, and explain the meaning of the longest and most obscure compositions. The superiority of his mental faculties to those of common men is most marked. He can accomplish intellectual feats where others fail. Possessed of such gifts and qualifications as these, a patriarch is the chief defender of Buddhism against the heretics and opposers of his time. Selected by the last patriarch from the crowd of common disciples, he takes the chief place ever after as champion of the Buddhist law and discipline. He cares nothing for luxurious living or social rank. He lives poorly, is meanly clad, and keeps up the dignity of his position by the influence of mind, of character, and of supernatural acts.

The succession was broken at the fifth Chinese patriarch, and has never been restored.

The rank of patriarch could be the more easily discontinued because he had no ruling power. He was simply a defender, teacher, and example of the Buddhist doctrine and life.

The following paragraphs are taken from papers I wrote many years ago.

After the death of Shakyamuni, or, to speak honorifically, his entrance into the Nirvâna at Kushinagara, a series of thirty-three patriarchs, if we include five Chinese holders of the dignity, superintended in succession the affairs of the religious community he had founded. Remusat has given an abstract of the biography of the patriarchs taken from a Japanese encyclopædia. He says, Buddha, before his death, committed the secret of his mysteries to his disciple, Maha Kashiapa. He was a Brahman, born in the kingdom Magadha, in Central India. To him was intrusted the deposit of esoteric doctrine, called Cheng fa-yen-tsang, "the pure secret of the eye of right doctrine." The symbol of this esoteric principle, communicated orally without books, is *man* or *wan*. This, in Chinese, means "10,000," and implies the possession of 10,000 perfections. It is usually placed on the heart of Buddha in images and pictures of that divinity. It is sometimes called sin-yin, "heart's seal." It contains within it the whole mind of Buddha. In Sanscrit it is called *svastika*. It was the monogram of Vishnu and Shiva, the battle-axe of Thor in Scandinavian inscriptions, an ornament on the crowns of the Bonpa deities in Thibet, and a favourite symbol with the Peruvians.

The appointment of Kashiapa to be successor of Buddha and patriarch is described in the following manner:—"The World-honoured teacher ascended the platform from which he gave his instructions, holding in his hand a flower, the gift of a king. His disciples were all regardless of his teaching. Only Kashiapa showed attention and pleasure in his countenance. Buddha understood what was passing in his mind, and gave him the pure mystery of right doctrine, the secret heart of the Nirvâna, that true knowledge of existing things which consists in knowing them not to exist, and the method of enlightenment and reformation."

Kashiapa distinguished himself by severely ascetic practices. Buddha knew his excellence, and wished him to sit on the same seat with himself, as being not inferior in merit. But to this he would not consent. He also easily comprehended the ideas of Buddha. Buddha, on one occasion, used the following illustration:—"A notable man's house took fire. He brought goat-carts, drawn by goats, deer, and bullocks, to rescue his sons. He afterwards gave them a lofty, broad waggon, drawn by white bullocks. The first are the methods of Hinayana. The last is that of Mahayana." Kashiapa understood that Buddha, when he thus alluded to the various modes of teaching employed by him to save men, wished to point out that the Mahayana is superior to the others in capacity, adaptability, and utility.

He taught at Rajagriha after the Nirvâna. The king, Ajatashatru, supplied daily with food for a whole summer a thousand Arhans, who were engaged under Kashiapa in collecting the book s containing the sayings of Buddha, *i.e.*, the *Tripitaka*. This is what is called by Koeppen the First Buddhist council.

Kashiapa taught after this for twenty years, and then intrusted to Ananda the secret of pure doctrine. After this we hear of his proceeding to the four places of pilgrimage to worship. These were—the place of Shakyamuni leaving his home to become a recluse, the place of his becoming Buddha, of first preaching, and of entering the Nirvâna.

The second patriarch, Ananda, figures in many narratives as the constant attendant and disciple of Buddha. In temples he is represented as the corresponding figure to the old man Kashiapa, where he stands on Buddha's right hand. He was the second son of Shakyamuni's uncle, and was therefore first cousin of the sage. His name means "joy." His face was like the full moon, and his eyes like the lotus flower. He became a disciple at eight years old.

At the assembly of the Lotus of the Good Law, Buddha foretold of Ananda that he would ultimately become Buddha. This was to be a reward for his joy at hearing the law, and his diligent listening to it. Buddha obtained knowledge and taught the law. The Bodhi was perceived; and the Dharma became its embodiment. The part of Ananda was to grasp, hold firmly, and save from destruction the Dharma as uttered by Buddha. In so doing he also saved from oblivion the Dharma which will be uttered by coming Buddhas, as foretold by Shakyamuni.

Kashiapa appointed that Ananda should sit on the lion throne, with a thousand secretaries before him. They took down his words while he repeated the Dharma as he had heard it from Buddha. Evidently he had a good memory. Kashiapa was an old man, and Ananda was comparatively young. Both were alike anxious to preserve the teaching of Buddha; and the thousand Arhans, who received the sacred Dharma, were selected from a vast multitude of those who had accepted Buddha as the lion of the law, the mighty hero of the new and popular religion.

It is not said that they wrote. They may have committed to memory the sacred Dharma as Ananda gave it, but writing became the common mode of preserving Buddhist teaching so soon after, that this narrative may describe actual dictation and the work of a diligent secretariat, or company of disciples, who acted as scribes.

The aged patriarch, Kashiapa, when he died, intrusted to Ananda the very victorious law, and told him the following story, which throws light on ancient Buddhism as represented by the Northern school. "Anciently, when Ting-kwang Fo was a 'Shamen' (*Shramana*), he had under his protection a 'Shami' (*Shramanera*) whom he required to recite prayers and meditations constantly, reproving him severely if he failed in reading the whole of his tasks. The Shami sometimes went out to beg for his instructor; but if he delayed beyond the due time, and did not complete his daily readings, he had to bear heavy blame from that very instructor for whom he begged. This led him to feel unhappy, and he commenced reciting on the road as he went his rounds. A kind and friendly man asked him the reason, and finding how matters stood, addressed him as follows:—'Do not be sad. In future I will provide for your wants.' The Shami ceased to beg, and gave his whole attention to recitations of the sacred books, and was never deficient in the number of pages read. This Shami afterwards became Shakyamuni Buddha. His kind friend became Ananda in a later birth, and his sagacity, his power of retention, and diligence in learning resulted from his meritorious treatment of the Shami."

The third patriarch was Shangnavasu of Rajagriha. In a former life he had been a merchant. On the road, as he travelled, he had met a Pratyeka Buddha, very sick, and poorly clad. He gave him medicine, and clothing of a beautiful grass-cloth. [2]

This is what, by Buddhists, is called sowing the "field of happiness" (*fu-t'ien*). Other ways of acting so as to reap happiness are improving roads, building bridges, respect to parents, care of the poor, and opening common wells.

The Pratyeka Buddha said, "This is called the *Shangna* robe. With it the acquirement of wisdom can be made, and with it the Nirvâna of destruction should be entered." He then took wing, performed the eighteen movements in the air, and entered the Nirvâna.

Shangnavasu collected fragrant wood, burned the body, and raised a dagoba over the relics. He also, as he wept, uttered a wish that in five hundred future births he might always wear a robe of this kind, and have a merit equal to that of his present life.

He went to sea, obtained valuable pearls, and became a rich man. He then invited large numbers to a free feasting assembly in a forest, such as was held once in three years. He built a tower at the entrance of the place of meeting. Ananda said to him, "You should learn our doctrine, and live to benefit mankind." To this he consented. He took the vows and became an Arhan.

Going away to the Manda mountain, he there by means of the *samadhi* of mercy, changed two poisonous young Nagas into beings having a good disposition.

Samadhi means ecstatic reverie, and as there is some uncertainty as to its nature in some writers on Buddhism, it may be well to draw attention to this instance of snake-charming. It means a mesmerising power, a fixing of the mind and eye which has an effect on the snake. To fix the faculties in Buddhist contemplation is to enter into *san-mei* or *samadhi*. Those phenomena which we call trance, brown study, reverie, are examples of an inactive *samadhi*. The addition of an effort of will makes an active *samadhi*, as that used in snake charming by Buddhists, and as that of mesmerists.

He founded a house to be used by monks as a contemplation hall at the spot, and perhaps the snakes he tamed may have been kept there in a box, as is sometimes done now in China. But the account does not say.

He went thence to Candahar, at that time called Kipin, and there propagated the doctrines of Buddhism about eighty years before the conquests of Alexander. He lived in the *Siang-*(elephant) *pe* (white) mountain, sat on his chair, and entered into a trance. While this was happening, Upagupta, his successor, was being much troubled with five hundred pupils, who were self-opinionated and proud. He felt that they were beyond his power to guide and elevate. There was not existing between him and them the "secret link of influence" (*yuen*, "cause." Sansc. *nidana*) that would have overcome this difficulty. This conviction he acquired in a *samadhi*, and learned or rather thought at the same time, while still in the ecstatic state, that only Shangnavasu could reform them. The *samadhi* here appears to be an elevated state of inspiration. But it has also a magical power. The next point in the narrative is the arrival of Shangnavasu himself flying through the air. He was habited most shabbily, and when he sat down on Upagupta's chair, the pupils stared angrily at him for daring to do this. But Upagupta came before him and bowed to him most respectfully. Shangnavasu pointed to the air, and fragrant milk fell as if from a spring on the side of a high mountain.

This was the result of a *samadhi*, which the patriarch said was the *samadhi* of a Naga rushing eagerly forward. He then exhibited five hundred different kinds of *samadhi*. At the same time he observed to Upagupta, that when Buddha performed any magical act by *samadhi*, his pupil Maudgalyayana did not know what *samadhi* it was. Nor did inferior disciples know the name of any *samadhi* by help of which Maudgalyayana might do anything wonderful. "Nor do I," he said, "understand that of Ananda. Nor do you understand mine."

"When I enter the Nirvâna," he continued, "77,000 Sutras will perish with me; also 10,000 Shastras and 80,000 works of the class of discipline."

After this the five hundred pupils bitterly repented, received the patriarch's instructions, and became Arhans. Upon this the patriarch entered into the Nirvâna.

Upagupta, the fourth patriarch, was a native of the Madura country. He had a noble countenance which indicated his integrity, and was highly intelligent and eloquent. His instructor, Shangnavasu, the third patriarch, told him to keep black and white pebbles. When he had a bad thought he was to throw down into a basket a black pebble; when he had a good thought he was to throw down a white pebble. Upagupta did as he was told. At first bad thoughts abounded, and black pebbles were very numerous. Then the white and black were about equal. On the seventh day there were only white pebbles. Shangnavasu then undertook to expound to him the four truths. He at once attained the fruit "Srôtâpanna" (*Sü-t'o-hwan*).

At that time a woman of wicked life in the same city with Upagupta, hearing of his upright conduct, sent messengers to invite him to go and see her. He refused. The son of a citizen in good repute at about the same time went to stay with her. This youth she slew, because a rich traveller came with presents of valuable precious stones and pearls, which he offered for her acceptance. She buried the youth in a court of her house. His relations came to seek him and dug up the body. The king, informed of what had occurred, ordered the woman to have her arms and legs cut off, and also her nose and ears. She was then thrown out among graves in the open ground beyond the city. When Upagupta went out on his begging round he arrived at the spot. She said to him, "When I invited you to come and see me I had a beautiful face, but you refused. Now that I am maimed, my beauty gone, and my death near, you have come to see me. Why is this?" He replied, "I have come to see you from a wish to know what you truly are, and not through evil desire. You have by your beauty corrupted and ruined many. You were like a painted vase always giving out evil odours. It was no pleasure to the truly enlightened to approach you. They knew that this beauty would not be permanent. Now all miseries have gathered on you like numberless boils and ulcers. You ought diligently to seek liberation by means which are in your power." The woman as she listened opened the eye of Dharma, and obtained the purification of her heart. At death she was born anew in paradise.

Upagupta, when still a youth, saw that all the common methods of redemption were marked by bitterness, emptiness, and non-permanence, and at once attained the fruit Anagamin, the third degree of saintship, or that from which there is "no" (*ana*) "return" (*gamin*). He was then seventeen. Shangnavasu at once received him to the vows on his application, and he became an Allan.

He was contemporary during the later years of his patriarchate with king Ashôka, who, hearing that he was on Mount Uda discoursing to a large audience of believers, sent messengers to him, inviting him to come to the city where the king was, and bless him, by touching him on the crown of the head. The king much desired to learn at what spots he should erect pagodas in honour of Buddha. To this the patriarch responded, by pointing out to him all the places where Buddha had done anything remarkable during his life.

The number of converts was immense. Each of them threw down a tally four inches long. The tallies filled a storehouse which was sixteen feet high. Upagupta became, in virtue and wisdom, almost a Buddha, lacking, however, the thirty-two points of characteristic beauty. When he had finished his journeys for reforming others, and the "accomplishment of destiny in meetings with them" (*hwa-yuen-yi-pi*, "renovating destiny already ended"), he performed the eighteen metamorphoses, and seized on the salvation that consists in destruction, *i.e.*, he died. The tallies in the house were used as offerings, *yajun* (*yajur*), to burn. The people all wept aloud, collected the "relics" (*sharira*), erected a *t'a* (*stupa*), and performed regular worship before it.

In this example of the saint worship of Buddhism may be observed the upgrowth of superstitious practices. It aptly illustrates the way in which the religious principle in man works outward. Buddha, a sort of human god, was first worshipped. Other highly venerated men of a secondary type were in succession added, and became the inferior gods of a new pantheon.

Drikata, the fifth patriarch, was given by his father to Upagupta as a disciple, to be in constant attendance on him as Ananda was upon Shakyamuni. Upagupta received him to the vows at twenty years old. It was in this way. Upagupta was on a religious journey. He came to the door of an elderly man, who asked him, "Why do you, a holy sage, travel unattended?" He replied, "I have left the world, and am without family ties. No one has given me an attendant disciple. It may be you who will bestow this kindness." The elderly man replied, "If I have a son I will respectfully offer him to you." He afterwards had a son whom he named Drikata, who devoted himself in youth to the study of the Sutras and other books, and then went in search of Upagupta.

When Upagupta was old, he said to Drikata, "My time for entering the Nirvâna is come. The Dharma which I have taught I intrust to you. It will be your duty to teach it in regions far and near." This he did in Central India, and when he died (seized on the Nirvâna) Devas and men were sad. Michaka was the sixth patriarch. When he met first with Drikata, he said to him, "I was formerly born with you in the heaven of Brahma. I met with Asita,[3] who taught me the doctrine of the Rishis. You met with good and wise teachers who instructed you in the principles of Buddhism. So your path differed from mine for a period of six kalpas. The record of the Rishis said, 'After six kalpas you shall meet with a fellow learner. Through him you shall obtain the holy fruit.' Today, in meeting with you, is it not the fulfilment of destiny?"

Drikata then instructed him in Dharma, and he made eminent attainments. The Rishis, his companions, did not believe, until Drikata performed before them various magical transformations, when they all believed and obtained the fruit of doctrine. When Drikata died, Michaka took his place in renovating mankind by teaching the Nirvâna.

The seventh (should be eighth) patriarch was Buddhanandi, a native of Northern India. When Michaka came to his country, Buddhanandi saw on the city battlements a golden-coloured cloud. He thought that there must be a sage beneath the cloud, who would transmit the Dharma. He went to search, and found Buddhanandi in the street leading to the market-place. Michaka said, "Formerly Buddha, when travelling in Northern India, said to Ananda, 'Three hundred years after my death there will be a sage named Buddhanandi. He will make the Dharma great in this region.'" Buddhanandi replied, "I remember that in a former kalpa I presented to Buddha a throne. It was on this account that he made reference to me, and foretold that I should in the 'kalpa of the sages' (*Bhadrakalpa*) spread the Dharma far and wide. Since this agrees exactly with what you have said, I wish to become a disciple." He at once obtained the four fruits of enlightenment.

The ninth patriarch, Buddhamitra, was found by his predecessor in the patriarchate in the following manner. Buddhanandi came to his country to teach. Seeing a white light over a house, he said to his disciples, "There is a sage here, who has a mouth, but does not speak, and has feet, but does not walk." He went to the door, and was asked by an old man why he came. The answer was, "In search of a disciple." The old man replied, "I have a son just fifty. He neither speaks nor walks." "That," said Buddhanandi, "is my disciple."

Buddhamitra rose, made obeisance, walked seven steps, and then pronounced the following *Gatha:*—"If my father and mother are not my nearest of kin, who is so? If the Buddhas are not my teachers, who are my teachers?" Buddhanandi replied, "You speak of your nearest relative being the heart. To this your love for your parents is not comparable. Your acting in accordance with 'doctrine' (*tau*) is the mind of the Buddhas. The Buddha of the *wai tau* (heretical teachers) belongs to the world of forms. Their Buddha and you are not alike. You should know that your real mind is neither closely attached nor separated." He further said to the father:—"Your son formerly met with Buddha, and, stimulated by compassion, had great longings to benefit others. But because he has thought too much of his father's and mother's love, who could not let him go, he has not spoken nor walked." The aged father hearing this, at once let him leave the family to become a monk.

When Michaka (in Eitel, Mikkaka; in *San-kiau-yi-su*, Misuchaka) was about to die, he intrusted to Buddhanandi the correct Dharma to teach to mankind.

Such is the statement of Chï-p'an of the Kiau-men in *Fo-tsu-t'ung-ki*. He rejects Vasumitra, the seventh patriarch of the contemplatist school. He does not even mention Vasumitra, who yet was very distinguished. He took a chief part in the last revision of the canon, as president of the third or fourth synod, under Kanishka, Rajah of Cashmere, B.C. 153. To this, Eitel adds, that he must have died soon after, though Chinese chronology places his death in B.C. 590.

The Kiau-men writers apparently say little about the synods or councils, perhaps because they were presided over by the patriarchs, who favoured the contemplatist school. Can this be the reason that Chï-p'an has neglected the seventh patriarch and caused Michaka to nominate Buddhanandi (the eighth) as his successor, making him the seventh?

From this point I prefer to follow *San-kiau-yi-su* and Eitel in numbering the patriarchs, while continuing to take the story of their lives from the interesting pages of *Fo-tsu-t'ung-ki*, because the author is full of anecdote.

Chi-p'an, to fill the vacancy caused by the omission of Vasumitra, mentions Madhyantika, a disciple of Ananda, who converted Cashmere. He was contemporary with Shangnavasu. Buddhamitra passed at once through the steps of enlightenment, and began to teach the correct Dharma.

There was a king then reigning who followed another school, and wished to destroy the influence of Buddhism, a religion which he despised. Buddhamitra, wishing to bring this king to submission, took a red flag in his hand, and carried it before the king for twelve years. The king at last asked who this man was. Buddhamitra replied, "I am a man of knowledge, who can discuss religion." The king ordered an assembly of Brahmans to meet him in a large hall, and discuss religion with him. Buddhamitra took his seat, and delivered a discourse. A man weak in knowledge was pitted against him, whose reasonings he at once subverted. The rest declined to argue. The king then entered himself into argument with him, but soon gave way, and announced his intention to follow the Buddhist religion.

In the same kingdom was a "Nirgrantha" (*Nikan*), who reviled Buddhism, and was an expert calculator. *Nirgrantha* means a devotee who has cut the ties of food and clothing, and can live without feeling hungry or cold. It is from *grantha*, "tie." Buddhamitra went to him and received information in regard to his calculations. The Nirgrantha spared no abuse in speaking of Buddha. The Buddhist then said, "You are now working [4] out punishment to yourself, and will fall into hell. If you do not believe what I say, try your calculations, and you will find whether it is so or not." The heretic calculated, and found that it was so. He then said to the Buddhist teacher, "How can I avoid this calamity?"

The reply was, "You should become a believer in Buddha. You may then have this demerit annulled." Nirgrantha (or the Nirgrantha) upon this, pronounced five hundred sentences in praise of Buddha, and repented of his former faults.

Buddhamitra then said, "Having performed these meritorious actions, you will certainly be born in one of the heavenly paradises. If you doubt this, make the calculations, that you may know it to be so." He did this, and found that his demerit was gone, and that he would be born in heaven. He and five hundred of his followers joyfully enrolled themselves as Buddhist monks, shaved their locks, and placed themselves under the protection of the Three Precious Things.

The tenth patriarch was Parshva, and the eleventh Punayaja. Parshva came to the city of "Pataliputra" (Chinese, *Hwa-shi*), and rested under a tree. He pointed to the ground and said, "If this earth should change to a golden colour, a sage must be here." As soon as he had said this, the ground changed its colour, and immediately Punayaja arrived. He was received to the vows by Parshva, and became his successor.

The twelfth patriarch was Ashwagosha, or *Maming*, "a horse neighing." In the city of Pataliputra, five hundred youths of princely families became at one time converts to his doctrine, and took the tonsure. The king feared that his kingdom would become depopulated, and issued an order that there should be no more chanting. This decree was levelled against the use of some very popular and sweet music introduced by Maming. The music must have excited great attention, and must have had its effect in leading many persons to resolve on leading the Buddhist life. This would lead to diminution in population. The country would become poorer. There would be fewer workers, fewer tax-payers, fewer soldiers, and fewer traders.

At this juncture the king of the Getæ (Indo-Scythians) besieged Pataliputra. There were 900,000 men in the city, and the besieging king required 900,000 pieces of gold as a ransom. The king of Pataliputra gave him Maming, a Buddha's rice bowl, and a cock, observing that each of these gifts was worth 300,000 gold pieces. Maming's wisdom was unrivalled. Buddha had boundless virtue, and a merciful heart. The cock would not drink water that had insects in it. All three would be able to drive away enemies.

The king of the Getæ was delighted, drew back his troops, and returned to his country. After a time, the Parthians attacked him. He gained a victory, and killed 900,000 of the enemy.

Maming was born at Benares, but taught chiefly at Pataliputra. One day, while he was causing the wheel of the wonderful law to revolve, an old man suddenly fell on the ground just before him. The patriarch said, "This is no ordinary person. There will be some remarkable appearance." No sooner was this said than he vanished. Then, in a trice, a man with a golden skin rose out of the ground. He soon became changed into a young woman, who pointed with her right hand at Maming and said, "I bow to the aged and honoured patriarch. Let me receive the mark of

Julai." She disappeared. The patriarch said, "A demon must be coming to struggle with me." There was a violent wind and heavy rain. The sky became dark. The patriarch remarked, "The demon is indeed come. I must expel him."

When he pointed into the air, a golden dragon appeared, who showed marvellous power, and shook the mountains. The patriarch sat calmly, and the demon's agency came to an end.

After seven days, a small insect appeared, which hid itself under the chair of the patriarch, who took it up and said to the assembly, "This is the demon in an assumed shape come stealthily to hear my teaching."

He set the insect free, and told it to go, but the demon in it could not move. The patriarch then said to the demon, "If you only place yourself under the direction of the Three Precious Things, you may at once obtain marvellous powers." The demon at once returned to his original shape, made a prostration and a penitent confession.

The patriarch, asking him his name, he replied, "Kapimara." When the inquiry, what was the extent of his powers, was addressed to him, he replied that to transform the sea was easy to him. "Can you," asked the patriarch, "transform the 'sea of the moral nature' (*sing-hai*)?" He answered that he did not know what was meant. Maming explained that the physical world rests on this moral nature for its existence. So also the powers of *samadhi*, and of far-reaching perception on the part of Buddhist proficients, also depend on this for all their value.

Kapimara became a believer, and three thousand of his adherents all entered the ranks of the shaven monks. The patriarch called in five thousand Arhans to aid in administering the vows to this large crowd of applicants.

Kapimara became the thirteenth patriarch. His numerous followers spread the Buddhist religion in Southern India. He compiled a Shastra (*Lun*), called the "Shastra of the Non-ego." It extended to the length of 100 *Gathas* (Kie). Wherever this Shastra came, the demons and heretics were pitiably discomfited. *Lung-shu*, or "Nagarjuna," was the fourteenth patriarch. He belonged to Southern India. A king there was very much opposed to Buddhism, and influenced by what that religion calls "depraved views" (*sie-kien*). Lung shu wished to convert him, and for seven years carried a red banner before him when travelling. The Rajah asked, "Who is this man?" He replied for himself, "I am a man possessing all kinds of knowledge." The Rajah asked, "What are the Devas now doing?" He replied, "Just now the Devas are fighting with the Asuras." In a moment they became aware of the conflict of swords in the sky, and, to the Rajah's astonishment, some ears and noses of the giants fell on the ground. The Rajah reverentially performed a prostration before Lung-shu. Ten thousand Brahmans who were at the time in the hall of audience all joined in praising the marvellous virtue of the patriarch, and at once submitted themselves to the tonsure, and entered on the monkish life.

Lung-shu wrote several important Shastras. Among them was that one called *Ta-chï-tu-lun*, "Shastra of the Method of Great Wisdom." He was one of the most prolific authors of the Mahayana school. On this account he became the object of the jealous dislike of the older school of the Lesser Conveyance.

When drawing near the end of his life, he unexpectedly fell one day into the trance called the *samadhi* of the moon's wheel, in which he only heard words of the Dharma, but saw no forms. His pupil, Deva, comprehended him, and said, "The Buddha nature which you, my teacher, make known to us, does not consist in sights and sounds." Lung-shu intrusted to him the care of the Dharma, and entered a vacant room. As he did not come out for a day, the pupils broke open the door. He had gone into a state of *samadhi*, and died. In all the kingdoms of India, temples were erected for him, and he was honoured as if he were Buddha.

The fifteenth patriarch was Kanadeva, a native of South India. The king of his country followed a form of depraved doctrine. When men were invited to act as guards, Kanadeva responded to the call, and took his place, spear in hand, in the front rank, discharging his duties in so regular and exemplary a manner that the king's attention was attracted. In reply to the king's inquiries, he said he was a man who studied wisdom and practised argumentative oratory. The king opened for him a discussion hall. Here Kanadeva proposed three theses:—(1.) Buddha is the most excellent of sages; (2.) No law can compare with the law of Buddha; (3.) There is no happiness (or merit) on earth equal to that of the Buddhist monk. "If any one can vanquish me in regard to these three theses, I consent to have my head taken off." In the discussion that ensued, all the heretics were worsted, and asked permission to become monks.

A follower of one of the scholars who were vanquished in argument felt ashamed for his master, was much enraged, and resolved to kill Kanadeva. He attacked him while engaged in writing a controversial work, and with his sword pierced him through. Before life was extinct, the patriarch said, "You can take my robe and rice bowl, and go quickly to my disciples and inform them, that if any among them have not made progress, they should keep firmly to their purpose without despairing." The pupils came to see their master with loud lamentation. He said to them, "All methods and systems are empty. I do not exist, and cannot be injured. I do not receive love or hatred from any. What that man has injured is the form of retribution for my past. It is not I myself." He then cast off the body, as a cicada does its outer covering.

His disciples collected the relics after his cremation, erected a dagoba, and paid him the regular honours of worship.

The sixteenth patriarch was Rahulata, a native of Kapila. When a certain Brahman wrote a work of 100,000 *Gathas*, extremely difficult to explain, Nagarjuna was able to understand the whole at first hearing, and Kanadeva at the second hearing. Rahulata was able to comprehend the whole when he had heard Kanadeva's explanation. On this, the Brahman said, under the influence of great astonishment, "The Shramana knows it as clearly as if he had known it all of old." He then became a believer.

After his destined work of reformation and instruction was done, Rahulata entered (the word is "took," "seized on") the Nirvâna.

The seventeenth patriarch, Sanghanandi, of the city Shravasti, was the son of the king. He could speak as soon as he was born, and read the books of Buddha when an infant. At seven years old he formed a dislike to a worldly life. His parents tried in vain to check him in resolving to be a monk. Two years later, Rahulata came to the banks of the Golden-water river and said, pointing with his finger, "At a distance of five hundred *li* from this spot, there is a holy person, named Sanghanandi, who will, a thousand years after Buddha, succeed him on the throne of purity." Rahulata led his disciples to see him. He had just awaked from a trance of twenty-one days, and at once desired to take the monastic vows. He very soon understood the principles of Buddha's teaching, and became himself an instructor.

One day Rahulata ascended to the heaven of Brahma with a golden rice bowl in his hand to obtain rice for a multitude of believing Buddhists. On a sudden they disliked its taste. Rahulata said, "The fault is not in me. It is in yourselves." He then desired Sanghanandi to distribute the food and eat with the others. All wondered. Rahulata then said, "He is a Buddha of bygone times, and you also were disciples of the law of Buddha in ages long past. However, you had not attained to the rank of Arhan, but only realised the first three fruits of the monastic life." They replied, "The marvellous power of our teacher can lead to faith. This Buddha of the past has still secret doubts." Sanghanandi observed that when Buddha was living, the earth was at peace and the waters made everything beautiful; but after his death, when eight hundred years had passed, men had lost faith. They did not believe the true form of beauty. They only loved marvellous powers and deeds that astonish.

He had no sooner ended, than he seized a crystal jar, and slowly entered the earth. He went with it to the boundary of the diamond wheel region, and filled it with the "drink of the immortals" (*kan-lu*). This he brought back to the assembly, and placed before them. They all repented of their thought, and thanked him.

An Arhan, full of all virtue and merit, came there. Sanghanandi tried his powers by a question. "One born of the race of the wheel kings was neither Buddha nor an Arhan. He was not received by after ages as real, nor was he a Pratyeka Buddha." The Arhan, unable to solve this problem, went to the paradises of the Devas, and asked Maitreya, who replied, "The custom of the world is to form a lump of clay, and with a wheel make it into a porcelain image. How can this image compare with the sages or be continued to later generations?"

The Arhan came back with this answer. Sanghanandi replied, "It must have been Maitreya that told you this."

When his destined course was finished, he grasped a tree with his right hand, and entered the state of destruction and salvation. The corpse could not be removed by his disciples on account of its great weight. A large elephant also came to try his strength, but was unable to move it. The disciples then piled up fragrant wood against the tree, and performed the process of cremation. The tree became still more luxuriantly beautiful. A dagoba was erected, and the relics were worshipped.

The eighteenth patriarch was named Sangkayasheta. When he heard the bells of a temple ringing on account of the wind blowing, his teacher asked him, "Is it the bells that make the sound, or the wind?" The youth replied, "It is neither the bells nor the wind, it is my mind." Walking on the sea-side, he came to a temple and went into it to beg food, saying, "Hunger is the greatest evil. Action is the greatest suffering. He who knows the reality of Dharma that there is in this statement, may enter the path of Nirvâna." He was invited to enter and supplied with food.

Sangkayasheta saw in the house two hungry ghosts, naked and chained. "What is the meaning of this?" he asked. His host said, "These ghosts were in a former life my son-in-law and daughter-in-law. They were angry because I gave away food in charity, and when I instructed them they refused to listen. I then took an oath and said, 'When you suffer the penalty of your sin I will certainly come and see you.' Accordingly, at the time of their suffering their retribution, I arrived at a certain place where monks, at the sound of the bell, had assembled for food. When the food was nearly all eaten, it changed to blood, and the monks began to use their bowls and other utensils employed at meals, in fighting with one another, and said, 'Why are you saving of food? The misery we bear now is a recompense for the past.' I asked them to tell me what they had done. They replied, that in the time of Kashiapa Buddha, they had been guilty on one occasion, when Bikshus came asking food, of concealing their store and angrily refusing to share it with them. This was the cause of their present retribution."

Sangkayasheta went on the sea and saw all the five hundred hells. This taught him fear, and the desire to avoid, by some means, such a fate as to be condemned to live there.

He attained the rank of Arhan, and finding in a wood five hundred "hermits" (*sien*) who were practising ascetic rules, he converted them to Buddhism by praising Buddha, the Law, and the Priesthood. When his destined course was run, he entered the Nirvâna, B.C. 13.

In the account of Kumarada, the nineteenth patriarch, is included an answer he gave to a youth who was puzzled at the inequality of rewards and punishments in the present life. The youth's parents were devout Buddhists, but in very feeble health. Their neighbour was a butcher, and enjoyed an immunity from all sickness and pain. Why should a man whose business it was to take animal life escape retribution from this sin?

Kumarada told him that the inequality of men's condition in the present life is mainly on account of sins and virtuous acts in a former life. Virtue and vice belong to the present. Happiness and misery are the recompense of the virtue and vice of the past. The virtue and vice of the present will be rewarded in the future life. Jayata was charmed with this conversation. His doubts were dissipated. He subsequently became the twentieth patriarch. Kumarada also said to him, "Activity, in which you have hitherto believed, comes from doubt, doubt from knowledge, knowledge from a man's not possessing the perceptive power, and the absence of perception from the mind's being in a morbid state. Let your mind be pure and at rest, and without life or death, victory or defeat, action or retribution, and you will then have attained the same eminence as the Buddhas of the past. All vice and virtue, action and inaction, are a dream and a delusion." Kumarada died A.D. 23.

The work of the patriarchs was to engage in a perpetual argument against unbelief. There were differences in localities. Some parts of India were more favourable to Buddhism than others. In the account of the life of Manura, the "twenty-first" patriarch, in *Fo-tsu-t'ung-ki* (but really the twenty-second), it is said that in the two Indias south of the Ganges, Western and Southern India, there was great perversity of view. Manura was well skilled in the analysis of alphabetic sounds, and was recommended by a learned Buddhist named Yaja, to proceed to Western and Southern India to teach Buddhism. Evidently he would aid in giving alphabets to the Tamil and other languages, which at that time were first committed to writing.

On the other hand, in Northern, Central, and Eastern India, all stated to be to the north of the Gauges, the work of Buddhist teaching is said to be easy. Yaja undertook to teach in this part of India.

The campaign of Manura is described as a long struggle with errors and heresies. He specially made use of a book by the twelfth patriarch called the *Sutra of the Not-me*. He found Western India under the control of king Teda, who one day when travelling passed a small pagoda. His attendants could not say what was the occasion of its being erected. He asked the "Brahmans of pure life" (*Fan-hing*), the "contemplatists" (*ch'un-kwan*), and the "utterers of charms" (*chen-shu*), who formed three classes of the community of that day. They did not know.

Manura was then asked; who said it was a pagoda erected by king Ashôka, and which had now come to light through the good fortune of the king. [5] The king was much impressed with Manura's teaching, and became a disciple. He gave over his royal authority to his son, and himself took vows as a monk. In seven days he advanced to the fourth grade of the understanding of Buddhist doctrine.

Manura gave the work of reforming the kingdom by Buddhist teaching into the hands of the king, and went himself to the kingdom of the Indian Get, who—retreating westward before the Hiung-nu, B.C. 180—conquered the Punjab and Cashmere in A.D. 126. Manura taught in Western India and in Ferghana in the third Christian century. He is author of the *Vibhasha Shastra*.

The twenty-third patriarch was Haklena. He was of the country of the Getæ (Candahar). At seven years old he began to rebuke those people who visited temples to sacrifice to the gods. He said they were deceivers of the people, by wrong statements of the causes of calamities and of happiness. "Besides, you are," he said, "wasting the lives of innocent cattle, which is a very great evil." On a sudden the temple and images fell down in ruins. At thirty-eight years of age he met with Manura, and was instructed. Manura told him that formerly five hundred of his disciples had, on account of small merit, been born as storks. "These are the flock that are now following you, wishing to delude you into showing them favour."

Haklena asked him, "How can they be removed?" Manura spoke some sentences in the form of Gathas. "The mind follows the ten thousand forms in their revolutions. At the turning-points of revolution, there really must be darkness. By following the stream and recognising the true nature, you attain a position where there is no joy or sorrow."

The birds hearing these words, flew away with loud cries. This is inserted by the Chinese biographer as an example of a patriarch's power over the animal creation.

Haklena went to Central India. While he was teaching in the presence of a Rajah, two men appeared dressed in dark red mantles and white togas. They came to worship, and stayed a long time. Suddenly they went away. The Rajah asked, "Who are they?" Haklena replied, "They are the sons of the Devas of the sun and moon."

His most promising disciple was Singhalaputra (Lion son; in Chinese, *Shï-tsï*), who had formerly believed in Brahmanism, and abandoned it in favour of the Buddhist faith. He asked Haklena, "To what must I give my chief attention if I would attain the true knowledge of things?" "Do nothing," was the reply. "If you do anything there is no merit in it. By doing nothing, you will comply with the system of Buddha." Haklena died A.D. 209 (Chinese chronology).

The twenty-fourth patriarch was Singhalaputra, a native of Central India. He went to Candahar (*Ki-pin*), and there brought over very many persons to Buddhism. Some heretics were guilty of gross crimes, and took the name of Buddhists. The king became angry against Buddhism, and cut off the head of the patriarch.

On account of this unhappy fate of the patriarch, the succession, according to some authors, was broken off at this point. Another reason for terminating the list of patriarchs here, is said, by the author of *Fa-tsu-t'ung-hi*, to have been that the remaining patriarchs were not foretold by Buddha by name, and did not equal in gifts and honour those that preceded.

The contemplative school, or school of Bodhidharma, however, have retained the twenty-eight names, and recognise no superiority in the twenty-four universally acknowledged patriarchs over the remaining four. For many centuries there was an active discussion on the claims of the last four and the Chinese patriarchs to the honour of the name. Chï-p'an, writing in A.D. 1269, at Ningpo, decides against them. Some of the friends who reviewed his work, and whose names are given, belonged to the contemplative school. The difference of views would not therefore be an unfriendly one.

The twenty-fifth patriarch, according to the contemplative school, was Basiasita. He was a Brahman, and a native of Candahar. He travelled into Central and Southern India, and died A.D. 328.

Putnomita was the next (twenty-sixth) that received the cloak and secret symbols of the patriarchs. He was a Kshatrya of Southern India. He visited Eastern India, where he found the king under the influence of heretical doctrine, and converted him. He died in A.D. 388.

His successor, the twenty-seventh patriarch, was Pradjñatara, a native of Central India, who travelled to the southern part of the peninsula, and there took under his instructions Bodhidharma, the second son of the king. He died A.D. 457, and left as his successor the pupil just mentioned, who, he foretold, would visit China sixty-nine years afterwards. Bodhidharma asked him, when under instruction, what he had to say about precious things, pearls, and doctrines, which are round and bright. The patriarch answered, "Among all precious things the Buddhist Dharma is the most precious. Among all bright things, knowledge is the brightest. Among all clear things, a clear mind is the clearest. Among all things, other men and I are the highest. Among all things, the "essential nature" (*sing*) of Dharma is the greatest."

Bodhidharma was the twenty-eighth patriarch. He represents a school that despises books and reduces Buddhist teaching to the simplest possible principles. He was an ascetic of the first water.

In A.D. 526, Bodhidharma left Southern India for China by sea. The sixty-nine years that passed between the death of his predecessor and his departure from India formed the basis of the prediction above mentioned, constructed we must suppose after the event. The cause of his departure was probably persecution and disaster. He was a sectarian even in Buddhism, and possibly his enemies were not only the Brahmans, but also fellow-Buddhists. The reading of books was the life and soul of many monasteries. Bodhidharma decried book reading. His system made the monasteries much less educational and much more mystical and meditative than before. Lovers of knowledge among the Buddhists would dislike his system. This would be the case in China and in India.

In China the dogmatic reason given for not acknowledging the last four patriarchs was that, in the "Dharmapitaka Sutra," Buddha had said, "After my entering the Nirvâna, there will be twenty-four honourable teachers, who will appear in the world and teach my law" (*Fo-tsu-t'ung-ki*, v. 1).

After this what could be done but take the statement as a final answer to the inquiry, How many patriarchs could there be?

Bodhidharma wished to return to India, but died in China before accomplishing this purpose.

The "Getæ" (Jats) mentioned in the account of Haklena are called *Yue-ti* by the Chinese. In the Cyclopædia *Fa-yuen-chu-lin*, it is said that the great kingdoms to the east, north, and west of India, are China, the Getæ, and the "Roman empire," *Ta-ts'in*. By the kingdom of the Getæ the Chinese author meant some great empire between Rome and China. This is a statement drawn from Indian sources.

Footnotes

1. This is stated in the life of Shangnavasu, the third patriarch. The word used is *hiang-ju*, "fragrant milk." This is the name of a milky plant, *Eschscholtzia cristata*, allied to the vervain.—*Williams.*
2. This cloth was brought to China from Thibet and other western countries in the T'ang dynasty. It was white, fine, thick, and strong. The plant of which it was made had nine stalks. When an Arhan is born this plant is found growing in some clean spot.
3. A Rishi who was able to detect the marks of Buddha on a child. Shakyamuni was his slave in a former birth.—*Eitel.*
4. *Tsau-tsui*, "creating sin," *i.e.*, the punishment of sin. Sin and its punishment are confused and loosely identified.
5. "Good fortune," *fu-li*, "power of the king's merit." *Fu*, "happiness," is in a Buddhist sense "merit." By the law of hidden causation, good fortune is always deserved by some good action done, either in the present or in some former life.

CHAPTER VI.

SKETCH OF THE HISTORY OF BUDDHISM IN CHINA.

The emperor Ming-ti sends an embassy to India for images, A.D. 61—Kashiapmadanga arrives in China—Spread of Buddhism in A.D. 335—Buddojanga—A pagoda at Nanking, A.D. 381—The translator Kumarajiva, A.D. 405—The Chinese traveller, Fa-hien visits India—His book—Persecution, A.D. 426—Buddhism prosperous, 451—Indian embassies to China in the Sung dynasty—Opposition of the Confucianists to Buddhism—Discussions on doctrine—Buddhist prosperity in the Northern Wei kingdom and the Liang kingdom—Bodhidharma—Sung-yün sent to India—Bodhidharma leaves Liang Wu-ti and goes to Northern China—His latter years and death—Embassies from Buddhist countries m the south—Relics—The Liang emperor Wu-ti becomes a monk—Embassies from India and Ceylon—Influence of Sanscrit writing in giving the Chinese the knowledge of an alphabet—Syllabic spelling—Confucian opposition to Buddhism in the T'ang dynasty—The five successors of Bodhidharma—Hiuen-tsang's travels in India—Work as a translator—Persecution, A.D. 714—Hindoo calendar in China—Amogha introduces the festival for hungry ghosts—Opposition of Han Yü to Buddhism—Persecution of 845—Teaching of Matsu—Triumph of the Mahayana—Budhiruchi—Persecution by the Cheu dynasty—Extensive erection of pagodas in the Sung dynasty—Encouragement of Sanscrit studies—Places of pilgrimage—P'uto—Regulations for receiving the vows—Hindoo Buddhists in China in the Sung dynasty—The Mongol dynasty favoured Buddhism—The last Chinese Buddhist who visited India—The Ming dynasty limits the right of accumulating land—Roman Catholic controversy with Buddhists—Kang-hi of the Manchu dynasty opposes Buddhism—The literati still condemn Buddhism.

IT was in the year A.D. 61, that the Chinese emperor Ming-ti, in consequence of a dream, in which he saw the image of a foreign god, sent messengers to India, a country several thousand miles to the southeast of the capital, to ask for Buddhist books and teachers.[1] A native of Central India named Kashiapmadanga, with others, accompanied them back. He translated a small but important Sutra, called the Sutra of Forty-two Sections, and died at Lo-yang. The religion had now long been established in Nepaul and Independent Tartary, as the travels of the patriarchs indicate. It had also extended itself throughout India and Ceylon, and the persecution of the Brahmans, instigated partly by controversial feeling, and more by a desire to increase their caste influence, had not yet commenced. Long before this, it is stated that in B.C. 217, Indians had arrived at the capital of China in Shen-si, in order to propagate their religion. Remusat, after mentioning this in the *Foě kouě ki*, adds that, towards the year B.C. 122, a warlike expedition of the Chinese led them to Hieou-thou, a country beyond Yarkand. Here a golden statue was taken, and brought to the emperor. The Chinese author states that this was the origin of the statues of Buddha that were afterwards in use.

At this period the geographical knowledge of the Chinese rapidly increased. The name of India now occurs for the first time in their annals. In the year B.C. 122 Chang K'ien, a Chinese ambassador, returned from the country of the Getæ, and informed the Han emperor Wu-ti, of the kingdoms and customs existing in the west. Among other things, he said, "When I was in the country of the Dahæ,[2] 12,000 Chinese miles distant to the south-west, I saw bamboo staves from K'iung and cloth from Si-ch'uen. On asking whence they came, I was told that they were articles of traffic at *Shin-do* ('Scinde,' a country far to the south-east of the Dahæ)." It is added in the commentary to the *T'ung-kien-kang-muh*, that the name is also pronounced, *Kan-do* and *T'in-do*, and that it is the country of the barbarians called Buddha.

Early in the fourth century, native Chinese began to take the Buddhist monastic vows. Their history says, under the year 335, that the prince of the Ch'au kingdom in the time of the Eastern Ts'in dynasty, permitted his subjects to do so. He was influenced by an Indian named Buddojanga,[3] who pretended to magical powers. Before this, natives of India had been allowed to build temples in the large cities, but it was now for the first time that the people of the country were suffered to become "Shamen"[4] (*Shramanas*), or disciples of Buddha. The first translations of the Buddhist books had been already made, for we read that at the close of the second century, an Indian residing at Ch'ang-an, the modern Si-an fu, produced the first version of the "Lotus of the Good Law." The emperor Hiau Wu, of the Ts'in dynasty, in the year A.D. 381, erected a pagoda in his palace at Nanking.

At this period, large monasteries began to be established in North China, and nine-tenths of the common people, says the historian, followed the faith of the great Indian sage.

Under the year A.D. 405, the Chinese chronicles record that the king of the Ts'in country gave a high office to Kumarajiva, an Indian Buddhist. This is an important epoch for the history of Chinese Buddhist literature. Kumarajiva was commanded by the emperor to translate the sacred books of India, and to the present day his name may be seen on the first page of the principal Buddhist classics. The seat of the ancient kingdom of Ts'in was in the southern part of the provinces Shen-si and Kan-su. Ch'au, another kingdom where, a few years previously, Buddhism was in favour at court, was in the modern Pe-chi-li and Shan-si. That this religion was then flourishing in the most northerly provinces of the empire, and that the date, place (Ch'ang-an), and other circumstances of the translations are preserved, are facts that should be remembered in connection with the history of the Chinese language. The numerous proper names and other words transferred from Sanscrit, and written with the Chinese characters, are of great assistance in ascertaining what sounds were then given to those characters in the region where Mandarin is now spoken.

Kumarajiva was brought to China from Kui-tsi, a kingdom in Thibet, east of the Ts'ung-ling mountains. The king of Ts'in had sent an army to invade that country, with directions not to return without the Indian whose fame had spread among all the neighbouring nations. The former translations of the Buddhist sacred books were to a great extent erroneous. To produce them in a form more accurate and complete was the task undertaken by the learned Buddhist just mentioned, at the desire of the king. More than eight hundred priests were called to assist, and the king himself, an ardent disciple of the new faith, was present at the conference, holding the old copies in his hand as the work of correction proceeded. More than three hundred volumes were thus prepared. [5]

While this work, so favourable to the progress of Buddhism, was proceeding, a Chinese traveller, Fa-hien, was exploring India and collecting books. The extension of the religion that was then propagated with such zeal and fervour very much promoted the mutual intercourse of Asiatic countries. The road between Eastern Persia and China was frequently traversed, and a succession of Chinese Buddhists thus found their way to the parent land of the legends and superstitions in which they believed. Several of them on their return wrote narratives of what they had seen. Among those that have been preserved, the oldest of them, the *Account of Buddhist Kingdoms*, [6] by Fa-hien, is perhaps the most interesting and valuable. He describes the flourishing condition of Buddhism in the steppes of Tartary, among the Ouighours and the tribes residing west of the Caspian Sea, in Afghanistan where the language and customs of Central India then prevailed, and the other lands watered by the Indus and its tributary rivers, in Central India and in Ceylon. Going back by sea from Ceylon, he reached Ch'ang-an in the year 414, after fifteen years' absence. He then undertook with the help of Palats'anga, a native of India, the task of editing the works he had brought with him, and it was not till several years had elapsed that at the request of Kumarajiva, his religious instructor, he published his travels. The earnestness and vigour of the Chinese Buddhists at that early period, is shown sufficiently by the repeated journeys that they made along the tedious and dangerous route by Central Asia to India. Neither religion nor the love of seeing foreign lands, are now enough, unless the emperor commands it, to induce any of the educated class among them to leave their homes. Fa-hien had several companions, but death and other causes gradually deprived him of them all.

The Ts'in dynasty now fell (A.D. 420), and with it in quick succession the petty kingdoms into which China was at that time divided. The northern provinces became the possession of a powerful Tartar family, known in history as the Wei dynasty. A native dynasty, the first of the name Sung, ruled in the southern provinces. The princes of these kingdoms were at first hostile to Buddhism. Image making and the building of temples were forbidden, and in the north professors of the prohibited religion were subjected to severe persecution. The people were warned against giving them shelter, and in the year 426 an edict was issued against them, in accordance with which the books and images of Buddha were destroyed, and many priests put to death. To worship foreign divinities, or construct images of earth or brass, was made a capital crime. The eldest son of the Tartar chief of the Wei kingdom made many attempts to induce his father to deal less harshly towards a religion to which he himself was strongly attached, but in vain.

The work of this king was undone by his successor who, in the year A.D. 451, issued an edict permitting a Buddhist temple to be erected in each city, and forty or fifty of the inhabitants to become priests. The emperor himself performed the tonsure for some who took the monastic vows.

The rapid advancement of Buddhism in China was not unnoticed in neighbouring kingdoms. The same prosperity that awoke the jealousy of the civil government in the country itself, occasioned sympathy elsewhere. Many embassies came from the countries lying between India and China during the time of Sung Wen-ti. whose reign of more than thirty years closed in 453. Their chief object was to congratulate the ruling emperor on the prosperity of Buddhism in his dominions, and to pave the way for frequent intercourse on the ground of identity in religion. Two letters of Pishabarma, king of Aratan, to this emperor are preserved in the history of this dynasty. He describes his kingdom as lying in the shadow of the Himalayas, whose snows fed the streams that watered it. He praises China [7] as the most prosperous of kingdoms, and its rulers as the benefactors and civilisers of the world. The letter of the king of Jebabada, another Indian monarch, expresses his admiration of the same emperor in glowing language. He had given rest to the inhabitants of heaven and earth, subjected the four demons, attained the state of perfect perception, caused the wheel of the honoured law to revolve, saved multitudes of living beings, and by the renovating power of the Buddhist religion brought them into the happiness of the Nirvâna. Relics of Buddha were widely spread—numberless pagodas erected. All the treasures of the religion (Buddha, the Law, and the Priesthood) were as beautiful in appearance, and firm in their foundations as the Sumeru mountain. The diffusion of the sacred books and the law of Buddha was like the bright shining of the sun, and the assembly of priests, pure in their lives, was like the marshalled constellations of heaven. The royal palaces and walls were like those of the Tauli heaven. In the whole Jambu continent, there were no kingdoms from which embassies did not come with tribute to the great Sung emperor of the Yang-cheu [8] kingdom. He adds, that though separated by a wide sea, it was his wish to have embassies passing and repassing between the two countries.

The extensive intercourse that then began to exist between China and India may be gathered from the fact that Ceylon [9] also sent an embassy and a letter to Sung Wen-ti. In this letter it is said, that though the countries are distant three years' journey by sea and land, there are constant communications between them. The king also mentions the attachment of his ancestors to the worship of Buddha.

The next of these curious memorials from Buddhist kings preserved in the annals of the same Chinese emperor, is that from "Kapili" (Kapilavastu), the birthplace of Shakyamuni, situated to the north-west of Benares.

The compiler of the Sung annals, after inserting this document, alludes to the flourishing state of Buddhism in the countries from which these embassies came, and in China itself. He then introduces a memorial from a magistrate representing the disorders that had sprung from the widespread influence of this religion, and recommending imperial interference. That document says that "Buddhism had during four dynasties been multiplying its images and sacred edifices. Pagodas and temples were upwards of a thousand in number. On entering them the visitor's heart was affected, and when he departed he felt desirous to invite others to the practices of piety. Lately, however, these sentiments of reverence had given place to frivolity. Instead of aiming at sincerity and purity of life, gaudy finery and mutual jealousies prevailed. While many new temples were erected for the sake of display, in the most splendid manner, no one thought of rebuilding the old ones. Official inquiries should be instituted to prevent further evils, and whoever wished to cast brazen statues should first obtain permission from the authorities."

A few years afterwards (A.D. 458) a conspiracy was detected in which a chief party was a Buddhist priest. An edict issued on the occasion by the emperor says, that among the priests many were men who had fled from justice and took the monastic vows for safety. They took advantage of their assumed character to contrive new modes of doing mischief. The fresh troubles thus constantly occurring excite the indignation of gods and men. The constituted authorities, it is added, must examine narrowly into the conduct of the monks. Those who are guilty must be put to death. It was afterwards enacted that such monks as would not keep their vows of abstinence and self-denial should return to their families and previous occupations. Nuns were also forbidden to enter the palace and converse with the emperor's wives.

The advances of Buddhism later in the fifth century were too rapid not to excite much opposition from the literati of the time, and a religious controversy was the result.

In the biography of Tsï Liang, a minister of state under the emperor Ts'ï Wu-ti (A.D. 483), there are some fragments of a discussion he maintained in favour of Buddhism. He says, "If you do not believe in 'retribution of moral actions' (*yin-kwo*), then how can you account for the difference in the condition of the rich and the poor?" His opponent says, "Men are like flowers on trees, growing together and bent and scattered by the same breeze. Some fall upon curtains and carpets, like those whose lot is cast in palaces, while others drop among heaps of filth, representing men who are born in humble life. Riches and poverty, then, can be accounted for without the doctrine of retribution." To this the advocate of Buddhism is said to have been unable to reply. He also wrote on the destruction of the soul. Personating the Confucianists, he says that, "The 'soul' (*shin*) is to the 'body' (*hing*) as sharpness to the knife. The soul cannot continue to exist after the destruction of the body, more than sharpness can remain when the knife is no more." These extracts show that some of the Confucianists of that age denied any providential retribution in the present or a future life. Whatever may be thought of notions connected with ancestral worship, and the passages in the classical books that seem to indicate the knowledge of a separate life for the soul after death, they were too imperfect and indistinct to restrain the literati from the most direct antagonism on this subject with the early Buddhists. Holding such cheerless views as they did of the destiny of man, it is not to be wondered at that the common people should desert their standard, and adopt a more congenial system. The language of daily life is now thoroughly impregnated with the phraseology of retribution and a separate state. All classes make use of very many expressions in common intercourse which have been originated by Buddhism, thus attesting the extent of its influence on the nation at large. And, as the Buddhist immortality embraces the past as well as the future, the popular notions and language of China extend to a preceding life as much as to a coming one.

A distinct conception of the controversy as it then existed may be obtained from the following extracts from an account of a native Buddhist, contained in the biographical section of the *History of the Sung dynasty:*—"The instructions of Confucius include only a single life; they do not reach to a future state of existence, with its interminable results. His disciple, in multiplying virtuous actions, only brings happiness to his posterity. Vices do but entail greater present sufferings as their punishment. The rewards of the good do not, according to this system, go beyond worldly honour, nor does the recompense of guilt include anything worse than obscurity and poverty. Beyond the ken of the senses nothing is known; such ignorance is melancholy. The aims of the doctrine of Shakya, on the other hand, are illimitable. It saves from the greatest dangers, and removes every care from the heart. Heaven and earth are not sufficient to bound its knowledge. Having as its one sentiment, mercy seeking to save, the renovation of all living beings cannot satisfy it. It speaks of hell, and the people fear to sin; of heaven, and they all desire its happiness. It points to the Nirvâna as the spirit's 'final home' (*ch'ang-kwei*, lit. 'long return'), and tells him of 'the bodily form of the law' (*fa-shen*),[10] as that last, best spectacle, on which the eye can gaze. There is no region to which its influence does not reach. It soars in thought into the upper world. Beginning from a space no larger than the well's mouth in a courtyard, it extends its knowledge to the whole adjacent mansion." These sentiments are replied to, in the imaginary dialogue in which they occur, by a Confucian, who says, "To be urged by the desire of heaven to the performance of virtue, cannot bear comparison with doing what is right for its own sake. To keep the body under restraint from the fear of hell, is not so good as to govern the heart from a feeling of duty. Acts of worship, performed for the sake of obtaining forgiveness of sins, do not spring from piety. A gift, made to secure a hundredfold recompense to the giver, cannot come from pure inward sincerity. To praise the happiness of the Nirvâna promotes a lazy inactivity. To speak highly of the beauty of the embodied ideal representation of Buddhist doctrine, seen by the advanced disciple, tends to produce in men a love of the marvellous. By your system, distant good is looked for, while the desires of the animal nature, which are close at hand, are unchecked. Though you say that the Bodhisattwa is freed from these desires, yet all beings, without exception, have them." To these arguments for the older Chinese system, the Buddhist comes forward with a rejoinder:—"Your conclusions are wrong. Motives derived from a future state are necessary to lead men to virtue. Otherwise how could the evil tendencies of the present life be adjusted? Men will not act spontaneously and immediately without something to hope for. The countryman is diligent in ploughing his land, because he expects a harvest. If he had no such hope, he would sit idle at home, and soon go down for ever 'below the nine fountains.'" [11] The Confucian answers that "religion" (*tau*) consisting in the repression of all desires, it is inconsistent to use the desire of heaven as a motive to virtue.

The discussion is continued with great spirit through several pages, turning entirely on the advantage to be derived from the doctrine of the future state for the inculcation of virtue. The Buddhist champion is called the teacher of the "black doctrine," and his opponent that of "the white." The author, a Buddhist, has given its full force to the Confucian reasoning, while he condemns without flinching the difficulties that he sees in the system he opposes. The whole is preserved in a beautifully finished style of composition, and is a specimen of the valuable materials contained in the Chinese dynastic histories for special inquiries on many subjects not concerned with the general history of the country. It was with fair words like these, the darker shades of Buddhism being kept out of view, that the contest was maintained in those days by such as would introduce a foreign form of worship, against the adherents to the maxims of Confucius. The author of the piece was rewarded for it by the reigning emperor.

In the northern provinces Buddhism was now flourishing. The prince of the Wei kingdom spared no expense in promoting it. History says, that in the year 467 he caused an image to be constructed "forty-three feet" in height (thirty-five English feet). A hundred peculs of brass, or more than five tons, were used, and six peculs of gold. Four years after, he resigned his throne to his son, and became a monk. When, about the same time, the Sung emperor erected a magnificent Buddhist temple, he was severely rebuked by some of his mandarins.

The time of Wu-ti, the first emperor of the Liang dynasty, forms an era in the history of Chinese Buddhism, marked as it was by the arrival in China of *Ta-mo* (Bodhidharma), the twenty-eighth of the patriarchs, and by the extraordinary prosperity of the Buddhist religion under the imperial favour.

At the beginning of the sixth century, the number of Indians in China was upwards of three thousand. The prince of the Wei kingdom exerted himself greatly to provide maintenance for them in monasteries, erected on the most beautiful sites. Many of them resided at Lo-yang, the modern Ho-nan fu. The temples had multiplied to thirteen thousand. The decline of Buddhism in its motherland drove many of the Hindoos to the north of the Himalayas. They came as refugees from the Brahmanical persecution, and their great number will assist materially in accounting for the growth of the religion they propagated in China. The prince of the Wei country is recorded to have discoursed publicly on the Buddhist classics. At the same time, he refused to treat for peace with the ambassadors of his southern neighbour, the Liang kingdom. Of this the Confucian historian takes advantage, charging him with inconsistency in being attached to a religion that forbids cruelty and bloodshed, while he showed such fondness for war.

Soon after this, several priests were put to death (A.D. 515) for practising magical arts. This is an offence attributed more than once by the Chinese historians to the early Buddhists. The use of charms, and the claim to magical powers, do not appear to have belonged to the system as it was left by Shakyamuni. His teaching, as Burnouf has shown, was occupied simply with morals and his peculiar philosophy. After a few centuries, however, among the additions made by the Northern Buddhists to popularise the religion, and give greater power to the priests, were many narratives full of marvels and impossibilities, falsely attributed to primitive Buddhism. These works are called the *Ta-ch'eng*, or "Great Development" Sutras. Another novelty was the pretence of working enchantments by means of unintelligible formulæ, which are preserved in the books of the Chinese Buddhists, as in those of Nepaul, without attempt at explanation. These charms are called Dharani. They occur in the Great Development classics, such as the "Lotus of the Good Law," *Miau-fa-lien-hwa-king* (*Fa-hwa-king*), and in various Buddhist works. The account given in the *T'ung-kien-kang-muh* of the professed magician who led the priests referred to above, says that he styled himself *Ta-ch'eng*, used wild music to win followers, taught them to dissolve all the ties of kindred, and aimed only at murder and disturbance.

The native annotator says that *Ta-ch'eng* is the highest of three states of intelligence to which a disciple of Buddha can attain, and that the corresponding Sanscrit word, *Mahayana*, means "Boundless revolution and unsurpassed knowledge." It is here that the resemblance is most striking between the Buddhism of China and that of other countries where it is professed in the north. These countries having the same additions to the creed of Shakya, the division of Buddhism by Burnouf into a Northern and Southern school has been rightly made. The superadded mythology and claim to magical powers of the Buddhists, who revere the Sanscrit as their sacred language, distinguish them from their co-religionists who preserve their traditions in the Pali tongue.

In the year A.D. 518, Sung-yün was sent to India by the prince of the Wei country for Buddhist books. He was accompanied by Hwei-sheng, a priest. He travelled to Candahar, stayed two years in Udyana, and returned with 175 Buddhist works. His narrative has been translated by Professor Neumann into German.

In A.D. 526, Bodhidharma, after having grown old in Southern India, reached Canton by sea. The propagation of Buddhism in his native country he gave in charge to one of his disciples during his absence. He was received with the honour due to his age and character, and immediately invited to Nanking, where the emperor of Southern China, Liang Wu-ti, held his court. The emperor said to him—"From my accession to the throne, I have been incessantly building temples, transcribing sacred books, and admitting new monks to take the vows. How much merit may I be supposed to have accumulated?" The reply was, "None." The emperor: "And why no merit?" The patriarch: "All this is but the insignificant effect of an imperfect cause not complete in itself. It is the shadow that follows the substance, and is without real existence." The emperor: "Then what is true merit?" The patriarch: "It consists in purity and enlightenment, depth and completeness, and in being wrapped in thought while surrounded by vacancy and stillness. Merit such as this cannot be sought by worldly means." The emperor: "Which is the most important of the holy doctrines?" The patriarch: "Where all is emptiness, nothing can be called 'holy' (*sheng*)." The emperor: "Who is he that thus replies to me?" The patriarch: "I do not know." The emperor—says the Buddhist narrator—still remained unenlightened. This extract exhibits Buddhism very distinctly in its mystic phase. Mysticism can attach itself to the most abstract philosophical dogmas, just as well as to those of a properly religious kind. This state of mind, allying itself indifferently to error and to truth, is thus shown to be of purely subjective origin. The objective doctrines that call it into existence may be of the most opposite kind. It grows, therefore, out of the mind itself. Its appearance may be more naturally expected in the history of a religion like Christianity, which awakens the human emotions to their intensest exercise, while, in many ways, it favours the extended use of the contemplative faculties, and hence the numerous mystic sects of Church history. Its occurrence in Buddhism, and its kindred systems, might with more reason occasion surprise, founded as they are on philosophical meditations eminently abstract. It was reserved for the fantastic genius of India to construct a religion out of three such elements as atheism, annihilation, and the non-reality of the material world; and, by the encouragement of mysticism and the monastic life, to make these most ultimate of negations palatable and popular. The subsequent addition of a mythology suited to the taste of the common people was, it should be remembered, another powerful cause, contributing, in conjunction with these quietist and ascetic tendencies, to spread Buddhism through so great a mass of humankind. In carrying out his mystic views, Ta-mo discouraged the use of the sacred books. He represented the attainment of the Buddhist's aim as being entirely the work of the heart. Though he professed not to make use of books, his followers preserved his apophthegms in writing, and, by the wide diffusion of them, a numerous school of contemplatists was originated, under the name of *Ch'an-hio* (*dhyana* doctrine) and *Ch'an-men* (*dhyana* school).

Bodhidharma, not being satisfied with the result of his interview with royalty, crossed the Yang-tsze keang into the Wei kingdom and remained at Lo-yang. Here, the narrative says, he sat with his face to a wall for nine years. The people called him the "Wall-gazing Brahman." [12] When it was represented to the Liang emperor, that the great teacher, who possessed the precious heirloom of Shakya, the symbol of the hidden law of Buddha, was lost to his kingdom, he repented and sent messengers to invite him to return. They failed in their errand. The presence of the Indian sage excited the more ardent Chinese Buddhists to make great efforts to conquer the sensations. Thus one of them, we are told, said to himself, "Formerly, for the sake of religion, men broke open their bones and extracted the marrow, took blood from their arms to give to the hungry, rolled their hair in the mud, or threw themselves down a precipice to feed a famishing tiger. What can I do?" Accordingly, while snow was falling, he exposed himself to it till it had risen above his knees, when the patriarch observing him, asked him what he hoped to gain by it. The young aspirant to the victory over self wept at the question, and said, "I only desire that mercy may open a path to save the whole race of mankind." The patriarch replied, that such an act was not worthy of comparison with the acts of the Buddhas. It required, he told him, very little virtue or resolution. His disciple, stung with the answer, says the legend, took a sharp knife, severed his arm, and placed it before the patriarch. The latter expressed his high approval of the deed, and when, after nine years' absence, he determined to return to India, he appointed the disciple who had performed it to succeed him as patriarch in China. He said to him on this occasion, "I give you the seal of the law as the sign of your adherence to the true doctrine inwardly, and the *kasha* (robe worn by Buddhists) as the symbol of your outward teaching. These symbols must be delivered down from one to another for two hundred years after my death, and then, the law of Buddha having spread through the whole nation, the succession of patriarchs will cease." He further said, "I also consign to you the *Lenga Sutra* in four sections, which opens the door to the heart of Buddha, and is fitted to enlighten all living men." Ta-mo's further instructions to his successor as to the nature and duties of the patriarchate are fully detailed in the *Chï-yue-luh*. He died of old age after five attempts to poison him, and was buried at the Hiung-er mountains between Ho-nan and Shen-si. At this juncture Sung-yün, who had been sent to India a few years previously for Buddhist books, returned, and inspected the remains of Bodhidharma. As he lay in his coffin he held one shoe in his hand. Sun;-yün asked him whither he was going. "To the Western heaven," was the reply. Sung-yün then returned home. The coffin was afterwards opened and found empty, excepting that one of the patriarch's shoes was lying there. By imperial command, the shoe was preserved as a sacred relic in the monastery. Afterwards in the T'ang dynasty it was stolen, and now no one knows where it is. The embassies from Buddhist kingdoms in the time of Liang Wu-ti afford other illustrations of the passion for relics and mementoes of venerated personages, encouraged by the Buddhist priests. The king of Bunam, the ancient Siam, wrote to the emperor that he had a hair of Buddha, twelve feet in length, to give him. Priests were sent from the Chinese court to meet it, and bring it home. Three years before this, as the *History of the Liang dynasty* informs us, in building, by imperial command, a monastery and pagoda to king *A-yo* (Ashôka), a *sharira*, or "relic of Buddha," had been found under the old pagoda, with a hair of a blue lavender colour. This hair was so elastic that when the priests pulled it, it lengthened *ad libitum*, and when let alone curled into a spiral form. The historian quotes two Buddhist works in illustration. The "Seng-ga Sutra" (*king*) says, that Buddha's hair was blue and fine. In the San-mei-king, Shakya himself says, "When I was formerly in my father's palace, I combed my hair, and measuring it, found that it was twelve feet in length. When let go, it curled into a spiral form." This description agrees, it is added, with that of the hair found by the emperor.

In A.D. 523, the king of Banban sent as his tributary offering, a true "sharira" (*she-li*) with pictures and miniature pagodas; also leaves of the Bodhi, Buddha's favourite tree. The king of another country in the Birmese peninsula had a dream, in which a priest appeared to him and foretold to him that the new prince of the Liang dynasty would soon raise Buddhism to the summit of prosperity, and that he would do wisely if he sent him an embassy. The king paying no attention to the warning, the priest appeared again in a second dream, and conducted the monarch to the court of Liang Wu-ti. On awaking, the king, who was himself an accomplished painter, drew the likeness of the emperor as he had seen him in his dream. He now sent ambassadors and an artist with instructions to paint a likeness of the Chinese monarch from life. On comparing it with his own picture, the similarity was found to be perfect.

This emperor, so zealous a promoter of Buddhism, in the year A.D. 527, the twenty-sixth of his reign, became a monk and entered the Tung-tai monastery in Nanking. The same record is made in the history two years afterwards. As might be expected, this event calls forth a long and severe critique from the Confucian historian. The preface to the history of the dynasty established by this prince, consists solely of a lament over the sad necessity of adverting to Buddhism in the imperial annals of the nation, with an argument for the old national system, which is so clearly right, that the wish to deviate from it shows a man to be wrong. In reference to the emperor's becoming a priest, the critic says, "that not only would the man of common intelligence condemn such conduct in the ruler of a commonwealth, but even men like Bodhidharma would withhold their approval."

A few years afterwards, the same emperor rebuilt the Ch'ang-ts'ien monastery five *le* to the south of "Nanking," in which was the *tope* (shrine for relics) of *A-yo* or Ashôka. The writer in the *T'ung-kien-kang-muh* adds, that a true relic of Buddha's body is preserved near "Ming-cheu" (now Ningpo). Ashôka erected 80,000 topes, of which one-nineteenth were assigned to China. The tope and relic here alluded to are those of the hill *Yo-wang shan*, well known to foreign visitors, and situated fifty-two *li* eastward of Ningpo. To Buddhist pilgrims coming from far and near to this sacred spot, the *she-li* is an object of reverential worship, but to unbelieving eyes it presents a rather insignificant appearance. The small, reddish, beadlike substance that constitutes the relic, is so placed in its lantern-shaped receptacle, that it does not admit of much light being thrown upon it. The colour is said to vary with the state of mind of the visitor. Yellow is that of happiest omen. The theory is a safe one, for there is just obscurity enough to render the tint of the precious remains of Shakya's burnt body somewhat uncertain.

King Ashôka, to whom this temple is dedicated, was one of the most celebrated of the Buddhist kings of India. Burnouf in his *Introduction à l'Histoire du Buddhisme Indien*, has translated a long legend of which

Ashôka is the hero, and which is also contained in the Chinese work, *Fa-yuen-chu-lin*. The commencement in the latter differs a little from that given by Burnouf. Buddha says to Ananda, "You should know that in the city 'Palinput' (Pataliputra), there will be a king named 'The moon protected' (*Yue-hu*; in Sanscrit, *Chandragupta*). He will have a son named Bindupala, and he again will have a son Susima." Ashôka was the son of Bindupala by another wife, and succeeded his father as king. The Indian king Sandracottus, who concluded a treaty with Seleucus Nicator, the Greek king of Syria, B.C. 305, was identified with Chandragupta by Schlegel and Wilson. According to the *Mahavanso*, the Pali history of the Buddhist patriarchs, there was an interval of 854 years from Buddha's death to the accession of Chandragupta, making that event to be in B.C. 389, which is more than half a century too soon. Turnour thinks the discrepancy cannot be accounted for but by supposing a wilful perversion of the chronology. These statements are quoted in Hardy's *Eastern Monachism*, from Wilson's *Vishnu Purana*. By this synchronism of Greek and Indian literature, it is satisfactorily shown that Ashôka lived in the second century before Christ, and Buddha in the fourth and fifth. The commonly received chronology of the Chinese Buddhists is too long, therefore, by more than five hundred years. [13] Probably this fraud was effected to verify predictions found in certain Sutras, in which Buddha is made to say that in a definite number of years after his death, such and such things would happen. The Northern Buddhists wrote in Sanscrit, made use of Sanscrit Sutras, and were anxious to vindicate the correctness of all predictions found in them. Burnouf supposes that the disciples of Buddha, would naturally publish their sacred books in more than one language; Sanscrit being then, and long afterwards, spoken by the literati, while derived dialects were used by the common people. By Fa-hien Ashôka is called *A-yo Wang*, as at the monastery near Ningpo. In Hiuen-tsang's narrative, the name *Wu-yeu wang*, the "Sorrowless king," a translation of the Sanscrit word, is applied to him.

The Liang emperor Wu-ti, after three times assuming the, Buddhist vows and expounding the Sutras to his assembled courtiers, was succeeded by a son who favoured Tauism. A few years after, the sovereign of the Ts'i kingdom endeavoured to combine these two religions. He put to death four Tauist priests for refusing to submit to the tonsure and become worshippers of Buddha. After this there was no more resistance. In A.D. 558 it is related that Wu-ti, an emperor of the Ch'in dynasty, became a monk. Some years afterwards, the prince of the Cheu kingdom issued an edict prohibiting both Buddhism and Tauism. Books and images were destroyed, and all professors of these religions compelled to abandon them.

The *History of the Northern Wei dynasty* contains some details on the early Sanscrit translations in addition to what has been already inserted in this narrative. [14] The pioneers in the work of translation were Kashiapmadanga and Chu-fa-lan, who worked conjointly in the time of Ming-ti. The latter also translated the "Sutra of the ten points of rest." In A.D. 150, a priest of the "An-si" (Arsaces) country in Eastern Persia is noticed as an excellent translator. About A.D. 170, Chitsin, a priest of the Getæ nation, produced a version of the *Nirvâna Sutra*. Sun K'iuen, prince of the Wu state, one of the Three Kingdoms, who, some time after the embassy of Marcus Aurelius Antoninus, the Roman emperor, to China, received with great respect a Roman merchant at his court, [15] treated with equal regard an Indian priest who translated for him some of the books of Buddha. The next Indian mentioned is Dharmakakala, who translated the "Vinaya" or *Kiai-lü* (Discipline) at Lo-yang. About A.D. 300, Chï-kung-ming, a foreign priest, translated the *Wei-ma* and *Fa-hwa*, [16] "Lotus of the Good Law Sutras," but the work was imperfectly done. Tau-an, a Chinese Buddhist, finding the sacred books disfigured by errors, applied himself to correct them. He derived instruction from Buddojanga and wished much to converse with Kumarajiva, noticed in a previous page. The latter, himself a man of high intelligence, had conceived an extraordinary regard for him, and lamented much when he came to Ch'ang-an from Liang-cheu at the north-western corner of China where he had long resided, that Tau-an was dead. Kumarajiva found that in the corrections he proposed to make in the sacred books, he had been completely anticipated by his Chinese fellow-religionist. Kumarajiva is commended for his accurate knowledge of the Chinese language as well as of his own. With his assistants he made clear the sense of many profound and extensive "Sutras" (*King*) and "Shastras" (*Lun*), twelve works in all. The divisions into sections and sentences were formed with care. The finishing touch to the Chinese composition of these translations was given by Seng-chau. Fa-hien in his travels did his utmost to procure copies of the Discipline and the other sacred books. On his return, with the aid of an Indian named Bhadra, he translated the *Seng-ki-lü* (*Asangkhyea Vinaya*), which has since been regarded as a standard work.

Before Fa-hien's time, about A.D. 290, a Chinese named Chu Sï-hing went to Northern India for Buddhist books. He reached Udin or Khodin, identified by Remusat with Khoten, and obtained a Sutra of ninety sections. He translated it in Ho-nan, with the title *Fang-kwang-pat-nia-king* (Light-emitting Prajna Sutra). Many of these books at that time so coveted, were brought to Lo-yang, and translated there by Chufahu, a priest of the Getæ nation, who had travelled to India, and was a contemporary of the Chinese just mentioned. Fa-ling was another Chinese who proceeded from "Yang-cheu" (Kiang-nan) to Northern India and brought back the Sutra *Hwa-yen-king* and the *Pen-ting-lü*, a work on discipline. Versions of the "Nirvâna Sutra" (*Ni-wan-king*), and the *Seng-ki-lü* were made by Chi-meng in the country *Kau-ch'ang*, or what is now "Eastern Thibet." The translator had obtained them at *Hwa-shï* or "Pataliputra," a city to the westward. The Indian Dharmaraksha brought to China a new Sanscrit copy of the *Nirvâna Sutra* and going to Kau-ch'ang, compared it with Chi-meng's copy for critical purposes. The latter was afterwards brought to Ch'ang-an and published in thirty chapters. The Indian here mentioned, professed to foretell political events by the use of charms. He also translated the *Kin-*

kwang-king, or "Golden Light Sutra," and the *Ming-king*, "Bright Sutra." At this time there were several tens of foreign priests at Ch'ang-an, but the most distinguished among them for ability was Kumarajiva. His translations of the *Wei-ma*, *Fa-hwa*, and *C'heng-shih* (complete) Sutras, with the three just mentioned, by Dharmaraksha and some others, together form the *Great Development* course of instruction. The "Longer Agama Sutra" [17] and the "Discipline of the Four Divisions" [18] were translated by Buddhayasha, a native of India, the "Discipline of the Ten Chants" [19] by Kumarajiva, the "Additional Agama Sutra" by Dharmanandi, and the "Shastra of Metaphysics" (*Abhidharma-lun*) by Dharmayagama. These together formed the *Smaller Development* course. In some monasteries the former works were studied by the recluses; in others the latter. Thus a metaphysical theology, subdivided into schools, formed the subject of study in the Asiatic monkish establishments, as in the days of the European school-men. The Chinese travellers in India, and in the chain of Buddhist kingdoms extending—before the inroads of Mohammedanism—from their native land into Persia, give us the opportunity of knowing how widely there as well as in China the monastic life and the study of these books were spread. About A.D. 400, Sangadeva, a native of "Cophen" (*Kipin*), translated two of the *Agama Sutras*. The "Hwa-yen Sutra" was soon afterwards brought from Udin by Chi Fa-ling, a Chinese Buddhist, and a version of it made at Nanking. He also procured the *Pen-ting-lü*, a work in the *Vinaya* or "Discipline" branch of Buddhist books. Ma Twan-lin also mentions a Hindoo who, about A.D. 502, translated some Shastras of the Great Development (*Ta-ch'eng*) school, called *Ti-ch'ï-lun* (fixed position), and *Shi-ti-lun* (the ten positions).

The Hindoo Buddhists in China, whose literary labours down to the middle of the sixth century are here recorded, while they sometimes enjoyed the imperial favour, had to bear their part in the reverses to which their religion was exposed. Dharmaraksha was put to death for refusing to come to court on the requisition of one of the Wei emperors. Sihien, a priest of the royal family of the Kipin kingdom in Northern India, in times of persecution assumed the disguise of a physician, and when the very severe penal laws then enacted against Buddhism were remitted, returned to his former mode of life as a monk. Some other names might be added to the list of Hindoo translators, were it not already sufficiently long.

About the year 460 it appears from the history that five Buddhists from Ceylon arrived in China by the Thibetan route. Two of them were Yashaita and Budanandi. They brought images. Those constructed by the latter had the property of diminishing in apparent size as the visitor drew nearer, and looking brighter as he went farther away. Though a literary character is not attributed to them, the Southern Buddhist traditions might, through their means, have been communicated at this time to the Chinese. This may account for the date—nearly correct—assigned to the birth of Buddha in the *History of the Wei dynasty*, from which these facts are taken, and in that of the Sui dynasty which soon followed.

According to the same history there were then in China two millions of priests and thirty thousand temples. This account must be exaggerated; for if we allow a thousand to each district, which is probably over the mark, there will be but that number at the present time, although the population has increased very greatly in the interval. [20]

Buddhism received no check from the Sui emperors, who ruled China for the short period of thirty-seven years. The first of them, on assuming the title of emperor in 581, issued an edict giving full toleration to this sect. Towards the close of his reign he prohibited the destruction or maltreatment of any of the images of the Buddhist or Tauist sects. It was the weakness of age, says the Confucian historian, giving way to superstitions that led him to such an act as this. The same commentator on the history of the period says, that the Buddhist books were at this time ten times more numerous than the Confucian classics. The *Sui History* in the digest it gives of all the books of the time, states those of the Buddhist sect to be 1950 distinct works. Many of the titles are given, and among them are not a few treating of the mode of writing by alphabetic symbols used in the kingdoms from whence Buddhism came. The first alphabet that was thus introduced appears to have been one of fourteen symbols. It is called *Si-yo hu-shu* or "Foreign Writing of the Western countries," and also *Ba-la-men-shu*, "Brahmanical writing." The tables of initials and finals found in the Chinese native dictionaries were first formed in the third century, but more fully early in the sixth century, in the Liang dynasty. It was then that the Hindoos, who had come to China, assisted in forming, according to the model of the Sanscrit alphabet, a system of thirty-six initial letters, and described the vocal organs by which they are formed. They also constructed tables, in which, by means of two sets of representative characters, one for the initials and another for the finals, a mode of spelling words was exhibited. The Chinese were now taught for the first time that monosyllabic sounds are divisible into parts, but alphabetic symbols were not adopted to write the separated elements. It was thought better to use characters already known to the people. A serious defect attended this method. The analysis was not carried far enough. Intelligent Chinese understand that a sound, such as man, can be divided into two parts, m and an; for they have been long accustomed to the system of phonetic bisection here alluded to, but they usually refuse to believe that a trisection of the sound is practicable. At the same time the system was much easier to learn than if foreign symbols had been employed, and it was very soon universally adopted. Shen-kung, a priest, is said to have been the author of the system, and the dictionary *Yü-p'ien* was one of the first extensive works in which it was employed. [21] That the Hindoo Buddhists should have taught the Chinese how to write the sounds of this language by an artifice which required nothing but their own hieroglyphics, and rendered unnecessary the introduction of new symbols, is sufficient evidence of their ingenuity, and is not the least of the services they have done to the sons of Han. It answered well for several centuries, and was made use of in all dictionaries and educational works. But the language changed, the old sounds were broken up, and now the words thus spelt are read correctly only by those natives who happen to speak the dialects that most nearly resemble in sound the old pronunciation.

To Shen Yo, the historian of two dynasties, and author of several detached historical pieces, is attributed the discovery of the four tones. His biographer says of him in the "Liang History:"—"He wrote his 'Treatise on the Four Tones,' to make known what men for thousands of years had not understood—the wonderful fact which he alone in the silence of his breast came to perceive." It may be well doubted if the credit of arriving unassisted at the knowledge of this fact is due to him. He resided at the court of Liang Wu-ti, the great patron of the Indian strangers. They, accustomed to the unrivalled accuracy in phonetic analysis of the Sanscrit alphabet, would readily distinguish a new phenomenon like this, while to a native speaker, who had never known articulate sounds to be without it, it would almost necessarily be undetected. In the syllabic spelling that they formed, the tones are duly represented, by being embraced in every instance in the final.

The extent of influence which this nomenclature for sounds has attained in the native literature is known to all who are familiar with its dictionaries, and the common editions of the classical books. In this way it is that the traditions of old sounds needed to explain the rhymes and metre of the ancient national poetry are preserved. By the same method the sounds of modern dialects that have deviated extensively from the old type have been committed to writing. The dialects of the Mandarin provinces, of Northern and Southern Fu-kien, and Canton have been written down by native authors each with its one system of tones and alphabetic elements, and they have all taken the method introduced by the Buddhists as their guide. The Chinese have since become acquainted with several alphabets with foreign symbols, but when they need to write phonetically they prefer the system, imperfect as it is, that does not oblige them to abandon the hieroglyphic signs transmitted by their ancestors. Never, perhaps, since the days of Cadmus, was a philological impulse more successful than that thus communicated from India to the Chinese, if the extent of its adoption be the criterion. They have not only by the use of the syllabic spelling thus taught them, collected the materials for philological research afforded by the modern dialects, but, by patient industry, have discovered the early history of the language, showing how the number of tones increased from two to three by the time of Confucius, to four in the sixth century of our era, and so on to their present state. Few foreign investigators have yet entered on this field of research, but it may be suggested that the philology of the Eastern languages must without it be necessarily incomplete, and that the Chinese, by patience and a true scientific instinct, have placed the materials in such a form that little labour is needed to gather from them the facts that they contain.

The Thibetans, and, probably, the Coreans also, owe their alphabets, which are both arranged in the Sanscrit mode, to the Buddhists. Corean ambassadors came in the reign of Liang Wu-ti to ask for the "Nirvâna" and other Buddhistic classics. It may then have been as early as this that they had an alphabet, but the writing now in use dates from about A.D. 1360, as Mr. Scott has shown. [22] The first emperor of the T'ang dynasty was induced by the representations of Fu Yi, one of his ministers, to call a council for deliberation on the mode of action to be adopted in regard to Buddhism. Fu Yi, a stern enemy of the new religion, proposed that the monks and nuns should be compelled to marry and bring up families. The reason that they adopted the ascetic life, he said, was to avoid contributing to the revenue. What they held about the fate of mankind depending on the will of Buddha was false. Life and death were regulated by a "natural necessity" with which man had nothing to do (*yeu-ü-tsï-jan*). The retribution of vice and virtue was the province of the prince, while riches and poverty were the recompense provoked by our own actions. The public manners had degenerated lamentably through the influence of Buddhism. The "six states of being" [23] into which the souls of men might be born were entirely fictitious. The monks lived an idle life, and were unprofitable members of the commonwealth. To this it was replied in the council, by Siau Ü, a friend of the Buddhists, that Buddha was a "sage" (*shing-jen*), and that Fu Yi having spoken ill of a sage, was guilty of a great crime. To this Fu Yi answered, that the highest of the virtues were loyalty and filial piety, and the monks, casting off as they did their prince and their parents, disregarded them both. As for Siau Ü, he added, he was—being the advocate of such a system—as destitute as they of these virtues. Siau Ü joined his hands and merely replied to him, that hell was made for such men as he. The Confucianists gained the victory, and severe restrictions were imposed on the professors of the foreign faith, but they were taken off almost immediately after.

The successors of Bodhidharma were five in number. They are styled with him the six "Eastern patriarchs," *Tung-tsu*. They led quiet lives. The fourth of them was invited to court by the second emperor of the T'ang dynasty, and repeatedly declined the honour. When a messenger came for the fourth time and informed him that, if he refused to go, he had orders to take his head back with him, the imperturbable old man merely held out his neck to the sword in token of his willingness to die. The emperor respected his firmness. Some years previously, with a large number of disciples, he had gone to a city in Shansi. The city was soon after laid siege to by rebels. The patriarch advised his followers to recite the "Great Prajna," *Ma-ha-pat-nia*, an extensive work, in which the most abstract dogmas of Buddhist philosophy are very fully developed. The enemy, looking towards the ramparts, thought they saw a band of spirit-soldiers in array against them, and consequently retired.

In the year 629 the celebrated Hiuen-tsang set out on his journey to India to procure Sanscrit books. Passing from Liang-cheu at the north-western extremity of China, he proceeded westward to the region watered by the Oxus and Jaxartes where the Turks [24] were then settled. He afterwards crossed the Hindoo-kush and proceeded into India. He lingered for a long time in the countries through which the Ganges flows, rich as they were in reminiscences and relics of primitive Buddhism. Then bending his steps to the southwards, he completed the tour of the Indian peninsula, returned across the Indus, and reached home in the sixteenth year after his departure. The same emperor, T'ai-tsung, was still reigning, and he received the traveller with the utmost distinction. He spent the rest of his days in translating from the Sanscrit originals the Buddhist works he had brought with him from India. It was by imperial command that these translations were undertaken. The same emperor, T'ai-tsung, received with equal favour the Syrian Christians, Alopen and his companions, who had arrived in A.D. 639, only seven years before Hiuen-tsang's return. The *Histoire de la Vie de Hiouen-thsang*, translated by M. Julien, is a volume full of interest for the history of Buddhism and Buddhist literature. As a preparation for the task, the accomplished translator added to his unrivalled knowledge of the Chinese language an extensive acquaintance with Sanscrit, acquired when he was already advanced in life, with this special object. Scarcely does the name of a place or a book occur in the narrative which he has not identified and given to the reader in its Sanscrit form. The book was originally written by two friends of Hiuen-tsang. It includes a specimen of Sanscrit grammar, exemplifying the declensions of nouns, with their eight cases and three numbers, the conjugation of the substantive verb, and other details. Hiuen-tsang remained five years in the monastery of Nalanda, on the banks of the Ganges, studying the language, and reading the Brahmanical literature as well as that of Buddhism.

Hiuen-tsang was summoned on his arrival to appear at court, and answer for his conduct, in leaving his country and undertaking so long a journey without the imperial permission. The emperor—praised by Gibbon as the Augustus of the East—was residing at Lo-yang, to which city the traveller proceeded. He had brought with him 115 grains of relics taken from Buddha's chair; a gold statue of Buddha, 3 feet 3 inches in height, with a transparent pedestal; a second, 3 feet 5 inches in height, and others of silver and carved in sandal-wood. His collection of Sanscrit books was very extensive. A sufficient conception of the voluminous contributions then made to Chinese literature from India will be obtained by enumerating some of the names.

Of the Great Development school, 124 Sutras.

On the Discipline and Philosophical works of the following schools:—

Shang-tso-pu (Sarvâstivâdas),	15	works.
San-mi-ti-pu (Sammitîyas),	15	,,
Mi-sha-se-pu (Mahîshâshakas),	22	,,
Kia-she-pi-ye-pu (Kâshyapîyas),	17	,,
Fa-mi-pu (Dharmaguptas),	42	,,
Shwo-i-tsie-yeu-pu (Sarvâstivâdas)	67	,,

These works, amounting with others to 657, were carried by twenty-two horses.

The emperor, after listening to the traveller's account of what he had seen, commanded him to write a description of the Western countries, and the work called *Ta-t'ang-si-yü-ki* was the result. [25]

Hiuen-tsang went to *Ch'ang-an* (Si-an-fu) to translate, and was assisted by twelve monks. Nine others were appointed to revise the composition. Some who had learned Sanscrit also joined him in the work. On presenting a series of translations to the emperor, he wrote a preface to them; and at the request of Hiuen-tsang issued an edict that five new monks should be received in every convent in the empire. The convents then amounted to 3716. The losses of Buddhism from the persecutions to which it had been exposed were thus repaired.

At the emperor's instance, Hiuen-tsang now corrected the translation of the celebrated Sutra *Kin-kang-pat-nia-pa-la-mi-ta-king* (in Sanscrit, *Vajra-chedika-prajna-para-mita Sutra*). Two words were added to the title which Kumarajiva had omitted. The new title read *Neng-twan-kin*, *etc*. The name of the city Shravasti was spelt with five characters instead of two. The new translation of this work did not supplant the old one—that of Kumarajiva. The latter is at the present day the most common, except the

"Daily Prayers," of all books in the Buddhist temples and monasteries, and is in the hands of almost every monk.

This work contains the germ of the larger compilation *Prajna paramita* in one hundred and twenty volumes. The abstractions of Buddhist philosophy, which were afterwards ramified to such a formidable extent as these numbers indicate, are here found in their primary form probably, as they were taught by Shakyamuni himself. The translation of the larger work was not completed till A.D. 661. That Hiuen-tsang, as a translator, was a strong literalist, may be inferred from the fact, that when he was meditating on the propriety of imitating Kumarajiva, who omitted repetitions and superfluities, in so large a work as this, he was deterred by a dream from the idea, and resolved to give the one hundred and twenty volumes entire, in all their wearisome reiteration of metaphysical paradoxes.

Among the new orthographies that he introduced was that of *Bi-ch'u* for *Bi-k'u*, "Mendicant disciple," and of *Ba-ga-vam* instead of *But* for "Buddha." This spelling nearly coincides with that of the Nepaulese Sanscrit, *Bhagavat*. In the Pali versions he is called "Gautama," which is a patronymic, in Chinese, *Go-dam. Ba-ga-vam* is used in the Sutra *Yo-sï-lieu-li-kwang-ju-lai-kung-te-king*. Modern reprints of Hiuen-tsang's translation of the Shastras called *Abhidharma*, are found in a fragmentary and worm-eaten state in many of the larger Buddhist temples near Shanghai and elsewhere at the present time. He lived nineteen years after his return, and spent nearly the whole of that time in translating. He completed 740 works, in 1335 books. Among them were three works on Logic, viz., *Li-men-lun, In-ming-lun, In-ming-shu-kiai*. Among other works that he brought to China, were treatises on Grammar, *Shing-ming-lun* and *Pe-ye-kie-la-nan*, and a Lexicon, *Abhidharma Kosha*. [26] The modern Chinese editor of the "Description of Western Countries" complains of its author's superstition. Anxiety to detail every Buddhist wonder has been accompanied by neglect of the physical features of the countries that came under review. Here, says the critic, he cannot be compared with

Ngai Ju-lio (Julius Aleni, one of the early Jesuits) in the *Chih-fang-wai-ki* (a well-known geographical work by that missionary). In truthfulness this work is not equal, he tells us, to the "Account of Buddhist kingdoms" by Fa-hien, but it is written in a style much more ornamental. The extensive knowledge, he adds, of Buddhist literature possessed by Hiuen-tsang himself, and the elegant style of his assistants, make the book interesting, so that, though it contains not a little that is false, the reader does not go to sleep over it.

The life and adventures of Hiuen-tsang have been made the basis of a long novel, which is universally read at the present time. It is called the *Si-yeu-ki* or *Si-yeu-chen-ts'euen*. The writer, apparently a Tauist, makes unlimited use of the two mythologies—that of his own religion and that of his hero—as the machinery of his tale. He has invented a most eventful account of the birth of Hiuen-tsang. It might have been supposed that the wild romance of India was unsuited to the Chinese taste, but our author does not hesitate to adopt it. His readers become familiar with all those imaginary deities, whose figures they see in the Buddhist temples, as the ornaments of a fictitious narrative. The hero, in undertaking so distant and dangerous a journey to obtain the sacred books of Buddhism, and by translating them into his native tongue, to promote the spread of that superstition among his countrymen, is represented as the highest possible example of the excellence at which the Buddhist aims. The effort and the success that crowns it, are identified with the aspiration of the Tauist after the elixir of immortality; the hermit's elevation to the state of Buddha, and the translation of those whose hearts have been purified by meditation and retirement, to the abodes of the genii.

The sixth emperor of the T'ang dynasty was too weak to rule. Wu, the emperor's mother, held the reins of power, and distinguished herself by her ability and by her cruelties.

In the year 690 a new Buddhist Sutra, the *Ta-yün-king*, "Great cloud Sutra," was presented to her. It stated that she was Maitreya, the Buddha that was to come, and the ruler of the Jambu continent. She ordered it to be circulated through the empire, and bestowed public offices on more than one Buddhist priest.

Early in the eighth century, the Confucianists made another effort to bring about a persecution of Buddhism. In 714, Yen Ts'ung argued that it was pernicious to the state, and appealed for proof to the early termination of those dynasties that had favoured it. In carrying out an edict then issued, more than 12,000 priests and nuns were obliged to return to the common world. Casting images, writing the sacred books, and building temples, were also forbidden.

At this time some priests are mentioned as holding public offices in the government. The historians animadvert on this circumstance, as one of the monstrosities accompanying a female reign.

About the beginning of the same century, Hindoos were employed to regulate the national calendar. The first mentioned is Gaudamara, whose method of calculation was called *Kwang-tse-li*, "The calendar of the bright house." It was used fur three years only. A better-known Buddhist astronomer of the same nation was Gaudamsiddha. By imperial command he translated from Sanscrit, the mode of astronomical calculation called *Kien-chï-shu*. It embraced the calculation of the moon's course and of eclipses. His calendar of this name was adopted for a few years, when it was followed in A.D. 721 by that of the well-known Yih-hing, a Chinese Buddhist priest, whose name holds a place in the first rank of the native astronomers. The translations of Gaudamsiddha are contained in the work called *K'ai-yuen-chan-king*, a copy of which was discovered accidentally, in the latter part of the sixteenth century, inside an image of Buddha. It has been cut in wood more than once since that time. The part translated from Sanscrit is but a small portion of the work. The remainder is chiefly astrological. Among other things, there is a short notice of the Indian arithmetical notation, with its nine symbols and a dot for a cipher. There was nothing new in this to the countrymen of Confucius, so far as the principle of decimal notation was concerned;

but it is interesting to us, whose ancestors did not obtain the Indian numerals till several centuries after this time. The Arabs learned them in the eighth century, and transmitted them slowly to Europe. Among the earlier Buddhist translations, a book is mentioned under the title of Brahmanical Astronomy," *P'o-lo-men-t'ien-wen*, in twenty chapters. It was translated in the sixth century by Daluchi, a native of the Maleya kingdom. Another is *Ba-la-men-gih-ga-sien-jen-t'ien-wen-shwo*, "An Account of Astronomy by the Brahman Gigarishi." [27]

The date of these translations, mentioned in the "History of the Sui dynasty," can be no later than the sixth century or very early in the seventh. The same should be observed of two works on Brahmanical arithmetic, viz., *Ba-la-men-swan-fa* and Ba-la-men-swan-king, each containing three chapters, and a third on the calculation of the calendar, *Ba-la-men-yin-yang-swan-li*, in one chapter. All these works, with one or two others given by the same authority, are now hopelessly lost, but the names as they stand in the history unattended by a word of comment, are an irrefragable testimony to the efforts made by the Hindoo Buddhists to diffuse the science and civilisation of their native land. The native mathematicians of the time may have obtained assistance from these sources, or from the numerous Indians who lived in China in the T'ang dynasty. In the extant arithmetical books composed before the date of these works, examples of calculation are written perpendicularly, like any other writing, but in all later mathematical works they are presented to the eye as we ourselves write them from left to right. The principle by which figures are thus arranged as multiples of ten changing their value with their position, was known to the Chinese from the most ancient times. Their early mode of calculating by counters, imitated more recently in the common commercial abacus, was based on this principle. [28] But it does not appear that they employed it to express arithmetical processes in writing before the Hindoos began to translate mathematical treatises into the language.

The next notice of Buddhism in the history is after several decades of years. The emperor Su-tsung, in A.D. 760, showed his attachment for Buddhism by appointing a ceremonial for his birthday, according to the ritual of that religion. The service was performed in the palace, the inmates of which were made to personate the Buddhas and Bodhisattwas, while the courtiers worshipped round them in a ring.

The successor of this emperor, T'ai-tsung, was still more devoted to the superstitions of Buddhism, and was seconded by his chief minister of state and the general of his army. A high stage for reciting the classics was erected by imperial command, and the "Sutra of the Benevolent King," *Jen-wang-king*, chanted there and explained by the priests. This book was brought in a state carriage, with the same parade of attendant nobles and finery as in the case of the emperor leaving his palace. Two public buildings were ordered to be taken down to assist in the erection and decoration of a temple built by Yü Chau-shï, the general, and named Chang-king-sï. A remonstrance, prepared on the occasion by a Confucian mandarin, stated that the wise princes of antiquity secured prosperity by their good conduct—not by prayers and offerings. The imperial ear was deaf to such arguments. The reasoning of those who maintained that misfortune could be averted and happiness obtained by prayer was listened to with much more readiness. Tae-tsung maintained many monks, and believed that by propitiating the unseen powers who regulate the destinies of mankind, he could preserve his empire from danger at a less cost than that of the blood and treasure wasted on the battle-field. When his territory was invaded, he set his priests to chant their masses, and the barbarians retired. The Confucianist commentary in condemning the confidence thus placed in the prayers of the priests, remarks that to procure happiness or prevent misery after death, by prayers or any other means, is out of our power, and that the same is true of the present life. One of those who had great influence over the emperor was a Singhalese priest named "Amogha," *Pu-k'ung*, [29] "Not empty," who held a high government office, and was honoured with the first title of the ancient Chinese nobility. Monasteries and monks now multiplied fast under the imperial favour. In the year 768, at the full moon of the seventh month, an offering bowl for feeding hungry ghosts was brought in state by the emperor's command from the palace, and presented to the Chang-king-sï temple. This is an allusion to a superstition still practised in the large Buddhist monasteries. Those who have been so unhappy as to be born into the class of *ngo-kwei*, or "hungry spirits," at the full moon of the seventh month, have their annual repast. The priests assemble, recite prayers for their benefit, and throw out rice to the four quarters of the world, as food for them. The ceremony is called *Yü-lan-hwei (ulam)*, "the assembly for saving those who have been overturned." It is said to have been instituted by Shakyamuni, who directed Moginlin, one of his disciples, to make offerings for the benefit of his mother, she having become a *ngo-kwei*.

The emperor Hien-tsung, A.D. 819, sent mandarins to escort a bone of Buddha to the capital. He had been told that it was opened to view once in thirty years, and when this happened it was sure to be a peaceful and prosperous year. It was at Fung-siang fu, in Shen-si, and was to be reopened the next year, which would afford a good opportunity for bringing it to the palace. It was brought accordingly, and the mandarins, court ladies, and common people vied with each other in their admiration of the relic. All their fear was, lest they should not get a sight of it, or be too late in making their offerings.

On this occasion Han Yü, or Han Wen-kung, presented a strongly-worded remonstrance to the emperor, entitled *Fo-ku-piau*, "Memorial on the bone of Buddha." He was consequently degraded from his post as vice-president of the Board of punishments, and appointed to be prefect of Chau-cheu, in the province of Canton. A heavier punishment would have been awarded him, had not the courtiers represented the propriety of allowing liberty of speech, and succeeded in mitigating the imperial anger.

In this memorial he appealed first to antiquity, arguing that the empire was more prosperous and men's lives were longer before Buddhism was introduced than after. After the Han dynasty, when the Indian priests arrived, the dynasties all became perceptibly shorter in duration, and although Liang Wu-ti was on the throne thirty-eight years, he died, as was well known, from starvation, in a monastery to which he had retired for the third time. [30] The writer then pleads to Hien-tsung the example of his predecessor, the first Tang emperor, and the hope that he himself had awakened in the minds of the literati by his former restrictions on Buddhism, that he would tread in his steps. He had now commanded Buddha's bone to be escorted to the palace. This could not be because he himself was ensnared into the belief of Buddhism. It was only to gain the hearts of the people by professed reverence for that superstition. None who were wise and enlightened believed in any such thing. It was a foreign religion. The dress of the priests, the language of the books, the moral code, were all different from those of China. Why should a decayed bone, the filthy remains of a man who died so long before, be introduced to the imperial residence? He concluded by braving the vengeance of Buddha. If he had any power and could inflict any punishment, he was ready to bear it himself to its utmost extent. This memorial has ever since been a standard quotation with the Confucianists, when wishing to expose the pernicious effects of Buddhism. The boldness of its censures on the emperor's superstition, and the character of the writer as one who excelled in beauty of style, have secured it lasting popularity. Among the crowd of good authors whose names adorn the T'ang dynasty, Han Wen-kung stands first of those who devoted themselves to prose composition. Christian natives in preaching to their countrymen often allude to this document.

Extraordinary superstition provoked extraordinary resistance. The sovereigns of the T'ang dynasty were so fond of Buddhism that it has passed into a proverb. [31] In the year 845 a third and very severe persecution befell the Buddhists. By an edict of the emperor Wu-tsung, 4600 monasteries were destroyed, with 40,000 smaller edifices. The property of the sect was confiscated, and used in the erection of buildings for the use of government functionaries. The copper of images and bells was devoted to casting cash. More than 260,000 priests and nuns were compelled to return to common employments. The monks of Wu-t'ai, in Shan-si, near T'ai-yuen fu, fled to "Yen-cheu" (now Peking), in Pe-chi-li, where they were at first taken under the protection of the officer in charge, but afterwards abandoned to the imperial indignation.

At this place there was a collection of five monasteries, constituting together the richest Buddhist establishment in the empire. There is a legend connected with this spot, which says that Manjusiri, one of the most celebrated of the secondary divinities of Buddhism, has frequently appeared in this mountain retreat, especially as an old man. By the Northern Buddhists "Manjusiri," *Wen-shu-shï-li* (in old Chinese, Men-ju-si-li), is scarcely less honoured than the equally fabulous Bodhisattwa, Kwan-shï-yin. The chief seat of his worship in China is the locality in Shan-si just alluded to, where he is regarded like P'u-hien in Sï-ch'wen and Kwan-yin at P'u-to the Buddhist sacred island, as the tutelary deity of the region. Wen-shu p'u-sa, as he is called, differs from his fellow Bodhisattwas in being spoken of in some Sutras as if he were an historical character. On this there hangs some doubt. His image is a common one in the temples of the sect.

The emperor Wu-tsung died a few months afterwards. Siuen-tsung, who followed him, commenced his reign by reversing the policy of his predecessor in reference to Buddhism. Eight monasteries were reared in the metropolis, and the people were again permitted to take the vows of celibacy and retirement from the world. Soon afterwards the edifices of idolatry that had been given over to destruction were commanded to be restored. The Confucian historian expresses a not very amiable regret at the shortness of the persecution. Those of the Wei and Cheu emperors had been continued for six and seven years, while in this case it was only for a year or two that the profession of Buddhism was made a public crime.

A memorial was presented to the emperor a few years after by Sun Tsiau, complaining that the support of the Buddhist monks was an intolerable burden on the people, and praying that the admission of new persons might be prohibited. The prayer was granted.

The line of the patriarchs had terminated a little before the period which this narrative has now reached, and the most influential leader of the Chinese Buddhists was Matsu, who belonged to the order of *Ch'an-shï,* [32] one of the three divisions of Buddhist monks. As such, he followed the system taught by Bodhidharma, which consisted in abstraction of the mind from all objects of sense, and even its own thoughts. He addressed his disciples in the following words, "You all believe that the 'mind' (*sin*) itself is 'Buddha' (intelligence). Bodhidharma came to China, and taught the method of the heart, that you might be enlightened. He brought the *Lenga Sutra*, exhibiting the true impression of the human mind as it really is, that you might not allow it to become disordered. Therefore that book has but one subject, the instructions of Buddha concerning the mind. The true method is to have no method. Out of the mind there is no Buddha. Out of Buddha there is no mind. Virtue is not to be sought, nor vice to be shunned. Nothing should be looked upon as pure or polluted. To have a sensation of an object is nothing but to become conscious of the mind's own activity. The mind does not know itself, because it is blinded by the sensations." He was asked, by what means excellence in religion should be attained? He replied, "Religion does not consist in the use of means. To use means is fatal to the attainment of the object." Then what, he was again asked, is required to be done in order to religious advancement? "Human nature in itself," he said, "is sufficient for its own wants. All that is needed is to avoid both vice and virtue. He that can do this is a 'religious man' (*sieu-tau-jen*)."

These extracts indicate that a great change had taken place in the popular teaching of Buddhism. In the first centuries of its history in China, retribution and the future life were most insisted on. But the tenets of Bodhidharma, who aimed to restore what he considered the true doctrine of Buddha, gradually diffused themselves and became the most powerful element in the system. The consequence was a less strong faith in the future life.

I-tsung, who ascended the throne A.D. 860, was devoted to the study of the Buddhist books. Priests were called in to discourse on their religion in the private apartments of his palace, and the monasteries were frequently honoured with the imperial presence. He was memorialised in vain by the Confucian mandarins, who represented that Tauism, speaking as it did of mercy and moderation, and the original religion of China, of which the fundamental principles were benevolence and rectitude, were enough for China, and the emperor should follow no other. This emperor practised writing in Sanscrit characters, and chanted the classics in the originals according to the musical laws of the land from which they came. Nothing could be more irritating to rigid conservatives, who hated everything foreign and lived to glorify Confucius, than to hear such sounds issuing from the imperial apartments. In this reign another bone of Buddha was brought to the palace. When it arrived the emperor went out to meet it, and prostrated himself on the ground before it, weeping while he uttered the "invocation of worship" (*namo*). The ceremonies were on a scale even greater than at the annual sacrifice to Heaven and Earth. Similar scenes occurred at about the same time in the West, when European kings were not ashamed to honour the relics of Christian romance, just as their contemporaries in the far East revered those of the equally luxuriant imagination of Buddhism. No one in the West, however, raised so loud a voice of warning against these superstitions as the Confucian mandarins at the court of Ch'ang-an.

Among the foreign Buddhists who took up their residence in China in the first T'ang dynasty was Bodhiruchi. He translated the *Hwa-yen* and *Pau-tsih* Sutras. Lenga, a second, came from the north of the Ts'ung-ling mountains; others from India. The usual story of these wanderers was that they were the sons of kings, and had resigned their title to the crown to free themselves from worldly cares, and cultivate the heart. These tales may have been true, but they should not be repeated too often, for fear of exciting suspicion in the mind of the reader. More than one of these *ci-devant* princes adopted the profession of rainmaker at the Chinese court, and saved the country from drought for a considerable period. On one occasion the emperor was assured that it would rain when certain images opened their eyes. After three days the images showed the same willingness to gratify the expectation of their worshippers as have those of another religion, and the prophecy was fulfilled.

Pu-k'ung, already mentioned, came from Ceylon. [33] As he was travelling, a herd of elephants rushed towards him. He sat quietly on the way side. The elephants all knelt down before him and retired. When he came to China, he produced, it is said, a great reformation of manners in court and country, and was reverenced as a divinity. If judged by his works, [34] however, consisting of unintelligible charms with pictures of many Bodhisattwas, he brought a grosser superstition than before. His book of directions for calling hungry spirits to be fed, by magical arrangements of the fingers, delineations of Sanscrit characters and such like means, vindicates for him the unenviable honour of being the chief promoter of Buddhist fetishism in China. From Sin-la, a kingdom now forming part of Corea, some priests also came. One of these, named Wu-leu, was retained by the emperor Hiuen-tsung, with Pu-k'ung, to pray for the imperial and national prosperity. When he approached his end he rose in the air a foot high, and so died. [35]

At this time some priests came from Japan, bringing ten of the monastic dresses denominated *Sanghali*, as presents to those in China who should best deserve them. Lan-chin praised the gift as evidence of the advancement made by the donors in the knowledge and dispositions of the true Buddhist. He determined to go to Japan, and after a tempestuous voyage he arrived there. The king came out to meet him, and assigned him a residence. From him the Japanese received their first instructions in the Discipline of Buddhism, or the rules of the monastic life.

Under the Later T'ang dynasty a native priest of Wu-t'ai, observing the mode in which the foreign Buddhists obtained their influence, felt a wish to share with them in the dominion of the atmosphere. He gave out that the dragon of the sky was obedient to him, and that wind and rain came at his call. The emperor and empress prostrated themselves before him, and he did not think it necessary to rise in their presence. Unfortunately a long drought arrived, and his prayers were unavailing to bring it to a termination. Enraged at his want of success, some proposed to burn him, but he was permitted to return home, and died of disappointment.

The last emperor of this short dynasty was much under the influence of Ajeli, a foreigner at Fung-siang, in Shen-si. He was memorialised by an officer of his court, on the subject of instituting examinations for those who wished to adopt the Buddhist life of reading and retirement. The monks and nuns should both be examined in the "Shastras" (*Lun*), the "Sutras" (*King*), and the daily duties of the monastery. In the same way he recommended that those who aspired to become Tauist priests should be examined in the literature of that sect. The emperor assented to these propositions. His successor of the Later Tsin dynasty distributed favours and titles very freely among the professors of the two faiths, and, as was natural, foreign priests, with teeth and other relics of Buddha, continued to arrive.

A little later a prince of the Cheu family and the immediate predecessor of the founder of the Sung dynasty, placed severe restrictions on Buddhism, and prohibited all temples except those that had received an inscribed tablet from former emperors. More than thirty thousand of these buildings were in consequence suppressed by edict; 2694 temples were retained. The same edict prohibited the monks and lay Buddhists from cutting off their hands and feet, burning their fingers, suspending lighted lamps by hooks inserted into the flesh, and from carrying pincers in a similar manner. "Let us not smile," says Mr. Watters, "at these self-imposed tortures, unless we can also weep to think that similar tortures have been practised by the followers of Jesus—not only by individuals on their own bodies, but also upon those of their fellows."

T'ai-tsu, the first emperor of the Sung family (A.D. 964), sent messengers to persuade his contemporary of the house of T'ang not to show such devotion to Buddhist superstitions as he had done. The latter took the remonstrance in good part, and ceased to look with his former regard on the crowd of priests that frequented his capital. T'ai-tsung, the second in the new succession, stopped the public examinations of candidates for monk's orders. He was an enemy to the delusions which he saw to be so popular among his subjects. Hearing that wood was being collected to form a death pyre for a priest who had determined to burn himself, he thought it was time to act, and issued an edict forbidding new temples. He changed his policy a few years after; for the history of the time relates the erection by his command of a pagoda 360 Chinese feet in height. It was completed in eight years, and relics of Buddha were deposited in it. A short notice of this class of structures will be here introduced.

The number of pagodas in China is very great. There are nine within thirty miles of Shanghai. When complete and well situated, the pagoda is without dispute the most ornamental edifice to be seen in this Eastern world. Perhaps no more beautiful single object could be added by the hand of man to hill and wood scenery. At Lo-yang, in the Tsin dynasty (A.D. 350), there were forty-two, from three to nine stories high, richly painted, and formed after Indian models. The word *t'a* (formerly *t'ap*), now in universal use, has displaced the older names *feu-t'u* (*budu*) and *fo-t'u* (*buddu*). The original purpose of the edifice was to deposit relics of Buddha. These relics might be a hair, tooth, metamorphosed piece of bone, article of dress, or rice vessel. When the bodies of deceased Bodhisattwas and other revered persons were burnt, the remains were placed in structures which received the same name, *t'upa* or *st'upa*, and it is these that have been described by travellers, in Afghanistan and other regions where Buddhism formerly prevailed, as topes.

"When there is no 'relic'" (*she-li;* in Sanscrit, *sharira*), says the cyclopædia *Fa-yuen-chu-lin*, "the building is called *chi-ti*" (in Sanscrit, *chaitya*), and it may be intended to commemorate the birthplace of Buddha, the spot where he became enlightened, where he taught, or where he entered into the Nirvâna. Footsteps of Buddha, an image of a Bodhisattwa or of a Pratyeka Buddha, are also honoured with the erection of a *chi-ti*.

When pagodas are without relics and unconnected with any legend, their erection must be attributed to reasons founded on the Chinese "geomancy" (*feng-shui*). These buildings are supposed to have a very important and happy influence on the districts in which they are situated. The charity of the contributors is also believed to be repaid in riches, longevity, and forgiveness of sins, as in the case of all Chinese almsgiving.

Most of the existing pagodas date from the time at which our narrative has now arrived. Those built in the T'ang and previous dynasties have many of then fallen a prey to the ruinous hand of time; while more recently the diminished favour which those possessing wealth and power have extended to Buddhism has caused an entire cessation of pagoda building, except when old ones were to be restored.

In the tenth century, [36] the royal family of the Min kingdom, bearing the surname Wang, were very much devoted to Buddhism. To them the city of Foochow owes the two pagodas which adorn it. The king admitted ten thousand persons to the vows in A.D. 940.

Anything that is precious in the eyes of the Buddhist devotee may be deposited in these structures. One was erected by the emperor for the preservation of the newly-arrived Sanscrit books at the request of Hiuen-tsang, lest they should be injured for want of care. It was 180 feet high, had five stories with grains of *she-li* (relics) in the centre of each, and contained monuments inscribed with the prefaces written by the emperor and prince royal to Hiuen-tsang's translations.

The great expense of large Buddhist structures sometimes led the more self-confident of the priests to rash resolutions. On one occasion a monk of T'ien-t'ai, a large and ancient establishment to the south of Ningpo, professed to the emperor his wish to commit himself to the flames when the erection of a certain temple was completed. His desire was granted, and an officer sent to see that the temple was built and the feat carried into execution. The pile was made and the priest called on to come forward. He excused himself, but in vain. He looked round on the assembled crowd for some one to save him; among priests and people, however, none offered to help the trembling victim of his own folly. The stern voice of the imperial messenger bade him ascend the pile. He still lingered, and was at length seized by the attendants, placed forcibly on the pile and burnt.

The conduct of the emperors towards Buddhism was then, as it has been more recently, very inconsistent. Favour was shown to priests, while occasional edicts were issued intended to check the progress of the system. The emperors gratified their private feelings by gorgeous erections for the practice of idolatry, while they paid a tribute to the Confucian prejudices of the literati by denouncing the religion in public proclamations.

In the reign of Chen-tsung, a favourer of Buddhism, a priest from India is mentioned as translating the "Sutra of Good Fortune," *Fo-ki-siang-king*, and other works, to the number of more than two hundred chapters.

Jen-tsung, in A.D. 1035, made an effort to preserve the knowledge of Sanscrit literature by appointing fifty youths to study it. A few years earlier, it is said in a notice of Fa-t'ien-pen, a native of "Magadha" (Bahar), in India, that he was assisted in translating the *Wu-liang-sheu-king*, the "Sutra of Boundless Age," and other works, by a native of China familiar with Sanscrit. These facts have a bearing on the possible existence of Sanscrit manuscripts in China. One old manuscript only has yet been discovered, in South China, in that mode of writing. Occasionally a few specimen characters are introduced in native works where foreign alphabets are treated of. [37] In an account of the Kwo-ts'ing monastery in the "History of T'ien-t'ai-shan" it is said that a single work was saved from a fire there several centuries ago, which was written on the *pei-to* (patra), or "palm" leaf of India. A visit to T'ien-t'ai—a spot abounding in Buddhist antiquities, the earliest, and except P'u-to, the largest and richest seat of that religion in Eastern China—by myself and two companions led to the discovery that this work is still there, but in the Kau-ming monastery, and that it is written in the Sanscrit character. I had a copy made which was sent to Professor Wilson; but the work of the copyist was found to be too incorrect to admit of its being read. T'ien-t'ai is about fifty miles south of Ningpo, and is celebrated for its beautiful scenery. As a monastic establishment it dates from the fourth century, while P'u-to is no earlier than the tenth. In the province of Che-kiang, where maritime and hill scenery are so luxuriantly combined, the picturesque homes of the Buddhist monks are clustered together more thickly, it would seem, than anywhere else. Like their English contemporaries whose mode of life was in many points so similar, they knew well how to choose spots where the rich landscape spread before their eyes would be some compensation for their banishment from social enjoyments. They were quite as inventive too in peopling the woods and rocks where they selected their place of retirement with supernatural visitors, whose rank or good deeds lent a mysterious sanctity to the place where traces of their presence were observed. And they framed with equal facility marvellous legends to form a ground for erecting temples in honour of the hero thus endowed with an imaginary immortality. The Bodhisattwas and "Arhans" (*Lo-han*) of Oriental religious fiction, correspond to the saints and martyrs venerated in the West. Those who chose the situations of many of the large Buddhist establishments must have had an eye for the loveliness of nature. The ignorant and unreflecting class of priests now usually met with, whose aim is no higher than to count beads, to chant the classics, and to perform the genuflexions according to rule, must not be taken as examples of the earlier race of Buddhist monks. There was in the flourishing days of Buddhism more devotion to the system, and a much better appreciation of its nature, than at present. It was quite in keeping with a more sincere belief in the religion, to choose beautiful solitudes high among hills for the practice of its rites, and to spare no expense in constructing appropriate edifices in the most magnificent style of Chinese architecture. It is only by supposing sincere attachment to the principles of the system, that cases of self-destruction by fire in imitation of the ancient Hindoo practice can be accounted for. History says that the emperor Jen-tsung, having as a high mark of favour introduced into the standard edition of Buddhist books some works by the priests of T'ien-t'ai, one of the monks performed this terrible feat to show his gratitude for the emperor's goodness. Another prevailing motive in uniting the utmost attainable beauty in nature and art, was undoubtedly the desire to produce popular effect, and to provide attractions for the rich and the superstitious when they went on a religious pilgrimage.

Among these spots none in all China is more famous than the island of P'u-to, to the east of Chusan. It was about A.D. 915 that it was taken possession of by the Buddhists, not many years before the time this narrative has reached. It is dedicated to "Kwan-shï-yin," a name translated from the Sanscrit *Avalokiteshwara*. P'u-hien (*Samantabhadra*), another fictitious Bodhisattwa, is honoured in a similar way at O-mei Shan, in Sï-ch'wen. At Kieu-hwa, in An-hwei, a little westward of Ch'ï-cheu fu, Ti-tsang another of the great Bodhisattwas, is honoured with special worship. The fourth and last of these establishments, the great gathering-places of the followers of Julai, is that of "Manjusiri" (*Wen-shu p'u-sa*) at Wu-t'ai in Shan-si, already referred to. The name "P'u-to" (*P'u-ta*) is the same as that known in Indian ancient geography as "Potala" or "Potaraka" (*P'u-ta-lo-kia*). Kwan-shï-yin is said in the *Hwa-yen-king* to have taught the Buddhist doctrines on that island. The original island was situated in the Southern sea of Indian geographers, and P'u-to is therefore denominated *Nan-hai p'u-to* (the P'u-to of the Southern sea). Through the Sung and Yuen dynasties buildings were added till they grew to their present magnitude. The number of priests from all parts of China who visit this sacred island is immense. [38]

The residents, however, are not so numerous as at T'ien-t'ai. T'ien-t'ai was at this time become famous for the origination of a new school. The works by Chinese authors mentioned above as placed parallel with the translations from Sanscrit, consisted of the productions of this school called *Chï-kwan-hio* or *T'ien-t'ai-kiau*. The common book of prayers, *Ta-pei-ts'an*, has the same origin. The object of this new school was to combine contemplation with image worship. While the regulations for kneeling and chanting by several persons in unison are most complicated and minute, the operators aim to fix their thoughts on certain objects of devotion. This system differs from Bodhidharma's school of pure mental abstraction, by adding to devotional thoughts the helps of the senses. The tawdry gaiety of the idols, the union of many persons under the direction of a time-keeper in kneeling and standing, mute thought and loud recitation, it was believed would have a highly useful influence, when combined with an intense effort after pure religious meditation. The union of these two elements was intended to be a great improvement on the previous methods. The first Buddhist worship had made no express provision for the meditative faculties, and it had in consequence degenerated into the driest of forms. The common ceremonial of the sect at the present time exemplifies it, exhibiting as it does postures devoid of all reverence and lifeless repetitions of foreign words destitute of all emotion. The founder of this new system, Chï-k'ai, lived at T'ien-t'ai in the latter half of the sixth century. It was not till after more than four centuries that the principal writings of the school he established were included among the standard books of Buddhism. The title by which he is known is T'ien-t'ai-chï-che. The ceremonial thus introduced still maintains its reputation, and is practised by those who wish to infuse a deeper feeling into the service of the religion than is aimed at by the every-day worshippers of Buddha.

These changing forms of Chinese Buddhism—and there are others that will subsequently be described—are facts not without significance for the religious history of mankind, that most interesting chapter in the chronicle of our race. Human nature, true to itself, will run the same round of varieties in connection with religions most different in their origin, principles, and geographical situation. Christianity has been greatly affected in the form that it has assumed in successive ages by the operation of the natural religious feelings inherent in man, which are the parents of all superstition and are independent of the new spiritual life bestowed by Divine power. This fact, which is clearly exhibited in Church history, renders the historical comparison between Christianity and other religions a possible one. The monastic institute, for example, which began in Buddhism, as its earliest books show, with Shakyamuni the founder of the religion, was in Christianity an innovation originating in the desire felt by many to engage constantly in religious contemplation, without being interrupted by the cares of secular life. In the history of both religions there have been leading minds that have elevated contemplation at the expense of external forms. Others have sought by sensible representations alone to call the religious feelings into action. Minds of a third class have combined the two. But when Buddhism proceeds to the negation of all thought, action, and individual existence, the parallel fails, for though philosophy has intruded frequently and extensively into the battle-field of Christianity, it has never been attempted to construct a new religious life on such a basis of philosophy as this. Philosophical scepticism in the West has been confined to the safer regions of speculation, without being brought, as Buddhism has tried to bring it, to a practical form. [39] Another subdivision of the Buddhist schools into *Tsung-men* and *Kiau-men* may be best characterised by using the terms *esoteric* and *exoteric* to distinguish them. The first of the former entered China when the patriarch Bodhidharma brought the traditional symbol, called in Chinese *cheng-fa-yen-tsung*, and the school he established is its highest kind. The magical formulæ *cheu* (dharani) also belong to esoteric Buddhism. These childish productions are as destitute of meaning in their original Sanscrit as they are in their transferred Chinese form, but all sorts of miracles are believed to be wrought by them. The classics and books of prayers, with the other parts of the literature, belong to exoteric Buddhism, which also embraces all rules for life and worship. For this classification the native terms in use are *hien*, "open," and *mi*, "secret."

The despotic nature of the Chinese government has been often shown in its treatment of religions. When persecution has not been resorted to, the right of interference in the internal regulations of Buddhism and Tauism has been often assumed. Thus the Sung emperor, Shen-tsung, ordered many of the "temples" denominated *sï* to be changed into the "monasteries" called *ch'an-yuen*, for the use of the monks who followed the system of Bodhidharma. His successor issued a similar decree. In 1119, Hwei-tsung, advised by Lin Ling-su, commanded the title of Buddha to be changed to one like those of the Tauist genii. He was to be styled *Ta-kio-kin-sien*, in which *kio*, to "perceive," is a translation of the word Buddha, and *kin*, *i.e.*, "golden," represents the substance of which his image is supposed to be formed. The other Indian titles were also ordered to be abandoned. The "priests," instead of being known as *seng*, were to be called *te-shi*, "virtuous scholars." The "temples," *sï*, and "monasteries," *yuen*, were to receive the designations *kung*, "palace," and *kwan*, "monastery," terms in use among the Tauists. This futile attempt to amalgamate the two religions was abandoned the following year.

The two brother philosophers, C'heng, in the city of Lo-yang, set themselves against the Buddhist burial rites. But an admirer compared them to the rock in the middle of a torrent, which can retard but for a moment the progress of the impetuous stream.

Sï-ma Wen-kung wrote soon after that men need not practise burial rites for deliverance from hell, because neither heaven nor hell are to be expected. The body decays at death, and the spirit flies off, carried away by a puff of wind.—(See Watters.)

At that time, as at the present day, Buddhist priests were invited by rich persons to go through a ritual for the dead. The follower of Confucius engages priests from both the other sects without scruple to offer prayers, in whose efficacy he does not believe, for the souls of deceased relatives.

By the Oriental, sincerity and independence in religious belief are without difficulty subordinated to the outward show of respect which is felt to be necessary while it is unreal. When, as death approached, a certain mandarin prohibited the employment of Buddhist priests at his funeral, the incident is commemorated as something remarkable. In justification of himself he quoted the saying of an author, "That if there were no heaven there was no need to seek it; and that if there were, good men would certainly go there. If there were no hell there was no need to fear it; and if there were, bad men would go there."

In the times of Buddhist prosperity persons received from the emperor a written permission to become *ho-shang* [40] or "monks." When this practice was abandoned, as by Kau-tsung, one of the emperors who reigned at Hang-cheu, A.D. 1143, the higher members of the Buddhist hierarchy undertook to distribute the usual certificates of membership in the order. Thus the aim of the emperor, who had argued that for want of imperial patronage the inmates of the monasteries would be thinned in numbers, until death effected what former emperors had sought to accomplish by persecution, was frustrated. When the neophyte visits the chief monk at some monastery, in order to go through the ceremonies of initiation, an indentation is usually burnt in at the top of his shaven head, and a new one is made at every repetition of the visit. A priest is proud to show these marks of distinction, arranged in a square on his naked cranium, as testifying to the self-denial he has practised in attaining his position.

There are various evidences of the continued influence of Indian Buddhism on that of China at this comparatively late period. The "History of the Sung Dynasty," in its account of India, details the arrival in A.D. 951 of Samanta, a monk, with a large party of companions from Western India, belonging to sixteen families. In 965 a Chinese priest, named Tau-yuen, returned from a journey to the Western countries with relics and Sanscrit copies of Buddhist books written on the "palm-leaf" *(pei-to)* to the number of forty volumes. He was absent twelve years, and resided in India itself half of that time. He returned by the usual route round the north-west of the great mountain mass denominated Ts'ung-ling. He gave an account of his travels to the emperor on his return, and showed him the Sanscrit books. The next year 157 Chinese priests set out together, with the emperor's permission, to visit India and obtain Buddhist books. They passed through Pu-lu-sha and "Cashmere" (*Ka-shi-mi-lo*), but nothing is said of their further proceedings. During the latter part of the tenth century Sanscrit manuscripts continued to arrive at court in great numbers. On one occasion the son of a king of Eastern India was a visitor. The reason of his abandoning his native land, continues our authority, was that it is customary for the younger sons of a deceased king to leave their eldest brother at home to succeed their father, and themselves become monks. They travel then to other countries and never return. These extracts from the "Sung History" are continued, because they are not only valuable in themselves, but because also there is some uncertainty as to the time when Buddhism was expelled from India, and they may be of assistance in determining that question. In 982 a priest of Western China returned from India with a letter from a king of that country to the emperor. It was translated by an Indian at the imperial command, and contained congratulations on the favour shown in China to Buddhism, together with geographical details on India and adjacent countries. The next year another Chinese monk returned by sea with Buddhist books from India. On his way he met at San-fo-t'si, a country bordering on Cambodia to the south-west, an Indian who wished to come to China to translate Buddhist books. He was invited by the emperor to engage in so doing. Other traces occur, not seldom in Chinese history, of the presence of Buddhist Indians in the Birmese peninsula, some of them of the Brahman caste. The rising influence of Brahmanism, and the more modern forms of religious belief in India, drove the followers of Shakya, not only into the northern regions, where they spread their system through Thibet and Tartary, and by which many of them found their way to China, but also into the islands and kingdoms that lay on the other side of the Bay of Bengal. A few years later than the last-mentioned date a Chinese, and with him a foreign Buddhist monk, came from the king of Northern India with a letter to the emperor. A Buddhist priest of the Brahman caste, with Aliyin, a Persian of another religion, are also mentioned as coming to the capital. The former, in the account he gives of his native country, mentions Buddhism as the religion favoured by the king. Some came by sea at this time who could not make themselves understood, but the images and books they brought showed that they were Buddhists. Several other arrivals of Hindoos are recorded, and if the books they are said to have presented to the Chinese emperor are still preserved in the state archives, there can be no lack there of Sanscrit manuscripts of Buddhist works.

Though the great mass of Buddhist literature was already translated, additions not a few were made in the Sung and Yuen dynasties, and the whole number of "chapters" (*kiuen*) raised from 4271 to 4661.

The account given of *Kau-ch'ang* (the Ouighour country north-west of China) says that the calendar there used was the one introduced by the Hindoo Buddhists at the court of the T'ang dynasty in the early part of the eighth century. More than fifty Buddhist temples had monumental tablets presented by emperors of the same dynasty, and, with the collected sacred books of Buddhism, are also preserved the early Chinese dictionaries [41] made with the assistance of the Hindoos. The reader is left to suppose that the Buddhist classics in the language of China were at that time used in the countries beyond its northwestern frontier, as they still are in Japan, Loo-choo, and Corea.

It is added, "Temples of Manes and Persian 'priests' (*senga*) are also found there, each following his own ritual. These are such as are called in the Buddhist Sutras 'heretics' (*wai-tau*)." This must be an allusion to the Manicheans, the fire-worshippers, and probably also to the Nestorians, who, on the Si-an inscription, call themselves by the Buddhist term *senga* in the sense of "priest."

From the extended sketch given of Japanese intercourse with China in the "Sung History," it appears that the object of the majority of the embassies then and previously was a Buddhist one. Monks were the ambassadors; books of that religion, such as were known in Japan only by name, were asked for; remarkable places, like the Wu-t'ai mountain in Shan-si, were visited; the doctrines of particular sects, such as that of T'ien-t'ai, were studied at the spots where they were principally cultivated; travellers like Hiuen-tsang were regarded with veneration, and the books that he intrusted to them, Sutras, Discipline, and Shastras, guarded with especial care. The impression left on the reader's mind by the narrative alluded to is, that the early and constant embassies from Japan were decidedly Buddhistic in their character. Perhaps this arose simply from the fact of the ambassadors having been monks, while some other cause led to the appointment of persons of that profession to the duty. At least, however, it indicates that the Buddhist priests in Japan possessed for a long period great political influence.

Kublai khan, the first Mongol emperor, was strongly attached to Buddhism. The imperial temples, for sacrificing to the objects of Chinese national worship, were converted to Buddhist uses; while Tauism was persecuted, injunctions were issued to all followers of Buddha to chant the sacred books diligently in all the monasteries. When Kublai was recommended by his courtiers to send an army to subjugate Japan, he refused on the ground that it was a country where the precepts of Buddha were honoured. A monk of that sect was sent as ambassador, but the king refused to follow the custom of his ancestor, by sending the tributary offering that pleases oriental vanity, and marks the submissive obedience of an inferior sovereign to his more powerful neighbour. A hundred thousand soldiers were sent to enforce the claim of supremacy over Japan, and their destruction in a storm while crossing the sea thither is a well-known fact of history.

The early attachment of the Mongols to Buddhism appears in the first notices of them in the annals of the dynasty that they overthrew.

While they still possessed only the northern parts of China more than one Buddhist monk was appointed to the office of *kwo-shï* (national instructor). The first of these was Namo, a native of one of the Western kingdoms. Another was *Pa-ho-si-pa* or "Baschpa," a "Thibetan" (*T'u-fan*), who introduced a new alphabet for the use of the Mongols based on that of his own language. It was issued by authority of Kublai khan, but failed to win its way, perhaps because the characters were less simple than the writing taken from the Syriac, which had already been adopted from the Nestorians.

In the reign of the successor of Kublai the historians complain that three thousand taels of gold were set apart to write Buddhist books in gilt letters, and other expenses for this religion were in the same proportion of extravagance. The "Yuen History" describes the politic aims of Kublai in his preference for Buddhism. Becoming sovereign of a country wild and extensive, and a nation intractable and quarrelsome, he resolved, in order to give his native wilderness a civilised aspect, and soften down the natural roughness of his subjects, to form cities on the Chinese model, to appoint mandarins of various ranks, and put the people under the guidance of a public instructor. A priest of Buddha held this post, and he was only subordinate to the chief lay mandarin. His orders were treated with the same respect as the imperial proclamations. When all the state officers were assembled he alone remained seated on the floor in the corner, and he was received at court with the highest honours that could be paid to a subject.

The remarks of Confucianist historians on such things are naturally bitter. It is not according to precedent to praise Buddhism. To censure it is the fashion of the literati. When they wield the historic brush, they deepen the colouring if superstitious emperors and Buddhist successes have to appear on the canvas. What they record of censure they record as a painful duty, and, as often happens when men have a painful duty to perform, they feel more pleasure in the performance than they like to acknowledge.

Towards the end of the thirteenth century, a census was taken by imperial command of the Buddhist temples and monks in China. Of the former, there were reported 42,318, and of the latter, 213,148. Three years after, at the close of Kublai's reign, when a priest came from "Thibet" (*Si-fan*) to become *kwo-shï* (national instructor), the emperor, regretting that he could not converse with him, ordered Kalutanasi, a Mongolian, to learn the Thibetan language from him. This task was accomplished in a year, and, says the narrative, the complete translation of the Buddhist Sutras and Shastras, from "Thibetan" (*Si-fan*), [42] and Sanscrit into Mongolian, and written in Ouighour characters, was presented to the founder of the Yuen dynasty in the year of his death, A.D. 1294. He ordered it to be cut on blocks, and distributed among the kings and great chiefs of his nation. The notices of Buddhism that occur in the reigns of the successive Mongol emperors are extremely numerous, but they belong perhaps more to Mongolian and Thibetan Buddhism than to that of China, and it will be only necessary, therefore, to take a brief review of them. The recitation of the classics was frequently practised in the Thibetan language in the monasteries of the capital at the emperor's command. In 1324 a second record occurs of the translation into Mongolian of the Buddhist books. It merely says that the translation from the *Si-fan* (Thibetan) language was then made in the "Ouighour" (*Wei-ngu-ri*) writing. Those who received the highest religious title, that of *kwo-shï* or *ti-shï*, "imperial instructor," were foreigners. One of these, Pi-lan-na-shi-li, of the Kan mu-lu kingdom, learned in his youth the Ouighour and "Sanscrit" (*Si-t'ien*, "Western heaven") writing. In 1312 he was ordered by the emperor to translate Buddhist books. From Chinese he translated the *Leng-yen-king*, a Sutra regarded by the Chinese literati as the best of all the Buddhist books. From Sanscrit he translated four Sutras, and others from Thibetan, in all a thousand "chapters" (*kiuen*). He was put to death for suspected treason, concerted with the son of the king of the An-si country on the eastern border of Persia. The Mongol emperors continued faithful to their adopted creed during the short continuance of their power in China. It was, as it has continued to be, one of their national institutions. The people accepted the religion that their chiefs appointed for them. While among the Chinese people, Buddhism has frequently had to struggle against direct and indirect hostility from the literary class and the government of the country, the Mongolians have beheld without envy the priests of this religion raised to the highest offices of state, and retaining unquestioned their position as the most influential body in the community.

The immoral pictorial representations introduced in the worship of Shiva were imitated by the Thibetan Buddhists. When brought to one of the Mongolian emperors by a Thibetan priest, he is said to have received them with approbation. The Chinese people were indignant when they heard that such representations were permitted to demoralise the inmates of the imperial palace. At present, although some authors have asserted the contrary, there appear to be no traces of any such practice in Chinese Buddhism, but they are found in the lama temples in Peking.

Curiosity to visit the first home of their religion had not yet entirely forsaken the Chinese Buddhists. Early in this period a Chinese priest named Tau-wu was excited by reading the accounts of Fa-hien and the early Buddhist travellers to try his fortune in a similar undertaking. He passed the Sandy desert, and through the kingdoms of Kui-tsi and Sha-la to *Kipin* (Cophen). He there learned the original language of the Buddhist books, obtained a Sutra on the admission of Kwan-shi-yin to the Buddhist life, and turning westward proceeded through the country of the Getæ and so into India. He returned by sea to Canton. This, however, is the last record of the kind.

There was no reaction against Buddhism for some time after the overthrow of the Yuen dynasty. Monks of that religion from the countries west of China were still welcomed at court, and decrees were promulgated applauding the beneficial tendencies of the system. When a mandarin ventured to reprove the third Ming emperor on this account, he was silenced by the inquiry, Did he wish to imitate Han Wen-kung?

In A.D. 1426 the next occupier of the throne ordered examinations to be instituted for those who wished to become monks. At this time, as had sometimes happened before, the attention of the government was called to the increasing property in land of the monasteries. In 1450 it was forbidden to any monastic establishment to have more than 60 *meu* (6000 feet square) of land. What was in excess of this was given to the poor to cultivate, they paying taxes to the emperor. Similar acts of interference with the property of the monasteries are recorded in the preceding dynasty. In the sixteenth century, in the time of Kia-tsing, some attempts to revive persecution were made by Confucian memorialists, but all they succeeded in effecting was the destruction of the Buddhist chapel belonging to the palace. High titles were still granted to certain priests who stated that they came from the West. They were called *shang-shï*, "superior teacher," instead of *ti-shï*, "imperial teacher," the title given in the Yuen dynasty.

In the latter years of the Ming dynasty, new enemies to Buddhism arrived in China. The Roman Catholic missionaries followed the Mohammedans in protesting against idolatry. The banner of hostility could be raised by Christians with more reason against this religion than against the national one, of which the worship of images forms no part. Matteo Ricci had a controversy with a noted Buddhist priest residing at Hang-cheu. It was with a show of reason pressed upon the Buddhists that if their theory of transmigration were true, it would be wrong to enter into wedlock for fear of marrying one's own father or mother. The Buddhists suggested in reply, that divination would reveal if such were the fact. Sü Kwang-k'i, Ricci's most illustrious convert, wrote a short tract against Buddhism, in which a few of its principal doctrines are discussed and condemned in a popular style. It is concluded by a chapter against ancestral worship. The work is called *P'i-shih-shï-chu-wang*, "The Errors of the Buddhists Exposed."

Of the Manchu emperors, Shun-chï was a friend to Buddhism, and wrote prefaces to some works of the followers of Bodhidharma, but his son K'ang-hi felt in his later life great repugnance to all religions except the Confucian. His sentiments are recorded in the "Sacred Edict," or Imperial book of moral instructions for the common people.

By insertion in the "Sacred Edict" these opinions have been widely spread, and are extensively approved of to the present time. The author cites the judgment pronounced by Chu Hi, the philosopher and critic of the Sung dynasty, saying that the Buddhists care nothing for heaven or earth, or anything that goes on around them, but attend exclusively each to his single mind. They are then condemned for fabricating groundless tales of future happiness and misery. They are charged with doing this only for gain, and encouraging for the same object the large gatherings of the country population at the temples; ostensibly to burn incense, but really to practise the worst forms of mischief.

Policy has led the Manchu emperors to adopt a very different tone in Mongolia and Thibet. The lamas of those countries are received at Peking with the utmost respect, and care has always been taken to avoid exciting a religious animosity that would be fraught with danger.

At the present time in the parts of China open to foreign observation, each country village has its annual festival, at which thousands assemble from distances of many miles to witness processions of the images, and join in the idolatrous ceremonies to which the day is consecrated. It is the same to the people whether it be a Buddhist or Tauist temple, where the concourse takes place. Their worship and offerings are presented with equal willingness in either, and whatever story is told of the power of any idol they are ready to believe.

The feeling of the educated is different from this. Despising the popular development of Buddhism, as consisting of image worship and procuring for money the protection of powerful unseen beings, they read with interest those of the Buddhist books that have in them a vein of metaphysical thought presented in elegant language. They study Buddhism for the profundity of its ideas, while they continue to adhere to Confucius, as their own chosen teacher in morals and religion. In the wide literature of this system there is room for readers of very various predilections. There are several works of which metaphysical discussion is the prominent feature, and they are read with pleasure by the intelligent, to whom a further attraction is the excellent native style adopted by the scholars who assisted in the translation. Such, for example, are the *Kin-kang-king* and the *Leng-yen-king*.

There are, however, not a few sincere Buddhists, chiefly in the middle class of society, who believe that there is a great merit and efficiency in the recitation of the sacred books. They have a higher aim than those who practise the mere burning of incense to secure particular forms of happiness. They engage in the reading of these books or enter on the life of a hermit or monk, hoping to quiet the passions and train the heart to virtue.

Hermits are not uncommonly met with in the vicinity of large Buddhist establishments. They occupy hill-side caves, or a closed apartment, which for a certain term of years they never leave. Their hair is allowed to grow unshorn. Their food is brought them by the monks of a neighbouring monastery. They employ their time in reciting the sacred books, meditation on Buddhist doctrine, care of their cell, and replenishing the incense urn placed before the image of Shakyamuni.

The preceding pages may be regarded as a sketch of the external history of Chinese Buddhism. A notice of the successive schools into which this religion has subdivided itself will now be presented to the reader.

* * * *

NOTE ON INDIAN SCIENCE AND ART.

The Hindoos borrowed copiously from Babylon and other western countries. If in the eighth and ninth centuries they used what we call the Indian arithmetical notation in giving mathematical instruction to the Chinese, it was because they had already learned it from Babylonian teachers. The decipherment of mathematical inscriptions from Mesopotamia shows that long before the age of David and Solomon this notation was in common use there. So in art the Hindoos copied the Greeks. After Alexander's invasion of India the Hindoos became sculptors. They carved Buddhist friezes by the help of Greek suggestion. Vincent A. Smith says in the volume for 1889 of the Journal of the Bengal Branch of the Royal Asiatic Society, that the Hindoos followed Greek prototypes when planning buildings, images, and pillars. This is the reason that the metempsychosis appears somewhat late in Indian literature. It too was of foreign origin.

Footnotes

1. He had the dream in A.D. 61. Eighteen men were sent. They went to the country of the Getæ, bordering on India, and there they met the two Brahmans. They came riding on white horses, with pictures, images, and books; and arrived in A.D. 67. On the thirtieth day of the twelfth month they saw the emperor.
2. *Ta-hia*, in old Chinese *Dai-he*. It was 207 years earlier that the Dale and Getæ were defeated in battle by Alexander. Dahistan borders on the Caspian, forming the south-east coast of that sea.
3. He foretold future events by interpreting the sound of pagoda bells as they were blown by the wind. On one occasion he placed water in an empty flower-pot, and burned incense, when a blue lotus sprang into view in full bloom.
4. The syllables *Sang-mun* are also employed. *Shramana* means the "quieting of the passions." *Sih-sin*, "to put the mind at rest," is the Chinese translation of it.
5. See the *Ts'in history*.
6. *Foĕ kouĕ ki*, translated by Remusat; from the preface to which, some of the facts given above are taken. The original work, *Fo-kwo-ki*, is contained in the collection denominated *Shwo-fu*, a *Ts'ung-shu* (selection of extracts and hooks old and new) of the reign of Shun-chï. Also in the *Han-wei-ts'ung-shu*.

7. The common Indian name of "China," written in Chinese *Chen-tan*, is here employed. Another orthography found in Buddhist books is *Chi-na*. It is clear from the use of these characters, that the Indians who translated into Chinese at that early period, did not regard the word "China" as the name of a dynasty, but as the proper name of the country to which it was applied. This leaves in great uncertainty the usual derivation of the term "China" from the *Dzin* dynasty, B.C. 250, or that of *Ts'in*, A.D. 300. The occurrence of the word as the name of a nation in the "Laws of Manu," supposed to date from some time between B.C. 1000 and B.C. 500, with the use of the term "Sinim" in the "Prophecies of Isaiah," indicate a greater antiquity than either of these dynasties extends to. Some have supposed that the powerful feudatory kingdom, Dzin, that afterwards grew into the dynasty of that name, may have originated the appellation by which the whole country subject to the Cheu emperors was known to the Hindoos. Dzin occupied the north-western tract now called Shen-si and Kan-su. It was that part of China that would be first reached by traders coming from Kashgar, Samarcand, and Persia. *Chen-tan*, the other Hindoo name of "China" used in the Buddhist books, may be the *Thinæ* of Ptolemy. When the first Buddhists reached China, the character used for writing the first of these two syllables would be called *Tin*, and soon afterwards *Chin*. In Julien's *Méthode*, &c., its Sanscrit equivalent is *Chin*. This would be somewhat late. Would it not be better, having traced the term to India, to make that country responsible for its etymology?

8. At that time the territory of Yang-cheu embraced Kiang-nan, with parts of Ho-nan and Kiang-si. Jambu, the southern continent, is one of the four Indian divisions of the world. India is in its centre.

9. *Shï-tsï-kwo*, the "Lion kingdom," translated from the Sanscrit name *Sinhala*, whence "Singhalese."

10. When the Buddhist has become sufficiently enlightened, an ideal picture of Buddhistic doctrine presents itself to his mind. It is called *Fa-shen* or *Fa-siang*. Elsewhere, as in the "Diamond Sutra," it is spoken of as a state that can be arrived at, but here it seems rather to mean an object of mental vision.

11. *Kiew-ta'euen-chï-hia*, a common phrase for "death."

12. *Pi-kwan* "*p'o-lo-men*" (in old Chinese, *Ba-la-men*).

13. The *Northern Wei History* gives the date of Shakyamuni's birth, B.C. 688, which is much nearer than the common date, to the time required by the evidence.

14. Of the interest felt by Sanscrit scholars in this subject, the letter of Professor Wilson, formerly Sanscrit Professor at Oxford, to Sir John Bowring is evidence. He invited the attention of the "China Branch of the Royal Asiatic Society" to the translations made by Hiuen-tsang in the T'ang dynasty, and the Sanscrit original works brought by that traveller to his native land.

    Of the Chinese translations I collected more than fifty while residing at Shanghai, for the library of the India House. Recently Rev. S. Beal has published an interesting account of these translations in the *Transactions of the Oriental Congress*, held in London, 1374.
15. In A.D. 226. This Roman was named Dzinlon. After describing his country to the Chinese prince, he was sent back honourably. His name looks in its Chinese form as if it were translated. See the "Liang History"—*India*.
16. In Sanscrit, *Saddharma Pundarika Sutra*.
17. *Ch'ang-a-han king.*
18. *Si-fun-lü.*
19. *Shih-sung-lü.*
20. Mr. Watters, citing the "Mirror of History," *Tung-kien*, chap. cccxvi., says, "Every household almost had been converted, and the number of those who had taken the vows was so great that the labours of the field were frequently neglected for lack of workmen."
21. See my *Introduction to the Study of the Chinese characters*.
22. Remusat supposed that this alphabet was borrowed by the Coreans from the Nü-chih and Kie-tan, who had invented a writing of their own, and ruled in Corea in the eleventh and twelfth centuries; but such an hypothesis is incompatible with the fact that the Corean letters are more like the Thibetan and Sanscrit letters.
23. The *lu-tau* here alluded to are the modes of existence into which, in the revolutions of the metempsychosis, all will be born who have not been saved by the teaching of Buddha. They are:—(1.) *T'ien*, the *Devas* of the Hindoos (Lat. *deus*); (2.) Man; (3.) *Asura* and *Mara*, superior classes of demons. Both these words are transferred. The former is transliterated by characters now read *sieu-lo* (in old Chinese, *su-la*), the latter by *mo* (*ma*), a character invented for the occasion by Liang Wu-ti, and which has passed into familiar colloquial in some dialects as *mo-kwei*, in the sense of "demon." (4.) "Hell," the prison of the lost, *ti-yu;* (5.) *Ngo-kwei*, wandering "hungry spirits;" (6.) Animals.

The use of *T'ien*, "Heaven," in a personal sense, as the translation of the Sanscrit *Deva*, whether in the singular or plural, is, perhaps, more common in Buddhist works than its use in a local sense. In explaining this new meaning of the word, *Deva* is transcribed as (*De-ba*) *T'i-p'o*.

24. It was about this time that the contests between Chosroes king of Persia, and the Turks on one side, and the Byzantine emperor on the other, occurred. The same events that have been described by Gibbon's luxuriant pen are found in a form more laconic and curtailed in the "History of the T'ang Dynasty." It might well be so, when Chinese travellers passed the eastern borders of Persia on their way to India, and when the imperial occupants of the throne of Constantinople sent embassies frequently to China. There are two records of these embassies preserved, the interest of which will be a sufficient excuse for a short digression. In A.D. 643, says the history, Pa-ta-lik, the king of the Fulim country, sent an embassy with presents of red glass. That this king was a Byzantine emperor is shown by the narrative of events in Persia just preceding it in the history. It says, "At the close of the Sui dynasty (ended A.D. 657), the "khan" (*k'a-han*) of the Western "Turks" (*Tu-kiue*) attacked "Persia" (*Pa-si*), and killed the king *K'u-sa-ha* (Chosroes I., or Nushirvan). His son *Shi-li* (Hormouz) succeeded him. After his death the daughter of K'u-sa-ha was made queen, but was killed by the Turks. Shi-li's son *Jen-ki* (Chosroes II.) fled to Fulim. (Gibbon says he took refuge with the Romans.) The people of the country brought him back and made him king. He was assassinated by *I-t'a-chi*, and succeeded by his brother's son *I-dzi-zi* (Yezdegerd)." This prince sent an embassy to China, A.D. 638. For misconduct he was driven away by his nobles, and fled to the *T'u-ha-la*, a tribe in Afghanistan. On his way he was put to death by the Arabs (*Ta-shih*). *Pi-lu-si* the son of *I-dzi-zi* appealed to the court at Ch'ang-an for aid against the irresistible Arabians, but in vain. These last details have been introduced by Gibbon into his narrative from De Guignes. It may be inferred, then, that the king *Pa-ta-lik* was the Byzantine emperor "Constans II." In the year 1081 there was also an embassy to China from the king of Fulim, who is called *Mih-li-i-ling kai-sa*. This *Kaisar* or "Cæsar" should be either Nicephorus Bataniares, who died this year, or his successor, Alexius Comnenus. In *Kin-shï-t'u-shu-pu*, a Chinese work on coins and other antiquities, there is a rude representation of a gold coin of this prince.

The word *Fulim* is evidently the same as the Thibetan *Philing* and the Indian *Feringi*, which, as Hodgson observes, must be variations of the word "Frank," commonly applied to all Europeans in Western Asia. Modern Chinese authors suppose Judæa to be *Fulim*, but the old passages in the Syrian inscription and elsewhere, in which the country is described as to its natural features, whether under this name or that of *Ta-ts'in*, read much more intelligibly if the Roman empire be understood.

25. This work has been recently reprinted, in the collection entitled *Sheu-shan-ko-ts'ung-shu*, at Sung-kiang, near Shanghai.

26. Vide Professor Wilson's letter published by the China Branch of the Royal Asiatic Society, at Hongkong.

    The changes in orthography adopted by Hiuen-tsang, may be made use of to show, that it was from Sanscrit and not Pali originals, that the Chinese Buddhist hooks were translated. He spells *tope* or "pagoda," *su-t'u-pa*. In Pali the word is *t'upa*, and in Sanscrit *st'upa*. Before Hiuen-tsang's time, the initial *s* was not expressed, probably for brevity, or through the influence of a local Indian dialect. Other examples might also be adduced. There is another use that may be made of these orthographical changes. As compared with preceding transcriptions, they are an index to the alterations that were taking place in the Chinese language itself. For convenience the age of Buddhist translations may be divided into three periods: (1.) A.D. 66, when Buddhism entered China, and the "Sutra of Forty-two Sections" was translated; (2.) A.D. 405, the age of Kumarajiva; (3.) A. D. 646, the age of Hiuen-tsang. The Sanscrit syllable *man* had been written with the character for "literature," *wen*. Hiuen-tsang adopted a character now as then heard, man. He changed the name of the Ganges from *Heng*, "Constant," to *Ch'ing-ch'ia* (*Gang-ga*). Comparison with existing dialects shows, that the Sanscrit pronunciation may be assigned without hesitation to the characters chosen, as nearly the sound that then belonged to them in Northern China, and one example is an index to a multitude of other words, passing through the same change at the same time. The three periods here given will help to supply the chronology of these changes, extending through almost all the sounds in the language. Thus, with other aid, the age of the Mandarin language may be fixed with comparative certainty.

27. A translation of a work by the same author, on the prophetic character of dreams, is also alluded to.

28. *Shanghai Almanac* for 5853—"Jottings on the Science of the Chinese."
29. Chief representative of the Tantra school in China, and author of the festival for hungry ghosts. He is also called Amogha Vajra, and his school is that called the Yogachara.(Eitel.)
30. Liang Wu-ti was eighty-six years of age when he died. His adopted son, whom he had appointed to succeed him, withheld the supplies of food that the aged emperor needed, and he died in consequence.
31. Watters, in *Chinese Recorder*, 1869, July, p. 40. The proverb *T'ang Fo*, "Buddha of the T'ang," means to be as devoted to Buddhism as was the T'ang dynasty.
32. The other two orders of Buddhist monks are (1.) *Lü-shï*, or "Disciplinists," who go barefoot and follow rigidly the rules enjoined in the early ages of Buddhism, for the observance of all who entered on the ascetic life; (2.) *Fa-shï*, or those who perform the common duties of priests, engage in popular teaching, and study the literature of their religion. The word *Ch'an* (in old Chinese, *jan* and *dan*), originally signifying "resign," had not the meaning to "contemplate" (now its commonest sense), before the Buddhists adopted it to represent the Sanscrit term *Dhyana*. The word in Chinese books is spelt in full *jan-na*, and is explained, "to reform one's self by contemplation or quiet thought." Perhaps an Eastern extension of the Jaina, or some lost sect, still existing in India, took place thus early. The marked difference between the Buddhism of Bodhidharma, and that already existing in China, requires some such supposition. These three orders still exist. The common priests met with in temples are not considered to deserve either denomination, but on the supposition that they fulfil their duties, they are *Fa-shï*. Distinguished priests are called *Ch'an-shï*. The emperors till very recently have always been accustomed to give names to distinguished priests. The early translators were honoured with the title *San-tsang fa-shï*. In common cases the title *Ch'an-shï* is all that is appended to the new name given by the imperial favour to those who, from their learning and character, are supposed to deserve it.
33. The Yoga or Yogachara school was founded by Asengha, and its system taught in China by *Pu-k'ung* (Amogha). It combined Brahmanism, Shivaism, and the doctrine of Dhyana Buddhas (derived from Nepaul), with the Mahayana philosophy.
34. See the work called *Ts'ien-sheu ts'ien-yen kwan-shï-yin p'u-sa to-pei-sin to-to-ni*, "The magical formula of the Bodhisattwa Kwan-shï-yin, who has a thousand hands and eyes and a merciful heart." "Da-la-ni" (*To-to-ni*) is in Sanscrit *Dharani*, "a

charm." See also the very popular work called *Yü-k'ia-yen-k'eu*, universally used by the priests as a mass-book for the benefit of the hungry dead, who come, in consequence of the priest's incantations, from hell, with "flaming mouths" (*yen-k'eu*) to receive "sweet dew" (*kan-lu*) and go back relieved.

35. These notices of foreign Buddhists are taken from the Supplement to the well-known cyclopædia *Wen-hien-t'ung-k'au*.
36. Watters, p. 42.
37. Sanscrit characters are also contained in such works as *Yü-k'ia-yen-k'eu*, which may be seen in any monastery. In Peking, Sanscrit sentences, chiefly charms, are seen written under the eaves of the roofs of temples. Some manuscripts have been brought to foreign residents for sale. They are written in a later *Devanagari* with the top line, from left to right, distinct in form. There are also Sanscrit inscriptions on "octagonal stones"(*shï-chwang*). The *Devanagari* is of an older style without the top line. They date from the Kin dynasty.
38. The Thibetan inscriptions at P'uto, which have frequently attracted the notice of foreign visitors, probably owe their origin to some far-travelled devotee from that country. Kwan-shï-yin is the national protector of the Thibetans, and, as Huc informs us, monuments with the words *Om-mani-padme-hum*, a sentence which occurs on the P'u-to stones, are everywhere seen there.
39. The attempt of Comte and his half-dozen followers to construct a religion on a basis of philosophy has been conspicuous only by its failure.
40. The word *ho-shang*, as the Chinese Life of Buddha informs us, is transferred from the language of "Udin" (*Yu-tian*) or "Khoten," south-east of Kashgar, and was originally translated from the Sanscrit *Upâsaka*. *Ho-shang* is now the universal term for the Buddhist monks. They themselves also use *ch'u-kia-jen*, a Chinese term convertible with it. It means "men who have left the family." *Upadhyâya* is a Sanscrit term for "a self-taught teacher," and *Hwa-shie* is a vernacular term in Kashgar and Kustana, and has become *ho-shang* in Chinese.—(Eitel.)
41. *T'ang-yün, Yü-p'ien*, &c.
42. See the "Supplement to *Wen-hien-t'ung-k'au*."

CHAPTER VII.

THE SCHOOLS OF CHINESE BUDDHISM.

The growth of esoteric sects in India—The Jains—Their series of twenty-four patriarchs—Bodhidharma headed a new school in Southern India, and was heretical as viewed from the Jains' standpoint—He founded the contemplative school in China—Nagarjuna, the author of the most revered books of this school—Tsung-men—Kiau-men—Divisions of Tsung-men—The Tsung-men sects are heretical in the view of the old orthodoxy—Specimen of the teaching of the Tsung-men—Lin-tsi school—Professes strict discipline—Its founder died A.D. 868—His monument on the bank of the Hu-to river in Chi-li—Resemblance to European speculation on the absolute—Is Buddhism pantheistic?—Exoteric sects—Lü-men, (Vinaya)—Yogachara—Fa-siang—Madhyamika—Fa-sing—Tsing-tu, or sect of the "Pure land" or "Western heaven"—T'ien-t'ai—Poetry of the Tsing-tu school.

BUDDHISM, as a religion of books and images, with the vow of celibacy and the monastic system, had entered China, and been widely propagated for several centuries, before anything was heard of schools. Gradually the Chinese Buddhists came to know of patriarchs, of the contemplative school, and of its many subdivisions.

We are told that when the use of books was carried to excess, and the true nature of humanity veiled from view, Bodhidharma arrived with a tradition of his own teaching, that men by becoming conscious of their own nature would attain the state of Buddha. He became the chief founder of the esoteric schools, which were divided into five principal branches. The common word for the esoteric schools is *dan*, the Sanscrit *Dhyana*, now called in the modern sound given to the character, *ch'an*.

Dr. Hamilton says, speaking of the Swaracs or Jains, a still existing Buddhist sect in India, that they worship twenty-four great teachers, who are called either *Avatars* or *Tirthancaras*. *Tirtha* is an incarnation or an heretical teacher or non-Buddhist ascetic of any sect. [1] Rhode supposed the Jains to be descendants of the Asuras and Rakshas, races hostile to the early Hindoos. [2] But they were rather a school.

The Chinese have the series of twenty-four patriarchs. They may be assumed to be the same with the Jaina twenty-four patriarchs. Bodhidharma will then be a heretic and continuator of an offshoot from the Jaina list of patriarchs, commencing with Basiasita. The location of this offshoot of the patriarchs, embracing the twenty-fifth, twenty-sixth, twenty-seventh, and twenty-eighth, was Southern India, for these four patriarchs were either natives of Southern India or were at least engaged in active labours there. Perhaps it will be better to say that the Jains and the school of Bodhidharma are both of them offshoots from a common stock, which recognised patriarchs from the time of Kashiapa, and maintained esoteric doctrine from that time.

The author of *Fo-tsu-t'ung-ki*, after describing the life of Buddha in four chapters, gives an account of the twenty-four patriarchs in his fifth chapter, and of nine selected patriarchs in his sixth and seventh chapters. Among the nine, Nagarjuna is the only foreigner, and the eight natives are not any of them among the five regular successors of Bodhidharma. Among them were (1.) Kau Hwei-wen, A.D. 550; (2.) Li Hwei-sï, founder of the Nan-ngo school; (3.) Chen Chï-k'ai of T'ien-t'ai and founder of that school. The five others I shall not mention.

Then he selects eight others. After this he gives the history of the succession in each case till he has related the lives of an immense number of teachers of schools, large and small, important and unimportant. After this he finds room for the school of Bodhidharma, on which, however, he is rather brief.

The author of *San-kiau-yi-su* places Bodhidharma in a much more important and elevated position. If Chi-p'an's view is a better representation of the old and orthodox Buddhist opinion, that of this later book is a better indication of the most prevalent opinions of modern Chinese monks.

Orthodox Buddhism has in China slowly but steadily become heterodox. The Buddhism of books and ancient traditions has become the Buddhism of mystic contemplation. The followers of Bodhidharma have extended themselves on every hand, and gained an almost complete victory over steady orthodoxy.

The history of ancient schools springing up long ago in the Buddhist communities of India, can now be only very partially recovered. Possibly some light may be thrown back by China upon the religious history of the country from which Buddhism came. In no part of the story is aid to the recovery of this lost knowledge more likely to be found than in the accounts of the patriarchs, the line of whom was completed by Bodhidharma. In seeking the best explanation of the Chinese and Japanese narrative of the patriarchs, and the seven Buddhas terminating in Gautama or Shakyamuni, it is important to know the Jain traditions as they were early in the sixth century of our era, when the patriarch Bodhidharma removed to China.

If it occur as an objection to this hypothesis that the discrepancies now existing between the school of Bodhidharma and of the Hindoo Jains are very great, the latter having temples and an external worship, and that their chronology also differs, in reply, it may be observed that the fame and influence of Bodhidharma in China mark him out as himself a great sect founder. In this character he would preserve only as much as he pleased of the traditions and observances of his fellow religionists, and in their view he was probably in many points a heretic. The absence of the esoteric element (at least that distinct and highly-developed form of it which belongs to China) from modern Jainism would follow the departure of the last patriarch. Further, his school keep images, and never think of dispensing with them, though they hold that they may be dispensed with. Their ritual also is most elaborate.

The second native writer, already quoted, thus compares Buddha and Bodhidharma. The former, "Julai" (*Tathâgata*), taught great truths and the causes of things. He became the instructor of men and Devas. He saved multitudes, and spoke the contents of more than five hundred works. Hence arose the *Kiau-men*, or exoteric branch of the system, and it was believed to be the tradition of the *words* of Buddha. Bodhidharma brought from the Western heaven "the seal of truth" (true seal), and opened the fountain of contemplation in the East. He pointed directly to Buddha's heart and nature, swept away the parasitic and alien growth of book instruction, and thus established the *Tsung-men*, or esoteric branch of the system, containing the tradition of the *heart* of Buddha. Yet, he adds, the two branches, while presenting of necessity a different aspect, form but one whole.

Though the two systems have worked harmoniously together, a line is readily drawn in their literature. Thus in the *Fa-yuen-chu-lin*, a large collection of miscellaneous Buddhist information coming down from the T'ang dynasty, nothing is said of Bodhidharma or his system. To separate the productions of these two great schools is then an important step in the classification of the Buddhist books in China. Among the traditions preserved in the history of the patriarchs are notices of some of the disciples of Buddha and other eminent persons, fabulous or real. They are given in an extended form in the work *Chï-yue-luh*. Manjusiri is the first. The others are *T'ien-ts'in p'u-sa* (Vasubandu Bodhisattwa), *Wei-ma*, *Shan-ts'ai* (good ability), Subhûti, *Wu-yeu-tso-wang* (the perfect king without any dissatisfaction), Sharīputra, Yangimara, Pindulo, *Chang-pi-*

mo-wang (the king who resists Mara), the prince *Na-t'o*, *Kwang-ngo-to-ri*, and *Dzin-ba-da*.

In tracing the rise of the various schools of esoteric Buddhism it must be kept in mind that a principle somewhat similar to the dogma of apostolical succession belongs to them all. They all profess to derive their doctrines through a succession of teachers, each instructed personally by his predecessor, till the time of Bodhidharma, and so further up in the series to Shakyamuni himself and the earlier Buddhas.

The sixth Chinese patriarch did not appoint a successor. The monastic habit and rice bowl that had descended to him were in accordance with what Bodhidharma had said, not communicated to a new patriarch. In the five petals the flower, as he had expressed it, would be complete, he himself, the first of the six, being the stem on which the others grew. The last of the patriarchs resided at Ts'au-k'i, in Kiang-si. Two schools were formed by his disciples, denominated Nan-ngo (South Mountain) and Ts'ing-yuen, from the spots where the teachers resided. The former is near Heng-cheu, in Hu-nan, the latter near Ts'iuen-cheu, in Fu-kieu. In these schools there was no very real difference in sentiment from the doctrine of the parent stem.

Heng-shan is the old Confucianist mountain known by that name, and also as Nan-ngo. The tablet of Yü was said to be discovered there, and we can see the reason of this. It was the southern limit of the Chinese empire of that time. He was the traditional civiliser, the canal maker and embankment engineer of the Hia dynasty, and of his work the geographical section in the "Book of History" is the record.

Though Bodhidharma was nominal founder of the esoteric schools in China, the real philosophic thinker, who gave them the impulse to reflection, was Nagarjuna, the most important founder of the Mahayana school. He specially originated the Madhyamika system, which reduces everything to bald abstractions and then denies them. The soul has neither existence nor non-existence. It is neither permanent nor non-permanent. Such was his teaching.—(See in Eitel). His system influenced

Kau Hweiwen, who studied the Shastra *Ta-chï-tu-lun*, and mastered the idea of "central gazing," *chung-kwan*, and also that of three branches of wisdom—viz. matter is nothing; the mind's annoyances are nothing; the temptations through the senses are nothing.

Li Hwei-sï, of the Nan-ngo school, built up his ideas on those of Hwei-wen, and transmitted to Chï-k'ai the "triple gaze," the empty, the hypothetical, and the medial.

Such is the statement of Chï-p'an, the orthodox authority. But, according to *San-kiau-yi-su*, the chief influence in the formation of the Nan-ngo and of the Ts'ing-yuen was that of the sixth patriarch upon the mind of Tu Hwai-jang and Lieu Hing-sï.

The founders of these two schools, the first of the Tsung-men, were Hwai-jang and Hing-sï. Their successors were Ma-tsu in Kiang-sï, and Hi-k'iau or Shï-t'eu, who, while they changed their residences and became themselves teachers of the esoteric doctrine, retained the names, Nan-ngo and Ts'ing-yuen, of the schools where they had been taught.

The biographical record of the Tsung-men teachers in the Chï-yue-luh contains notices of priests trained by the predecessors of the sixth patriarch, and sent out to teach the doctrine of Bodhidharma. Two were instructed by the successor of Bodhidharma, eight by the fourth patriarch, and six by the fifth. One of the latter, Shin-sieu, was styled the sixth patriarch for North China, while Hwai-neng, the legitimate successor of Bodhidharma, from residing in the southern provinces, was called the sixth patriarch for the South. Nothing is said of the schools originated in various provinces by these teachers. It is only the successors of Hwai-neng, the last-mentioned hierarch, that are regarded as deserving a memorial. From him a series of disciples, all becoming "teachers" (*ch'an-sï*) in their turn, are counted to the sixteenth generation. This mode of expression is used instead of mentioning, according to custom, the years of imperial reigns and dynasties. The biography in the *Chï-yue-luh*, a book of the Ming dynasty, ceases at the sixteenth descent. This was at the beginning of the twelfth century, and the whole series embraces about four hundred years. Modern monks of these schools trace their succession in a similar manner, according to a more recent arrangement, in twelve divisions. The reason for this careful record of ecclesiastical ancestry is to be sought in the principle of unbroken lineal descent, which is indispensable to the maintenance of esoteric tradition. Yet it does not appear that there was any secret doctrine which those who knew it would not divulge. What they held was simply a protest against the neglect of the heart, and dependence on book knowledge and the performance of outward rites. Since their object was to draw neophytes away from the inordinate study of the books of the religion, instruction was given orally. An extensive series of works containing records of the instructions of these teachers has been the result. They are called *Yü-luh*, "Records of the sayings" of celebrated teachers.

Several branch schools were originated by the successors of the sixth patriarch. In the fourth generation from him the Hwei-niang school was formed. In the fifth appears that of Lin-tsi and Ts'au-tung. The Yün-men belongs to the eighth generation. That called Fa-yen belongs to the ninth. These names are taken from the places where the founders of the respective schools resided. They are denominated collectively the Wu-tsung, or "Five schools," to distinguish them from those which preceded them, and adhered more closely to the tradition of the patriarchs. The differences that existed between these schools and the parent doctrine were not great. But it is not essential that differences should be great to make them the subject of controversy and the cause of division. An example of the mode in which the contemplative Buddhists carried on their discussions will here be given. Shin-sieu taught his doctrine in the following verses:—

> "The body is like the knowledge tree.
> The mind is like a mirror on its stand.
> It should be constantly and carefully brushed,
> Lest dust should be attracted to it."

His teacher, the fifth patriarch, was pleased with this mode of representing the importance of watching over the heart. But Hwai-neng, the sixth patriarch, opposed it with vehemence. He also wrote his view in verses:—

"There is no such thing as a knowledge tree.
There is no such thing as a mirror-stand.
There is nothing that has a real existence.
Then how can dust be attracted?"

In the former appears very distinctly the practical part of the esoteric system, attention to the heart. In the latter its speculative tendency—denying everything external to the mind—is brought to view.

According to the system held in common by these schools, the heart is Buddha. There is no mode of attaining to the state called Buddha but by the mind itself. This mind has neither beginning nor end, colour nor form. To look outward is to be a common man. To look in ward is to be Buddha. In reality man is the same thing as Buddha. To rely on the performance of particular acts is not true knowledge. To make offerings to all the past Buddhas is not to be compared with offering to one man who has become superior to mental passions and sensational influences.

All that the great Bodhisattwas have taught, men have in themselves. The pure vacancy of Manjusiri, the withdrawal of the thoughts from the world of sensations recommended by P'u-hien, the mercy of Kwan-yin, the knowledge of Shï-chi, the purity of "Vimakita" (*Wei-mo*)—all these various principles are in the heart. To know it, is all that is needful. To become Buddha the mind only needs to be freed from every one of its affections, not to love or hate, covet, rejoice, or fear. To do, or aim at doing, what is virtuous or what is vicious is to leave the heart and go out into the visible tangible world. It is to become entangled in the metempsychosis in the one case, and much trouble and vexation in the other. The right method is in the mind; it is the mind itself. The fountain of knowledge is the pure, bright, self-enlightening mind. The method taught by all the Buddhas is no other than this. Let the mind do nothing, observe nothing, aim at nothing, hold fast to nothing; that is Buddha. Then there will be no difference between living in the world and entering the Nirvâna. Then human nature, the mind, Buddha, and the doctrine he taught, all become identical. [3]

While revising these papers, and adding to them, so that they may form a distinct book on Chinese Buddhism (August 11, 1899), I here insert a brief account of the Lin-tsi school.

The Lin-tsi school has been very successful. It has pushed out the other sects, and spread over the north and south of China to an enormous extent. Beginning in Shantung, it has been accepted throughout the eighteen provinces, and in Japan, as the most popular exponent of the teaching of the contemplative school.

They say, "Within the body which admits sensations, acquires knowledge, thinks, and acts, there is the 'True man without a position,' *Wu-wei-chen-jen*. He makes himself clearly visible; not the thinnest separating film hides him. Why do you not recognise him? The invisible power of the mind permeates every part. In the eye it is called seeing, in the ear it is hearing. It is a single intelligent agent, divided out in its activity in every part of the body. If the mind does not come to conscious existence, there is deliverance everywhere. What is the difference between you and the sages of antiquity? Do you come short in anything? What is Buddha? *Ans*. A mind pure, and at rest. What is the law? *Ans*. A mind clear and enlightened. What is *Tau? Ans*. In every place absence of impediments and pure enlightenment. These three are one." The object of the Lin-tsi has been to teach Buddhism, so that each monk should feel that there is difficulty in the paths of self-improvement, and that he has in himself the power to conquer that difficulty.

The "true man without a position," *Wu-wei-chen-jen*, is wrapped in a prickly shell like the chestnut. He cannot be approached. This is Buddha, the Buddha within you.

The sharp reproof of discipline is symbolised by slaps on the cheek with the palm of the hand, and blows with the fists under the ribs. This treatment gives an improved tone to the mind and feelings.

An infant cannot understand the seven enigmas.

These enigmas are given in dark language difficult even for adepts to explain. Thus: "Is it to search in the grass where there is the shadow of the stick that you have already come here?" "To kill a man, to strike with the sword a dividing blow, and the body should not enter the water."

The explanations of these enigmas are not given in the book I have consulted. Doubtless they mean something quite in harmony with the fundamental principles of Buddhism, otherwise the Lin-tsi school would not be so popular as it is.

They have the "Three 'dark,' *hiuen*, principles," the "real," *shï*, the "formal," *t'i*, and the "practical," *yung*. They have also the "Three 'important,' *yau*, principles." These are, "illumination," *chau*, "utility or use," *yung*, and the combination of the two. In their discipline they have three blows with the cane, three successive reproofs, and the alternation of speech and silence. They have a play on the words "guest" and "host." The guest may learn from the host by seeing how he meets circumstances, and imitating him. The host may learn from the guest, as when those who are already profound in wisdom make constant inquiries from their visitors, and seize ardently on what they approve. The host may learn from another host, as when those who are already wise discuss points, and such as are learning throw away what they had been grasping firmly. The guest may learn from another guest, as when the learner is laden with the heavy wooden neck collar and iron lock, and all discussion ceases.

Where the meaning of such mysterious teaching is not clear, there will be an oral explanation by the tutor; and so step by step the pupils will acquire a knowledge of the Lin-tsi school doctrines and discipline, and of the enigmatical language in which they are couched.

The founder of the Lin-tsi school died A.D. 868. A dagoba was erected over his ashes in the south part of the province of Chi-li, near Ta-ming fu, on the north-west angle not far from the city.

He resided for some years on the banks of the river Hu-t'o, which rushes with great force of current out of Shan-si into Chi-li, at the distance of a mule's journey of five days from Peking on the south-west. This river flows through the prefecture of Chen-ting fu to the Grand Canal. On the banks of this river to the south-east of the city of Chen-cheu, as Chen-ting fu was then called, the founder of the Lin-tsi school spent much of his life in a small monastery. Here he was in a quiet spot surrounded by the objects of a well-cultivated plain, where wheat and millet have been sown from time immemorial; and here he acquired a reputation for magical powers. He could stroke the beard of a fierce tiger, split rocks, burst open precipices, walk upon ice, and move along the edge of a sword. The main features in the landscape on which he looked were the blue mountains of Shan-si, forming a broad and continuous chain on the west, with the swift river which flowed by his monastery with a full and foaming stream in the summer months, and sinking to a much smaller one in the winter, when it is frozen hard enough to be passed by loaded waggons. It was this river that gave a name to the school, for *Lin-tsi* means "Coming to the ford."

To the kind of philosophy springing up in India, and further developed by the Chinese in the esoteric schools above described, there is much that is similar in recent European speculation. We see here the Finite going back into the Absolute, the denial of the existence of everything but self, the identity of self and God, and of the subject and object. That abstraction which is the pantheist's God, may, without violence to the meaning of words, be considered as the corresponding term to Buddha in this system. For God, as the Absolute, is the state towards which nature and man are returning, a description which answers to the notion here alluded to of the state called Buddha. When, however, in the manner of the older schools, Buddha is looked upon as having historical personality, it becomes at once incorrect to say that he is God; his personality being strictly human, and not divine. There is, however, a difference. The Asiatic speculator undertakes to realise his system, and employs the monastic institute or other aids for the purpose, hoping thus to escape from the chains of sense and passion into the freedom of pure abstraction. The European theoriser, on the other hand, even if he attempts to show how a practical religion may be based on a system of abstractions—as was done by Fichte—never seriously thinks of carrying it into execution.

Neander, following Schmidt and Baur, represents Buddhism as one form of pantheism, on the ground that the doctrine of metempsychosis makes all nature instinct with life, and that that life is the Deity assuming different forms of personality, that Deity not being a self-conscious free acting First cause, but an all-pervading spirit. The esoteric Buddhists of China, keeping rigidly to their one doctrine, say nothing of the metempsychosis, the paradise of the Western heaven, or any other of the more material parts of the Buddhist system. The Indian Buddhists were professed atheists; but those of China, instead of denying the existence of God, usually content themselves with saying nothing about Him. To deny or affirm any special existence, fact or dogma, would in their view be equally inconsistent. Their aim is to keep the mind from any distinct action or movement of any kind. They look, therefore, with pity on worshippers of every class as necessarily missing what they aim at, and that because they aim at it; and as having no prospect of escaping from the misery of life until they abandon all special dependencies and doctrines, look within instead of without, and attend to the voiceless teaching of the mind itself.

This system also exists in Japan, and the same subdivisions into schools occur there among its followers. (See Burger's account of religious sects in Japan, *Chin. Rep.*, vol. ii. pp. 318-324.)

It is in high estimation among the reflecting class of Chinese, who look with contempt on the image worship of the multitude.

An account of the "Exoteric sects," the *Kiau-min* of Chinese Buddhism, will now be presented to the reader.

Shakyamuni is said to have foretold that, for five centuries after his death, the true doctrine would be followed. After that, for a thousand years, a system of forms or "Image worship," *Siang-kiaou*, would prevail. This would subsequently give place to another called the "final system," which would terminate the present *kalpa*. The popular Buddhism of China belongs to the second of these developments. It was this form that it first assumed on entering China. Buddha is said to have taught the doctrines of this system in early life, while the more abstruse and mystical parts of his teaching were delivered when he was become an old man. After his entrance into the Nirvâna, Ananda compiled the "Sutras" (*King*). In the council that was then held, these Sutras were adopted as an authentic account of the Buddhist doctrine, and they are the first of the Three collections that constitute the standard books of Buddhism.

The biographical notices of the principal translators of the Sutras, and founders of the Kiau-men, are by the author of the *San-kiau-yi-su* placed before the five schools into which he divides the exoteric Buddhists. The first of the eight who are thus distinguished is Kashiapmadanga. When he came to Lo-yang in the first century of our era, he lodged in the *Pe-ma sï* (White horse temple). Hence the residences of Buddhist priests were called *sï* (*ga-lam*, "monasteries;" for the Sanscrit, *sangarama*). Associated with his countryman Chu-fa-lan, he translated five Sutras. The latter afterwards translated five more, consisting of thirteen "chapters" (*kiuen*). "Kumarajiva's" (*Kieu-mo-to-shi*) name is the third, and the fourth that of "Buddojanga" (*Fo-t'u-cheng*), who is better known as a wonder worker and a founder of monasteries (he erected 893) than a translator. A commentary on the *Tau-te-king* of Lau-tsi came from his pen. The remaining four names most noted in the early history of Chinese Buddhism are Chï-tun, Tau-an, Pau-chï, and Shan-hwei. They were all natives of China, noted for their writings and public discussions in explanation and defence of the Buddhist system.

The five subdivisions of exoteric Buddhism will now be considered. (1.) That named from the Vinaya or second division of the sacred books, is the first. The writer of the "Vinaya" (*Lü*) and founder of this school was "Upáli" (*Yeu po-li;* in old Chinese, *U-pa-li*), one of the ten chief disciples of Shakyamuni. He wrote the Si pu-lit, which was admitted into the "Three pitaka" (*San-tsang*) at the council held after Buddha's death (*vide* Hardy's *Eastern Monachism*). Among the nine leaders of this school, two other Hindoos are mentioned. The first Chinese among them is in the fifth century. He taught the system of the work called "Discipline of Four Divisions." The name of this school is *Hing-sï-fang-fei-chï-ngo*, indicating that its aim is in action to guard against error and check vice. It is also called the *Nan-shan* (Southern hill) school. Priests of this school at the present time dress in black. There was at Nanking, before the T'ai-ping rebellion, a monastery where this system was in operation.

(2.) Yo-ga-mi-kiau, "The secret teaching of Yoga." The founder of this system is called *Kin-kang-sat-wa* (Vajrasattwa). It was brought to China about A.D. 720 by *Kin-kang-chï* (Vajramati), who was succeeded by Pu-k'ung. Seventy-two works came from the pen of the latter, and were placed in the national collection of Buddhist books. His numerous disciples learned to repeat charms with great effect, and this seems to be the proper business of the school. The word *Yoga* is explained as "Correspondence" and, it is added, is employed as a general term for books "containing secret doctrines" (referring to magic). To this school belongs the very popular festival of the hungry ghosts, held in the seventh month.

The Yoga or Yogachara school is also called the Tantra school, because it taught the use of magic formulæ or unintelligible charms used for rain, for protection in storms, &c. They are written in Sanscrit or Thibetan letters.—(See in Eitel, under the word "Yogatchara.")

(3.) Wei-shi-siang-kiau. This school occupied itself with the study of the Shastra *Wei-shï-lun*, and similar works. These books were written by the two Bodhisattwas Wu-cho [4] and T'ien-ts'in. Kiai-hien, a Hindoo residing at the monastery Nalanda, was their most distinguished disciple, and was principally concerned in establishing this school, and arranging those forms of Buddhist instruction called the Three "Developments" (*Yana*). Next to him was the traveller Hiuen-tsang, who received the Shastra mentioned above from Kiai-hien, and originated the school in his native country. He was succeeded by his pupil Kwei-ki. This school is called *Fa-siang-tsung*, or the "School that exhibits the nature" and meaning of the Buddhist written doctrines.

(4.) Another of these schools derives its name from the Shastra called *Chung-lun*. That work was written by the Hindoo *Lung-shu*, "Nagarjuna" (Dragon tree). The founder of the school based on the doctrines of that book was a Chinese of the Northern T'si kingdom in the sixth century. His successor was a monk of one of the sects that followed the teaching of Bodhidharma, Hwei-sï of Nan-ngo. He was succeeded by Chï-k'ai of T'ien-t'ai shan, who developed the system to a much greater extent, and divided it into four subordinate schools, named from their subjects, those of the written doctrine, true human nature, the use of the senses, and action.

(5.) The last exoteric school is that which was founded by Fa-shun, a native of Tun-hwang, an ancient kingdom in what is now Thibet. He gave his chief attention to the "Hwa-yen Sutra." The third leader of the school was Hien-sheu, the best known of them all. His name is often given to the system that he with his predecessors and successors recommended. It is called usually *Fa-sing-tsung*, the "School of the true nature" of the written doctrine.

Another exoteric school parallel with these, but placed separately in the classification, is that called *Lien-tsung* (Lotus school), or *Tsing-tu* (Pure land). To it belongs the popular legend of the Western heaven, the abode of "Amida Buddha" (*A-mi-to Fo*), a fabulous personage worshipped assiduously—like Kwan-yin—by the Northern Buddhists, but unknown in Siam, Birmah, and Ceylon. The founder of this school in China was a native of Shan-si, Hwei-yuen, of the Tsin dynasty (fourth century). The second "patriarch" (*tsu*) of this school was Kwang-ming of the seventh century. For more than thirty years he taught the doctrine of the "Pure land," persuading multitudes to adopt it. Pan-cheu, his successor, was honoured with the title *Kwo-shï* (National instructor) in the reign of T'ai-tsung (760 A.D.). The sixth in order was Chï-kio. His views differed little from those of T'ien-t'ai, Hiuen-tsang, and Hien-sheu. He was very fond of saving fish and crabs from being killed and eaten. Seven chiefs of this sect are enumerated. To the same school belongs Chu-hung, the priest who opposed Matteo Ricci. in works and letters still extant, and founded the Yün-tsi monastery near Hang-cheu.

The Western paradise promised to the worshippers of Amida Buddha is, as has been pointed out by Schott in his work on the Buddhism of High Asia and China, inconsistent with the doctrine of Nirvâna. It promises immortality instead of annihilation. The great antiquity of this school is evident from the early date of the translation of the *Amida Sutra*, which came from the hands of Kumarajiva, and of the *Wu-liang-sheu-king*, dating from the Han dynasty. Its extent of influence is seen in the attachment of the Thibetans and Mongols to the worship of this Buddha, and in the fact that the name of this fictitious personage is more commonly heard in the daily conversation of the Chinese people than that of the historical Buddha Shakyamuni.

The only remaining school is that of T'ien-t'ai, already partially described. In the latter part of the sixth century Hwei-wen, a native of "Northern China" (*Pe-ts'ï*), studied the *Chung-lun* (Central Shastra), written by the Hindoo called "Conqueror of the Dragon" (*Lung-sheng* or *Lung-shu*), the fourteenth patriarch. Convinced of its excellence, he instituted "three sorts of meditation" (*san-kwan*), viewing the world as (1.) empty, (2.) false, or (3.) central. This he regarded as the limit of religious meditation on the surrounding universe, and therefore called his system *Chï-kwan*, "Reflection carried to its limiting point." He also founded his doctrine partly on the *Fa-hwa-king*, and was followed by Hwei-sï and Chï-che of T'ien-t'ai, who gave his name to the school.

The following verses translated from the poetry of the Tsing-tu sect will serve to illustrate the doctrine of that school. It is not much of the Buddhist system that easily admits of being put into this form of composition. There is nothing akin to the spirit of poetry in the turgid splendour and wearisome reiteration of the legends that abound in the books of this religion. Chinese versifiers have, however, found some materials more to their taste in the Western heaven of Amida Buddha. If the reader should think the conceptions are poor, they are at least a genuine description, so far as they go, of the heaven of the Northern Buddhists.

"THE WESTERN HEAVEN.

"The pure land of the West, say what language can tell
Its beauty and majesty There ever dwell
The men of this world and the Devas [5] of heaven,
And to each has the same wreath of glory been given.
The secrets of wisdom unveiled they behold,
And the soil that they tread on is bright yellow gold.
In that land of true pleasure the flowers never fade,
Each terraced ascent is of diamond and jade.
The law of Tathâgata [6] sung by each bird
From thicket and grove in sweet music is heard.
The unwithering Upata, [7] fairest of flowers,
Sheds fragrance around in those thrice lovely bowers.
There, each from the world that he governs, are found
Assembled in conference long and profound,
The ten supreme Buddhas who cease not to tell

The praise of the land where the genii [8] dwell.
For there is no region so happy and blest,
As the heaven of great Amida far in the west.
On the moment of reaching it by a new birth,
The material body of men while on earth
Is exchanged for another ethereal and bright,
That is seen from afar to be glowing with light.
Happy they who to that joyful region have gone!
In numberless *kalpas* their time flows on.
Around are green woods, and above them clear skies,
The sun never scorches, cold winds never rise,
Neither summer nor winter are there ever known
In the land of the Law and the Diamond Throne;
All errors corrected, all mysteries made clear,
Their rest is unbroken by care or by fear.
And the truth that before lay in darkness concealed
Like a gem without fracture or flaw is revealed."

The word "diamond" is used in the sense of "unconquered and unconquerable," and may refer either to Buddha's power as a teacher, or to the divinities that support his throne and act as his protectors.

"AMIDA BUDDHA.

"See where, streaming forth radiance for thousands of miles,
Ever sits the compassionate Buddha, and smiles,
Giving joy to the victims of sorrow and strife
Who are saved by his law from the sorrows of life.
All his features of beauty no words can express,
For the sands of the Ganges in number are less;
Mark the flowers of the lotus encircling his seat
As if of themselves they sprang up round his feet.

Whoever would enter the home of the blest
In his innermost thoughts should incessantly rest
On that beautiful form like the clear moon on high
When she marches full-orbed through an unclouded sky.
By that halo of light that encircles his head,
On all living beings a radiance is shed.
The sun at noonday is less glorious than be,
His compassion resembles a bottomless sea.
Without ceasing his arms are outstretched to relieve
The afflicted that weep, and the orphans that grieve,
For his mercy is such as none else can display,
And long ages of gratitude cannot repay."

These descriptions are taken from a collection of poems called Tsing-tu-shï. The measure in the original is the usual one of seven words in a line. The Chinese words are monosyllables, and the diction consequently very terse. Our English tongue is different. A metre like that here adopted has more room in it than others for unaccented syllables. This circumstance renders it convenient. It has often been used by translators.

In these descriptions there is a prominent materialism in the expressions. Buddha in the Western heavens is thought of as like the monstrous gilt image seen by the worshippers as they go to a temple on a gala day. Idolatry loves to borrow from nature. Here there are flowers, and singing-birds, and the favourite jade-stone. Buddha is here made popular; there is no abstruse speculation. The boasted Nirvâna is abandoned, and a paradise gratifying to the senses takes its place. Many a simple-minded dreamer spends his days in meditating on this picture, and indulging his imagination with the hope that he will one day be born from a lotus flower, in the very joyful world of Amida, and live there for ever gazing on his sacred form.

Footnotes

1. *Transactions of the Royal Asiatic Society*, vol. i p. 538.
2. Rhode, *Réligiose Bildung u. s. w. der Hindus*.
3. This description is taken from a little work of the T'ang dynasty, called *Twan-tsi-sin-yau*.
4. *Asengha*, "Without attachment," was originally a follower of the Mahashasaka school. He first taught the Mahayana system, and wrote the books which contain the Wei-shi doctrines. Then he because the founder of the Yoga school, and wrote a book which he said was dictated to him by Maitreya in the Tushita paradise.—(See in Eitel.)
5. *Devas*, the "gods" of the Hindoos (in Chinese, *t'ien*). They are inferior in power and splendour to human nature when elevated to the rank of the Buddhas and Bodhisattwas.
6. *Tathâgata*, a title of Buddha; in Chinese, *Julai*. "The law," is the doctrine proclaimed by Buddha.
7. Also spelt Utampatala.
8. "Genii." In Sanscrit, *Rishi;* in Chinese, *Sien-jen*.

CHAPTER VIII.

ON CHI-K'AI AND THE T'IEN-T'AI SCHOOL OF BUDDHISM.

T'ien-t'ai, a place of great note in Chinese Buddhism—Chï-k'ai resided there in the sixth century—His cloak and rice bowl—Fu-lung-feng—Fang-kwang sï and the rock bridge—Legend of the Lo-hans—Twelve monasteries founded—He taught the Fa-hwa-king—System of threefold contemplation—Six connectives—Eight modes of characterising Buddhism—Ten steps in progress—Derived much from Nagarjuna—T'ien-t'ai, a middle system—Regulations.

THERE is no Buddhist establishment better known in China than T'ien-t'ai. It has much natural beauty, but its interest, so far as it is historical, centres chiefly round the ancient monk who is the subject of this notice. It had been visited before by Tauist recluses, but it was he that by selecting it for his abode gave it its high reputation as a spot consecrated to the meditative life.

The cluster of hills that compose T'ien-t'ai terminate abruptly to the south-west. Ch'ih-ch'eng,[1] an imposing hill crowned with a pagoda, is conspicuous from the timeworn walls of the city of T'ien-t'ai, 180 miles south-east of Hang-cheu. This is the southern extremity of the hilly region known by the same name. From a valley on its left flows a mountain stream, which, increasing in width as it traverses the plain, is capable of bearing boats of considerable size when it reaches the busy little city just mentioned. Passing on it bends to the south-east, and arriving at T'ai-chen, an important sea-port, pours its waters, after a short course of ten or fifteen miles, into the ocean.

It was up one of the feeders of this stream that, near the end of the sixth century, Chï-k'ai wended his way in search of a lonely mountain residence suited to his meditative cast of mind. Leaving the beautiful site where afterwards stood the Kwo-ts'ing monastery, just below four hills now covered to their summits with rich foliage, he ascended a long and romantic valley. He was travelling in a region threaded by few paths, and in a direction that seemed to lead nowhere but farther away from the habitations of men. In this wilderness of hills and valleys, occupying many square miles, which he now entered, although unknown to the agriculturist, he yet found some few residing whose views of human life were congenial to his own. Local traditions point out where he lived and reflected. An antique mausoleum, with a long inscription of the Sui dynasty, marks the place where his ashes were deposited. At a little distance from it the Kau-ming monastery comes into view. It is in a deep valley shut all round by wooded heights. The building has an old look, befitting the relics of our hero still preserved there. The visitor will have shown to him a large square silk garment. It is said to have been the cloak worn by Chï-k'ai. It is handsomely embroidered after a pattern evidently very antique. A metal bowl, worn by long use, and capable of holding several meals of rice for an abstemious monk, is another curiosity. These memorials of this early Buddhist will appear, however, to one who is not a special admirer of the monastic life, secondary in interest to a Sanscrit manuscript which escaped a fire some centuries ago, and is one of the few remains of that literature still existing in China. The history of the manuscript, its name and contents, are unknown to the resident priests.

This monastery is even now difficult of access. But the valley where it stands, in Chï-k'ai's time had scarcely ever been visited. [2] It was filled with forest trees and thick brushwood, and formed a favourite cover for deer. The woodcutter and herdsman seldom wandered to this wild spot. An accident led our hero there. On the hill above—Fu-lung-feng—near where the "st'upa" (*t'ah*) that contains his ashes is still standing, he was one day explaining to his disciples the *Tsing-ming-king* (Sutra of Pure name) when a gust of wind blew away the leaves far into the deep hollow below. With his tin-headed staff in his hand to assist him in the search, he set out to recover the fugitive book. After a pursuit of a mile and a half the wind ceased, and the book fell to the ground. He caused a building to be erected at the spot, in commemoration of the circumstance, which became one of the twelve establishments that owe their origin to him. It was not, however, till many years after that the present monastery was erected and its modern name assigned to it. When the Kwo-ts'ing monastery was destroyed by fire, the manuscript spoken of above was removed to Kau-ming for greater safety.

After penetrating several miles farther to the northwest in this hilly and desolate region, Chï-k'ai arrived [3] at the remarkable rock bridge where the Fang-kwang monastery now stands. The loud roar of the waterfall, and the close-set woods on the hills around, the two mountain brooks uniting before they reach the cataract, then passing beneath the natural bridge down the fall, and thence pursuing their way to the north, united to give this spot an air of grandeur in the hermit's mind. It seemed a home for supernatural beings. It is they that cause the unusual appearances of nature. The Lo-hans, those exalted disciples of Buddha whose power and knowledge are so great, might reside here. In fact a legend on the subject soon grew into public belief, and the music of the Lo-hans was said to be heard at times a little before dawn by priests lying awake in their cells. A choir of five hundred at that silent hour made the woods resound with harmony. Such a colony of Buddha's superhuman disciples served to invest this wild mountainous district with a sacred character. In every monastery of this region a hall devoted to images of the five hundred Lo-hans now exists, and on the side of the natural bridge is a small shrine containing five hundred small stone figures, which are worshipped by those who venture to cross by the narrow and dangerous path that spans the cataract.

Our hero continued his wanderings in this elevated region, where the valleys do not sink farther than 1500 feet above the sea-level, and which is by its loneliness well suited for the ascetic. Solitude reigns here for many miles round, in one of the most densely-populated provinces of China. He did not take up his abode at one place exclusively. No fewer than twelve monasteries mark the spots where he formed a cottage of stones and straw, or caused a modest building to be erected.

As he approached the peak of Hwa-ting, nearly 4000 feet high, and five miles to the east of the natural bridge, he met on the T'ien-feng ridge an old man who said to him, "Sir, if you seek a residence for contemplation, select the place where you meet a rock." The monk soon after encountered a Buddhist from Corea named *Pan-shï* (Rock), who encouraged him to stay there, and give himself up to study. He accordingly constructed a hut there, in which he remained sixteen years, and composed a commentary on the "Book of the Nirvâna."

A little farther to the north is Hwa-ting, the highest ground in Che-kiang excepting T'ien-mu shan. The monastery, bearing the same name as the mountain, had already been erected by Te-shau, a celebrated Buddhist who lived a century anterior to Chï-k'ai. Several hundred monks now belong to the society, a large part of them residing in hermitages on the hill. The monastery is an extensive thatched range of buildings, more comfortable than the bleak huts where, out of sight of any human being, the more self-denying spend their days and nights chanting in honour of Buddha. Certainly theirs is a gloomy home. A thick mist usually rests on the summit and spreads down the sides of the mountain, enveloping these rude cottages with their visionary inmates; and snow often remains unmelted for many months. It is hard to explain how a people so social as the Chinese, so fond of cities and crowds, and so averse to mountain travelling, can supply hermits to live in residences like these. That Chï-k'ai, the founder of a flourishing sect, a man of deep reflection, and in love with solitude, should choose such an abode, is not so surprising as that common Chinese minds, without his profound thinking, or his love of wild nature, should still follow his example.

Another spot where Chï-k'ai once resided is Si-tso, at some distance to the west of the rock bridge, and near the Wan-nien monastery. Here he composed his system of doctrine called *Chï-kwan*, "Limited or perfected observation."

Chï-k'ai had in early life followed the teaching of the school established by Bodhidharma, the Hindoo patriarch who had died in Northern China thirty years before. He afterwards became dissatisfied with the *Ch'an-men* (Contemplative school), as that sect is called, not agreeing with its principle that book learning should be discarded, even that which consisted of Buddha's own words, and the heart nurse itself into a state of perfection by rejecting everything external and giving itself up to an unconscious sleep-like existence.

Chï-k'ai grew tired of this system, and formed the outlines of another, which he taught to multitudes of admiring disciples. He resided at Nanking, the capital of the kingdom (Ch'en dynasty), and maintained a high reputation. When he determined on removing to T'ien-t'ai, the emperor forbade him, but allowed him to leave when he saw that his mind was made up. Three times afterwards an imperial message required his attendance at court, but he pleaded indisposition and remained at T'ien-t'ai. He complied on one occasion only, and explained the sacred books of his religion to the emperor and his court. He also made one visit home to Hu-nan, but returned to die at the mountain residence to which he was so much attached. He expired while sitting cross-legged and giving instruction to his followers.

He wrote commentaries on the *Fa-hwa-king, Kin-kang-king*, and *A-mi-ta-king*, with several original works. These books were in the year A.D. 1024, all included in the Buddhist Tripitaka (Collection of sacred writings) of China.

His school continued to flourish for a long period at the Kwo-ts'ing and Fu-lung monasteries.

The *Miau fa-lien-hwa-king* (Lotus of the Good Law) was his favourite book. He thus explained its name:—"As the lotus grows out of the mire and yet preserves its freshness and purity, so the doctrines of this book, the good law, assist men to retain their original nature unsullied and undisturbed amidst the misery and corruption around them." In the course of the book, he added: "Truth is sometimes taught in abstract, at other times by illustration, sometimes it is explained and elsewhere defended, just as the lotus flower buds, blossoms, fades, and falls by a succession of changes, and at last produces fruit."

Chï-k'ai divided the teaching of Shakyamuni into five periods. beginning with the *Hwa-yen-king*, and ending with the *Fa-hwa-king* and the Nirvâna. After this classification of the sacred books, he introduced to his followers his own system. To restore man's true moral nature there must be "observation" (*kwan*, "to see") of human actions. In regard to opinions, there are three kinds—the true, the common, and the mean. The true is "destructive of all methods and doctrines" (idealism), the popular brings them into existence, and the mean places them all together and chooses the middle path. The deceptions that prevent men from perceiving the truth are threefold: ignorance, the dust of the world, and the activity of the thoughts and senses. These taken in their order hide from view the beauty of the religious life, prevent moral improvement, and operate against pure mental vacancy. The feeling of Buddha, on observing the world in this state, was that men's own notions are false and not to be trusted; that in true knowledge there is no distinction of what is myself and what is not myself, and that the conception of a living personal Buddha should be abandoned. Otherwise men could not return to their true moral nature.

Having proceeded thus far, Chï-k'ai developed his threefold system of observation, which, as he believes it to be conclusive of controversy and perfectly satisfactory, he called *Chï-kwan*, "Perfected observation." This observation is "empty" (*k'ung*), "hypothetical" (*kia*), or "medial" (*chung*). For removing the deceptions that blind men's minds, the most successful method is to view all things in "vacancy" (*k'ung*). For constructing doctrines and institutions, the "inventive" (*kia*) method is the best. For establishing and confirming man's moral nature, the medial method is the most effective. These three modes of viewing the world are complete in each other and inseparable, resembling the three eyes of the god Maha Ishwara. The vacant mode destroys the illusions of the senses, asserting their nothingness, and constructs the virtue of *Prajna* (Knowledge). The inventive mode destroys the deluding effects of the dust of the world, and constructs the virtue of "rescue (from all errors and evils)," *kiai-t'o*. The medial method destroys the delusion that results from ignorance, and constructs the "religious character" (*fa-shen*).

Still fearing lest his followers should be in error as to the method of self-reformation, and fall into one-sided views, he formed a series of what he called the Six connectives.

1. "Reason" (*li*). All living beings, down to the smallest insects, have received a moral nature, and have Buddha within them. Constantly resting in this, they attain their perfection, because the gift of reason is equally bestowed.
2. Names and terms. Although reason is the same in all beings, yet in the course of the world, they will not come to the knowledge and use of it, and therefore instruction is necessary to produce belief and remove what is false.
3. Observation of human action. Instruction having been imparted and belief produced, the threefold mode of viewing the world, as already explained, must then be employed.
4. Likeness. Perfection itself being difficult to gain, the likeness to it may be reached.
5. The true development of human nature.

6. Confirmation. Ignorance is for ever gone. The mind becomes perfectly intelligent.

Each of these six steps being Buddha, the three embodiments of the religious life are thus completed—viz., "embodiment" (*shen*) of the "law" (*fa*), of "recompense" (*pau*), of "renovation" (*hwa*). [4]

Chï-k'ai divided the Buddhist system according to its characteristics into "Eight parts" (*Pa-kiau*):—(1.) The compliant; (2.) The gradual; (3.) The secret; (4.) The indeterminate; (5.) Collection; (6.) Progress; (7.) Distinction; (8.) Completion. The last four are called Chï-k'ai's "Four modes of contemplation" (*Sï-kwan*).

With regard to *Collection*, the sacred books were embraced in three divisions, *king*, *lü*, *lun*, or *sutra*, *vinaya*, and *abidharma*. These include, under the head of suffering, the twenty-five classes of beings that inhabit heaven, earth, and hell; also the eighty-eight causes of human delusion; and further, thirty-seven steps in self-knowledge and improvement. They also embrace the five classes of instructed and enlightened beings:— (1.) The disciple, in several subdivisions; (2.) The wise, in four grades— Sudawan, Sidagam, Anagam, Arhan; (3.) The perfectly intelligent; (4.) The Bodhisattwa; (5.) The Buddha. With regard to *Progress*, there are ten steps—viz., unproductive knowledge, moral nature awaking, the eight convictions of the true sage, perception, first advances, conquest of the passions, the wrong set right, the Pratyeka Buddha, the Bodhisattwa, and the Buddha.

In these successive steps of moral improvement there is some resemblance to the common Buddhist view of the material universe. They regard it as divided according to a moral scale into stages accurately definable. The metempsychosis, by a rigid law of moral retribution, assigns at death the position of every soul in the fifty or sixty grades of being belonging to heaven, earth, and hell. Above these are found the states of Buddha's disciples and that which is itself called Buddha.

With regard to the excellence termed *Distinction*, which is reached by the Bodhisattwa only, there are embraced in it Ten modes of faith, Ten modes of firm adherence, Ten modes of action, Ten inclinations, Ten mental states, together with the highest knowledge in two separate forms.

In reference to the last class, that of *Completion*, everything is viewed as perfect. There are five states which the student may occupy—viz., pleasure. recitation, instructing, putting in practice the ten rules, correct practice of the ten rules.

A series of twenty-five auxiliaries to knowledge and virtue, and of ten modes of observing the true nature and end of human actions, follow the preceding. 5

To give these numerous divisions of Buddhist doctrine more minutely is here unnecessary. So much as is here presented will illustrate the manner in which reflecting Buddhists comment on the doctrines of their religion. It contains a sketch of the opinions of one of the oldest and most influential schools in China, and exhibits the same fondness for a numerical arrangement of propositions ramifying endlessly, which also belongs to other Buddhist schools. This symmetrical classification of doctrines in round numbers pervades the whole Buddhist literature, and suggests a resemblance to the habits of the European schoolmen.

The fundamental subdivision of the T'ien-t'ai system into three modes of contemplation, the empty, the inventive, and the medial, originated with "Nagarjuna" (*Lung shu*), who lived in North-western India about two centuries after Christ. The views which the T'ien-t'ai-kiau have borrowed from him are contained in the "Medial Shastra" (*Chung-lun*), a work in five hundred stanzas based on the principles of the Prajna paramita, and translated into Chinese early in the fifth century. This work gave rise to the *Madhyamika* school (the Central philosophy) in Thibet. The author says in this work: "The methods and doctrines springing from various causes, I declare to be all 'emptiness' (*k'ung*). They may also be called 'invented' (*kia*) names. Further, they may be said to contain the meaning of the medial (*chung*) path." Hwei-wen erected a system on this, as the basis, and Chï-k'ai, following him, moulded it to its present form as the T'ien-t'ai-kiau.

The following extract from a commentary on the *Fa-hwa-king* will illustrate the way in which the principles of this school are applied in interpreting the sacred books:—"All were 'Arhans' (*Lo-hans*) whose defects were obliterated, for whom there was no more suffering, who had obtained benefits for themselves, who had broken all ties, and in their hearts possessed peace." This is the text. The commentator says: "The word Arhan expresses *rank*, and what follows, *character*. Arhan is variously explained as the 'true man,' or the 'extricated man.' Some say it contains three meanings, viz., freedom from birth, killer of robbers in the sense of being delivered from perceptions and sensations, the robbers of the mind, and deserving honour. This is the sense according to the principles of (1.) Collection, and (2.) Progress. But for the two higher principles, (3.) Distinction, and (4.) Completion, the word implies, not only the killing of robbers, but of non-robbers, *i.e.*, the Nirvâna, which in the higher region of these two principles is also deserving of extinction. Freedom from birth expresses their complete rescue from life and death, and that is the meaning of their defects having been obliterated. Because they can give happiness to all the nine classes of beings, therefore they are said to deserve honour. By their embodiment of the religious life, they benefit themselves. By their wisdom, they obtain deliverance from life and death. By expelling ignorance and evil, they kill robbers.

"Interpreting according to the Threefold contemplation, empty, inventive, and medial, the first is exemplified in their wisdom, the second in their expulsion of evil, and the third in their embodiment of the religious life. In the transition from the inventive to the empty, there are also three modifications of the sense, viz., arrival at the central point of contemplation, killing the thieves of ignorance, and keeping the heart from a one-sided position.

"Interpreting according to the contemplation of the heart, following the middle path, and taking the correct view, they do not err on the side of the empty or inventive mode of observation. The sorrow of the heart is gone. When a man sees the true moral nature of his mind, that is called the higher state of confirmation. Like a hidden treasure, reserved for myself, is the benefit which the Arhans have obtained."

When Brahma appears before Buddha as a disciple, the commentary says: "The word *Brahma* means 'leaving the desires, abandoning earthly ties, and ascending to the coloured heavens.' It is also said to mean 'high' and pure.' This Brahma is one of the wheel kings of a single generation, who asks instruction of Buddha, which he receives according to his wish and capacity. Interpreting the idea of *Brahma*, according to that method which observes the heart, it means 'contemplating the removal of all pollutions.'" [6]

These extracts exemplify how the mythological apparatus of the Buddhist Sutras, or "Sacred books of the first class," is explained away. The whole machinery of Buddhas and Bodhisattwas, kings and divinities, disappears under this process. Eastern and Western pantheism are alike in this, that they will not be content with an independent self-evolved structure of metaphysical thought, but assuming the critical office, aim at the overthrow of all the objects of popular belief. Knowledge, self, the absolute—these are the only existences allowed by this arrogant philosophy to remain in the universe. Even these are made identical, and finally explained into nothing.

While the reflecting Buddhists hold these views, they encourage the faith of the vulgar in the Hindoo mythology and the more recent inventions of their own system. Their denial of the reality of worldly phenomena, and of the validity of the information afforded by our senses, has not been a check to popular image worship, but rather promoted it, from the license that it gave them to countenance lying legends and invent new additions *ad libitum* to the Hindoo pantheon.

The special object of the T'ien-t'ai school has been to strike a middle path between the credulous acceptance of the sacred books as literally true, and their entire rejection by extreme idealism. It was thought best to recognise both these modifications of Buddhism as genuine developments of the system, and to add a third reconciling principle which distinguishes the others, compares and combines them, and then chooses the path between them.

In conformity with this view, regulations for the practice of his followers were instituted by Chï-k'ai:—(1.) Constant sitting, to attain the state of *samadhi* or reverie taught to Manjusiri; (2.) Constant moving, to attain another state of *samadhi* taught by Buddha; (3.) Partly sitting and partly moving, to attain the state of *samadhi* taught by him to P'u-hien; (4.) Neither sitting nor moving, to attain still another form of religious reverie.

The regulations for chanting as followed by this school were elaborated by a priest named Fa-chï who lived some centuries after Chï-k'ai. They are very minute, and are intended to produce more reverential feelings in the minds of those engaging in the ceremonial than is common in Buddhist worship. [7]

Footnotes

1. The "Red wall," so called from its colour and precipitous appearance.
2. *T'ien-t'ai-shan-chï.*
3. A.D. 575, Biography in *T'ien-t'ai-han-chï.*
4. *Chï-yue-lu.*
5. *San-kiau-yi-su.*
6. *Fa-hwa-hwei-i.*
7. Regulations of the T'ien-t'ai-kiau, in the liturgical work called *Ta-pei-ts'an.*

CHAPTER IX.

THE BUDDHIST MORAL SYSTEM.

The Ten virtues and Ten vices—The cause of human stupidity is in the passions—The Five prohibitions—The Ten prohibitions—Klaproth's praise of Buddhism—But it is atheistic, and therefore this praise should be qualified—Kindness to animals based on the fiction of transmigration—Buddhism teaches compassion for suffering without inculcating obedience to divine law—Story of Shakyamuni—Sin not distinguished from misery—Buddhists teach that the moral sense is innate—They assign a moral nature to animals—The Six paths of the metempsychosis—Hindoo notions of heaven and hell—Countless ages of joy and suffering—Examples—Exemption from punishment gained by meritorious actions—Ten kings of future judgment—Fate or Karma—Buddhism depreciates heaven and the gods—Buddha not God, but a Saviour—Moral influence of the Paradise of the Western heaven—Figurative interpretation of this legend—The contemplative school identifies good and evil—No moral distinctions in the Nirvâna—Buddhism has failed to produce high morality—The Confucianist condemnation of the Buddhists—Mr. P. Hordern's praise of Buddhism in Birmah—The Birmese intellectually inferior to the Chinese—Kindness to animals known to the Chinese before they received Buddhism—Buddha's reasons for not eating flesh.

THE books of primitive Buddhism exhibit a higher moral tone than is found in the larger works full of metaphysical abstractions, which succeeded them. The "Book of Forty-two Sections," translated in the first century, and belonging to the former class, speaks of Ten vices and Ten virtues as belonging to mankind. The vices are: three of the body—killing, stealing, and adultery; four of the lips—slandering, reviling, lying, and elegant words (uttered with a vicious intention); three of the mind—jealousy, hatred, and "folly" (*ch'i*), the last of which includes not believing in "the Honoured Three" (*Buddha, Dharma, Sanga*), and holding erroneous opinions. The opposites of these are the Ten virtues.

In the same work Buddha says: "That which causes the stupidity and delusion of man is love and the desires." "Man having many faults, if he does not repent, but allows his heart to be at rest, sins will rush upon him like water to the sea. When vice has thus become more powerful it is still harder than before to abandon it. If a bad man becomes sensible of his faults, abandons them and acts virtuously, his sin will day by day diminish and be destroyed, till he obtains full enlightenment."

In the work *Kiau-ch'eng-fa-shu*, the three vices of the mind are described as—covetousness, hatred, and folly. The Ten virtues that correspond to the Ten vices are there stated to be—preserving life, almsgiving, a "pure and virtuous life" (*fan-hing*), peaceful words, yielding words, truthful words, plain unadorned words, abstinence from quarrelling, mercy, and "acting from good causes" (*yin-yuen*).

Hardy, in describing the Buddhism of Ceylon, states the four sins of speech to be—lying, slander, abuse, and unprofitable conversation. The three sins of the mind he states to be—covetousness, malice, and scepticism.

The disciple of Buddha, whether he enters a monastery or wears the prescribed dress and continues in the family, must pledge himself to the five following things:—(1.) not to kill; (2.) not to steal; (3.) not to commit adultery; (4.) not to lie; (5.) not to drink wine. These are called *Wu-kiai*, "The five prohibitions." In Hardy's *Manual of Buddhism*, five evils to be avoided are mentioned—viz., (1.) drinking intoxicating liquors; (2.) gambling; (3.) idleness; (4.) improper association; (5.) frequenting places of amusement.

In the work called *Sheng-t'ien-shih-kiai-king*, "The book of birth in heaven through keeping the ten prohibitions," a Deva informs Buddha that he was born in the "heaven of the Thirty-three Devas" (that of Indra Shakra), as a reward for reverencing the "Three Precious Ones" (Buddha, the Law, and the Priesthood), for not inflicting death, or stealing, or committing adultery, or slandering, or deceiving, or lying, or drinking wine, or eating flesh, or coveting, or holding false opinions.

In the work *Kiau-ch'eng fa-shu*, the Ten prohibitions are stated to be:—(1.) killing; (2.) stealing; (3.) adultery; (4.) lying; (5.) selling wine; (6.) speaking of others' faults; (7.) praising one's-self and defaming others; (8.) parsimony joined with scoffing; (9.) anger, and refusing to be corrected; (10.) reviling the Three Precious Ones.

In the comment on the *Fan-wang-king*, a work of the Great Development school in the Discipline division, by Chĭ-hiü, the Ten prohibitions are identified with the Ten vices, but in the text the prohibitions are given as in the last quotation.

Other lists of prohibitions might be transcribed amounting to two hundred and fifty, and even higher numbers. For these it will be sufficient to refer to the works already mentioned.

Klaproth, having in view these moral precepts, and their effects on the character of nations, speaks of Buddhism as being of all religions next to Christianity in elevating the human race.

He says: "The wild nomades of Central Asia have been changed by it into amiable and virtuous men, and its beneficent influence has been felt even in Northern Siberia."

The beneficent influence of this religion would have been much greater had it recognised the love and fear of God as the first of all the virtues. Buddhism, by ascribing the creation, continuance, and destruction of the world to an ever-changing fate, avoided the necessity of admitting a supreme God. This was the side the Buddhists took in their controversies with the Brahmans in India. Atheism is one point in the faith of the Southern Buddhists. By the Chinese Buddhists each world is held to be presided over by an individual Buddha, but they do not hold that one supreme spirit rules over the whole collection of worlds. Klaproth affirms that, according to, the Buddhists and the other Hindoos, "the universe is animated by a single spirit, individualised under innumerable forms, 'by' (*par*) matter which does not exist except in illusion." This spirit, however, is not God, the universal Creator and Preserver, and separated from the world by His everlasting personality.

Good has resulted doubtless in many instances from the prominent exhibition made by this system of the virtues and vices enumerated. But much more good would have been done if they had rested on a better basis, and been supported by a different view of the future state. The crime of killing rests chiefly on the doctrine of metempsychosis, which ascribes the same immortal soul to animals that it does to man. Faithful Buddhists are told not to kill the least insect, lest in so doing they should cause death to some deceased relative or ancestor whose soul animates the insect. On this account the corresponding virtue is stated to be *fang-sheng*, "to save life," constantly applied by the Buddhist priests and common people of China to the preservation of the lives of animals. The monks are vegetarians for the same reasons. They abstain from flesh because they will not share in the slaughter of living beings. They also construct reservoirs of water near the monasteries, in which fish, snakes, tortoises, and small shell-fish, brought by worshippers of Buddha, are placed to preserve them from death. Goats and other land animals are also given over sometimes to the care of the monks, and it is a custom in some monasteries, as at T'ien-t'ung, near Ningpo, to feed a bird with a few grains of rice just before the morning meal has commenced. When the priest appears at the door, the little bird, which is watching in the neighbourhood, and knows how to act on the occasion, flies to receive the gift.

In the Buddhist account of human sins and duties no obligation is included except the duty of lessening the sum of human misery and promoting happiness. This accords with the anecdote already related of Shakyamuni in his youth. His father, remembering the forewarning of a hermit, that the prince his son would wish to abandon the world, erected for him three palaces, where everything fascinating was placed to keep him from such a purpose. The son of a Deva came down to praise the beauty of the gardens and groves.

But the prince, then eighteen years old, wished to go out and see the city. The king sent him with a wise minister to attend him. A Deva appeared at one of the city gates transformed into an old man resting on a staff. At another gate a Deva appeared as a sick person in pain and helpless. At another gate he saw a corpse attacked by ravens—also a Deva. The prince asked in each case the reason of what he saw. The wise counsellor told him these sufferings came from the natural state of the world, and could not be avoided. People must grow old, must suffer from sickness, and must die. The prince was not satisfied, and the next day, seeing a Deva dressed as a monk, he dismounted from his horse and asked him who he was. The reply was, "A Shamen [1] who has left the world." The prince asked him why he had left the world. He said, because he saw men exposed to the evils of birth, old age, sickness, and death; he therefore left the world to seek truth and save living beings. The disguised Deva then ascended into the air and disappeared.

At nineteen, assisted by the Devas, Shakyamuni is said to have gone through the air on horseback two hundred and fifty miles to Baga, a mountain belonging to the Himalayas. Here he lived as a hermit for six years, and became prepared for the office he was to assume.

According to the view thus presented of the great object of Buddha's teaching, it is to deliver men from suffering. This is done by persuading them to enter on the monastic or hermit life, and act in obedience to the directions of Buddha. This system looks on mankind as involved in misery rather than guilt. The Ten vices are rather to be regarded as faults, into which men fall from delusion and ignorance, than positive sins. The common people in China, whose phraseology is extensively infected with Buddhist ideas, see in every attack of sickness, and in other misfortunes, a close connection with "sin" (*tsui*). They hold that sin is the cause of suffering. Yet they do not mean by this wilful sin, but some improper act done unconsciously, or in childhood, as treading on an insect, wasting rice-crumbs, or misusing paper that has the native characters upon it. Or they refer the calamity to the sins of a former life. Hence they regard themselves as more to be pitied than blamed for the *tsui* or "sin" of which their ill fortune gives evidence.

This is an example of the mode in which the better tendencies of the Buddhist system are neutralised by its omissions. Its moral precepts, good as most of them are, would have more power, and the true character of sin be more felt by the people, if the authority of God were recognised as the great reason for acting well—the source of moral obligation.

Buddhism shook the faith of the Chinese in Heaven as a personal ruler, and put the Buddhas and Bodhisattwas in the place of that personal ruler. The effect of Buddhism in part was to urge the Chinese mind to see in Heaven only impersonal and material power. Thus the good effect of its moral teaching was neutralised; and then the Chinese had good moral teaching before.

The question that has been raised by European moralists as to whether man has from his natural constitution an inborn moral sense, is decided by the Buddhists, though without holding a controversy on the subject, in the affirmative. They may be said to appeal to a natural conscience, when they teach that all men have within them a good moral nature, and that this principle of good is only prevented from making men virtuous and happy by contact with the world and the delusions of the senses. This is similar to the Confucian doctrine, that all men are born good, and it is only by falling into evil habits subsequently that they become vicious. Most systems of morals, indeed, [2] in words or by implication, admit the existence of conscience, because all men possess it, and cannot be made to understand moral distinctions without it.[3] The existence of a system of virtues and vices shows the operation of conscience on the maker of it, as the use of that system in moral instruction involves an appeal to conscience in the disciple. The identification of conscience, however, with natural goodness, by the Confucianists and the Buddhists, obscures its true character as the judge between right and wrong. And to tell men that they are naturally good is not only assuming, in compliment to human nature, a fact that should be proved, but it is also likely to induce those who are thus taught to look leniently on their own vices as originating solely in the influences of the outside world. The feebleness of the Buddhist appeal to conscience, as the source of moral obligation, is further increased by its assigning the same originally good nature to each member of the animal creation that it does to man.

The motives to well-doing, drawn from a future state of retribution in this system, are derived from the Hindoo popular account of heaven and hell. The Six life-paths into which living beings can be born are—(1.) "Devas" (gods); (2.) men; (3.) "Asuras" (monsters); (4.) "hell" (naraka); (5.) hungry ghosts; (6.) animals. The first three are assigned to the good, the latter three to the wicked. The moral action is called *yin* (cause), and its recompense *kwo* (fruit). All beings, whether virtuous or vicious, continue to be re-born in one of these six states, until saved by the teaching of Buddha.

Buddha said: "To leave the three evil states is difficult. When the state of man has been attained, to leave the female sex and be born in the male, is difficult. To have the senses and mind and body all sound is hard. When this is attained, to be born in Central India is hard." He continues to say, that to meet Buddha and be instructed, to be born in the time of a good king, to be born in the family of a Bodhisattwa, and to believe with the heart in the Three Honoured Ones, are all difficult.

Buddha said,[4] in a discourse delivered in the heaven of Indra Shakra, that whatever good man or woman heard the name of Ti-tsang Bodhisattwa, and in consequence performed an act of praise or worship, or repeated that Bodhisattwa's name, or made an offering to him, or drew a picture of him, such a person would certainly be born in the heaven of Indra Shakra.

The same Bodhisattwa tells the mother of Buddha, who resides in the paradise just mentioned, that "disobedience to parents, with slaying, and wounding, are punished with an abode in the place of suffering called *Wu-kien-ti-yü*. Slandering the Three Precious Ones, or wounding the person of Buddha, or dishonouring the sacred books, or breaking the vows, or stealing from a monk, are punished in a similar way. Their punishment will last for ten millions of millions of *kalpas*. Then their sin being compensated for by sufficient suffering, they will be released.

"If a woman with an ugly countenance and sickly constitution prays to this Bodhisattwa, she will, for a million of *kalpas*, be born with a beautiful countenance." If any men or women perform music before the image of the same deity, sing, and offer incense, they shall have hundreds and thousands of spirits to protect them day and night, so that no unpleasant sound may enter their ears. Any one who slanders or ridicules a worshipper of this Bodhisattwa will be transported to the "Avichi naraka" (*O-pi ti-yü*) till the end of this *kalpa*. He will then be born a wandering hungry ghost, and, after a thousand *kalpas* become an animal. After a thousand kalpas more he will again become a man.

Such are a few specimens of the doctrine of retribution as taught to the popular mind. It is easy to see that such sensual conceptions of the future existence of man must degrade the common notions of the people on duty and virtue. The objects for which the common people in China worship in the Buddhist temples are almost all of a very inferior nature. Religious worship, which ought to concern the recovery of man to pure virtue, and the restoration of direct communication with God by the forgiveness of sin, is changed into an instrument for acquiring various kinds of material happiness.

The opinion the Buddhists hold on the forgiveness of sin is, that it can be attained by repentance and meritorious actions. A definite amount of gifts and worship will gain the removal of a corresponding amount of sin and its attendant suffering. Thus, a filial daughter, by a certain number of days spent in worshipping a Bodhisattwa, or a Buddha, can obtain the rescue of a mother from hell.

In the popular view of the future state, the Hindoo king of death, "Yama" (*Yen-lo*) holds a high place as the administrator of the punishments of hell. Nine others are joined with him of Chinese origin. They are called the Ten kings. The wicked at death are conducted to them to receive judgment.

The decree by which men are born into the Six states of the metempsychosis is merely that of fate, expressed in the words *yin-kwo*, "cause and effect," or, employing one factor only, *yin-yuen*, "causation," or "fate" (*karma*). "Good actions" are also sometimes called *yin-yuen*, because they ultimately bring happiness to the doer.

The motive to a good life, drawn from heavenly happiness, cannot be considered a strong one, when the Devas and their felicity are systematically depreciated, as they are in Buddhism. The "Devas" (or popular Hindoo gods; in Chinese, *t'ien*) are all mortal, and limited in power. The state of man may be so elevated as to approach to that of the paradise of the Devas. Some men attain to nearly the same power as the gods, *e.g.*, Krishna. Southey, in the *Curse of Kehama*, has made that personage, although a man, a terror to the kings of the Devas, and such a representation is in accordance with Hindoo notions. So in Chinese Buddhist temples, the visitor sees the highest of celestial beings listening humbly to Buddha.

It may be said that it is not correct to institute or imply a parallel between God as He is in the view of the Christian, and the Hindoo deities. It may be said that a parallel between God and Buddha would be more just. But Buddha is a world-born man, who washes away his sins like others, by penances, offerings, and the teaching of some enlightened instructor. He is not said to create the universe, nor to act as the judge of mankind. He is simply a teacher of the most exalted kind, who, by superior knowledge, passes out of the world of delusion, and gradually attains the Nirvâna. His attitude towards his disciples is simply that of an instructor, not an authoritative superior. The tie by which the disciple is attached to him is that of voluntary not compulsory obedience.

In fact, the character ascribed to Buddha is rather that of a Saviour than that of God. The object of his life and teaching is to rescue living beings from their misery. While such is the character of Buddha as he is described in books, he is, as an object of popular worship, like the great Bodhisattwas, simply regarded as a powerful divinity. A brief notice will here be taken of the ethical views of some of the Chinese sects. The Tsing-tu school substitutes a paradise of purely Buddhist invention for that of Hindoo mythology. It makes birth in the Western heaven, the abode of Amitabha Buddha, the reward of virtue. The description of this paradise consists entirely of things pleasing to the senses. It is popularly regarded as real, but the founder of the Yün-ts'i school in his commentary on the "Amitabha Sutra," [5] explains it as figurative. According to this explanation, the Western heaven means the moral nature, confirmed, pure, and at rest. Amitabha means the mind, clear, and enlightened. The rows of trees mean the mind cultivating the virtues. The music means the harmony of virtues in the mind. The flowers, and particularly the lotus, mean the mind opening to consciousness and intelligence. The beautiful birds mean the mind becoming changed and renovated.

It is evident that, on adopting this mode of commenting on the fable of the Western heaven, it cannot any longer be honestly held out as a future state of reward, to attract men to good actions.

The object of this figurative interpretation of the Western paradise of Amitabha was, doubtless, to redeem the Tsing-tu school from the discredit into which it had fallen, by abandoning the Nirvâna in favour of a sensual heaven. The original inventors of the fiction must also have had such a notion of it as that here given, while they did not try to prevent its being accepted as real by the ignorant and uninquiring.

In the contemplative school, founded by Bodhidharma, the distinction of vice and virtue is lost. To the mind that is given up to its own abstract meditations, the outer world becomes obliterated. A person who attends simply to his own heart may revile Buddha without sin, for nothing is sin to him. He does not make offerings or pray. All actions are the same to him. This system; however, is not in opposition to ethical distinctions. It only aims to enter a higher sphere. It seeks to attain a sort of Nirvâna even in the present life.

In the books of this school, as in others where the unreality of all sensible phenomena is maintained, virtue and vice occupy an inferior position. These notions only come into existence through the imperfection of the present state. They disappear altogether when an escape from it is effected, by admission into the higher region of pure enlightenment. Virtue and vice, life and death, happiness and misery, the antithetical states originated in the world of delusions to which we belong, are all condemned together as constituting a lower state of existence. All beings should strive to be freed from them, and to rise by Buddha's teaching to that perfection where every such diversity, moral or physical, will be lost in unity. The Nirvâna does not admit any such distinctions as those just mentioned. It is absolute and pure illumination, without anything definite attached to it, whether good or evil, pain or pleasure. Thus there is no place for ethics, except in the lower modes of life.

It is common for intelligent priests in China of the contemplative school to defend their system of idolatry by saying that they do not worship images themselves. They are intended for the ignorant who cannot comprehend the deeper principles of their religion. Religion being purely a matter of the heart, offerings and prostrations are really unnecessary. This exemplifies how what is regarded as a highly virtuous action in the common people, ceases to be so in the case of one who, as he thinks, has made some progress towards the state of Buddha. According to this view the consistent Buddhist will offer worship to no being whatever. He simply aims to raise himself above all the common feelings of human life.

We cannot wonder that the Buddhist system of ethics having such deficiencies and such faults as have been pointed out, has failed to produce high morality among its votaries. The mass of the people have gained from it the notion of a future retribution, but what is the use of this when the promised state beyond death consists merely of clumsy fiction? The metempsychosis, administered by a moral fate, has only provided them with a convenient means for charging their sinfulness and their misfortunes on a former life. What virtue the people have among them is due to the Confucian system. Buddhism has added to it only idolatry, and a false view of the future state, but has not contributed to make the people more virtuous.

Klaproth complains of "a worthy and learned English missionary" (Dr. Marshman of Serampore) for saying, "Unhappily for mankind, Buddhism... was now fitted to spread its baneful influence to any extent."

These modes of expression are not, however, by any means too strong to describe the effects of this religion in China if we accept the Confucianist view of Buddhism. No thorough-going disciple of Confucius would think this language too strong if only Buddhism be judged from the standpoint of political and social morality. Surely if the Confucianist cannot see how the monk, who forsakes his family and his duties as a working citizen, is to be excused from heavy condemnation, the Christian also may be permitted to criticise with severity a system which denies the authority of God, identifies the moral nature of men and animals, teaches mankind to look to man instead of to God for redemption, and amuses the imagination with the most monstrous fictions of the unseen world and of the future state.

The morality of Buddhism has received very high praise from more recent writers. Professor Max Müller says, "The moral code of Buddhism is one of the most perfect the world has ever known." Mr. P. Hordern, the Director of Public Instruction in Birmah, says, "The poor heathen is guided in his daily life by precepts older and not less noble than the precepts of Christianity. Centuries before the birth of Christ men were taught by the life and doctrine of one of the greatest men who ever lived lessons of the purest morality. The child was taught to obey his parents and to be tender of all animal life, the man to love his neighbour as himself, to be true and just in all his dealings, and to look beyond the vain shows of the world for true happiness. Every shade of vice was guarded by special precepts. Love in its widest sense of universal charity was declared to be the mother of all the virtues, and even the peculiarly Christian precepts of the forgiveness of injuries and the meek acceptance of insult were already taught in the farthest East.

"Throughout Birmah it is a daily thing to see men, women, and children kneeling on the road side, their hands clasped, and their faces turned devoutly to a distant pagoda; while at the weekly festivals, or the full moons, the devotions of the mass of the population is among the most interesting spectacles in the whole East."

It is otherwise in China. Though the Buddhists have good precepts they are very much neglected, even in the teaching. Books containing hard metaphysical dogma such as the non-existence of matter, form much more the subject of daily reading. The monks are subject constantly to the Confucianist criticism that they are not filial to parents nor useful working members of the commonwealth. A widely-extended monastic system does not approve itself to the Chinese political consciousness any more than it has done to European governments in times of revolution. The charge of laziness and neglect of social duties was made the ground of persecution in former days. At present, while Confucianism has ceased to persecute Buddhism, it has never withdrawn its indictment against it on the ground of morality. Indeed, all the force of the moral teaching of the Chinese is in Confucianism and not in Buddhism. It is the moral sense of the Chinese themselves that is energetic and influential so far as they are really a moral people. The Buddhist moral code is feebleness itself compared with the Confucianist. This is partly because it is entangled by the coexistence with it of monkery as a life, and of the metempsychosis and metaphysical nihilism as dogma.

Then in regard to the power of Buddhism to elevate a people above the vain shows of the world and render then devotional, the conclusion to be drawn from the effect of this religion in the Chinese is very different from that adopted by Mr. Hordern in regard to Birmah. The Chinese intellect is strong and independent in its judgments, and it does not accept the fictions of Buddhism. The Hindoo mind cannot dominate the Chinese mind, and the contemplative life has no attractions for the countrymen of Confucius. The foreign resident in China does not witness the appearance of devotion which has won the admiration of Mr. Hordern in Birmah.

The power shown by Buddhism to win the faith of the Birmese I should rather trace to the superiority of the Hindoo race over the mountain tribes of the Indo-Chinese peninsula. The Birmese belong, with the Thibetans, to the Bod race, which, having no intellectual development of its own, accepted the Hindoo religion when brought them by the Buddhist teachers. The superiority of Hindoo arts and civilisation helped Buddhism to make this conquest. Bishop Bigandet [6] says: "The Birmese want the capability to understand the Buddhist metaphysics. If the Buddhist moral code in itself has the power to influence a people so far as to render them virtuous and devotional, independently of the element of intellectual superiority, we still lack the evidence of it.

"The success of Buddhism is in this respect the reverse of the success of Christianity, which, originating in Judea, subjugated both Greece and Rome without aid from intellectual superiority."

I just add here that the Confucianists do not allow that kindness to animals was first taught them by Buddhism. They find it in their own ancient books. Thus Mencius made the compassion felt by a prince, Tsi Siuen-wang, for a bullock about to be slaughtered, a ground for his exhibiting compassion still more for the people he governed.

He had been distressed at the shuddering of the bullock chosen for sacrifice, and ordered it to be changed for a sheep, which was done. Confucianism assumes that pity for animals is natural for the human heart. The mother of Mencius moved her residence from the neighbourhood of a butcher's shop because she would not have her boy, while of tender years, witness daily that which would make him cruel.

Yet it cannot fairly be denied that beneficial effects must follow from the great prominence and publicity assigned to compassion as an attribute of Buddha to be imitated by every devout believer. The salvation of multitudes from suffering is held up as his great achievement, and to this he was prompted by disinterested pity.

This the Confucianists would probably admit, while they would never allow that there is any ground to believe in the Buddhist metempsychosis, on which pity for animals is often made to rest for its basis. With Buddhist temples and monks everywhere, the Chinese do not accept the teaching that the souls of men migrate into animals, nor do the monks cordially maintain it.

Among the reasons the Buddhists give for sparing the life of all animals, they do not mention the duty of not inflicting unnecessary pain, nor do they say that Buddha has a sovereign power to make laws, and he having made this law it must be obeyed.

Their reasons are of a lower sort, or they are based on dogmatised necessity. This, like other matters, is by the Buddhists treated in a thoroughly utilitarian and selfish way. Only in one point it is not so. They are invariably conscious of "moral fate," the *karma*, pervading the universe by an inevitable and unconquerable force. Kindness to animals is sure to bring happiness, as cruelty will cause misfortune.

The following are the reasons given by Buddha for abstinence from animal food:—

First, In the endless changes of the metempsychosis, persons in the relation to me of any of the six divisions of kindred have become, from time to time, some of the animals used for food. To avoid eating my relations I ought to abstain.

Second, The smell and taste are not clean.

Third, The smell causes fear among the various animals.

Fourth, To eat animal food prevents charms and other magical devices from taking effect.

The writer who invented these reasons and put them in the mouth of Buddha, did not add the certainty of the retribution of the *karma*, as an additional motive for showing compassion to objects possessed of life, but this is understood and lies underneath all Buddhistic thought.

Footnotes

1. In Sanscrit, *Shramana;* but according to the commentator on the "Life of Buddha," Shakamananga, meaning "Diligence and cessation."
2. Paley and those who side with him, who have attempted to construct a moral system without a natural sense of right and wrong in man, must be excepted.
3. Morality is now accounted for by evolution. The School of Darwin and Spencer refuses to accept moral law as eternal. Yet all the Asiatic religions make it their basis.
4. Vide *Ti-tsang-king*.
5. *O-mi-to-king-su-ts'au*, by Lieu-sï-ta-shï.
6. See *Vie de Gaudama*, p. 412.

CHAPTER X.

THE BUDDHIST CALENDAR.

National festivals—Festivals in honour of celestial beings—In honour of the Buddhas and Bodhisattwas—In honour of characters in Chinese Buddhist history—Supplemental anniversaries—Singhalese Buddhists keep a different day for Buddha's birthday—In the T'ang dynasty Hindoo astronomers reformed the calendar—Gaudamsiddha—The week of India and Babylon known to the Chinese—Word mit for Sunday—Peacock Sutra—The Hindoo Rahu and Ketu.

ONE of the most instructive illustrations of a religion is its calendar. Not only do the fasts and festivals kept by a people point out in succession who are the personages held by them in the highest honour; they also contain an epitome of the history and doctrines of the religion they believe, and especially aid in opening to observation the popular religious life.

The work called *Ts'ing-kwei*, "Regulations of the Priesthood," contains instructions for the observance of all fasts and festivals through the year. From it are extracted the following details of anniversaries:—

1. NATIONAL.

Emperor's birthday.—The ceremonial for this anniversary lasts a week, embracing three days before and three after the day in question. It is called *Sheng-tsie*, "Sacred festival."

Empress's birthday.

Day of receiving an imperial message at the monastery.—Six persons are sent out "five *li*" (nearly two miles) to meet it. On its approach, the monks, headed by their chief, issue from the monastery, and bow their foreheads to the ground three times.

Four monthly feasts.—These are at the new and full moons, and on the 8th and 23d of the month. They are called *Kin-ming sï-chai*, "The four feasts illustriously decreed." The last two words refer to a decree of an emperor of the Sui dynasty in A.D. 584, requiring the special observance of the monthly feasts in the 1st, 5th, and 9th months; because then the great Southern continent was prayed for, in which China is included.

Anniversaries of emperors' deaths.—Those of the present dynasty only are included.

2. CELESTIAL BEINGS

Day of worshipping the Devas (Kung-T'ien).—All the chief personages, whether Devas, spirits, demons, Asuras, Rakshas, &c., of the Hindoo older mythology, are worshipped on this occasion. This observance rests for its authority on the *Kin-kwang-ming-king*, "The Bright Sutra of Golden Light."

Eclipses of the Sun and Moon.—In the services for these days, the sun and moon are addressed as "Bodhisattwas" (*P'u-sa*), and the power of Buddha is invoked to deliver them. Hence the name of the service, *Hu-jï, Hu-yue,* "Delivering the sun and moon." The prayers offered for them are considered as gratitude for their light.

Sacrifice to the Moon, 8th month, 15th day.—The ground for this observance is that this day is, according to national tradition, the moon's birthday. As in the service for eclipses, *Namo,* "Honour to," the introductory formula of worship, is used in addressing the moon. She is called in full *Yue-kung-t'ai-yin-tsun-t'ien-p'u-sa,* "The moon in her mansion, luminary of night, honoured Deva and Bodhisattwa."

Prayer for fine weather.—Prayer to various Buddhas, and other divinities.
Prayer for rain.—Worship is performed towards the East, and prayers offered to the Dragon king, the various Buddhas, &c.

Prayer for snow.—Ditto.

Prayer against locusts.—To various Devas and spirits.

Prayer to Wei-to (Veda).—The Deva Wei-to is the protector of the Buddhist religion. When the supplies of the monastery fail, he is prayed to, to replenish them. He is chief general of the army of the four Mahadevas.

Birthday of Wei-to, 6th month, 3d day; according to some the 13th day.—Wei-to is a deity of Hindoo mythology, who protects three of the four continents into which the world is divided. (See Remusat's Notes to *Foĕ kouĕ ki*.)

Birthdays of the divine protectors of the monasteries.—They are three:—(1.) Hwa-kwang, 9th month, 28th day; (2.) *Lung-wang*, or *Naga-raja*, the "Dragon King;" (3.) *Kwan-ti*, the "God of war," 5th month, 13th day, according to the common account; but according to his biography in the national annals, 6th month, 24th day. These three personages take the place of eighteen worshipped in India. One of them is the well-known hero of the "Three Kingdoms." They receive the same honours that are awarded to Wei-to.

Birthday of the Kitchen god, 6th month, 24th day, 8th month, 3d day, and 12th month, 24th day.—The Buddhists say, to excuse themselves for adopting a Tauist superstition, that the Kitchen god they worship is not the Tsau-kiün venerated commonly by the people, but a king of the "Kinnaras" (a fabulous race of celestial beings), who became a Chinese priest in the T'ang dynasty, and was appointed at death to preside over the vegetarian diet of the monks. This is a lame defence of what is evidently a self-interested accommodation to popular notions.

3. THE BUDDHAS AND BODHISATTWAS.

Birthday of Shakyamuni, 4th month, 8th day.—He is also called Buddha, "Tathâgata" or *Julai*, and Gautama, and is revered as *Pun-shï*, the "Teacher of the world during the present *kalpa.*"

Anniversary of Shakyamuni's elevation to the rank of Buddha, 12th month, 8th day.—The phrase in use is *Ch'eng-tau*, "Attained the summit of knowledge and virtue."

Anniversary of Buddha's entrance into the Nirvâna, 2d month, 15th day.

Birthday of Yo-shï Fo (The Buddha who instructs in healing, Bhaishajyaguru Buddha), *9th month, 30th day.*—The world governed by this Buddha is in the East.

Birthday of O-mi-to Fo or "Amida" (Amitabha) *Buddha, 11th month, 17th day.*—The Buddha who rules in the universe to the west of that governed by Shakya, and grants the request of all those who pray to him to admit them to the Western heaven.

Birthday of Mi-li Fo (Maitreya Buddha), *1st month, 1st day.*—The Buddha who is to succeed Shakyamuni in the government of the world. Maitreya was visited in one of the paradises by Shakyamuni, and foretold his destiny.

Birthday of the female Buddha, Chun-ti, 3d month, 6th day.—Great powers of sorcery are attributed to this personage.

Birthday of "Wen-shu p'u-sa" (Manjusiri Bodhisattwa), *4th month, 4th day.*—One of the Bodhisattwas of Northern Buddhism.

Birthday of "P'u-hien p'u-sa" (Samantabhadra), *2d month, 21st day.*—A fictitious Bodhisattwa of Northern Buddhism.

Birthday of "Kwan-shï-yin p'u-sa" (Avalôkitêshwara), *2d month, 19th day.*—This fabulous Bodhisattwa has in China been usually represented with female attributes. In the *Fa-hwa-king*, *Kwan-yin* is described as being able to assume any form at pleasure, whether that of Buddhas, Devas, men, or others, and as being guided in such voluntary metamorphoses by a constant desire to proclaim the Buddhist doctrine to those who need it, in the form most likely to effect the object. Kwan-yin is thus able to save any of the inhabitants of the *Saha* (or Saba) world, *i.e.*, the present race of mankind. When *Kwan-yin* is translated, not inappropriately, "Goddess of mercy," it should be remembered that female attributes are only temporarily assumed by the Bodhisattwa in question. (See the "Kwan-yin" section, near the end of the *Fa-hwa-king*.)

Birthday of Ta-shï-chï p'u-sa, 7th month, 13th day.—The position of this Bodhisattwa is to the right of Amitabha Buddha, while Kwan-yin takes the left. They are styled together, "the Three Sages of the West" (*Si-fang-san-sheng*).

Birthday of Ti-tsang p'u-sa, 7th month, 30th day.

4. CHARACTERS IN CHINESE BUDDHIST HISTORY.

Anniversary of the death of "Bodhidharma" (Ta-mo), 10th month, 5th day.—The first of the six patriarchs.

Death of Pe-Chang, 1st month, 19th day.—He was a teacher of Bodhidharma's system in the T'ang dynasty. He wrote the work *Ts'ing-kwei* from which these notices of fasts and festivals are taken.

Death of Chï-k'ai, 11th month, 24th day.—The founder of the T'ien-t'ai school.

Death of Hien-sheu, 11th month, 14th day.—A founder of a school bearing his name, and advocating the "Great Development" system (*Ta-ch'eng*).

Death of Tau-siuen, 10th month, 3d day.—A founder of the Discipline school.

Death of Hwei-yuen, 8th month, 6th day.—A founder of the Tsing-tu school.

Death of the founder of the monastery,—also of a priest's own religious instructor, of the priests who admitted him to the vows, and of his parents.

5. SUPPLEMENTARY ANNIVERSARIES.

Commencement of summer (Li-hia), 4th month, 16th day.—This anniversary is traced to the usage of the earliest Hindoo Buddhists, who, when summer arrived, came together and remained associated under strict monastic rule during the hot months. This period over, they began their begging excursions afresh.

"Yü-lan-p'en" (U-lam) ceremony, for feeding hungry ghosts, 7th month, 15th day.—The authority for this festival is the *Yü-lan-p'en Sutra*, translated into Chinese about A.D. 270. It terminates the summer, as the preceding began it.

End of summer, 7th month, 16th day.

Commencement and end of winter (Li-tung, Kiai-tung), 10th month, 15th day, and 1st month, 15th day.

First day of the year.—Special worship.

Birthday of Shakra, 1st month, 9th day.—Shakra, or Indra, god of the atmosphere, is, in the modern editions of *Pe-chang-ts'ing-kwei*, "Manual of Buddhist Regulations and Festivals," identified with the well-known Tauist divinity *Yü-ti*. Oriental religions are so mutually complimentary, that they sometimes adopt each other's divinities without scruple. The Sanscrit 'Indra Shakra' is rendered in Chinese *Ti-shï* (formerly *shak*).

Birthday of "Yo-wang p'u-sa" (Bhâishajyarâja), "Medical king and Bodhisattwa," 4th month, 15th day.

Birthday of the Bodhisattwa "Lung-shu" (Nagarjuna), or "Dragon-tree," 7th month, 25th day.—He was the fourteenth patriarch, and author of the "Hundred Discourses," one of the most noted of the Buddhist Shastras.

Birthday of the ancient Buddha Jan-teng, "Light lamp" (Dipankara Buddha), 8th month, 22d day.—Shakyamuni in a former kalpa was a disciple of this Buddha.

Winter solstice.—Special worship.

Birthday of the Bodhisattwa Hwa-yen, 12th month, 29th day.

The method of observing these anniversaries, and the prayers to be used, are very minutely detailed in the book from which these notices are translated.

The dates are those of the lunar months of the Chinese national almanac. It may be doubted whether more than a very few of them are identical with the festivals of the Southern Buddhists, viz., those of Ceylon, Siam, and Birmah, there being several of the great Bodhisattwas who are not mentioned in works by foreign authors treating of the Buddhism of those countries.

In Ceylon the prevalent legend of Gautama's life states that he was born on the day of the full moon in the second month of spring. This differs irreconcilably.

In this popular calendar, there is no mention of anything astronomical; yet in the T'ang dynasty Buddhist calculators from India were invited to undertake the improvement of the imperial calendar.

Gaudamsiddha, in the eighth century, published a work called *Kieu-chï-li*. It is a translation from a Hindoo original. In it the days of the week are apportioned among the planets in the following order: *Yung-hwo*, "Mars;" *Ch'en-sing*, "Mercury;" *Sui-sing*, "Jupiter;" *T'ai-pe*, "Venus;" *Chen-sing*, "Saturn." [1]

These planets, with the sun and moon, form the *ts'i-yau*, "seven bright celestial objects." They constitute the mythological week of seven days, which sprang up in Babylonia, and spread to India, and also to Europe in the days of the Roman empire.

Some Chinese almanacs call Sunday the day of *Mit*, the Persian "Mithras," a name for the sun. *Mit* is spoken of as a *Hwei-hwei* word. This term *Hwei-hwei* is one of the names for the Persian language among the Chinese. It is the word *ouighour*.

In the *Kung-ch'io-king*, "Peacock Sutra," the days of the week are also given. This work is a translation by a Chinese priest named Yi-tsing. When Mr. Wylie was visiting Peking on one occasion, he went with me to a monastery to consult the "Peacock Sutra" in the library. We were courteously received, and allowed to take it home with us for a few days.

Many superstitious beliefs and observances native to India were imported to China by the Hindoo Buddhists. They taught much that was not at all purely Buddhist. The education they received embraced a wide range. Metaphysics, astronomy, medicine, and other subjects were taught in India in the old times of Buddhist prosperity, probably much as they are now in the lamaseries of Mongolia.

Thus the ascending and descending nodes of the moon's orbit were known as two monsters, called "Rahu" and "Ketu," in modern Chinese, *Lo-heu* and *Ki-tu*. At eclipses, the Chinese story of a wild dog eating the sun and moon is derived from this piece of Hindoo mythology. In native almanacs these names are preserved in the nomenclature of astrology, and the conception is encouraged that the earth's shadow crossing the moon is a dark heavenly body, and a sort of planet of a dark nature, becoming risible only at eclipses.

The Indian year of three seasons is described, but no attempt has been made to interfere with the Chinese seasons of three months each. The Buddhists have arranged their calendar of festivals and fasts to suit the Chinese months.

Footnotes

1. See *Chinese Recorder*, 1872. Mr. Wylie, "On the Knowledge of a weekly Sabbath in China," pp. 40-45. But add to Mr. Wylie's very full and interesting statements, that *Mit* is "Mithras" here, and in page 8.

CHAPTER XI.

RELATION OF BUDDHISM TO THE OLDER HINDOO MYTHOLOGY.

Buddhism accepted the Hindoo mythology, with the sacred books of the Brahmans, so far as it agreed with its own dogmas—The gods Indra, Brahma, and Ishwara listen as disciples to Buddha—Eight classes of Devas—Four kings of Devas—Yakshas—Mahoragas—Pretas—Maras—Yama, king of the dead—Creation is denied to the Hindoo gods in the Chung-lun and other works.

FOLLOWING the guidance of the Buddhist books, the existence of the Vedas and their mythology at least five or six centuries before the Christian era must be regarded as an established fact. Religious divisions had then already arisen in the social life of the Hindoos, and numerous adherents of all castes were joining the newly-raised standard of Buddhism. Colonel Sykes and others have maintained the hypothesis that Buddhism was the original religion of Hindostan, and that the Vedas with their religion, the four castes, and the Sanscrit language itself were all invented at a later date by the Brahmans. This conjecture has little to support it from any source of evidence, and is perfectly untenable when recourse is had for information to the Buddhist books. From them it is clear that the Brahmans were in antagonism with the system of Shakyamuni from the first, that the four Vedas were already venerated as the sacred books of the nation, and that the truth of their mythology was not denied by the founder of Buddhism or his followers. So far from opposing the popular belief in such beings as Indra and Yama, the Asuras, Devas, and Gandharvas, they are included in the mythological *personnel* of the new religion, and these names have thus become known from Japan to Persia, and from Java to the Altai mountains. No mythology perhaps has ever spread so far as the Hindoo, forming as it does a part of the people's religion in all Buddhist countries, as well as in its mother-land.

An account of the opening scene of the *Saddharma-pundarika*, or "Lotus of the Good Law," in Chinese *Fa-hwa-king*, will show the place assigned in the Sutras of the Great Development class to these fictitious beings. The Sanscrit names in most instances are taken from Burnouf's translation of the Nepaulese original.

"Thus have I heard. On a time Buddha was residing at the city 'Rajagriha' (*Wang-she*), on the mountain Gridhrakuta, with two thousand Bikshus, all of them Arhans." Here follow the names of many of Buddha's disciples. "There were also two thousand more, some having knowledge and some having none. *Ma-ha-pa-ja-pa-ti*[1] (Mahâprajâpatî) came with female disciples and their followers, in all six thousand." "Of Bodhisattwas, eighty thousand also came." "Their names are Manjusiri, Kwan-shï-yin, &c." There came also *Shak-de-wan-yin* (Shakra, the Indra of the Devas),[2] with a retinue of twenty thousand sons of Devas. There were also the sons of the Devas Chandra, Samantagandha, and Ratnaprabha. Besides these there were the four "Great kings" of the Devas (*Maharaja*), with a suite of ten thousand sons of Devas. Then there were the sons of the 'Deva Ishwara' (*Tsï-tsai-t'ien*) and of the 'Deva Mahêshwara' (*Ta-tsï-tsai-t'ien*), and their retinue of thirty thousand sons of Devas. The lord of the universe "Saba" (*Saha*), the 'King of the Brahma heaven' (*Fan-t'ien-wang*) also came, with the two great Brahmas, Shikhin and Jyotishprabha, and their retinue of twenty thousand. There were also eight 'Dragon kings' (*Nagaraja*), with their retinues, four kings of the Kinnaras, four of the Gandharvas, four of the Asuras, and four of the

Garudas. The son of Waîdêhî, Ajatashatru king of Magadha (Bahar) and father of Ashôka, with a suite of many thousands, was also there."

These constitute Buddha's audience while he delivers the instructions contained in this Sutra. Most of the names, the descriptive passages, and many notices of the retinues of the kings, are omitted for brevity. The whole account, however, in the Chinese version is one-third shorter than in that of the French translator, who has followed the Sanscrit text. Kumarajiva did not scruple to pare off the redundancies of this and other works that he translated, which is perhaps one reason of their permanent popularity.

Two of the principal Hindoo divinities occur in this extract, Shakra and Brahma. The latter is the first in the well-known triumvirate of gods, *Brahma, Vishnu,* and *Shiva,* or the "Creator," "Preserver," and "Destroyer." Here he occupies a humbler position, being merely the disciple of Buddha. Shakra or Indra is met with in Buddhist legends more frequently than Brahma. In some Chinese temples their images are said to form a pair among the auditors of Shakyamuni. The Buddhist compilation, *Fa-yuen-chu-lin*, contains an extract from the "Central Agama Sutra," where several names by which Shakra is commonly known are explained. Indra, his most frequent appellation, is a term of office, "Lord" or "Ruler," and as such is translated into Chinese by *Ti* or *Chu*. It is often applied to others of the chief Devas or gods with distinctive names. Two other Brahmas will be observed to accompany the chief Brahma.

The word Ishwara, rendered by *tsï-tsai*, "self-existent," is the term used by missionaries in India for God, in the Christian sense. Mr. Wenger's letter, inserted in Dr. Legge's *Notions of the Chinese concerning God and Spirits*, says, that this term is applied to Shiva and Vishnu as a title of authority; "but should any other of the innumerable *devatas* be called Ishwara, it would be an unusual thing, and call for something like an explanation." In the Buddhist passage cited above, the term is applied as a distinctive name to two of these *devatas*, indicating a difference in the Brahmanical and Buddhist use of the word. The commentator on the "Fan-wang Sutra" identifies the great Ishwara with Brahma, but this is not authorised by the text, and disagrees with common usage, which makes them different personages. He adds, "In the whole universe there is but one king, and this is he." According to the Chinese rendering, "Self-existent," the term *Ishwara* strongly resembles the Hebrew name *Jehovah*.

The four *Maharajas*, or "Great kings" of the Devas, preside each over one of the four continents into which the Hindoos divide the world. Visitors in Chinese temples will have noticed two warlike images on each side, just within the entering door. They are the Devas here alluded to. Each leads an army of spiritual beings to protect mankind and Buddhism. At the head of the Gandharvas and Vaishajas is Dhritarâshtra, for the Eastern continent. The inhabitants of the South, Jambudvipa, are protected by Virudhaka with an army of Kubândas. In the West, Virupaksha commands an army of "dragons" (*nagas*) and Putanas. In the North, Vaishramana is at the head of the Yakshas and Rakshasas.

The names of various classes of mythological beings are sometimes translated, and at other times transferred, in Chinese Buddhist works. The "Nagas," from their form, are rendered by the word *Lung*, 'Dragon.' The Apsaras are called *T'ien-nü* or "Female Devas." The Devas, including all the Hindoo gods that are mentioned, whether great or small, are called *T'ien* (Heaven). The Kinnaras are celestial choristers looking like horses with horned heads. The Gandharvas are also musicians who play and sing for the amusement of the Devas. The Asuras are beings of gigantic size, dwelling in solitary woods and mountain hollows. They make war with the Devas, and are connected with eclipses (*vide* Hardy's *Manual of Buddhism*). The Garudas are golden-winged birds who are large enough to devour the Nagas. Beings inferior to the Devas are called collectively the "Eight classes" (*Pa-pu*). They are called *Nats* by the Birmese.

It will be observed that all these beings, including the most venerated and powerful of the gods, are introduced as disciples of Buddha. The combination of ascetic eminence and profound philosophy in Shakyamuni raise him to a position higher than any of them. Beings of every rank in earth or heaven confess their inferiority to the human Buddha by becoming his humble and attentive auditors.

The Hindoos having become acute metaphysicians, thought themselves superior to every being in the universe.

Further on in the same work other names occur. The Yakshas are a species of demons living in the earth and waters, often represented as malignant in their disposition towards man. The Mahoragas are the genii of the large serpent called in Chinese the Mang. The Rakshasas resemble the Yakshas, but they have not the power like them to assume any shape at pleasure. When they appear to men it must be in their own form. They live in the forest of Himâla, and feed on the flesh of the dead (*vide* Hardy's *Manual of Buddhism*). The "Brahmas" (*Fan;* formerly *Bam*, or *Vam*) are the inhabitants of the heaven called "Brahma-loka" (*Fan-t'ien*), over which *Fan-t'ien-wang* (Mahabrahma) or the chief Brahma presides. The Pretas, in Chinese, *kwei*, "demon," are the inhabitants of the *narakas* or "subterranean" and "other prisons" called *ti-yü*, "hell." Many of them formerly belonged to the world of men. Some are condemned by Yama to certain prisons. Others haunt the graves where their former bodies are interred. The Pretas, hunger for food, and hence the custom so prevalent in China of feeding the hungry ghosts both of relatives and of others. The Maras are enemies of Buddha's doctrine. On this account they are considered as demons, although they inhabit one of the *lokas* or "heavens" of the Hindoo cosmogony. The king of the "Maras" (*Mo-kwei*) is called *Po-siün* and *Mo-(Ma) wang*. The word *Mara* is explained, "he who kills," also "the culprit." The *kwei* are, in some instances, of a good disposition. Among such are reckoned—as a Buddhist work quoted in the *Fa-yuen-chu-lin* informs us—the *shen* or "genii" of mountains, seas, and other natural objects. The word *shen* is also used generically for the eight classes of beings before mentioned, from the dragons downwards, and is very frequently employed by the Buddhists for the soul of man, perhaps more than in any other sense. The early Buddhist apologists,

243

in pleading for the immortality of the soul as a part of the doctrine of metempsychosis, constantly used *shen* for "soul."

The king of the *kwei* or "demons" is Yama, in Hindoo mythology the ruler of the dead. From his office as judge of future punishments, his name constantly occurs in the conversation of the common people in China. He is called *Yen-mo-lo-she* (formerly *Jam-ma-la-ja*), which is abbreviated to *Yen-lo*. The usual Hindoo name may be recognised in *Yen-ma* and *Yem-ma*, which are other designations applied to him in Chinese books. *Jam-ma-raja* means the "Royal pair," a brother and sister, who judge men and women respectively. Associated with Yen-lo are nine kings who preside together over the state of the dead. His image is placed with theirs in temples, accompanied with various representations suited to remind the spectator of the world of torment. In the *Ti-tsang Sutra*, he is described as coming from the iron mountain wall where the Buddhist hell is situated, to the Tau-li heaven, to hear Shakyamuni Buddha deliver a Sutra there. He is classed among the sons of Devas, and is attended by many thousand kings of demons. He may be pointed to as the most remarkable example of the influence of Hindoo mythology on the popular mind of China. The common people all expect to meet *Yen-lo-wang* (Yama) after death, and be judged by him with the strictest impartiality. They believe that he fixes the hour of dissolution, and that the decision once made, nothing can alter or postpone it.

These various beings, when in the Sutras they appear before Buddha, perform to him an act of worship, and ask for instruction like any other of his auditors. Their power is great, but it is surpassed by that of Buddha, and it is all employed to extend his fame and doctrines. Their authority as rulers of the world is still recognised, but Buddhism by a simple stretch of the imagination makes a universe a thousand times as large to form the kingdom of Buddha. They promote virtue and the Buddhist religion. For this they live and rule. The very highest acts of deity, such as the creation of all things, or in the language of idealism the causation of all sensational phenomena, are denied them. The "Central Shastra" (*Chung-lun*) sets out with proving that creation was not the act of the great "Self-existent god" (*Ishwara Deva*), nor of the god "Vishnu" (*Ve-nu Deva;* also written *Ve-shi-nu*); nor did concourse and commixture, or time, or the nature of things, or change, or necessity, or minute atoms, cause the creation of the universe. In the Buddhist view, these deities are also subject to death, and men by certain virtuous acts which are specified, may be born at some future period to become their successors.

Buddhism, while it thus aimed to find some intelligence and power higher than those of the popular divinities, failed to perceive that the creation and government of the universe are united in one all-wise eternal mind. It looked no further than the wisdom of a human sage, and the innate goodness and self-elevating power of the human mind. It gives to the wise man the honour that is due only to God.

In forming an estimate of the extent to which the older Hindoo mythology has been spread in China, it should be remembered that the Tauists have copied from the Buddhist books in the most slavish manner. Some names are new, but the majority are adopted without alteration. Brahmas, Devas, Asuras, and Maras figure in the writings of this native sect. The prayer-books used in chanting by the Tauist priests are from beginning to end an imitation of the Buddhist Sutras. By the combined influence of these two religions, the Hindoo view of the universe, with its numerous classes of beings higher than and inferior to man, and its multiplicity of worlds, some for happiness, and others for torment, has become the common belief of the Chinese people.

Other Hindoo gods, such as the modern Shiva and Durga, Rama and Krishna, do not occur, unless concealed under names which closer examination may decipher. The rise of their worship in India was at too recent a date to allow of their being introduced into the early Buddhist literature. The unexampled viciousness of the recent Hindoo worship would also he an insuperable bar to its adoption in China. In the Buddhist books of China there is abundance of what is puerile, superstitious, and incredible, but nothing openly opposed to good morality. In such a country only what is decorous in the images and worship of any sect could be tolerated.

Since neither Vishnu nor Shiva occur among the auditors of Buddha, on occasions when all the chief persons in the universe are present, it must be supposed that the extended popular worship of both these well-known deities was subsequent to the time when the Buddhist books were written, and within the Christian era.

Footnotes

1. This was Shakyamuni's aunt, who took care of him when an infant at the death of his mother. She became a leader in the female propaganda of Buddhism, and acted a conspicuous part in the scene of Buddha's entrance into the Nirvâna.
2. *De-wan* is "the Devas." *Yin* is "Indra."

CHAPTER XII.

THE BUDDHIST UNIVERSE.

The universe passes through incessant changes—Kalpas of various lengths—Kalpas of establishment, of destruction, &c.—Saha world—Sumeru mountain—The Southern continent is Jambudvipa—Heaven of the thirty-three—Tushita paradise—Upper tier of paradises—Heavens of form and of desire—Heavens without form—Brahma's paradise—No wise man is born there, because Brahma says he created the universe—The hells—Story from the "Ti-tsang Sutra."

THE universe, according to the Buddhists, is in a constant state of change. The periods in which its changes take place are called *kalpas* (*kie-po* or *kie.*) Eighty small *kalpas* make one large *kalpa*. The inhabitants of the Brahma heaven live through twenty small *kalpas*, and their chief, Mahabrahma, through sixty. *Kalpas* are divided into the small *kalpa*, the *kalpa* of establishment and destruction, and the great *kalpa*. In the small *kalpa*, the age of mankind diminishes from an immeasurable length to ten years, and then increases to a length of from ten to eighty thousand years. In twenty of such periods the world is completed. Through twenty more it remains in the same state. After twenty more the world is destroyed, and there remains nothing but vacancy during twenty more. The first forty mean *kalpas* make up the *kalpa* of establishment. The other forty compose that of destruction. All of them taken together form a great *kalpa*. We live in the second intermediate *kalpa*, or that in which the world continues in its completed state, in a period called the *hien kalpa* or "Age of wise men" (*Mahabhadra-kalpa*. There are still eleven small kalpas to be passed before the age of destruction commences. During the "eighth *kalpa*" (*Mandu-kalpa*), immediately preceding the present, a hundred Buddhas successively appear. Shakyamuni is the fourth Buddha of the *Mahabhadra-kalpa*. In his time the age of man had already gradually diminished to a hundred years, and the same process of gradual subtraction by one year at a time is still going on. In the centre of the Saha world, or that ruled by Shakyamuni, is the Sumeru mountain. A wide sea separates this from eight other mountains. Outside these mountains, beyond another wide sea, is a great circular mountain mass of iron. A thousand such circular iron mountain chains constitute one "small world" (*siau-ts'ien-shï-kiai*). Three thousand such walls form a "great world" (*ta-ts'ien-shï-kiai*). This is the Saha world.

Within each iron wall are four continents, and a sun and moon to shine upon them. It is in the southernmost of these continents, Jambudvipa in the case of our own world, that India and all countries known to the Hindoos are situated. Far to the north is the Sumeru mountain, one million one hundred and twenty thousand miles high, and whose depth in the sea is equally great. It is composed of gold on its east side, of "lapis-lazuli" (*lieu-li*, spelt in full, according to the old pronunciation, *be-lu-li* and *be-du-li;* in Sanscrit, *vaiduria* [1]) on the south, of "crystal" (*p'o-li,* "glass;" in Sanscrit, *sp'atika*) on the north, and silver on the west.

Travelling south from Jambudvipa across the Southern ocean, there are three hundred and sixty thousand six hundred and sixty-three "yojanas" [2] (*yeu-siün*) to the circular mountain mass of iron. This mountain's depth in the sea is three hundred and twelve yojanas, and its height about the same. Its circumference is three million six hundred and ten thousand three hundred and fifty yojanas. Each iron-bound world has a Sumeru mountain in its centre. Supposing the world to be under the eternal law of change sketched above, Buddhist authorities give no account of its first origin, not feeling the need of a doctrine of creation. The physical causes engaged in its periodical formation and destruction are water, wind, and fire. These are three of the four elements *ti, shui, hwo, feng,* "earth, water, fire, and air," which are supposed to form the basis of all things. They are perhaps to be taken in the sense of elemental causes rather than elemental atoms.

Over and under this world of mountains, seas, and continents are two others, heaven and hell. Of celestial regions there are thirty-two inhabited by the divinities of the older Hindoo mythology. For the Buddhas and Bodhisattwas, peculiar to Buddhism, other abodes are found. Among the thirty-two heavenly regions, ten are called worlds of desire; including, among others, the heaven of the sun and moon, the heaven of the four kings of Devas, and the heaven of the thirty-three or paradise of Indra Shakra, who has under him thirty-three powerful Devas. There are also the Yama paradise, the Tushita paradise, the "Nimala paradise" (*Hwa-lo*), and the paradise of "Paranimita" (*T'a-hwa-tsï-tsai*).

At the base of the Sumeru mountain reside *shens*, "spirits," and Yakshas. Half-way up the mountain is the paradise of the Four kings of Devas. On the summit is the *Tau-li* or "Trayastrinsha" (thirty-three) heaven, *i.e.*, the paradise of Shakra, king of the gods. The rest of these celestial abodes are fixed in vacancy, each as high again as the one beneath it.

The next tier of these paradisiacal regions consists of eighteen. They are called heavens of form, denoting that the senses are still in activity there, though there is freedom from that influence of the passions which is still felt in the regions of desire near the world of men. The eighteen heavens of form are divided into stages of contemplation. Three belong to the first, second, and third stages, and nine to the fourth. The first stage is appropriated to the Brahmas, divided into three classes, the (Mahabrahma or) "king," officers of state, and people. Each of these classes has a paradise assigned to it. The heavens above these have various names compounded of the ideas of purity, light, virtue, abstraction, and tranquillity. In the highest of them all, Akanit'a, resides "Maha Ishwara," or *Ma-he-shwa-ra*.

The uppermost tier of four, "formless," as they are called, derive their names from the notions of vacancy, knowledge, destitution of all properties, and negation of all thought.

Of these thirty-two heavens, five are inhabited only by sages, twenty-five by sages and common men together, and two by common men alone. One of the latter is the paradise of Mahabrahma. A wise man can never be born in the abode of Brahma, say the Buddhist cosmogonists, because that deity, in his ignorance of causes, asserts that he can create heaven, earth, and all things. He being so arrogant as this, no wise man would go to live in his heaven. The other is the paradise of abstraction, where those heretics who disbelieve in the Nirvâna, but aim to gain a state of perfect mental abstraction, will hereafter be born. They will there enjoy five hundred years of freedom from the sufferings of life in a state of mindless vacancy; but since they will not tread the path of the Nirvâna, evil desires must afterwards arise, and they must be born subsequently in hell. No wise man, therefore, would willingly go to that heaven.

One of the higher worlds is assigned for the residence of those disciples of Buddha who have attained the rank of Anagamins and Lohares. Those who are shortly to become Buddha are first born into the Tushita paradise.

Mara, king of the "demons" (*mo-kwei*), resides in the space below the Brahma heaven.

These heavens are peopled by Devas. Men from the four continents of our own world may be born into them by transmigration into the body of a Deva. The Devas are born and die, their bodies are of great stature, they wear clothing, have horses and elephants to ride upon, marry, eat and drink, and perform many other actions resembling mankind. Above the worlds of desire, there is no distinction of sexes.

To become an inhabitant of these worlds is regarded as a reward for good actions, for those who have lived previously in lower states of existence. But it is still a punishment when viewed in comparison with the attainment of Nirvâna or any of the higher grades of discipleship under the teaching of Buddha.

The Buddhist "hells" (in Sanscrit, *niliya* or *naraka*), the prisons of the lost, are in some cases situated under the region inhabited by man. Twenty thousand yojanas (280,000 miles) below the Jambu continent is one called the *Avichi naraka*, or the "Hell of unintermitted torments." The Yama naraka is half-way between. Others are among fabled mountains, or on the shores of a great sea. In Chinese books they are called by a common name *ti-yü*, "earth-prisons."

In the "Ti-tsang Sutra" is a story of a maiden of the Brahman caste, whose mother had been condemned to the *Wu-kien ti-yü*, or "Avichi naraka." Full of distress, she went to a temple to pray for help from an ancient Buddha whose image was there adored. In reply to her offerings and prayers a voice addressed her—that of the Buddha represented by the image. She was told to sit at home and meditate on the name of the same Buddha. While doing so she fell, after a day thus spent, into a state of deep reverie, and found herself on the banks of an ocean. Here she saw many beasts of prey with iron bodies, flying and walking on the sea. Multitudes of unhappy men and women were also swimming there, and were constantly bitten by these ferocious animals. The maiden, supported by the power of Buddha, did not feel terrified. A demon king addressed her kindly, and informed her that she was come to the great iron mountain girdle that surrounds the world. "I have heard," said the maiden, "that hell is here; how can I reach it?" *Ans.* "Only by spiritual power, and of merit self-acquired." *Qu.* "And who are these unhappy criminals suffering in this sea?" *Ans.* "They are the wicked inhabitants of the Jambu continent who have recently died. After forty-five days, if no one performs any meritorious act for their benefit, they must first be transported to this place. Eastward are two other 'seas of misery' (*k'u-hai*), where the punishment inflicted is still greater." *Qu.* "But where is hell?" *Ans.* "Within these three seas there are many thousand prisons, but of the larger kind only eighteen." *Qu.* "My mother died not long since; where now is her soul?" The good-hearted demon king answered this question by another. *Qu.* "O Bodhisattwa, what sort of life did your mother formerly lead?" *Ans.* "My mother held heretical opinions. She ridiculed and slandered the 'Three treasures' (Buddha, the Law, and the Priesthood). If she became a believer for a time, she soon ceased to honour them." *Qu.* "What was her name?" *Ans.* "My father and mother were both of the Brahman caste. Their names were Shira and Yetili." The demon king, holding up his joined hands respectfully to the Bodhisattwa, said, "Holy maiden, return. Dismiss all sad thoughts. It is now three days since the sinful Yetili was born an inhabitant of paradise. The filial love that prompted such acts to save a parent, and such piety towards an ancient Buddha, are sufficient not only to preserve a mother from hell, but also to raise innumerable other persons to heaven." The Brahman maiden then returned to consciousness as from a dream. Reflecting on what had happened, she visited again the shrine of the ancient Buddha, and made a vow that through innumerable coming *kalpas* she would perform acts of merit for the deliverance from suffering of multitudes of living beings. Shakyamuni Buddha added, addressing Manjusiri, "That demon king and Brahman maiden have now become the Tsai-sheu Bodhisattwa and the Ti-tsang Bodhisattwa."

This story must serve instead of a detailed description of the Buddhist hells. It will be sufficient to say of them that they combine all that is horrible to each of the senses. Every form of torment, mental and physical, that can befall the unhappy violators of a good conscience and of the Buddhist law, are found there. The extremes of cold and heat, cutting, flaying, biting, insulting, and tantalising, have to be endured by such persons according to their deserts. Demons of the most monstrous shapes and most cruel dispositions terrify them in every possible way. All that fire and water, knives and clubs, can by ingenuity be made to do in tormenting, is there done.

The preceding brief sketch of the "three worlds" (*san-kiai*) almost all refers to what is common to the other native Hindoo sects. Buddhism adopted the national belief in regard to the form of the universe, including the worlds of reward and punishment. It belongs to all forms of Buddhism in China or elsewhere.

The Northern Buddhists have, however, gone further, and framed a much more extensive cosmogony, which deserves a separate consideration.

Footnotes

1. The *d* and *t* in these two Sanscrit words are the cerebral *d* and *t*, usually printed with a dot under them. They approach the sound of *l*. The Buddhist dictionary, *Yi-ts'ie-king-yin-i*, says, that the word *p'o-li* is in its full Sanscrit form, *sa-p'a-ti-ka*. In K'ang-hi, we are told, "the Roman empire has glass of five colours," *ta-ts'in-yeu-wu-se-p'o-li*. In Buddhist books it means "rock crystal." Why the aspirate is not preserved in the common colloquial term *po-li* "glass," is not clear.
2. There are two kinds of *yojana*. One consists of four *goshalas*, the other of eight. A *goshala* is the distance at which the bellowing of a bull can be heard, or nearly two miles.

CHAPTER XIII.

THE EXTENDED UNIVERSE OF THE NORTHERN BUDDHISTS.

Primitive Buddhism aimed at moral improvement and the Nirvâna—Its mythology was of popular growth—The Mahayana mythology was introduced by the metaphysicians of Buddhism itself—Nagarjuna, the chief inventor—Hwa-yen-king—An extended universe invented to illustrate dogma—Ten worlds beyond the Saha world in ten different directions—New divinities to worship—Amitabha—His world in the West—Kwan-yin and Ta-shï-chï—The world of Ach'obhya Buddha in the East—World of Yo-shï Fo, the healing teacher—Mercy, wisdom, &c., are symbolised in the Bodhisattwas—Wu-t'ai shan in China is introduced in the Hwa-yen-king.

ABOUT four centuries after the time of Shakyamuni, or Gautama as he is more commonly called in Birmah and Ceylon, a great increase to the Sanscrit literature of the Buddhist religion began to be made. Very little had been added to the national mythology by the founder and first propagators of this system, except what respected Buddha himself. Their aim was to inculcate virtue, encourage the ascetic life, and urge persons of all castes and both sexes to aim at deliverance from the evils of existence and the attainment of the Nirvâna. They based their teaching on the existing doctrine of metempsychosis, of the gods and other classes of beings, and of heaven and hell. These had been united from the earliest infancy of the Hindoo nation in one system. By the transmigration of souls, all in heaven or earth, whether gods, men, demons, or inferior animals, are linked together into one chain of animated existence, and compose one world. It is the business of a Buddha and a Bodhisattwa to instruct these beings in moral truths, and assist them to escape from all the six forms of life, into a state of perfect enlightenment and tranquillity. The mythological element, as it existed in early Buddhism, was even then an old creation of the popular mind that had grown up with the first literary efforts of the nation. In this respect it agrees with most other mythologies, in the fact of its originating, not in philosophical schools, but among the people themselves.

To this was added a legendary element. Long tales were invented to illustrate the great merits and powers of Buddha. Free use was made in these narratives of those vast periods of time into which the Hindoos divide the past history of the world. The biography of the great sage was extended by attributing to him numberless previous lives. The manner in which, from small beginnings, he rose by self-sacrificing and meritorious acts to be lord of the world, and "teacher of gods and men" (*t'ien-jen-shi*), is minutely recorded. But the scene is not extended in any other way. New worlds are not invented in far distant space. The writers of these legends, while they represent their hero as visiting the celestial regions to instruct their inhabitants, or as becoming by transmigration an inhabitant of those paradisiacal residences for long terms of years, do not transgress the limits of the popular Hindoo universe.

The Northern Buddhists, however, about the beginning of the Christian era, pushed the bounds of their system much further. Men appeared at that time in Northern India devoted to metaphysical discussion, who aimed to develop to the utmost the principles of Buddhism.[1] In adding to the number of Buddhas and Bodhisattwas, they felt it necessary to frame new worlds to serve as suitable abodes for them. With their peculiar philosophy it was easy to do this. Not believing in the existence of the world of the senses, there was no more difficulty in admitting to their system an unlimited number of fictitious worlds and fictitious Buddhas than in continuing to recognise the universe of their predecessors. They named their system Mahayana, *Ta-ch'eng*, or "Great Development." Among these teachers the leading mind was *Lung-shu*, or "Nagarjuna," as he is called by the Thibetans. Csoma Körösi, cited in Hardy's *Manual of Buddhism*, says, "With Nagarjuna originated what is known in Thibet as the Madhyamika system in philosophy. The philosophers in India had taught either a perpetual duration or a total annihilation with respect to the soul. He chose a middle way, hence the name of this sect." The Chinese "Central Shastra" (*Chung-lun*), which bears his name as the author, contains this system, and his opinions may therefore be regarded as nearly those of the T'ien-t'ai school, whose doctrine is based on that work, and of which Lung-shu is consequently regarded as the first founder.

This circumstance throws light on the objects of Lung-shu in composing the Sutras of which he was the author. For this school gives a symbolical interpretation to the mythology of the Buddhist books. The very popular and influential Sutra called *Hwa-yen-king* came from the pen of Lung-shu. The Chinese preface to that work says that Lung-shu p'u-sa, having exhausted the study of all human literature, entered the Dragon palace to examine the Buddhist "pitaka" (*san-tsang*). He there found three forms of the *Hwa-yen-king*. The largest was divided into sections whose number is expressed by the particles contained in a world of dust. The next consisted of twelve hundred sections, and the smallest of forty-eight sections. The last and least he gave to the world with its present title, and he must therefore be regarded as its author.

This and other works of the Great Development class contain a great extension of the mythological element of Buddhism. Many new Buddhas and Bodhisattwas here appear, distinguished by various high attributes of goodness, knowledge, and magical power. To afford room for the display of these attributes, new worlds are located at pleasure in the boundless regions of space. But the whole of this imaginative creation was probably intended by the authors to be symbolical. According to the explanation of the T'ien-t'ai school, and of the esoteric Buddhists, the whole of this fictitious universe was meant to illustrate certain Buddhist dogmas. It was the extreme scepticism of the Buddhist philosophers that paved their way to this mode of teaching their system. In the T'ien-t'ai commentary on the *Fa-hwa-king*, the symbolical method of interpreting this mythological creation of the fancy may be seen exemplified.—(See *Fa-hwa-hwei-i*).

Some specimens of this mythology will now be given.

The *Hwa-yen-king* says that, on one occasion, Buddha was presiding over an assembly at a place of meeting called Aranyaka, in the kingdom of Magadha. He saw approaching a multitude of Bodhisattwas from distant worlds. They asked to be instructed in regard to the "lands where the Buddhas resided." (*Fo* "*ch'ah*," spelled in full in the old pronunciation, *ch'a-ta-la;* in Sanscrit, *kshêtra*, "land." 2) Buddha accordingly entered on a description of the kingdoms of the Buddhas. To the east, after passing worlds equal in number to the dust of ten of these kingdoms, there is one termed the golden-coloured world. The Buddha of "wisdom unmoved" presides there. *Wen-shu* (Manjusiri) and a crowd of other Bodhisattwas attend his instructions, as he sits on a lion dais surrounded by lotus flowers. To the south, west, and north, and to the north-east, south-east, south-west, and north-west, are other worlds at a distance equally great. Towards the zenith and nadir two other worlds make up the number ten, each having a governing Buddha, and a countless number of Bodhisattwas, who perform to him an act of worship, and humbly receive his instructions.

The same work also describes the ten worlds that come next to the one in which we live, on the east, south, west, and north, and the other directions as before. Each of them is ruled by a Buddha, to whom prayers are to be offered, in which he is to be addressed under ten different names.

The moral import of these worlds and their Buddhas is contained in the names that are given them. These names are formed symmetrically, and carry the reader and the worshipper round a circle of Buddhist ideas.

Thus the significations of the appellations given to the Buddhas are such as surpassing wisdom, self-possessed wisdom, Brahmanical wisdom, &c. The leading Bodhisattwas receive such denominations as chief in the law, chief in merit, chief in visual power, &c.

It was thus that these Buddhist philosophers employed the imagination as an instrument of moral instruction, just as western authors write a poem or a novel for a similar end. They were men whose minds were cultivated to the utmost subtlety in argument, as the Shastras, works by the same authors, and taken up exclusively with philosophical discussions, abundantly show. They did not, therefore, believe in the truth of these fanciful creations. Their metaphysical creed would prevent it, and there is not wanting such indirect evidence to the fact as has been already adduced. But what shall be said to the morality of such modes of teaching a religion? These sceptical writers cannot be shielded from the charge of practising a vast and systematic deception on the common people, in inducing them to regard these imaginary beings with religious reverence. Falsehood is involved in the very form of the Buddhist Sutras, for they are attributed unhesitatingly in all their multitudinous variety and voluminous extent to Shakyamuni himself. Ananda, the cousin and favourite disciple of the sage in his declining years, is put forward as the compiler from memory of all these works. The practice of worshipping the divinities introduced in these new mythological creations was also directly encouraged, and this new idolatry spread with great rapidity throughout the countries where Northern Buddhism prevails.

To illustrate these statements more fully, reference must be made to the more popular personages and better-known worlds in the new mythology. Among these fabled worlds located in distant space, the best known is the paradise of Amitabha. In the *Wu-liang-sheu-king* (Amitabha Sutra), Buddha tells a tale of a king in a former *kalpa* who left the world, adopted the monkish life, assumed the name *Fa-tsang*, "Treasure of the law," and became, by his rapid growth in knowledge and virtue, a Bodhisattwa. To the Buddha who was his teacher he uttered forty-eight wishes, having reference to the good he desired to accomplish for all living beings, if he should attain the rank of Buddha. Ten *kalpas* since, he received that title with the name "Amitabha" (*O-mi-to Fo*), and now resides in a world far in the West, to fulfil his forty-eight wishes for the benefit of mankind. Ten million kingdoms of Buddhas separate his world from our own. It is composed of gold, silver, lapis-lazuli, coral, amber, a stone called *ch'a-ku*, and cornelian. There is there no Sumeru mountain, nor iron mountain girdle, nor are there any prisons for punishment. There is no fear of becoming a hungry ghost, or an animal by transmigration, for such modes of life are unknown there. There are all kinds of beautiful flowers, which the inhabitants pluck to present as offerings to the thousands and millions of Buddhas that reside in other parts of space. Birds of the most beautiful plumage sing day and night of the five principles of virtue, the five sources of moral power, and the seven steps in knowledge. The listener is so affected by their music, that he can think only of Buddha, the Law, and the Priesthood. The life-time of this Buddha is without limit, lasting through countless *kalpas*, and therefore he is called "Amitabha" (*Wu-liang-sheu*, "Boundless age"). Two Bodhisattwas reside there, anxious to save a multitude of living beings, who, with Amitabha, are worshipped assiduously by the Northern Buddhists. They are, says the *Wu-liang-sheu-king*, Kwan-shï-yin and Ta-shï-chï. They radiate light over three thousand great worlds. They attained their rank by good deeds performed in our own world, and were rewarded by birth into the Western paradise of Amitabha.

The *Amitabha Sutra*, after minutely dilating on this paradise, describes nine other worlds at a corresponding distance from our own, and occupying, as in the former case, the cardinal points and intermediate positions, with the zenith and nadir. Ach'obhya and other Buddhas rule in the East, numerous as the sands of the Ganges, each proclaiming the doctrine that instructs and saves to the inhabitants of his own kingdom. A similar account is given of the other worlds and their Buddhas.

The two Sutras already cited, together with one called *Kwan-wu-liang-sheu-king*, are entirely occupied with Amitabha and his paradise. These three works form the textbooks of the Tsing-tu school, whose very numerous publications, suited to the popular taste, and based on the doctrine of these Sutras, are very widely disseminated among the Chinese people at the present day.

In the last-mentioned work, Buddha, when seated in the midst of his disciples, is said to have poured forth from his eyebrows a flood of golden light which shone to all the surrounding worlds. This light returning was seen by the assembly to form itself into a golden tower on Buddha's head. It was like the Sumeru mountain, and by its splendour many kingdoms of Buddhas were revealed to view. One was constructed of the Seven precious stones and metals, another of lotus flowers, another was like the palace of Ishwara, another like a crystal mirror. A disciple, struck by this magnificent display, expressed a desire to be born in the Western heaven, and Buddha told him how he might have his desire gratified. This is an example of the manner in which the inventors of this mythology intended, by scenes of vastness and splendour, to affect the reader's or listener's mind. Feelings favourable to the influence of Buddhist ideas were thus to be called into action.

Another of these creations which has gained considerable notoriety is a world in the East ruled by *Yo-shï Fo* (Bhaishajyaguru Buddha). There intervene between that world and ours, kingdoms of Buddhas to the number of ten times the sands of the Ganges. This personage, when he was a Bodhisattwa, uttered twelve great wishes for the benefit of living beings, including the removal of various bodily and mental calamities from those who are afflicted with them, and the lengthening of their life. Hence his name, "The healing Teacher." In attendance on him are two leading Bodhisattwas, whose names, *Ji-kwang-pien-chau*, and *Yue-kwang-pien-chau*, signify the "Far-shining light of the sun" and "of the moon." The world in which he resides is composed of lapis-lazuli, its walls and palaces of the seven precious stones and metals, its streets of gold, thus resembling, as is observed by the author of the *Yo-shï-king*, the *Ki-to-shï-kiai*, or "Paradise of Amitabha." He is worshipped as a deity who removes sufferings and lengthens life, and is in fact the symbol of these ideas. While many of the fabulous beings introduced in the literature of Northern Buddhism have no image or shrine in the temples of the present day, Yo-shï Fo is one of those who are very seldom omitted in the arrangement of these edifices.

The freedom of imagination in creating new worlds and new deities, in which the authors of this literature indulged, would naturally lead to incongruities. Newly-invented worlds would be located in regions already appropriated by previous writers. In the *Fa-hwa-king*, a circle of eight worlds, with two Buddhas to each, is described. Amitabha and Ach'obhya occur in the west and east respectively, the account agreeing in this respect with that in the *Amitabha Sutra*, but the other names do not harmonise; so that in several cases new Buddhas are imagined in regions preoccupied by those created at an earlier date.

Accounts of many more of these fancied worlds might be collected from other works. For example, in the *Pei-hwa-king*, one in the south-east with its Buddha, is described with minuteness.

The symbolical character of this mythology is seen very clearly in the attributes of the Bodhisattwas, who play in it such an important part, and who are the objects of such extended popular worship in the Buddhist countries of the North. In Kwan-yin, mercy is symbolised; wisdom, in Wen-shu; and happiness, in P'u-hien. To the philosophic Buddhists, these personages, with Amitabha, Yo-shï Fo and the others are nothing but signs of ideas. The uninstructed Buddhists believe in their real existence, but all the evidence goes to show that they were invented by the former class of Buddhists, and palmed upon the people by them as real beings proper to be worshipped.

A near parallel to this is the setting up of the image of Reason to be popularly adored, by the atheists of the first French revolution. If, as some think, the pantheism of Germany will, according to the common law of progress in human perversity, result in polytheism, we have here an example of the way in which such a new idolatry will possibly be introduced.

I append here some further account of Manjusiri, the Bodhisattwa honoured at Wu-t'ai shah in North China.

These notices will also show how in the expansion of the mythology which we meet with in the Sutras of the Great Development, even China is made one of the countries, and Wu-t'ai one of the mountains, where Buddha delivered discourses.

We learn from the Mongol account of Wu-t'ai, that Manjusiri is addressed in prayer as the enlightener of the world. His wisdom is perfect, and is symbolised by the sword he holds in his right hand; because his intellect pierces the deepest recesses of Buddhist thought, and cuts knots which cannot otherwise be solved.

He is also represented as holding in his hand a volume of Buddha's teaching, of which a flower is the symbol. He is styled also the lamp of wisdom and of supernatural power.

He is said to drive away falsehood and ignorance from the minds of all living beings, and on this ground the lama who compiles the books prays to him for knowledge in reverential terms.

The *Hwa-yen-king*, called in Mongol *Olanggi sodar*, is cited in this work as recording an assembly of numberless Bodhisattwas at Wu-t'ai, among whom Manjusiri is conspicuous in power and in honour. To faithful Buddhists, the mention, in a discourse of Buddha, of a Chinese mountain, is evidence of the superhuman knowledge of the sage. But as we know that Nagarjuna was the real writer of this work, we look upon it rather as proof that the geography of China was known to the translators of the works of this copious author, and that they lived in a time when this mountain had already become a favourite abode of the devotees of this religion in that country.

In another book quoted by the author, Manjusiri is informed by Buddha, that it is his duty to seek the instruction and salvation of the

Chinese by making his home at Wu-t'ai, and there causing the wheel of the law to revolve incessantly on the five mountains of the five different colours, and crowned by five variously-shaped pagodas.

The lotus will not grow at Wu-t'ai. It is too cold. How shall Manjusiri be born from its ample couch of leaves? The magical power of Buddha causes a lotus to grow from the seed of a certain tree. Thus he was without father or mother, and was not stained with the "pollution of the common world" (*orchilang*). The legend of Manjusiri at Wu-t'ai seemed to require the authority of Buddha. The translators of the Mahayana Sutras in the T'ang dynasty—in order to supply this want—did not scruple to insert what they pleased in their translations. Certainly Wu-t'ai was not a Buddhist establishment till some centuries after Nagarjuna. If some Sanscrit scholar would consult the Nepaulese *Hwa-yen-king*, he would probably find nothing there about Wu-t'ai shan. It would be curious to note what the original says in those passages where China is introduced by the translators.

Footnotes

1. *Vide* Burnouf's account of the third Buddhist council held in Cashmere, in his *Introduction à l'Histoire du Buddhisme Indien*.
2. The dictionary *Yi-ts'ie-king-yin-i* adds, that this word, used for "land or "kingdom," is the root of the word *Kshatrya*, the second of the four castes, to which belong the royal families of India, the *Kshatryas* being Lords of the soil.

CHAPTER XIV.

BUDDHIST IMAGES AND IMAGE WORSHIP.

Temples—Entering hall, Sï-ta-t'ien-wang—These four kings described—The laughing Buddha, Mi-li Fo—Behind him, Wei-to—Chief hall Ta-hiung-pau-tien—Shakyamuni—Ananda—Kashiapa—Kwan-yin, Wen-shu, and other Bodhisattwas—Buddha represented as teaching—Buddha of the past, present, and future—Chapels to O-mi-to Fo, Ti-tsang, and the Ten kings—Representation of the eight miseries from which Kwan-yin delivers—Temples in Ceylon—Images in temples near Peking—Tan-cho-sï snake—Pi-yün-sï—Hall of Lohans—Diamond throne of Buddha—Colossal images of Maitreya—Musical instruments—Reflections.

THE temples of the Buddhists, like other Chinese structures, usually look south. Their architecture also is similar. Temples cut in rock, like those of the same religion in India and Java, are not found. In natural caves, however, and on hill sides images are sometimes cut from the stone. Temples consist of several halls and chapels called by a common name, *tien*. In the "entering hall" (*sï-i'ien wang-tien*), two colossal wooden statues meet the eye on each side. These are the *Mahârâjas*, or "Four great kings of Devas," or *Sï-ta-t'ien-wang*.

The Sanscrit names are explained: "Vaishramana" (*Pi-sha-men*), "He who has heard much;" "Dhritarashtra" (*T'i-to-lo-to*), "Protector of kingdoms;" "Virudhaka" (*Pi-leu-le-cha*), "Increased grandeur;" and Virupaksha (*Pi-lieu-pa-cha*), "Large eyes." They are called in Chinese *To-wen*, *Ch'ï-kwo*, *Tseng-chang*, and *Kwang-mu*.

They govern the continents lying in the direction of the four cardinal points from Mount Sumeru, the supposed centre of the world. In the *Kin-kwang-ming-king*, they are described as actively interfering in the affairs of the world. When kings and nations neglect the law of Buddha, they withdraw their protection. They bestow all kinds of happiness on those that honour the *San-pau* (Three treasures), viz., Buddha, the Law, and the Priesthood.

Properly they are all warlike, but as seen in temples they are dressed in different modes. He of the South holds a sword. He has a black countenance and ferocious expression. The others have blue, red, and white faces. One holds in his hands a "guitar" (p'i-pa), at the sound of which all the world begins to listen, or, as some say, the camps of his enemies take fire. Another has an umbrella in his hand, at the elevation of which a violent storm of thunder and rain commences; or, according to others, universal darkness ensues. Another holds in his hand a snake, or some other animal hostile to man, but by his power made submissive and instrumental to the wishes of its conqueror.

Between them and the south wall are sometimes placed two figures in military attire and with fierce countenances, called *Heng-Ho-er-tsiang*, "the two generals *Heng* and *Ho*."

In the same building, opposite the door, is usually an image of Maitreya Buddha" (*Mi-li Fo*), or the Buddha to come. The Sanscrit name, Maitreya, means the "Merciful one." He is always represented as very stout, with the breast and upper abdomen exposed to view. His face has a laughing expression. After three thousand years he will appear in the world and open a new era.

An image of Kwan-fu-tsï the Chinese deified hero, in his capacity as protector of the Buddhist religion, is also sometimes placed in this hall on one side of the north door. Behind Maitreya is the image of *Wei-to*, a

Deva who is stiled *Hu-fa-wei-to*, or the "Deva who protects the Buddhist religion." He is represented clad in complete armour and holds a sceptre-shaped weapon of assault usually resting on the ground. He is general under the Four kings.

The shrine in which these two idols are placed forms a screen to a door behind, which opens into the court of the "Great hall" called *Ta-hiung-pau-tien*. This is appropriated to the images of Shakyamuni Buddha and a select number of his disciples. He is represented in an attitude of contemplation, sitting on a lotus-leaf däis; Ananda, a young-looking figure, and Kashiapa, an old man, are placed on his right and left. On the east and west sides of the hall are arranged eighteen figures of "Arhans" (*Lo-hans*). They are represented as possessing various kinds of supernatural power, symbolised in some instances by wild animals crouching submissively beside them. They listen to Buddha, some with thoughtfulness, some with pleasure. Along the north wall are often to be seen the images of Jan-teng, an ancient Buddha, and of six Bodhisattwas and disciples of Shakyamuni, viz., Kwan-yin, P'u-hien, Shï-chï, Wen-shu, Shariputra, and Maudgalyayana. This is the arrangement at the Kwang-fu-sï, the principal monastery in Shanghai. Wen-shu and P'u-hien often take the right and left of the central Buddha. Behind the three central images, and looking northwards, is usually placed an image of Kwan-yin with rock, cloud, and ocean scenery rudely carved in wood and gaudily painted. This Bodhisattwa, with Wen-shu and P'u-hien, is sometimes placed in front, as at Lung-hwa, near Shanghai, Kwan-yin occupying the centre, immediately behind Shakyamuni, who then sits alone on his däis in the midst of the hall. This hall, the highest and largest building in the whole monastery, takes its name from one of Buddha's titles, *Ta-hiung*, or "Great hero"—in Sanscrit, *Virah*—with the addition of the word *pau*, "precious."

The image of Kwan-yin has several forms corresponding to the various metamorphoses which he or she assumes. Two of the commonest are those of the Northern and Southern sea. In the large cloud-and-water picture in alto-relievo, of which he so often forms the principal figure, several smaller personages are added to lend variety to the scene. The Four kings of Devas are occasionally employed for this purpose, and still more frequently a female figure, *Lung-nü*, "Daughter of the Dragon king," and a youth called *Shan-ts'ai*, who form interlocutors in some of the Sutras. Another metamorphosis of Kwan-yin is represented in a female figure, holding in her arms a child. It is in reference to this image that a parallel has often been instituted between Kwan-yin and the Virgin Mary. A stranger who did not take notice of minute peculiarities in dress, would very naturally have the idea of similarity presented to him, and mistake the child which the goddess presents to mothers praying for posterity, for the infant Saviour. It is in part from such resemblances that Hue has adopted the hypothesis that the modern form of Buddhism in Thibet arose from a mixture of Christianity with that religion. Sometimes Kwan-yin appears with a thousand hands, symbolising his desire to save all mankind.

The interval between the hall of the Four great kings of the Devas, and that of Shakyamuni, is occasionally occupied by another hall. Kwan-yin of the Southern sea may be seen here pictured with his usual attendants. Behind, looking northwards, is often found a scene in honour of Ti-tsang Bodhisattwa. He is surrounded with cloud and rock carving, on the abutments of which are seen the ten kings of hell. They all listen to the instructions of this Bodhisattwa, who seeks to save mankind from the punishments over the infliction of which they preside. The Hindoo god "Yama" (*Yen-to-wang*) is the fifth of them. Sometimes in this intermediate space there is a structure called the hall of the Lo-hans, where are found on the east and west walls, small carved figures of the five hundred Arhans of Buddhist legends. They are placed on the protuberances of a rough alto-relievo scene such as those above described. In other instances this representation of the five hundred Arhans is placed over the more powerful and better known eighteen Arhans in the hall of Shakyamuni.

In the central hall, representatives of all the four ranks above the range of the metempsychosis are found, as will be seen from the preceding details. Disciples of the lower ranks, who are, however, delivered from the world of life and death, and are called *sheng-wen*, "listeners," are represented in Ananda and Kashiapa; the one holding a written scroll emblematic of his great work, the compilation of the Sutras; the other resting on a staff, the symbol of his office, as successor of Buddha in the patriarchate. They are bareheaded and close shaved. The "Arhans" (*A-lo-han*), eighteen in number, speak for themselves as to the extraordinary power, knowledge, and gratification which they have gained through listening to the teaching of Buddha, by their attitudes as conquerors of evil, and defenders of good, and by the expression of intelligence and pleasure which the artist has attempted to depict on their countenances. The rank above this, that of Bodhisattwa, uniting great knowledge and power with strong desire to save those beings who are still involved in the metempsychosis, is represented in Wen-shu and P'u-hien wearing crowns gilt and ornamented in the lotus-leaf shape. To the highest rank of all in wisdom and power, that of Buddha, belong Shakyamuni, and his instructor in a former life, Jan-teng. They have short curly hair formed of shells, and painted a dark blue. Devas sometimes appear there, *e.g.*, "Brahma" (*Fan-t'ien*) and "Shakra" (*Ti-shih*), who in some temples make two of six auditors of Buddha, the others being Ananda and Kashiapa, P'u-hien and Wenshu.

As the principal hall is appropriated to the four highest classes of beings recognised by Buddhism, so the hall of the Four Diamond kings, or kings of the Devas, contains the images of those beings still involved in the wheel of the metempsychosis, so far as they are considered by the Buddhists as proper to be worshipped. Wei-to and the Four kings with their attendants all belong to the class of Devas or inhabitants of heaven. The presence of Maitreya there may be accounted for by the fact, that he as the predicted successor of Shakyamuni in the office of Buddha, now resides in the Tushita paradise, from which at the appointed time he will descend to the earth, to assume the duties assigned him. He is not yet therefore exempt from the metempsychosis.

In the monasteries of Ceylon, a small temple termed Dewâla is placed before the chief building, and dedicated to the worship of the Devas (*vide* Hardy's *Eastern Monachism*). Thus in both cases, the visitor arrives first at the hall where the metempsychosis still prevails, and afterwards passes on to the abode of the Buddhas and Bodhisattwas.

Looking at the arrangements of these two parts of a Buddhist temple from another point of view, the large central hall already described is intended to symbolise Buddha giving his instructions to an assembly of disciples, while the leading idea of the entering hall is the representation of the powerful protection by celestial beings enjoyed by the Buddhist religion and its professors. In some large temples, Wei-to, and a king of the Devas, holding a pagoda in his hand, stand with the usual figures on the right and left of Shakyamuni. Twenty Devas, ten on each side, are also sometimes placed at the south end of the two rows of Arhans that line the eastern and western walls. This accords with the descriptions given in the Sutras of the audience gathered round Buddha on remarkable occasions, when the inhabitants of the various celestial mansions hold a conspicuous position among the crowd of his disciples. The carrying out of this thought is doubtless the prevailing aim in the choice of personages, attitudes, dress, and positions, and all is in agreement with the "Developed" Sutras or those of the Mahayana class used by the Northern Buddhists. Exceptions to this rule occur. For example, figures illustrating the thirty-two points of personal beauty belonging to Buddha are in some temples placed where the Arhans are usually found. So also, in large temples, instead of the two disciples on each side of Julai, are two other figures of Buddha, representing the future and the past, as the central one does the present. The three images are much alike, and each of them wears the close-fitting skull-cap of painted shells which is always appropriated to Buddha.

Facts of this latter class point to another aim as influencing the arrangement of the figures, that of presenting to the mind of the visitor a picture of the conception of Buddha, in its most expanded form, each image exhibiting a distinct feature of the ideal whole to the contemplation of the worshipper. This principle of arrangement is, however, followed much less frequently than the former.

The idea of celestial protection as prevailing in the arrangement of the entering hall, has already been illustrated in the description of the Four kings and of Wei-to. It may be further observed, that the beings called *K'ia-lan* (Ga-lam) or protectors of the "monasteries" (*sangarama*), viz., Kwan-ti, the god of war, and others, are placed here in vacant spaces, as in a suitable spot.

The other "chapels" (*tien*) or halls are erected on the side of or behind the central structure. They are appropriated to Yo-shï Fo, O-mi-to Fo, Ti-tsang p'u-sa, and the ten kings of hell. Other names occur, such as the hall of the thousand Buddhas, &c., but these are the most common.

In some instances, as for example in the Kwan-yin-tien, there are two images, one light enough to be carried in a sedan chair for processions, another larger for daily worship. Kwan-yin is sometimes represented in eight metamorphoses, assumed for the purpose of saving men from eight kinds of suffering. Shipwrecked sailors, in one part of the carving, are seen reaching the shore. In another some traveller escapes from a wild beast. The deliverer Kwan-yin stands by. In a scene of this kind, the image of this divinity is thus repeated eight times, besides the larger one in the centre. The whole is called *Pa-nan Kwan-yin*, "the Kwan-yin of eight kinds of suffering."

Kwan-yin is also occasionally found in a subordinate position, as one of the two supporters of "Amitabha Buddha" (*O-mi-to Fo*), Shï-chï being the other. They are called together the three sages of the west. O-mi-to is also called *Tsie-yin Fe*, or the "Buddha who *receives* suffering mortals to the rest of the Western paradise over which he presides, and to which he *guides* them."

The usual right and left supporters of Yo-shï Fo, the Buddha of the East, are Yo-tsang p'u-sa and Yo-wang p'u-sa. These preside over medicine, but the jurisdiction of the Buddha himself is not limited to healing; it includes all kinds of calamity. He is sometimes represented like Shakyamuni with three images, denoting the past, present, and future.

Ti-tsang is often attended by the ten kings of hell, from whose punishments he seeks to save mankind. All of them, except Yama, have Chinese names. Some of them point to particular localities, as Pien-ch'eng, or the city of K'ai-feng fu. T'ai-shan is a mountain of Shan-tung. Others refer to attributes, as *p'ing-teng*, "even," *chuen-lun*, the "turner of the wheel (of doctrine)." Criminals receiving punishments and attendants are also represented by small earthen or wooden figures. The ten kings all stand when in the presence of Ti-tsang p'u-sa; but if Tung-ngo-ti-kiün, a Tauist divinity, presides, they may sit, he being little superior to them in rank. Most of the names of these ten kings are of Chinese origin and not many centuries old.

Ti-tsang is represented by the priests as the son of a king of Siam. He has a full round countenance of mild aspect, with a lotus-leaf crown, the usual head furniture of a Bodhisattwa. The figures on his right and left are sometimes Muh-kien-lien and P'ang-kü-shï, disciples of Shakyamuni Buddha. Elsewhere Min-kung and Min-tsi take this position. The former was a Chinese who gave the land at Kieu-hwa, the hill some miles west of Nanking, on which is erected a large monastery in honour of Ti-tsang. Min-tsi is his son. Two other disciples, who act as "servants" of the Bodhisattwa (*shï-che*), are also represented by two other smaller figures.

The idols called P'u-sa sit when in their own shrines, but if in the presence of Buddha they stand.

Tauist idols are numerously employed in the Buddhist temples. Kwan-ti, Lung-wang, and Hwa-kwang have been formally adopted by the sect as protecting divinities. Several of a medical character are also extensively made use of, obviously to attract those who in time of sickness seek aid from supernatural sources. Diseases of the eye, ulcers, the small-pox, and bodily ailments in general are assigned to the care of various heavenly beings, and the sick in large numbers seek their assistance. "He who presides over riches," *Ts'ai-shen*, whose popularity is unrivalled among all the Chinese divinities, has also a shrine bestowed on him. There are also many others, such as *San-kwan*, *Yü-ti*, &c., which, as properly belonging to Tauism, will not be described here.

Celebrated Chinese Buddhists have also images where the arrangements of a temple are complete. That of "Bodhidharma" (*Ta-mo ch'u-shi*) is frequently met with in temples where priests of the tsung-men reside, as also that of the founder of the monastery.

According to the explanations of the philosophic Buddhists, the principle of arrangement and the use of idols tit all must be viewed as symbolical, as already remarked. When the worshipper enters he is met with the idea of "protection" from celestial beings. As he advances into the presence of Buddha, he sees in his image "intelligence," the fruit of long and thoughtful contemplation. In the Bodhisattwas are exhibited "knowledge and mercy" combined. In the Arhans he sees those who have become "venerable" by years, wisdom, and a long course of asceticism. In the *sheng-wen*, the bareheaded "disciple," he sees the first step in progress towards the Nirvâna, the introduction to the other three. When he bows before these images, and makes his offering of incense, candles, and gilt paper, this also is a symbol. It only means the reverence with which he receives the instructions of Buddhism.

The common people, however, as happens in Christian countries where the worship of images prevails, see in each idol a powerful divinity, and losing sight of the moral and intellectual objects of the system, pray to be freed from sickness, poverty, childlessness, an early death, and other dreaded evils. Such a faith in the objects of their idolatry is of course encouraged to the utmost by the priests, whose prosperity depends upon the number of the worshippers.

In April 1858, I visited at Galle, in Ceylon, two Buddhist temples. The image of Buddha is remarkably like what it is in China. The skull-cap, the posture, and the form of the body are the same. It is made of mud and gilt in the same manner. Three Buddhas were represented, and they were all called Godam and Shakyamuni. The disciples were Mogallana, Shariputra, Ra-hula, Ananda, and Kashiapa. The last two of these do not, as in China, occupy the nearest place to Buddha. Brahma and Vishnu were the kings of the Devas represented.

I noticed a pictorial representation of heaven and hell, and I know not what more, upon the four faces of a square screen that completely surrounded Buddha's image. On the inside face of the screen were images of Vishnu and Brahma, with other Devas. A Garuda attended Vishnu.

Beside the smaller temple was a *stupa* or "tomb" of Buddha. It was a handsome circular mausoleum, apparently of stone, twelve or fourteen feet in height. In China this would be a pagoda.

In the series of painted tableaux, hell was on the left, and heaven on the right. Heaven was also on the back of the screen.

Beside each temple lives a priest in a yellow kasha, with his pupils, whom he teaches to read. Fresh flowers of the strongest odours are constantly placed in abundance on the altar before Buddha. There were also oil lamps, which were not lit. Both temples were on an eminence in secluded spots and encircled by trees.

A few cottages of the Singhalese were near. They looked wretchedly poor.

A friend with me from Siam, Mr. Alabaster, informed me that the temples in Ceylon are entirely different in appearance from what they are in Siam. The following is the arrangement of the images in a temple at the Western hills near Peking. In the centre, Shakyamuni; on his right, Kwan-yin; on his left, Shï-chï. In front there are three large fans (a cylindrical cloth is so called), embroidered with inscriptions, hanging from the roof-beams. The däis on which are the three images is supported by lions, elephants, and griffins. The horse-shoe shaped aureole which encircles Buddha's head is carved with winged monsters and warriors.

Paper rubbings of the sixteen Lohans from Hang-cheu hang on the side walls. These are celebrated as having been carved in the T'ang dynasty. They were made eighteen at a later period. The sixteen were Hindoo, and there are Sanscrit characters on the fifth in order. The addition of two is due to Chinese love of change, originating with we do not know whom.

If the observer is reminded in the carved entablatures of stone pagodas of old date, that there is a resemblance to Greek and Roman sculpture, let him meditate on the idea that Alexander's conquest of Persia and invasion of India was a signal for a host of new thoughts to originate in the countries conquered. Stone sculpture may have come in this way into India, and elevated the ruder art there prevailing.

In Peking and its neighbourhood metal images are not uncommon. Shakyamuni and the two favourite disciples who usually accompany him are sometimes seen made of copper or white copper, about six feet high, with hanging bands of yellow cloth suspended in front of them. To these bands small bells are attached, which ring when shaken with the wind, or when touched by the priests or by visitors coming forward to burn incense.

In North China it is also common to see pictures of Buddhist subjects painted more or less rudely on the walls of the halls where the images are seen.

One of the forms, as said already, in which the goddess of mercy is adored is as the "Kwan-yin of the eight misfortunes" which attend unprotected travellers. In painting them on walls travellers are seen, for example, on a mountain attacked by robbers, who draw their bows at their intended victims. Just at this moment the goddess and her attendant appear in the air, and save the travellers by rendering them invisible. This is accomplished by pouring a fluid from a bottle which becomes a cloud in its descent, and intervenes between the travellers and the banditti.

In the monasteries in North China are sometimes found a tooth of Buddha, or some other relic. One tooth I saw at the temple called Teushwai-sï was two inches and a half thick and ten by thirteen in width. Relics are kept in bottles and shown to visitors.

In the T'ang dynasty a vast number of temples and pagodas were erected. It became the fashion then, under the influence of the superstition of *feng-shui*, which came into vogue in the time of that dynasty, to build pagodas for luck as well as to contain relics. The pagoda of T'ien-ning-sï, near Peking, on the south-west, and dating from the Sui dynasty, must have been then in the old city. The Pa-li-chwang pagoda would be a *feng-shui* protector on the north of the ancient city. On both these pagodas, which are strongly built of stone, there are carved Buddhas and Deva kings on large entablatures. The former and older of these pagodas grows narrower as it rises. The other is almost as wide above as below.

The Peking custom in making large images, whether they are of brass, iron, wood, or clay, is to construct them with the internal organs as complete as possible. While the smaller images are filled with Thibetan incense or cotton wool, the larger have the interior arranged according to Chinese notions of anatomy. The heads are always empty. The chief viscera of the chest and abdomen are always represented. They are of silk or satin, and their shape is that found in drawings of the organs in native medical works. A round red piece of silk represents the heart, whose element is fire. It is the size of a dollar. It and the lungs, which are white, and divided into three lobes, are attached to a piece of wood, round which is wound a piece of yellow paper, having on it a Thibetan prayer. To the wood is attached, by silk threads of five colours, a metallic mirror called *ming-king*. This represents intelligence, the heart being regarded as the seat of mind. The lungs cover the heart as an umbrella or lid, as if to preserve it from injury.

In the abdomen the intestines are made of long narrow pieces of silk with cotton wool stitched along the concave border. This may represent fat or the mesentery. Embracing all, like the peritoneum, is a large piece of silk covered with prayers or charms. Inside are also to be found little bags containing the five kinds of grain, with pearls, jade, small ingots of silver, and gold of five candareens' weight, and bits of solder of various shapes to represent silver.

The larger and older idols have, in very many cases, been rifled of these little valuables, no one knows when. Poor priests in want of money, if the fear of sacrilege is not strong in their minds, know where to get help, so that idols, in the interior of which gold and silver were once deposited, have now none. In the metallic images, the way to get to the inside is from the bottom. As they are very heavy, they have usually escaped being robbed. But the clay and wooden images are packed from a hole in the back, and are more liable to thievish depredation.

When the idols are set up there is a ceremony of consecration. The priests prostrate themselves before them, and a film of clay or some other substance is cleared away from the eyes of the idols. It is called the ceremony of opening to the light, and the day is spoken of as *k'ai-kwang-jï-tsï*.

I am indebted to Dr. Dudgeon for the preceding statement of the contents of Buddhist images in Peking.

The richest temple at the Western hills near Peking is that called Tan-cho-sï. It has a revenue of twelve thousand *taels* of silver a year. This is between three and four thousand pounds. In 1866 I arrived there one evening with some friends and slept in a guest room. At the evening service there were about forty priests performing. In addition to chanting they struck the wooden fish, clashed cymbals together, and had several other kinds of simple instruments. At the end of the service they all walked in single file round the hall twice behind the images. The reason why the three principal images in front of the great central door are placed with a space behind them is, that a procession behind may be practicable. It is also convenient to have a door there, and in front of the door an image or picture, which is, consequently, at the back of the three principal idols.

In a box given a century ago to this monastery by the emperor, and placed near the western wall of the large hall, is a snake two feet long.

Beside it is a porcelain tray of fresh water. When a rap on the box is given by the attendant priest, the snake moves its tongue out about half an inch, vibrating it in token of reverence and submission. It takes nothing but water. So the priest assured us. If we are to believe him, it had been there for two thousand years. The snake is not worshipped as a divinity, but rather represents the power of Buddha in charming and taming a savage nature. It was a snake with brown body and black spots, and its head was small. The power of Buddha keeps the animal in subjection. That is the theory. If the snake goes out of the box, as it does occasionally to take an airing, it returns to it as to its home.

We also saw a structure called the *Leng-yen-tan*. It has eight sides, and is used as an altar to represent in its carved ornaments the scenes of the *Leng-yen-king*. The central figure is what is called a Pratyeka Buddha. Round it on the eight sides are carved eight representatives of Shakyamuni. Above them are crowns of flowers. Singularly enough there are placed here six Portuguese sailors, with iron cuirasses and broad-brimmed hats, in European fashion. Each of them kneels on one knee, and holds up with both hands an offering to Buddha. They are small iron figures, made in the time of the Ming dynasty, and are called *Si-yang-jen*. This is the name by which the Portuguese are known in China.

There is behind the *Leng-yen-t'an* an altar for receiving new monks to the vows, that is, a *Kiai-t'an*, consisting of two stories. On the upper story or terrace are arranged chairs for the abbot and his assessors. The abbot sits on the central chair, and six monks on each side. The neophyte kneels with his face toward the "abbot" or *fang-chang*, from whom he is separated by a table. The rules are read by the abbot while the neophyte kneels.

T'an also belongs to the school of the "Vinaya" or *Lü-men*.

There had been a storm of rain, and we were invited by a friendly priest to go and see the foaming and dashing water near the great gate of the monastery. The bed of the stream is steep, and filled with large stones. The water coming down the mountain after a storm rushes madly over boulders and gravel to the bridge, and is shown to every visitor.

Near this spot is a small temple in honour of Pratyeka Buddha. The temple is called *An-lo-yen-sheu-tang*. The terrace on which is placed the image of Pratyeka Buddha is supported by four protectors of the law of Buddha. These four personages were once in a robber band of five hundred men, and they lived at that time for nothing but crime. They were subdued to virtue by the teaching of Buddha. In gratitude for the enlightenment they received, they offered to carry Buddha henceforth on their shoulders.

The Pratyeka Buddha wears the skull-cap of the ordinary Buddha. It is supposed to be the form assumed by the hair after several years of ascetic retirement in mountain solitudes.

At Pi-yün sï, a temple twelve miles west of Peking, there is a hall of five hundred Lo-hans. The building is a large square, and contains six galleries. It is entered from the north. The first figure met by the visitor is Maitreya. He faces the door. Beyond and behind him is the central north and south gallery. On each side of it, as of the other five galleries, are seated full-sized figures of Lo-hans. They are of clay and seated on a stone terrace two feet in height. To the right and left are parallel galleries. Four small courts in the centres of the four quarters of the large square give light by continuous rows of paper windows to the galleries. On a beam overhead, near the entrance, is a small figure, the five hundred and first, which was placed there as a supplementary image. The story is that this Lo-han came too late, the places were all filled, and, therefore, he was accommodated with a seat in the roof.

In another court are representations of the future state. Mountain scenery, clouds, bridges, lakes, as well as men and other living beings, are represented in clay. The five principal Bodhisattwas preside, and especially *Ti-tsang*. Good Buddhists are seen crossing a bridge with happy faces. Bad men are pushed by demons into a place of torture below. Various cruel punishments are represented. Everything is in carefully moulded and coloured clay. *Kwan-yin* is associated with *Ti-tsang* in presiding in the side halls. Along with the three other divinities, *Wen-shu*, *P'u-hien*, and *Ta-*

shï-chï, they preside with equal honour in the centre hall. On the coloured rock-work, the tortures of the wicked and the happiness of the good are mixed, to indicate the results of Buddhist teaching as imparted by the five divine instructors.

Above these courts is the chief court of the temple with Shakyamuni's hall, the residences of the priests, and the guest rooms. In the principal guest room there is a large picture hung on the wall descriptive of an ancient Chinese princess, Chau-chiün, who was demanded by the king of the Hiung-nu Tartars as an indispensable condition of peace, and was sent to Tartary accordingly. She leaped into the Black River and was drowned. In the picture she looks unhappy at the forced exile from her home and country. At some distance behind her is the Shan-yü or emperor of the Hiung-nu.

Above this hall is a very handsome marble gateway. It is flanked by large stone lions. The pillars are surmounted also by lions. The cross-beams are carved with phoenixes above and dragons below. Two large entablatures have carved scenes representing the triumph of the four virtues—*hiau*, "filial piety," *chung*, "loyalty," *lien*, "official purity uncorrupted by bribes," and *tsie*, "chastity." Certain celebrated persons are here represented. Above this is a pagoda of the shape called *Kin-hang pau-tso*, "Diamond throne." It is very massive and is built with blocks of marble. On the square flat summit are seven small pagodas surmounted with bronze caps. The larger ones have thirteen stories, but they are very shallow. There are various inscriptions cut in the stone, Thibetan and Chinese. The view of Peking from the summit is very fine.

In the province of Che-kiang I have seen two large stone images of Buddha cut out of mountain rock. One is at Hang-cheu, and the other at a town called Sin-chang. The second of these is the larger of the two. The road to it extends a mile and a half to the south-east of the city, and it is seventy feet high. That at Hang-cheu is not, I believe, more than forty. The Sin-chang image is more than a thousand years old, and was cut by the labour of a father, son, and grandson, requiring the chiselling of three generations. It is an image of Maitreya, the coming Buddha. Being so majestic in height, the sight of this image is very impressive. It is about the height of Nebuchadnezzar's image on the plains of Dura, and has a reflecting benevolent aspect.

The wooden image of Maitreya in Peking, at the large lamasery, Yung-ho-kung, is still higher.

The traditional height of Shakyamuni, the historical Buddha, is sixteen feet. That of Maitreya appears to be sixty. Let it be remembered that teeth of Buddha and also his footsteps in rocks are of monstrous size.

In Hiuen-tsang's travels he mentions a statue of wood at Dardu, to the north of Cashmere and the Punjab. It was a hundred feet high, and was executed by the Lo-han Madhyantika, who converted to Buddhism the king of Cashmere and all his people. By magic he raised a sculptor to the Tushita paradise to see for himself the wonderful form of Maitreya. After going up three times he executed this image.

An enormous tope, or Buddhist tower, was seen by the traveller ten *li* east of Peshawur, in the Punjab. It was three hundred and fifty feet round, and eight hundred feet high. Every Buddhist structure in China is dwarfish beside this. From its erection till the year A.D. 550, a period of eight hundred and forty-two years were said to have passed. This would show that in B.C. 292 Buddhism was the prevalent faith in the Punjab (Koeppen, p. 191). Modern travellers have found it west of the city, and still remarkable for its immense size. It was built—if this statement can be accepted—in the reign of Chandragupta ($\Sigma\alpha\nu\delta\rho\alpha\kappa\omicron\tau\tau\omicron\varsigma$), with whom Seleucus concluded a treaty, and at whose court at Pataliputra, the Greek historian Megasthenes appeared as an ambassador. But the Chinese travellers ascribe it to Kanishka; and this can be believed, for it is only in the time of powerful monarchs that monuments of this size can be erected; and Kanishka was a most devoted Buddhist. He was a contemporary of Augustus and Antony, as is known by coins. (See in Koeppen, p. 192.)

The prayers are chanted by the priests either sitting, kneeling, or standing. They consist of extracts from Sutras, or special books containing charms. The extracts are statements of doctrine, of the mercy and wisdom of Buddha, and the glory attaching to him.

The prayers are not prayers in our sense. They work a sort of magical effect. The law of a secret causation connects itself with the act of the reader of the law, or the offerer of incense, flowers, and fruits.

Music accompanies the worship. The following instruments I have noticed:—the drum, small bells, cymbals, *tang-tsï*, *ch'ing*, wooden fish, *yin-ch'ing*, and the large bell.

The drum has a clapper called *ku-ch'ui*.

The cymbals are of brass. Each has a cloth holder through the centre tied inside. The "cymbal" is called *kwo*.

The *tang-tsï* is a small gong, and is held by a half cross, to which it is tied by strings. It is of brass, and is struck by a small clapper.

The *ch'ing* is a flat metallic plate cut in the shape of flowers. It is supported by a wooden cylindrical box, and this again rests on a low table. It has a cloth-covered clapper.

A small kind of *ch'ing* is called *yin-ch'ing*. A thin iron rod strikes it to keep time for the chanters. This *yin-ch'ing* is two inches long by one deep, and is fastened tightly to a long carved wooden handle.

The large bell is struck by a wooden mallet.

In the images and the worship offered to them by the Buddhist monkish community, may be found a key to the solution of the question, how Buddhism as a religion has lasted so long.

It does not need faith, or conviction, or zeal. The monk's life is a quiet one. His work is very light. Nothing is expected of him but orderly conduct, and the chanting of the instructions of Buddha, with invocations and the beating of the wooden fish. The indolent become monks. Of real religious activity there is none. There is no God to worship but

Buddha, and Buddha is a teacher, an uncrowned god, in the sense in which Confucius was an uncrowned king.

The monks kneel to adore images, not to pray. When seated in a large hall, they recite together the teachings of their Shakyamuni, it is to favour contemplation and reflection. The reflex influence of the images on their minds is all-important.

Good luck is expected, not through the will of any god, but through an impersonal fate.

Yet they go beyond this, and rest their faith on the legends, with which their books are crowded, relating the powerful interference of the Buddhas and Bodhisattwas; and thus these personages become, in the religious faith of the people, virtual divinities.

If however this is so, there are no printed prayers. If O-mi-to Fo, or Shï-kia Fo, or *Kwan-yin p'u-sa*, are believed in as gods by the more credulous, the worship is not altered on that account. The monks still read the traditional passages out of the books of Buddha which teach the nothingness of the universe, and seem to be so many sermons on the old text in Ecclesiastes, "Vanity of vanities, all is vanity." In the Buddhist literature, prayers with special ends in view, directly addressed to either of these personages, I do not remember ever having seen more than once or twice. There is nothing but praise and invocation in an exceedingly brief form. It is a prayerless and godless religion, if looked at from the Christian point of view.

CHAPTER XV.

MONASTERIES AT P'U-TO.

This establishment more modern than T'ien-t'ai and Wu-t'ai—Many Thibetan inscriptions—Frequent visits of Peking lamas—Dedicated to Kwan-yin—Gifts by K'ang-hi—Images—Caves—Pagodas—Inscriptions—Resident defenders of Buddhism—The Potala of Jehol in Mongolia—It is also the name of the palace—Temple of the Dalai Lama—In China an island was preferred to be the tau-ch'ang of Kwan-yin.

THIS island has long been known to foreigners as a celebrated spot, to which multitudes of zealous Buddhists make pilgrimages. It has of late years been a favourite summer residence of foreigners, and has been frequently described in recent books on China, so that its natural features need not be here repeated.

The peculiarities of the monasteries, however, need some remarks, for travellers have hitherto said nothing to explain them. Their interest is modern compared with that of some other celebrated seats of the Buddhist religion. For antiquities they cannot vie with T'ien-t'ai, or with Wu-t'ai shan in Shan-si. They are remarkable rather as forming a connecting link with the lama Buddhism of Thibet and Mongolia. This connection is seen in several circumstances. Kwan-yin is the patron deity of Thibet and also of P'u-to, leading to a peculiar arrangement of the images in the monasteries, and the substitution of this deity for

Shakyamuni Buddha in the centre of the great hall. Lama priests at Peking have always been accustomed to visit the island, and perform worship there till recently, of which Thibetan inscriptions still on the island are monuments. The monastic establishments now on the island date principally from the Mongolian dynasty in the fourteenth century, and the Manchu emperors have, from motives of policy, always shown favour to the national religion of their Western tributaries.

Yet the regulations of the monasteries are all Chinese, and the schools to which the monks belong are those which have sprung up in China itself. One establishment belongs to the Lin-tsi school, and the other to that of Ts'au-tung. The following is the mode of teaching in these schools. The instructor utters a few sentences to his pupils adapted to enlighten them on some point considered of importance. The pupils in the Tsung-men division of Chinese Buddhism, to which both these schools belong, depend not on books or on a regular course of study, but simply on the living teacher. The founder of the Lin-tsi once said, in answer to a disciple's questions, "What is really Buddha? What is *dharma* (the law)? What is religious progress?"—"That the heart be pure and calm, is Buddha. That the mind be clear and bright, is *dharma*. That hindrances in all directions be removed, and the mind calm and bright, is 'religious progress' (*tau*)." There appear to be more monasteries now belonging to this school than to any other.

The visitor to the Buddhist sacred island will notice the green and yellow tiling of the two large monasteries. The same material was employed in the Nanking porcelain tower now destroyed, and is found in the monasteries of the lamas in Peking. This glazed pottery is of the five colours at Nanking, viz., blue, yellow, red, black, and white. Here it is only green and yellow. It is called *lieu-li-wa*. *Lieu-li* is a word introduced to China, like *po-li* "glass," by the Buddhists. It is one of the Eight precious things, and is called at full length in Sanscrit *Vaiduria*. This name appears to be given by the Hindoos to a natural and an artificial substance (as in the case also of "sp'atika" or *po-li*, "glass"). The buildings are on a large scale. Thus the great hall of Kwan-yin, in the first monastery, is fifty yards long and thirty wide.

Both the large monasteries are dedicated to Kwan-yin p'u-sa, instead of to Shakyamuni Buddha. In other monasteries the central position and the most monstrous image are always assigned to Shakya, the Buddha reigning in the present *kalpa*, and the teacher to whom every monk unites himself when he takes the vows. Here, however, Kwan-yin presides, and is therefore called *Chu Fo*, "the Ruling Buddha," of the monasteries and of the island.

Instead of the usual name *Ta-hiung-pau-tien*, "The precious hall of the great hero," alluding to Shakyamuni, we have the *Ta-yuen-t'ung-tien*, "The hall of the complete and correct doctrine," referring to Kwan-yin.

In this hall is a large image of earthenware with pedestal and canopy, all brought from Thibet, by order of the emperor K'ang-hi, and presented to each of the monasteries. The figure is gilt, and is that of a female sitting cross-legged in the Buddhist manner. There is no dress on it except rings on the arms, a few lotus leaves, and the usual crown of the Bodhisattwas. In one of the monasteries, a yellow silk cloak is thrown over the image. Round the canopy, which is of wood, are figures of Bodhisattwas, and on the pedestal several white elephants and lions carved in wood, which are also foreign.

Behind the Thibetan image is a monstrous male Kwan-yin, with the P'i-lu crown, representing the ruler of the monastery. Over his head is a large circle, on which nine dragons twine themselves. From them the hall is also sometimes called *Kieu-lung-tien*. Above, on a tablet, is a sentence given by K'ang-hi, *P'u-tsi-k'iün-ling*, "The universal saviour of all living beings." This is said in praise of Kwan-yin.

On the left of this image is a figure of wood, representing Amitabha, the fictitious Buddha of the Western heaven, whose name is constantly on the lips of the Chinese and Thibetan priests, and is seen everywhere painted on walls and carved on stone. Kwan-yin plays a principal part in the legend of the "Peaceful land" or *Tsing-tu*, "The Western heaven," and is one of the "three sages" (*san-sheng*) supposed to reside there, the other two being *Ta-shï-chï p'u-sa* and Amitabha.

On the right is another Kwan-yin, called *Kwo-hai* Kwan-yin, alluding to a "passage across the sea" of this deity to the island Putaloka, the Indian archetype of *P'u-to* itself. Along the east and west walls of the hall are ranged thirty-two images, representing the metamorphoses of Kwan-yin. They are called *Kwan-yin san-shï-rï-siang;* they are all male, and are individualised by varieties in posture, dress, and head-coverings.

The name Kwan-tsï-tsai is used in some of the inscriptions for Kwan-shï-yin. This is a new name introduced by Hiuen-tsang the traveller, from the Sanscrit Avalôkitêshwara, in place of the older one translated by Kumarajiva from the shorter Hindoo name Avalokite.

There are other representations of this deity. The Eight-faced Kwan-yin, the Thousand-handed Kwan-yin, and "The giver of sons" are found here, and commonly in Buddhist temples. The last of these, *Sung-tsï-*Kwan-yin, is a female figure.

Before the principal idol is a stand for an incense urn, &c. It is called *Wu-shï-hiang-pau*, "The five-vessel-incense stand." The five vessels are—an incense urn in the middle, two candle supporters, and two urns for flowers.

The same five vessels are also placed on the pavement in front of the hall. Artificial flowers only are used.

There is much similarity in the arrangements of the two monasteries. Both have two imperial tablets with halls specially erected for their reception. When these buildings are injured by time, it is not permitted to repair them without an order from the emperor. Hence some of them have become much dilapidated. Lamas used to be sent every year from Peking to the island, to worship Kwan-yin in the emperor's name, and investigate the condition of the monasteries. None, however, have gone there during the last forty years. The two Thibetan inscriptions on the road side leading to the first monastery were made by these lamas. The older one dates from the time of Kia-k'ing, A.D. 1796 to 1819. The other is no earlier than the reign of Tau-kwang.

In both monasteries the eighteen *Lo-hans* (Arhans), usually placed in the central hall of temples, are found in side chapels, their place being occupied by the thirty-two figures of Kwan-yin. These supposed beings are a step inferior to the rank of Bodhisattwa; both are inferior to Buddha. The reverence paid to Kwan-yin is not, however, less on this account. Like other deities of the same rank, Kwan-yin has refused for a time to become Buddha, preferring to save mankind by discoursing to them on the doctrines of this religion, and inducing them to enter on the path to the Nirvâna.

In a small temple called Hung-fa-t'ang, just beyond the first monastery, is an interesting representation of the eighteen Arhans crossing the sea. They are seated on various sea animals. The proper names of these personages are all Hindoo, and unfamiliar in their sound, from the circumstance that they do not occur in current legends, but only in more recondite ones, contained in some among the great collection of works termed *Tsang-king*. The names of well-known deities are therefore frequently substituted for them, such as Kwan-yin, Maitreya, and Ti-tsang-wang. The last of these is seated on a large sea quadruped in the representation here referred to. While he sleeps, a star with a stream of light issues from his head. Beside him, sitting on a dragon, are two youths called "Joy" (*Ki-k'ing*) and "Rest" (*B'ing-an*). The one, in a playful humour, wishes to wake his sleeping neighbour, but he is checked by his companion. Bodhidharma, the founder of the contemplative school in China, is introduced seated on what is termed a "one-horned immortal bull." He carries a pole on his shoulder with one shoe suspended on it. The story is that, on crossing the Yang-tsze keang, he dropped the other, which was picked up by a countryman, and was found to possess wonderful powers. Manjusiri is seated on a sea demon. A tiger is whispering at his ear. He thus learns what people at a distance are doing. It should be remembered that the attribute of this great Bodhisattwa is wisdom. In the same representation Kwan-yin sits on some other sea animal. He is pouring the elixir of life from a gourd. As it flows out it becomes the genius of a star.

There is no difficulty felt by the arrangers of temples in placing the Bodhisattwas among the Arhans, because they have all necessarily passed through that state before arriving at their present position. So the Arhan is only such after passing through three grades of discipleship, which are the first steps on the road to the Nirvâna. The Buddha himself must go through all these stages from the first introduction to the sacred life up to the state of Bodhisattwa. They form the ladder from the actual world of human life to that cloud-land of abstractions which the contemplative Buddhist hopes to reach at last. In accordance with this, the hermit life of Shakyamuni Buddha is depicted on the walls of the same temple. Above the eighteen Arhans just described, is a representation, in painted clay, of the Himalayas. Here is seen a hut of rushes inhabited by the future Buddha. Monkeys and sacred geese bring him food, and dragons, tigers, and white rabbits are his near neighbours.

In the third monastery, high on the hill called Fo-ting shan, is a somewhat remarkable representation of the Hindoo gods. They are presided over by Yü-hwang of the Brahma heaven. I could not, however, obtain an intelligent account of them from the illiterate priest who was residing there. He was an artisan from Kieu-kiang in Kiang-si, who had left his wife and family in charge of his eldest son, and become a monk. At another smaller temple, where there are several caves, each with one or more small stone Buddhas seated inside, shown to visitors as emblematic of the hermit life, I found a young priest very ready to defend his system. When the worship of Buddha was objected to, on the ground that it substituted the creature for the Creator, he replied that Shakyamuni Buddha, being at the head of the Hwa-tsang universe, was far higher in dignity than

He who ruled this lesser universe. He was reminded in reply that the vast *Hwa-tsang-shï-kiai*, a congeries of an immense number of lesser worlds, was nothing but an invention of the author of the *Hwa-yen-king*, and that in reality there was no existence or world not included within the dominions of God. He did not attempt to continue the argument.

Facing the first monastery is a small pagoda, dedicated to the Ming emperor, known as Wan-li hwang-ti. This prince before ascending the throne had conferred benefits on the institutions of the island, and this pagoda was named after him *T'ai-tsï-t'a*, "Pagoda of the crown prince." On its four sides are placed stone images of the four great Bodhisattwas, to each of whom one of the four elements is assigned. Ti-tsang, under whose jurisdiction hell is supposed to be, presides over earth. He is said to have become incarnate in a former Siamese prince. He is worshipped specially in the South at Kieu-hwa, near Nanking. Kwan-yin presides over water. His attribute is mercy, and he is worshipped in the East at P'u-to. P'u-hien presides over fire. His attribute is happiness, and he is worshipped in the West at the Woo-wei mountain in Sï-ch'wen. Manjusiri presides over air (wind), and is worshipped in Shan-si. His attribute is wisdom.

Inscriptions on rocks lining the paths are very numerous at P'u-to. Most of them are Buddhistic. Some specimens of them will be now given. *Hwei-t'eu-shï-an*, "You have but to turn back and you will have reached the shore." *Teng-pei-an*, "Go up on that shore." The Buddhists say that salvation is in knowledge. The disciple is led by the teaching of Buddha, from the sea of ignorance to the "Shore of true wisdom" (Prajna paramita, *Po-je po-lo-mi-to*), *Kin-sheng-kio-lu*, "The golden thread that guides into the path of intelligence." *Hwei-jï-tung-sheng*, "The sun of wisdom rises in the east." *Teng-ta-yuen-cheu*, "Ascend the ship of great wishes." The great wish of a Buddha or a P'u-sa is to save mankind and all living beings. They rescue those who are struggling in the sea of life and death, and vice and virtue, and convey them to the shore of true knowledge. Hence Kwan-yin is called *Ts'ï-hang*, "Vessel of mercy." *Fa-lun-ch'ang-chwen*, "The wheel of the law constantly revolves." This refers to the unceasing proclamation by books and monks of the doctrines of Shakyamuni. The metaphor by which Buddhist preaching is called the revolving of the wheel, is seen practically exemplified in the praying-wheels of Mongolia, by the turning of which an accumulation of merit is obtained. So in China, the whole Buddhist library of several thousand volumes is placed in a large octagonal revolving bookcase, which is pushed round at the instance of the visitor.

At Jehol, about a hundred and twenty miles north-east of Peking, there is a nest of lama monasteries, in a valley close to the emperor's hunting-lodge and summer palace. Among these monasteries are some of Thibetan architecture, the chief of which is Potala. It is modelled after the Potala in which the Dalai Lama lives at Lhassa in Thibet. The Dalai Lama is a living incarnation of Kwan-yin, and therefore his palace-temple was called Potala. This name is applied variously to a sea-port at the mouth of the Indus, the seat of Shakyamuni's ancestors, and to a mountain range near or part of the Nilgherries where Avalôkitêshwara was fond of going, in addition to the island in the Indian Ocean, the palace at Lhassa, and the Chinese P'u-to. For particulars, see in Eitel, p. 93.

Perhaps the island may have been at the mouth of the Indus, and left its name in the present Tatta, the *Pattala* of the Greeks.

The setting apart of the island P'u-to, in the Chusan Archipelago, is proof that the Buddhist imagination, in selecting a place for the special worship of Kwan-yin in China, preferred an island. This agreed best with the legends.

Here Kwan-yin would, in expounding the *dharma* that is to save living beings, seem more in her place than on a mountain of the mainland. This is an appropriate *tau-c'hang*[1] for her, where she can be at hand to rescue sailors from the dangers of the sea, and where crowds of pilgrims will in fair weather not be wanting to receive the benefit of her instructions.

Footnotes

1. *Tau-c'hang*, "Place of doctrine."

CHAPTER XVI.

BUDDHIST PROCESSIONS, ASSOCIATIONS, PILGRIMAGES, AND CEREMONIES FOR THE DEAD.

Yü-lan-hwei, "Association for giving food to the dead"—Worship of ancestors—Liturgical services in the houses of the rich, for the liberation of the souls of the dead from hell—Village processions—Based on the old rural processions of classical times—Masquerades—Plays—Pilgrimages to Miau-feng shan—Pilgrims wearing iron chains—Supposed efficacy of the prayers of the priests—Zeal of the laity in promoting pilgrimages to celebrated shrines.

A STRIKING example of the popular influence of Buddhism is found in the associations called *Yü-lan-hwei*. The day for feeding hungry ghosts, the professed object of this association, is the 15th of the seventh month. The original hungry ghosts were the Hindoo Pretas. In China the hungry ghosts are the spirits of the dead, especially of ancestors. Buddhists are appealed to on behalf of the dead who have no descendants to worship them, and feed them by sacrifices. Thus the sentiment of compassion for the neglected dead and of ancestors is ingeniously made by Buddhism into an instrument for promoting its own influence among the people.

The belief in the metempsychosis among the Hindoos connected itself with the Chinese sacrifices to ancestors. The two things combined formed an engine of great power for affecting the public mind.

When the rich die in Peking, priests are invited to read liturgies for three days in their houses. Eight men are sent. A priest told me that they read five books in particular on one occasion recently, when I made inquiry. They were the *Leng-yen-king*, the *Kin-kang-king*, the *Fa-hwa-king* (Lotus of the Good Law), the *Ti-tsang-king*, and the *Ta pei-ch'an*, a *Tantra* of the T'ang dynasty. They read for about six hours each day, with a particular intonation, which is determined by a certain musical notation and is learned specially. They took with them candlesticks, a picture of Buddha, and the wooden fish, and had no musical instruments. Their object was by prayers to liberate as early as possible the soul of the dead from misery. Buddhism found village processions of a religious character already existing in the country, and accepted them so far as seemed fitting. When it is considered that in the old religion of Greece and Rome, rural processions were in those countries a favourite amusement mixed with religious ideas, the examination of similar customs in China is of special interest.

In the discourses of Confucius it is said, that when the agricultural labourers came out to drink wine, or to perform a ceremony intended to drive away pestilential diseases, and the old men appeared leaning on their crooks, Confucius himself also came from his house in his court robes and stood on the east side on the stone steps. This was an indication of his desire to conform to the habits of the country. He abhorred all irregularity. The play or spectacle here alluded to was a procession of singers. It was called *No*.

The custom at present representing the ceremony of the No is called *Yang-ko*. The performers, about ten in number, go about the villages and hamlets on high stilts in fancy costumes. One is a fisherman, another is a wood-gatherer called *Chai-wang*, "Prince of fuel." There is a "begging priest," or *ho-shang*, and an old woman called *tso-tsï*, and some others. They sing as they go. The word *ko* is "song," and yang is "to raise." The "stilts" are called *kau-k'iau*. These processions are seen in the country at the end of February. The old custom of Confucius' age has died out, to be revived afresh in this modern form with a Buddhist priest as one of the performers. It is regarded by the literati as a mere theatrical performance and an amusement of the rural population. Some trace it to the son of Lieu Pei, who reigned in Sï-ch'wen, A.D. 280. But then there were few priests, which is an objection to this view.

In the *Cheu-li*, the ancient sovereigns of China or their deputies are represented as performing certain ceremonies for the removal of pestilential diseases four times in the year—once for each season. The view then held was that the *wen-yi* or "sickness," prevailing at certain times of the year, is caused by demons called *li* or *dit*.

These customs could only be introduced on their present basis at a time when Buddhism was rife and shorn priests were found in every village. Probably they are earlier than the T'ang dynasty. Some natives think they belong to the Sung, because it is customary to represent in masquerade the robbers of the novel called *Shuî-hu*, the scene of which is laid at the mountain Liang-shan in Shan-tung. These robbers all at last submit to control, and are made officers of the government, which was that of the Sung dynasty, when Pien-liang was the capital. But the main object of these village amusements being religious, it is perhaps better to regard them as Buddhist, and as parallel with the theatrical shows of the lamas in their monasteries in Peking and Mongolia.

Buddhist nunneries in Peking have theatrical shows once a year. A large mat shed is erected, and play actors are invited to perform an ordinary play. The nuns wait on the spectators of the play, and the money collected helps to defray the expenses of the nunnery for the current year. Plays are considered religious, because they are supposed to be performed to amuse the gods in whose temples they are performed.

Every year, in the third and ninth months,—our April and October,—a procession is organised in Peking to Miau-feng shan, a Buddhist place of pilgrimage; the journey to which by the pilgrims occupies three, four, or five days. Money is subscribed, and is placed in the hands of a committee who erect lofty mat sheds on the line of route for the entertainment of the pilgrims. The worship consists of bowings, kneelings, head-knockings, burning incense, and offering of money to the attendant priest. Large pits are filled with copper money to a depth of two, three, or five feet. With the money thus obtained the priests return to their monasteries, leaving this particular temple shut up and unoccupied at the end of the season, till the time of pilgrimage comes round again, six months later, in the autumn or spring as the case may be. The chief divinity is Pi-hia Yuen-chiün, a Tauist personage, but the temple is cared for by Buddhist priests. It is placed among the mountains to the north west of Peking.

On one occasion I passed a pilgrim going from Peking to Miau-feng shan to fulfil a vow. He was a Manchu of twenty-seven years of age. He had been ill, and while ill had vowed to walk in chains to the temple and back. An iron chain bound his feet and hands. It was borrowed from a temple where such gear is kept for the occasional use of pilgrims.

The next day I met another such pilgrim returning, but stronger in body and livelier in appearance than the one I conversed with the day before. Both were attended by a companion, and both wore a red dress in token of their being malefactors; for the pilgrims style themselves on these occasions criminals, and the chain is a sign of voluntary bondage undertaken in the spirit of confession of demerit. They at first look like prisoners in charge of police, but their submissive air and the red dress show that they are devotees.

Three sisters, called the three *niang-niang*, are worshipped at Miau-feng shan. The second of the three is chiefly worshipped there. The eldest is honoured at some place in Shan-tung with special reverence.

The prayers of the *ho-shang* are supposed to have the power to break open the caverns of hell. They chant together in the houses of the rich to which they are invited, proceeding through a selection of favourite liturgical books. This is called *tso-kung-te*, "performing meritorious acts."

Every act of merit is a *fu-yuen*, "cause of happiness." There never yet was a good man whose goodness was left without reward. The prayers of the priest must have their effect. The chanting of the books cannot fail to bring happiness. Such is the operation of the *karma*, or "moral necessity."

I conversed, in the spring of 1879, with a woman who brought a sick member of her family to Peking to be under the care of Dr. Dudgeon, at the London Mission Hospital. They stayed for some days, and learned Christian doctrine from a Bible-woman. The woman had been an organiser of Buddhist pilgrimages to a monastery called Si-yü sï in the mountains west of Peking. She lives at a small town in the country two days' travelling from the monastery. Every spring she has exerted her influence for many years past to persuade her neighbours to go together to this monastery to worship. She headed the arrangements. The procession usually consisted of mule carts to the number of about fifteen. She expressed her determination to give this up and become a Christian.

Lay Buddhists appear to be far more active in stirring up the people to go on pilgrimage to mountain temples than the priests themselves. When money is to be collected for the repair of temples, the priests take the lead; but in voluntary associations for a religious jaunt in spring or autumn weather, the zeal of the laity is much more conspicuous.

CHAPTER XVII.

BUDDHIST LITERATURE.

Buddhist libraries presented to monasteries by emperors—Ch'eng-tsu, of the Ming dynasty, was the first to print the entire series of the Buddhist accepted books—Prajna paramita, eighty times as large as our New Testament—The Pei-tsang, or second printed edition, dates from the sixteenth century—The Kia-hing edition of the Pei-tsang—Division into King, Lü, Lun—First Council—Work of Ananda—The Mahayana of Northern Buddhism—Council of Cashmere—Authors of the Mahayana—Lung-shu wrote the Hwa-yen-king—Contrasts between the primitive and Mahayana books—List of translators A.D. 70 to A.D. 705—Sixteen hundred works are classified, inclusive of those by Chinese authors—On the councils for settling the canon—Translations by Burnouf and others—Lotus—Book of Forty-two Sections—Character of this and other early works—Stories illustrative of ancient life—Fan-wang-king—Chan-tsï-king translated by Beal—Pratimoksha.

THE first fixing of the Buddhist canon was at the Councils of Rajagriha and Pataliputra. The Northern and Southern Buddhists held together till the Council of Pataliputra, under Ashôka. When an immense missionary development followed on the meeting of this Council, the separation was a natural result, because of the vast extent of country over which Buddhism shortly became the prevalent religion.

The origin of the primitive Buddhist books which are Common to the Northern and Southern Buddhists is, then, anterior to B.C. 246; and the addition to the canon of the Mahayana books containing the legends of Kwan-yin and of the Western heaven with its Buddha, Amitabha, was also previous to the Council of Cashmere, a little before the beginning of our era.

When the first books were translated into Chinese from Sanscrit, it was before the time of the introduction of paper. Bamboo tablets were still employed, and they were painted on with a brush. Paper-making soon came into use, and in the fourth century the present system of Chinese writing was fully in use. From that time till the invention of printing, seven hundred years later, copies of the sacred books would be made from time to time in the monasteries. As in countries where the palm grows the monks have continued to write on the palm-leaf, so in China, till printing was known, transcribed copies of all needed books would be made and preserved in monasteries.

The library of the larger Buddhist monasteries consists of a complete collection—presented by some former emperor—of the "books of the religion" (*tsang-king*). The visitor will see them in eight or ten large bookcases. In many instances they are preserved with great care and are highly valued. Even if worm-eaten and injured by damp, the priests always express unwillingness to part with any portions of them. Though they seldom make use of this library themselves, they consider that it would be an offence against the emperor to allow any of the books it contains to be removed.

The preface to one of the last imperial editions is dated A.D. 1410, in the *Yung-lo* period of the third emperor of the Ming dynasty. In addition to the erection of the porcelain tower at Nanking, previous to the removal of his residence from that place to Peking, he further signalised his zeal for Buddhism by causing blocks to be cut for the first time for the entire series of Buddhist books. They reached the number of 6771 *kiuen* or "sections." A little more than three-fourths of this extensive literature consists of translations from Sanscrit. According to a rough calculation, the whole work of the Hindoo translators in China, together with that of Hiuen-tsang the traveller, amounts to about seven hundred times the size of the New Testament in Chinese form. In this estimate lost translations, which are numerous, are not included.

One of these works, the *Maha Prajna paramita* (*Ta-poh-je-king*), consists of a hundred and twenty volumes. It is perhaps the most extensive single book ever translated in any age or country, being about eighty times as large as the New Testament. The celebrated Chinese translator, Hiuen-tsang, was engaged on it four years.

The edition of Buddhist books printed in the period Yung-lo is called *Nan-tsang*, the "Southern collection." There was another made in the time of Wan-li in the closing part of the sixteenth century. The imperial residence having been already removed from Nanking to Peking, this edition was called the *Pei-tsang* or "Northern collection."

A new set of blocks was cut at the expense of private persons from this last, by a priest called Tsï-pe to-shï, not many years after. They were placed in the Leng-yen monastery at Kia-hing near Hang-chew, and were still there before the T'ai-ping rebellion.

In 1723, a former governor of Che-kiang repaired the blocks, and wrote a preface to a catalogue of these books under the title of *Pei-tsang-mu-lu*. It contains a reprint of the imperial preface to the first complete edition dating in the seventh century (T'ang Chung-tsung). This document alludes to the labours of the successive translators, and dwells especially on the adventures of Hiuen-tsang who had recently returned from his twenty years' travels in India, and had come to be regarded, on account of his successful journey and literary labours, as the most remarkable of all the Chinese Buddhists.

The primary division of the Buddhist books is into three parts, *King, Lü, Lun*, or "Sutra, Vinaya, and Abhidharma." The first contains the immediate instructions of Buddha on dogma. It details those present as listeners, any remarkable circumstances that occurred, the conversations that took place between Buddha and any of his audience, and the direct instructions that he communicated to them. The Vinaya relates the discipline appointed by Buddha for his followers, and the circumstances that led to the establishment of particular rules and observances. The scene, audience, and conversations are detailed much in the manner of the Sutras or works of the first class. The word *king* is indeed often applied to works that are placed in the Vinaya division. The third part, Abhidharma, consists of discussions, in many instances by known authors, on the Buddhist creed and on heresies. They are not then like the works found in the first and second classes, necessarily spoken—according to Buddhist faith—by Shakyamuni; but include many that were written, in the first centuries after his death, by the more distinguished of his followers.

After Buddha's entrance into the Nirvâna, we are told his disciples met to agree on the books that should be regarded as the true traditions of their master's instructions. Kashiapa assembled them at the mountain *Gi-ja-ku-ta* (Gridhrakuta). They came there by the exercise of miraculous power. Ananda, who was young, had not yet attained to the rank of Arhan when the meeting began, but just at this time he was raised to the necessary elevation and took his seat with the rest. Kashiapa then said: "The 'Bikshu Ananda' (*O-nan Pi-Neu*) has great wisdom. Like a vessel receiving water, he imbibed the doctrine of Buddha, retaining no more and no less than what the teacher uttered. Let him be invited to compile the *Sutra Pitaka* (Collection of the king or discourses of Shakyamuni)." The assembly remained silent. Kashiapa then addressed Ananda: "It is for you now to promulgate the 'eye of the doctrine' (*fa-yen*)." Ananda assented, and after observing the countenances of the audience, said: "Bikshus and all here present. Without Buddha nothing is noble or beautiful, as in the expanse above, the stars cannot spare the moon." He then bowed to the assembly, and ascended the rostrum. He began: "Thus have I heard—At a certain time, when Buddha was a certain place, he delivered such instructions." In each instance Kashiapa asked the Bikshus if such were really the words of Buddha, and they all replied, "They were just these words." [1]

A similar account is retained by the Singhalese of the origin of the Sutras. [2] The Vinaya division of the books was, according to their traditions, prepared by Upali, and the Shastras or Abhidharma by Kashiapa.

So far as this threefold arrangement of the books, the Northern and Southern Buddhists are at one. But for the literature of the North a further division must now be noticed. The distinction of *Mahayana (Ta-ch'eng)*, or "Great Development," and *Hinayana (Siau-ch'eng)*, or "Lesser Development," runs through the works of all the three classes above described. The works of the "Lesser Development" (or vehicle) there can be little doubt are the original books of Buddha, for their dogmas and legends agree with the religion as it is still professed in Ceylon and by all the Southern Buddhists. The Mahayana is, on the other hand, unknown there. Burnouf attributes the books of the Lesser Development to the first Buddhist council already described, and those of the Greater Development to another held a little more than four hundred years after Shakyamuni's death. It is his opinion that the Mahayana books were composed in Cashmere, in the reign of Kanishka, [3] a king of Northern India (Cabul). A council—the third or fourth—was then called to decide what books should be canonical, and it was then that these extensive additions to the *Tripitaka* or "Three collections" were agreed upon. The same learned writer interposes another council a hundred and ten years after the first, in the reign of Ashôka also called Piyadasi. This prince, from his extensive empire and his patronage of Buddhism, is called a wheel-king, *i.e.*, a Buddhist king to whom the world is subject, and who causes the wheel of the holy doctrine to be kept turning.

There need be no hesitation in adopting Burnouf's view, for we know the names and many of the writings of influential Buddhists who lived at the time and place indicated, and whose opinions and qualifications were such as to render them fitted for the authorship of the *Ta-ch'eng* or "Mahayana" books, and much presumptive evidence of the fact will be found to exist.

Among them were—(1.) *Ma-ming*, or "Ashwagosha," the twelfth patriarch, who wrote *K'i-sin-lun*, the "Shastra for awakening faith." [4] (2.) *Lung-shu*, or "Nagarjuna," the fourteenth patriarch, author of *Vibhasha-lun, Chung-lun, Ta-chi-tu-lun, Prajna-teng-lun, Shï-er-men-lun*, and several other works, including the most venerated of all the Buddhist books in China, the *Hwa-yen-king*. (3.) *T'ien-ts'in*, or "Vasubandu." It is said of him, that when he first became a monk he was a bitter enemy of the Mahayana books, and destroyed them whenever he had opportunity. By the influence of his elder brother Asengha, [5] he was brought to change his views. His remorse was such that he would have wrenched out his tongue, but Asengha said to him, "as he had formerly used his tongue to revile the Great Development books, he should now employ it to praise them. This would be an expiation for his fault." After this he wrote more than a hundred works, which were placed in the third division of the sacred books. [6] (4.) *Wu-cho*, or "Asengha," brother of the last. (5.) *Hu-fa*, or "Dharmapara" (Protector of the law). He was born in the Dravida country in South India. He wrote the Shastra *Ch'eng-wei-shï-lun*. (6.) Maitreya. (7.) Deva. (8.) Sheng-t'ien. These and one or two more are mentioned among the authors of Shastras. All these persons are dignified with the name of Bodhisattwa.

The authorship of the *Hwa-yen-king* may be ascribed to Lung-shu, on the ground that he is said in a Chinese preface to have discovered it in the "Dragon palace," and first promulgated it as one of the Mahayana Sutras, or books of the "Great vehicle." He could not prefix his name to it as to works of the third division, because it is essential to a Sutra that it be a discourse of Buddha. In conformity with this principle, the Great Development "Sutras," or as they are called in Chinese *King*, are by a fiction ascribed to Shakyamuni, though their real authors were, as there is every reason to suppose, the acute-minded Hindoos whose names have just been given.

Two principal divisions of the Buddhist books, in reference to the time of their composition, are thus obtained. The former belonging to the fifth century B.C. contain, among other things, the monastic institutions, the moral code, the ascetic life, the metempsychosis, and the Nirvâna, of which the first two are Buddhist, and the latter three common to the native religions of India. The whole is interwoven with the fantastic notions of the Hindoos on geography, astronomy, and supernatural beings.

The second division embraces later developments in metaphysics and cosmogony. In the *Prajna paramita*, through a hundred and twenty volumes, the favourite dogma of extreme idealism, the non-existence of mind and matter in all their forms, is reiterated to satiety. In the legends of the Eastern and Western paradise—that of Ach'obhya and that of Amitabha—and regarding the formation of various other vast worlds and powerful divinities, the new mythological tendencies of this system are exhibited. These books must be assigned to about the first century B.C.

By help of the catalogue of Buddhist books published A.D. 730 (*K'ai-yuen-shi-kiau-lu*), the earliest and most noted translators may be divided between these two schools. Works of the *Siau-ch'eng* or "Lesser Development," *i.e.*, primitive Buddhism, were introduced by the following persons:—

Translator.	Country.	Date A.D.
Kashiapmadanga	Central India	70
Chu-fa-lan	Central India	70
An-shï-kau	Ansi	147
Chi-yau	India	185
K'ang-meng-ts'iang	K'ang-ku (Thibet)	194
Dharmati	Ansi	254
Chu-liü-yen	India	230
Chi-kian	"Massagetæ" or Ta-yue-chi	250

Name	Country	Date A.D.
K'ang-seng-hwei	K'ang-ku (Thibet)	250
Fa-kü	India	300
Chu-dharma-lan		380
Gaudamsenghadèva	Cophen	390

Among the translators of the books of the Larger Development, were the following individuals:—

Name.	Country.	Date A.D.
An-shï-kau	Ansi	147
Chi-lu-ka-ts'an	Massagetæ	147
K'ang-seng-k'ai	India	254
Peh-yen	India	258
Chi-kian	Massagetæ	250
Chu-dharmaraksha	Massagetæ	313
Malach'a	Udin	299
Dabadara	Central India	400
Kumarajiva	India	401
Fa-hien	China	414
Dharmaraksha	Central India	433
Gunabadara	Central India	435
Paramoda	Western India (Oujein)	540
Hiuen-tsang	China	650
Bodhiruchi	Southern India	705

To assist in numbering and distinguishing the books belonging to the great threefold collection, the characters contained in the "Book of a Thousand Characters" (*Tsien-tsï-wen*) are made use of.

The first subdivision of the "Sutras" or *King* under the heading, *Ta-ch'eng*, "Great Development," is that of "Prajna" (*Po-jè*). It contains the work *Maha-prajna-paramita* in six hundred chapters, to mark which, sixty characters from the "Thousand Character Classic" are employed. Eighteen other works are placed in the same subdivision.

These are followed by books containing the legends of Amitabha and Ach'obhya, the Western and Eastern Buddhas. These, with others, compose the *Pau-tsi* subdivision. After this comes that called *Ta-tsi*, or "Great Collection." Then succeed those called *Hwa-yen*, so named from the common book of that title in eighty chapters. The fifth comprises books on the Nirvâna. After these five chief subdivisions are arranged the names of many others, whether translated once or oftener. With the preceding they make in all five hundred and thirty-six Sutras of the Great Development class.

Of the Smaller Development school two hundred and twenty-eight works are contained in the collection, the chief of them belonging to the *Agama* subdivision. There were added in the Sung and Yuen dynasties three hundred altogether. Their names follow in the catalogue.

Many of these works are very small, ten or more being often placed together under one letter.

Under the denomination "Vinaya" or *Lü*, "Discipline," twenty-five works belong to the Great Development school, while fifty-nine are assigned to the *Siau-ch'eng* department.

Among the works belonging to the third class, "Abhidharma" or *Lun*, are ninety-three of the Great Development school, and thirty-seven of the Lesser. To these twenty-three were added in the Sung and Yuen dynasties.

After this occur works by various Western authors, in number ninety-seven, which do not admit of being classed with those that precede. Many of these consist of liturgical regulations and biographies of Hindoo Buddhists.

At the end of the collection are placed works by Chinese authors, in all a hundred and ninety-six. These consist of commentaries, biographical works, cyclopædias, travels in Buddhist countries, apologetic treatises, liturgical works, and the original works of authors belonging to the various native schools of Buddhism. Of these forty were appended in the Ming dynasty—as in all such cases—by imperial order.

These numbers give a total of about sixteen hundred separate works, of which fourteen hundred are translations from Sanscrit. Several hundred others are lost.

Many productions of less importance, probably amounting to several hundreds in number, by native authors, are commonly read. In an estimate of the extent of Chinese Buddhist literature these should be included. They consist of popular treatises, with anecdotes of the power of the Buddhas and Bodhisattwas, and the benefits of chanting the sacred books. Woodcuts are much used in these books, illustrative of the Buddhist future state, of Shakyamuni instructing his disciples, and of the Hindoo cosmogony and geography. Descriptions of remarkable monasteries and sacred places, and many works on the various schools of this religion in China, should be added to the list.

I place here some remarks on the councils held by the early Buddhists.

Professor Max Müller says: "The Northern Buddhists know but one Ashôka, the grandson of Chandragupta, and but one council held in his reign, viz., the Council of Pataliputra, under Dharmashôka, and this they place a hundred and ten years after Buddha's death."

The Singhalese Buddhists speak of two Ashôkas, viz., Kalashôka and Dharmashôka. Twelve kings intervened between them. A council was held under each Ashôka.

If we admit the last, it must have taken place either B.C. 242 or B.C. 246 at Pataliputra.

The fourth council, under Kanishka, presided over by Vasumitra, was probably a little before the Christian era. Nagarjuna's works and system were recognised, and from this time the "Great Development" spread among all the Northern Buddhists.

The attention of the student of Buddhism may be directed especially to those works in the *San-tsang*, or "Three pitaka," of which translations have been made.

Of these the most elaborate is that of the *Fa-hwa-king*, "Lotus of the Good Law," by Eugene Burnouf. It is rendered from the Sanscrit, and illustrated by a vast body of notes.

On comparing it with the Chinese version of Kumarajiva, I found considerable lacunæ in the Chinese copy. Kumarajiva came under the influence of the Chinese literati, to whom the ponderous verbosity and extensive repetitions of the original were intolerable. He wisely cut it down, and made a much shorter book of it. Burnouf would have been wise to do so too.

The small books with a prominent moral element are extremely interesting. Some of these are translated by Mr. Beal in his *Catena*.

The "Book of Forty-two Sections" was translated from Sanscrit by the first Hindoo missionaries. An edition in five volumes, with very full notes, by Sü Fa, and published a century and a half ago, is a signal example of the industry and fulness of illustration and comment of a Chinese scholar when editing an ancient book.

In this and other small but interesting works may be seen the principles of primitive Buddhism as taught by Shakyamuni.

The monastic life is here portrayed, and the duties of those who entered upon it are clearly pointed out. But though vows of celibacy, and living in society with fellow-believers in the Buddhist doctrine, or in solitude in woods and caves, were recommended by Shakyamuni as the most suitable mode of carrying out his system, he did not make them absolutely essential. In the "Wei-ma Sutra," *Vimakita* (*Wei-mo-kie*), a layman native of Vaishali, living in society, is represented as having made great progress in the knowledge of the principles of Buddhism. He is contrasted with many who had taken the vows, but were far inferior to him. "Manjusiri" (*Wen-shu p'u-sa*) and Vimakita are held up as equally good models of Buddhist excellence: the one, as to form, being without a rival in the monastic society; the other, as to action, being the most advanced student of the Buddhist law outside the circle of those who had taken the vows.

Many of the Buddhist books are valuable, on account of the stories illustrative of ancient life which they contain.

The following story of travellers killing a guide, to sacrifice to the Devas of a certain place, reminds the reader irresistibly of the narrative of Jonah.

"A company of merchants undertaking a journey selected a guide. With him they set out across an uninhabited region. On the way they arrived at a temple to the Devas, at which it was the custom, that a man must be sacrificed before the travellers could pass on.

"They consulted as to what should be done, and said one to another: 'We are all friends, neighbours, and relations. None of us can be sacrificed. Only the guide can be.' When they had put him to death and finished the offering, they proceeded and lost their way. Weary and brokenhearted, all one by one died.

"So it is with men. They wish to enter the sea of doctrine in order to get the pearls hidden in its depths. They must take virtue for their guide. If they slander and destroy virtue they will be sure to lose their way, and never emerge from the desert of life and death. Their sufferings must last for long ages."

A story of the shadow of gold in water is told to illustrate how ignorant men seek for golden doctrine in places where they will never find it. The story says that "formerly a foolish man went to a lake and saw at the bottom of the water a shadow of what seemed true gold. He called out, 'Here is gold.' He then went into the water and sought it in vain till he was tired and the water grew muddy. He sat down and waited till the water was clear, when he saw it again, and once more he tried fruitlessly to get it. At last the father came to look for his son, and asked him why he was so weary. On learning, he said, after seeing the shadow, 'This gold is on the tree above. A bird must have taken it in his beak and placed it there.' The son climbed the tree and found it."

To illustrate the difficulty of creating, a story is told against the Brahmans, who ascribe creation to Brahma. They call him Maha Brahma Deva, and say that he is the father of the world, and can create all things. The story states that "this so-called creator had a disciple who said he could create all things. He was foolish, but thought himself wise. He said one day to Brahma, 'I desire to create all things.' Brahma replied, 'Do not think of it. You cannot create. Without being able to use the language of the Devas, you have the desire to create things.' Brahma saw what his disciple had made, and noticed that the head was too large and the crown too small, or the hand too large and the arm too small, or the foot too large and the leg too small. In fact, it was like the Pishâcha demons." [7]

"We thus learn," continues the narrator, "that what every one brings into existence is not the creation of Brahma."

THE STORY OF THE BRAHMAN WHO KILLED HIS SON.

"Once there was a Brahman, who, according to his own statement, was extremely wise, and knew all the arts of astrologers and jugglers. Wishing to show his powers he went to another country, carrying his son in his arms, and weeping. When asked, 'Why do you weep?' he replied, This young child is to die in seven days. I mourn over his short life.' The people of the country remarked, 'It is hard to know when men will die. It is easy to err in such calculations. Wait till the seven days are past, and perhaps he will not die. Why weep now?' The Brahman answered, 'The sun and moon may be darkened, the stars may fall, but what I have said cannot fail of fulfilment.' On the seventh day, for the sake of fame and profit, the Brahman killed his son to confirm the truth of his own words. When men heard that the Brahman's son was dead precisely seven days after the time of the prediction, they all admired the wisdom of the Brahman, whose words proved true, and came to listen to his instructions. It is so among the four classes of Buddha's disciples, with those who for gain say they have attained eminent enlightenment. By their foolish doctrine they destroy the son of the good, falsely assume a benevolent character, and must in consequence endure much suffering. They resemble the Brahman who killed his son."

The book proceeds to speak of the Buddhas and their teaching. They are not liable to the errors of such men. The Buddhas in giving instruction keep a middle path, without encroachment on either side. They are neither too constant on the one hand, nor are they too interrupted and inconstant on the other. There is in their actions and teaching no disproportion. Various pretenders, however, try to imitate them, and fall into the errors of boasting, lying, and extravagance. Men, in exhibiting the form of the law, fail to present to view the true law.

These extracts are taken from the "Book of a Hundred Parables," *Pe-yü-king*, chapter ii., translated by Gunabidi.

There is a book of moral instructions, arranged in the form of the *Gâtha*, with headings, such as teaching, conversation, mercy, &c. It is called *Fa-kü-king*, "Book of the Dharma in Sentences." There are five hundred of these sentences. In India every student read this book at the beginning of his course. If he did not read this among the many books of his religion, he omitted the preface.

The sentences are of the following nature:—When rising in the morning you should think, "My life will not last long. It is like the vessel of the potter, easily broken. He who dies does not return." On this is grounded an appeal to men to learn Buddha's law.

It was translated from the work of *Tau-lio* by Kumarajiva. There are some other works specially devoted to fables and parables, such as *Tsa-yü-king*, "Book of Miscellaneous Parables."

Among works specially deserving attention is *Fan-wang-king*. This book on the "Discipline" or *Vinaya*, is the Brahmajala, "Net of Brahma."

Mr. Gogerly, in the *Ceylon Friend,* published a brief translation of the work. See Beal in *Second Congress of Orientalists,* p. 134. It states the rules which guide the Bodhisattwa.

The Chinese *Fo-pen-hing-tsi-king* is in Sanscrit "Abhinishkramana Sûtra." It has been translated by Beal, who thinks the narratives it contains will explain the "Sanchi topes," the inscriptions on which are hard to identify in any books. It is a life of Buddha, with many episodes, which may also illustrate the inscriptions at Bharhut, Amravati, &c.

Mr. Beal finds in the *Chan-tsï-king* the "Sâma Jâtaka," which contains part of the story of Dasaratha and Rama, and refers to an allusion in the travels of Fa-hien, to a festival in Ceylon, which may have light thrown on it by this book.

Sâma was Shakyamuni Buddha in a former life, living in a forest with his father and mother, who were blind. He fed them with fruits, fetched water for them, and was beloved by the deer and other wild animals of the woods. At last the king came on a hunting expedition, shot an arrow into a large herd of (leer by the water side, and killed Sâma with it, who happened to be in the middle of the herd. Sâma died, and the king was most penitent, while the parents wept over their son. The gods seeing this sad spectacle—the parents lamenting over their son, and the sympathising Raja—came and restored him to life.

The work *Pratimoksha* is mentioned in the last instructions of Buddha. It contains the rules of discipline for the disciples of Buddha. He left this, when dying, in the hands of his followers, as their guide for holy conduct.

A translation of the first chapter of the *Leng-yen-king* and of a short Shastra here follow.

The *Leng-yen-king* is praised by Chu Hi and other Confucianists as the best worth reading of the Buddhist sacred books.

Footnotes

1. *Chï-yue-luh.* "Biography of 'Kashiapa' (*Kia-she*)."
2. Hardy's *Eastern Monachism*.
3. Kanishka conquered the greater part of India. He was a second Ashôka in his patronage of Buddhism. He reigned B.C. 15 to A.D. 45, during the patriarchate of Vasumitra and others.
4. *Tsing-tu-sheng-hien-luh* contains notices of (1) to (4).
5. Eitel separates Vasubandu from Asengha by an interval of some centuries. My authority for making them brothers is the introduction to *Ch'eng-wei-shï-lun*. They were natives of Purusha in Gandhara (north end of the Punjab).
6. For the names of several of his works and those of Asengha, see *K'ai-yuen-shi-kiau-lu*, a catalogue of Buddhist books published in the T'ang dynasty.
7. A sort of vampires. Retinue of the Deva king Dhritarashtra.

CHAPTER XVIII.

THE LENG-YEN-KING.—FIRST CHAPTER.

The Sutra of firm establishment in all doctrine, describing clearly the secret merit and attainments in the religious life of Tathâgata, who appears as Buddha in his great and unsurpassed stature; also the many acts of the Bodhisattwas.

IT is called also *Chung-yin-tu-na-lan-to-ta-tau-ch'ang-king*. "The Sutra of Nalanda, the great seat of worship, in Central India."

The monastery of Nalanda, in the kingdom of Magadha, the present Bahar, was of great size, and lasted through more than seven centuries. The Chinese traveller Hiuen-tsang visited it. He found there ten thousand monks living in six buildings erected by as many monarchs, forming together one great ascetic establishment, the most splendid in India. It was celebrated as a place of study both for the Brahmanical books and those of Buddhism, and was devoted to the study of that branch of Buddhist doctrine called the "Greater Development." For legends connected with this flourishing seat of Buddhism, the translation by M. Julien of Hiuen-tsang's travels, from which I have derived these facts, may be consulted. It lay about thirty miles south-east of the modern Patna.

The Chinese translation of the *Leng-yen-king* was made in the year 705 A.D., by Paramiti, a Hindoo Buddhist monk at Canton. He was assisted by Yung-pi, a Chinese, and Migashakya, a native of Udyana, a country lying northwest of Cashmere.

TRANSLATION.

Thus have I heard:—On a time, Buddha was at the city Shravasti, in the chapel in the grove of Jeta. He was there with twelve hundred and fifty Bikshus, his disciples, who had all attained the rank of Arhan. These children of Buddha were at rest in their minds, grasping firmly the doctrine of their master, and excelling in goodness. They might in any country be patterns of virtue and dignity. They attended to the "monastic rules" (*Vinaya*) with exemplary carefulness. Assuming without limitation whatever bodily form was needed, they could save men from misery. Their names were Shariputra, Maha Maudgalyayana, Maha Kuhila, the son of Puruna, Mitarani, Subhûti, Upanishata, and others.

Besides these, innumerable Pratyekas, together with many who had just begun to desire improvement in knowledge, came to the place where Buddha was, at the close of summer, repenting of their former evil acts.

Remarks.—Shravasti was situated in what is now the province of Oude. Pratyekas are called in Chinese either *P'it-ti*, or *P'it-ti-ka-la*. They are in Sanscrit denominated "Pratyeka" Buddha, and in Chinese *Yuen-kioh*, "those who have attained intelligence by the study of causes," When a period occurs in the world's history without a Buddha, the Pratyekas appear, and, arriving at the perception of doctrine in his absence, take his place as teacher till he arrives.

It happened to be the time when the Bikshus at the close of summer were released from restraint. From every region Bodhisattwas came to ask questions and have their doubts removed. They listened respectfully, and sought to know the secret thoughts of their teacher. Tathâgata sat in a tranquil attitude, and addressed to his audience profound doctrines which they had not before heard. His voice, like the singing of the Kalavingka, penetrated to the boundaries of the world. Bodhisattwas, numerous as the sands of the Ganges, crowded to the assembly, and Manjusiri was chief among them.

At this time king Prasenajit had, in memory of his father's death, prepared a vegetable repast for Buddha. He invited Buddha to the interior apartments of his palace, and came himself to conduct him in. He also invited the Bodhisattwas.

In the city there was a man of rank who had also bidden the monks to a feast, and was waiting the arrival of Buddha. Buddha directed Manjusiri to send some of the Bodhisattwas and Arhans to attend the feast in place of himself.

Ananda alone had been invited elsewhere at some distance, and had not returned. He was too late to take his place with the others, and there was no older monk with him nor an A-je-li to admonish him. He was coming back alone and empty-handed. As he passed along the streets he held in his hand a rice bowl, and asked alms from door to door. He was desiring that he might be entertained by some one who had not already invited the monks. He would not ask if the viands were pleasant to the taste or not, whether the host was of the Kshatrya caste, or belonged to the Chendaras. Feeling the same kind disposition towards rich and poor, he did not choose honour in preference to poverty, but was anxious that all with whom he met should obtain unmeasured happiness (by almsgiving).

Ananda knew that Buddha had blamed Subhûti and Kashiapa, because they had not obtained the evenhanded justice of the Arhans, and he had reverently listened to his wise advice for relieving scruples and preventing suspicions and slanders.

He crossed the moat, and slowly approached the gate. His demeanour was grave. It was that of one who reverently observed the dietetic regulations.

He passed on his way the house of a prostitute, and fell under the influence of enchantment. Matenga, by means of a charm obtained from

Brahma by one of the Sabikaras, drew him to her couch, and he was about to break his vow of chastity.

Tathâgata knew that he had been enthralled by the charm. On returning from the repast to which he had been invited, the king, his courtiers, and many persons of reputation in the city, came to hear Buddha discourse. Light shone from the head of Tathâgata, seeming to combine the several rays of all precious stones. Out of this mild radiance was seen to spring a lotus flower with a profusion of petals, and upon it Buddha sat crosslegged with metamorphosed body, uttering a mighty charm. He sent this charm by the hand of Manjusiri to save Ananda. The messenger went, and the influence of the wicked charm being broken, he brought Ananda with Matenga to the presence of Tathâgata.

Remarks.—The bird called Kalavingka had a very soft, rich voice.

Prasenajit, the king of Shravasti, was very favourable to the Buddhist religion. It was his minister Sudatta who bought the garden of Jeta from the prince of that name, and erected in it a residence for Buddha. (See Julien's *Memoires sur les Contrées Occidentales.*) Many of the Sutras attributed to Buddha are said to have been delivered here. At the time of Hiuen-tsang's visit the city was mostly in ruins. He observed the remains of the monastery formerly standing on the site of the garden of Jeta, two miles below the city. (See Julien's *Histoire de la Vie de Hiouen-thsang*). It was here that the Bikshus assembled to listen to Buddha.

During three months in summer the Bikshus lived in seclusion, forbidden to travel or to see Buddha. At the end of this time they met before Buddha, and gave liberty to each other to point out any faults in their conduct, in order that they might undergo a penance appointed by Buddha.

The word A-je-li means an instructor in the ascetic discipline. It was required that, in going to a distance, at least three should be in company. A monk in the position of Ananda should have had with him a superior in rank and also an A-je-li.

When Buddhism was flourishing in India, the Kshatryas and Chendaras were at the two extremes of the social scale. The kings and nobles belonged to the Kshatrya caste. The Chendaras were butchers, and belonged to various humble trades.

Subhûti asked alms only from the rich, because they were able to give. Kashiapa preferred to beg of the poor, desiring to increase their happiness. Buddha blamed them both for transgressing the rule of justice.

The Sabikaras were a heretical sect, with brown hair, who fasted on rice. They obtained this charm by special worship of the god Brahma. It was capable of being communicated to others, and Matenga made use of it.

The commentator, Te-ts'ing, a Chinese Buddhist monk of the Ming dynasty, says that a superficial reader might wonder why this Sutra, which unveils the hidden nature of man, points out a secure place of rest, and unfolds a doctrine in all respects complete, should make such an ordinary incident as the temptation of Ananda its point of departure. He says, in explanation, that it is the passions which prevent men from attaining the Nirvâna. Among the passions sensual lust is the most powerful, and therefore it needs a remedy of corresponding strength to remove it.

Ananda, on seeing Buddha, bowed his head to the ground and bitterly wept. He grieved that he had not yet made a successful beginning, and that, after all the instruction he had received, he should still be deficient in moral strength. With earnestness he asked to know how the Buddhas of all worlds had obtained entrance to the region of rest and contemplation.

The auditors, numerous as the sands of the Ganges, sat silent, waiting for Buddha to address them.

He then said to Ananda:—"You and I are akin by birth. We are thus caused by heaven to love each other. You formerly felt a desire to follow my teaching. What beautiful appearance was it which led you to forsake the world's deep love?" Ananda replied: "I saw the thirty-two beauties of Tathâgata. [1] They are inexpressibly lovely, and the bodily form to which they belong is transparent as crystal. I reflected that such a form cannot be produced by earthly love. Because the bodily desires are coarse and ill-smelling lusts, and they cannot give origin to a pure bright form radiating a purple golden light like that of Tathâgata; therefore I thirsted to follow Buddha and be shorn of my hair, in token of my abandonment of a worldly life."

Buddha replied:—"You speak well, Ananda. All men continue to live and die, and live and die again, because they do not know that the mind should rest in a state of constant purity, and their nature be kept clear and true to itself. Ideas arise in their minds which are not true, and perforce they enter the wheel of ceaseless revolution. If you would attain the highest knowledge and develop your true nature in its clearness, answer honestly my inquiries. The Buddhas have trodden one path to escape from life and death. They have kept their hearts right. Their hearts and words were right, and they have therefore begun well and ended well. Thus they have no wrong thoughts or pernicious changes. I now ask you, Ananda, when your heart was attracted towards the thirty-two beauties of Tathâgata, what was it that saw, and what was it that loved?" Ananda replied: "This love came from the use of my heart and my eye. My eye saw the transcendent beauty of Buddha, and my heart felt love. Therefore it was that I desired to become freed from life and death."

Buddha answered:—"Since this love came from the heart and the eye, you must know where these organs reside; otherwise you cannot overcome the evils caused by the 'objects of sense' (*ch'en*). When a country is ravaged, the troops sent to chastise the marauders must know where they are to be found. I ask, then, where the heart and eye, the enemies who have done you harm, reside?"

Remarks.—The passions are the cause of men being subject to life and death. To set them at rest is the means of attaining to the state of Buddha. Ananda had been led away by passion, and he asks to be reinstructed in the mode of escape. He felt the evil to be great, and that some very powerful agency was needed to destroy it. He desired to commence self-reformation afresh, but not knowing where to begin, he asks for information. The first step is to observe, contemplate, and loosen the heart from its attachments.

Buddha does not proceed at once to describe the three modes of contemplation, but first inquires of him why, in the first instance, he had commenced the ascetic life. The answer of Ananda revealed the cause of his want of success. Love had been awakened in his mind by the sight of beautiful forms. This was because his mode of thinking was wrong. He had only exchanged one love for another. His heart had been attracted by a beautiful vision; but he had not seen Buddha in his higher character. If he was right in loving Buddha, might he not also love Matenga?

Not only is Ananda the victim of wrong thoughts. All men are so; and therefore it is that they do not emerge from the region of life and death. But man's true nature cannot be developed where wrong thoughts prevail. The exciting causes of this wrong state of things must be examined into. It is the work of the senses. The senses are the six enemies that disturb the original tranquillity of man's nature. These six thieves, as they are called, are ruled by the heart and the eye. The place where they reside must be discovered.

The answer of Ananda was that "living beings, of all the ten different kinds, without exception regard the perceiving faculty and the heart or mind as being within the body. They also see that Buddha's eye forms a part of Buddha's countenance. This eye of mine and three other organs of sense are a part of my face. My 'heart' (mind), then the perceiving organ, is certainly within my body."

Buddha replied to him:—"You are sitting in this house. You see the grove of Jeta. I ask you where it is?" "It is," answered Ananda, "outside of this hall. This house is in the garden of Anáthapindika. And assuredly the grove is outside of the house." Buddha again inquired: "In this house what do you first see?" Ananda replied: "I first see Tathâgata, then the audience, and farther off the trees and the garden." Buddha continued: "In looking towards the trees and the garden, how do you perceive them?" Ananda replied: "By the door and other openings." Buddha then stretched out his golden arm, and touching the head of Ananda, said: "There is a *samadhi* called that of the *Sheu-leng-yen* Rajah, who is Buddha-like in size and stature. It embraces all good actions, and describes how all the Buddhas were rescued from the world of sense and entered the glorious path that leads to confirmed rest. Listen!" Ananda made a prostration, and waited to hear.

Remarks.—Hiuen-tsang relates that the grove of Jeta is "six *li*" (two miles) south of the city Shravasti. In this grove was the garden of Anáthapindika or Anáthapindada. At the time when the Chinese traveller visited it, the convent which was formerly there was in ruins. Jeta sold the land to Sudatta, and himself gave the grove. *Anáthapindika* means "He who gives to orphans." Sudatta was so named on account of his charities.

Samadhi is a sort of waking dream or reverie, occurring to Buddha or his disciples when engaged in deep contemplation, and in which an impression or vision teaching certain religious dogmas seems present to the mind's eye.

The commentator Te-ts'ing remarks that men generally fall into the error of Ananda. They think that the mind is enclosed in the visible body. Continuance in the sphere of the metempsychosis arises from men's mistaken opinion that the body, the mind, and "their actions" (*wu-yün*) constitute myself. This false view must be first combated. Buddha, being about to subvert the cherished opinions of Ananda, kindly placed his hand upon his head to inspire him with confidence, lest he should feel pained.

Buddha:—"According to what you say you are in this hall, and through the open doors you see the garden and the grove. If you could not see Tathâgata, would you be able to see what is outside of the hall?"

Ananda:—"That could not be."

Buddha:—"This to your mind is perfectly clear. Now, if that mind which perceives it be within the body, men ought first to see what is within the body and afterwards what is outside. Since we do not see the heart, liver, and other viscera, while we can perceive the growth of nails and hair, and the movements of muscles and pulses, the heart cannot reside within the body."

Ananda (bowing):—"As I hear the instructions of Tathâgata, I am made to perceive the truth, that my mind resides outside of my body. For it is like a lamp lighted in a house. It first shines on what is within the house, and then through the door upon the portico. Since men see only what is outside the body, the perceiving mind cannot reside within them. This statement is incontrovertibly right."

Buddha:—When these Bikshus come to seek me in this city of Shravasti, and assemble at the grove of Jeta, should you see one of them eating, would all of them be thereby relieved from hunger?"

Ananda:—"No! for although they were Arhans and share in a different kind of existence, how could one man's taking food remove hunger from the rest?"

Buddha:—"The mind and body being entirely separate from each other, neither of them can know what is known to the other. I now show you my hand. Your eye sees it, but does your mind distinguish it?"

Ananda:—"Yes, Honoured Chief of the world!"

Buddha:—"If both perceive it, then it is wrong to say that they are separate from each other, and that the mind dwells outside of the body."

Ananda:—"Buddha has said that the mind, not seeing what is within the body, cannot reside there. Further, he has said that when the mind and body both know what is known to the other, they cannot be outside of each other, but must be in one place."

Buddha:—"Where, then, is the mind placed?"

Ananda:—"I think it must be hidden in the organs of sense. The eye is to the mind like a piece of glass which does not interfere with vision. Whenever the eye sees, the mind at once distinguishes. The reason why the mind does not see the interior of the body is because it resides in the sensorial organs, and its position there enables it to notice objects outside of the body."

Buddha:—"Supposing that it is so, I ask what a man will see when a glass is placed before his eyes? When he sees the hills and mountains beyond, will he see the glass also?"

Ananda:—"He will see the glass."

Buddha:—"If so, why should not the eye be seen at the time when hills and rivers are visible through it? But if the eye be seen it is a part of the scenery observed by the mind, and there is no interdependence between the two, so that the mind should at once perceive what is an object of vision to the eye. But if the mind does not see the eye, then it cannot be said that the mind resides in the organs of sense."

Ananda:—"I have now thought upon another thing. The viscera are in the interior of the body, while the various apertures are outside. There is darkness in the one and light in the other. While I look at Buddha my eye is open and sees light. In this case I see what is external. When I close my eyes I see darkness. In this case I see what is internal. Is this a correct distinction?"

Buddha:—"When you close your eyes and look on darkness, is the darkness which you see 'objective to the eye' (*wei-ü-yen-tui*), or not? If the darkness be objective, it is something before the eye, and it is therefore wrong to say that it is internal. If, on the other hand, the darkness be internal, then the darkness you see in a room where no light can enter is nothing but the interior of your body. If, however, the darkness be not 'objective' (*tui*) to the eye, it cannot be said to be seen. If the darkness be internal, and is yet seen objectively by the eye, why do you not see your face when with open eyes you look on brightness? If you see your face, the perceiving mind with the organ of vision must be in vacancy. They cannot then be within the body, nor can they be a part of it. For if they were a part of your body, then I who now see your face should be part of your body. By means of your eye which is in vacancy, you know that your body does not perceive objects. You must therefore hold that there are two acts of perceiving and two perceiving agents. You would thus become two persons. It cannot therefore be said, that in closing the eye and looking on darkness you see what is within."

Ananda:—"I have heard Buddha say that actions spring from the mind, and the mind from action (*i.e.*, mind and action are necessary to each other, and equally unreal). It appears to me that my thoughts are my mind, and that wherever my thought is, there is my mind. Thus the seat of the mind need not be within or without, or in an intermediate position."

Buddha:—"The mind, Ananda, cannot be where the thought is; for it is without 'substance' (*t'i*), and cannot be at any place. For if an unsubstantial thing could be said to be at a place, the eighteen limiting points which excite sensations would become nineteen, and the six objects of sense would become seven. But that the mind is unsubstantial can easily be shown. When I touch myself with my hand, the knowing mind (the resulting act of knowledge) must come from within outwards, or from without inwards. If the former, the interior of the body would be visible; if the latter, I should first see my face. Since I see neither, my mind must be unsubstantial."

Ananda:—"It is the eye that sees; though it is not the eye that knows. To say that the mind sees is incorrect."

Buddha:—"If the eye could see, the door of the house in which you are might also be able to see. The eye of the dead sees nothing. Further, Ananda, the mind, if it has substance, must be one substance or many. Your mind must pervade your entire body or not. If your mind be a single substance, when you touch one limb all the limbs should feel the pressure. If it were felt everywhere, the sensation would not be referred to any particular spot. If the sensation belongs to one part, you who are the subject of it cannot form a single substance. But neither can you be many substances, for then you would be many men. If the substance of your mind pervade your entire body, a sensation of pressure would be felt in every part. If it pervaded the body partially, a portion of it would be susceptible to touch, while the remaining parts were not so. Since this is not the case, your supposition, that the mind is wherever thought is, falls to the ground."

Ananda:—"Formerly I heard Buddha discoursing with Manjusiri and others on the true nature of things which appear. You then said the mind is neither within nor without the body. It seems to me that without interior perception there can be no external knowledge. What is in the body must be perceived, if we are to know what is outside of the body; else the mind cannot be within the body at all. As it is, we only perceive what is outside, and not what is within. The mind, therefore, must be neither within nor without, but between the two."

Buddha, in his reply, argues that Ananda is wrong, and that the place of the mind is not between the inside and the outside, any more than it is within the body or without in the material things which are the objects of sensations.

So ends the first chapter of this book.

Remarks.—The eighteen limiting "boundaries" (*kiai*) of the sensations are—eyes, ears, nose, tongue, body, mind, colour, sound, smell, taste, "contact" (*chu*), law, seeing, hearing, smelling, tasting, feeling, and thinking. These eighteen items are otherwise arranged as six roots, the sensorial organs, six kinds of dust, colour, taste, smell, &c., and six kinds of sensational knowledge.

The second group of six are also called the six thieves, as being the causes of delusion to all mankind who believe in matter. The first six are also called the six subjects that "love" (*ai*), and the six things that "feel" (*ts'ing*).

Footnotes

1. "Tathâgata," an appellation of Buddha, is, in Chinese, *Ju-lai*, "Calmly approaching."

CHAPTER XIX.

THE EKASHLOKA SHASTRA.

The "Ekashloka Shastra," translated from the Chinese, with an analysis and notes. [1]

THE author of the original work, of which a translation is here given from the Chinese version, was the patriarch "Nagarjuna" (or *Lung-shu*), of whom much has been said in the preceding part of this book. Beside being the writer of many of the more important Shastras, he also composed several of the Sutras, though these works are generally attributed to Shakyamuni Buddha. A keen reasoner, acute thinker, and voluminous author, such as Nagarjuna, deserves to be better known, and it is hoped that the following translation of one of his lesser works will prove not altogether useless in the elucidation of Buddhism.

It is called *Yih-shu-lu-kia-lun*, the "Shastra of One shloka." The three characters *shu-lu-kia* are in old Chinese pronunciation *sho-lo-ka*. When a double consonant begins a syllable, it is usual to employ the same vowel after each consonant in transcribing them in Chinese characters.

Shloka is a Sanscrit term for "verse," and particularly for a couplet of a certain kind. I take the following account of it from Williams' Sanscrit Grammar:—"The Institutes of Manu are written in the *Sloka*, or *Anushtubh metre*. This is the commonest of all the infinite variety of Sanscrit metres, and is that which chiefly prevails in the great epic poems of the East. It consists of two lines of sixteen syllables each, but the rules which regulate one line apply equally to the other." "The 1st, 2d, 3d, 4th, 9th, 10th, 11th, and 12th syllables may be either long or short. The 16th, as ending the line, is also common; so too the 8th." "The 5th syllable ought always to be short. The 6th may be either long or short; but if long, then the 7th ought to be long also; and if short, then the 7th ought to be short also." "The last four syllables form two iambics."

The Hindoo author has in the present instance taken a single couplet as his theme, and hence the name of his short treatise. This couplet, consisting in its Chinese form of four short sentences, appears at the commencement.

We are also informed by an introductory note that the treatise was translated into Chinese, from the original of Lung-shu p'u-sa, by the Brahman Gaudama Prajnaluti, at the city of Lo-yang, in the reign of the Yuen-Wei dynasty. This city is that now called Ho-nan fu, on the south bank of the Yellow River, in Ho-nan province. The time of the translation is the fourth century of our era.

TRANSLATION OF "YIH-SHU-LU-KIA-LUN" (THE SHASTRA OF ONE SHLOKA).

"My body (or substance) in its nature is not permanent;
Thus, then, my body is not a body.
My body in its nature not being a body,
I therefore say that it is empty and not permanent."

"It is asked, Why write this "stanza" (Gâtha)? What is its meaning? What man's opinions is it intended to overthrow? I reply, It is written on account of those, who in reading Shastras of great length grow weary; and also for those intelligent persons, who have studied many Shastras, and exercised their thoughts (deeply) in the sea of Buddha's law, but growing fatigued have begun to doubt about the doctrine, not by any means to be questioned or suspected, of the non-permanence of things and the nothingness of my own body. To destroy such doubts I have composed this Shastra.

"What says my doctrine? That all kinds of "acting" (*fa*) are non-permanent, and my own body is nothing. The non-reality of my body is not separate from the non-permanence of all action, my nature and my body being nothing. Therefore there is no such thing as permanence.

"All the Buddhas, and their disciples of the two classes *Yuen-kioh* and *Sheng-wen* ("Listeners," *Shrâvaka*), have obtained their liberation from ignorance by means of this principle of nothingness; not by the opposite principle, which maintains the existence of breaking off, and of permanence in actions. The *Gâtha* says:—

"Lose sight of this principle of nothingness, and prefer to reside in body;
You then obtain a view of things as permanent.
If you say that afterwards they are to be destroyed,
You thus come to see things as having cessation."

"With this meaning I speak of all actions as being in themselves without real embodiment. The Buddhas, the 'Enlightened' (Yuen-kioh), the Listeners, and the Arhans have gained their benefits and successes by believing in this principle.

"I will now speak of what men are to be opposed. If a man who has gained some knowledge says that, without reference to 'action' (*hing*), there is non-permanence, his view is not the correct one. If the so-called non-permanence is separated from 'existence,' *yeu-wei*, or (actuality), in order to be called non-permanent, then permanence becomes nothing. Thus, then, actuality and non-reality are not essentially different. If actuality and non-reality combine, the actual being joined to the unreal, a bottle cannot be broken (which is absurd, a bottle being an *actual* thing). If the unreal and the actual combine, the unreal being joined to the actual, the Nirvâna is destructible (which is absurd, the Nirvâna being not an actual thing). If the actual and the unreal are, as thus argued, identical, all kinds of 'teaching' (or 'action,' *fa*) are indestructible, like the Nirvâna, which is permanent, and is, therefore, not produced from any cause. If 'actions' (*hing*) are not produced from causes, they do not differ from the empty Nirvâna. In this case, the method or state of 'actuality' (*yeu-wei*) need not be called constant. But if the things done, being not produced from causes, are still non-permanent, then the empty Nirvâna is not called permanent, If this be true, the methods of actuality and of non-reality are neither of them good. If the non-permanent is parted from actuality and is still called non-permanent, then actuality apart from constancy ought to be called constant. But this is not correct reasoning. In which of the Sutras are there such words as these?

"What ideas are to be discoursed upon? What meaning is there in that which you now say? There is much in it that is unreasonable, such as your crooked mind cannot fathom. Therefore what you say, is not correct doctrine. If men, who have gained some knowledge, maintain that the (action or) 'law' of the past, present, and future is in each case completed from and in itself, this is to be regarded as a false view. Why so? Because it is a view which omits the notion of cause. If we speak of the future as not being produced from causes, but as formed from and in itself, then the present is also not produced from causes, but is formed from its own nature. For the future and the present are, in their own nature, even and equal, without any difference. If so, and the law of the present comes from causes, why, in this case, should not the law of the future come from causes also? You ground this view either on the Sutras, or upon your own judgment. But the statement is incorrect and unreasonable. Being unreasonable, it is not to be believed. If the law that regards the future is not produced from causes, but comes from its own nature, it must be an empty thing. Being cut off from any connection with causes, it cannot be produced from any cause. It is, therefore, not truly future in itself. But if the future is non-existent, then the present and past are also non-existent. The present and the past being non-existent, then time in its threefold aspect is really nothing in itself. If it be said that it has a real existence, this is to say that it is permanent, and is produced without a cause.

"If the disciple of Buddha thinks so, who has reached some depth in perception, he does not differ from the heretical teachers, Kapila and others. This Shastra, however, is not made for such as Kapila and Uluka, but for you who hold the same views with me. What I have thus far said, in opposition to the opinions of certain persons, is for the sake of you who have made some advancement, that you may reject incorrect views.

"It is on this account that I have compiled this Shastra and the 'Gâtha of one *shloka*' (Yi-sho-lo-ka-lun), which commences my book. I shall now explain the meaning of this *Gâtha*.

"When it is said, 'My body, in its nature, is not permanent,' 'my body' refers to that which is born and acts, and which is, therefore, called 'my body.' He who has made advancement in right perception, being in the midst of this acting, thinks out for himself that this is the body (or takes it to be the body). This acting commences in the region of the physical and mental operations. [2] In it are involved also the *Sheng-wen* and *Yuen-kioh*, who wander circuitously (in this lower region). Thus, when we speak of bodies, as one, two, or several; or of men, as one, two, or several; each is considered as having a body independent of the rest, and they are commonly spoken of as such. As earth, water, fire, and wind are respectively hard, moist, hot, and movable, each according to its nature; so every man (and thing) has his own form and substance. Hence the expression, 'my body.'

"If he who has made some advancement in knowledge says that man in his birth, in his continued life, and in his death, is the same in form, he speaks erroneously. The body of man is, in its nature, not permanent, and, therefore, its being called body has arisen from the circumstance that men who have advanced somewhat in true knowledge have made this distinction. Therefore apart from the various modes of action, there is no non-permanent body; because man is, in his form, not permanent.

"Therefore Buddha, in instructing the Bikshus respecting various acts, represents them all as not constant. This is on account of what has been already said.

"If it be maintained that, apart from acting, men and things are non-permanent, retaining their own form, such an opinion is wrong. Should you not understand why the phrase non-permanent is used, I will now explain it. It is because of what is said in the opening stanza, 'Body is not body.' The notions of body and not body you easily distinguish. The non-permanent, what is it? It is without body. Therefore it is, that body is not body. In its own nature it is not body, and therefore it is formally stated to be without body.

"When it is said, 'My substance, in its nature, is not substance,' it is asserted that there is no substance but that which is 'not substance' (*wu-t'i*). For this reason it is said that substance in itself is not such. If you hold that there is some substance existing beside *wu-t'i*, you are wrong; this mode of arguing is not that of the Sutras. If you assert that the 'absence of body' (*wu-t'i*) is what constitutes substance, this also is incorrect; because the Sutras do not say so. In what Sutra has Buddha, the World's Honoured one, taught such a doctrine? It is not to be found in any Sutra, for it is not 'correct teaching' (*king-shwo*, the 'teaching of the classics'); such arguments cannot succeed, because they are not the doctrine of the great holy Sutras; they ought not, therefore, to be believed. It is, then, not only my own words that I bring as evidence.

"The last sentence says, 'Therefore it is stated to be empty and not permanent.' Refer, for example, to the Sutra, *Tiau-fuh-san-mih-t'i-king*, 'Narrative of Buddha pacifying and subduing Samidhi,' which says, that Buddha addressed Samidhi with the words, 'The eye of man is empty and not permanent. There is no eye that does not move, that does not perish, that does not change. And why? It is its nature so to do. The ear, nose, tongue, body, and mind have all the same changeable and destructible nature.'

"Buddha, the World's Honoured one, speaking in this Sutra of emptiness and of non-permanence, on this account expressed the opinion here stated. Thus we know that all acts are empty and non-permanent. Being not permanent, they are without 'body' (*t'i*). Consequently all acts are, in their nature and of themselves, without bodily form. It is in this way that the meaning of the words *wu-t'i*, 'without body,' is established.

"If, in this manner, an opinion be tested by the Sutras, it will be well established. If it will not bear this test, it must fall to the ground. In my view, what is in the Sutras must be completely satisfactory. Therefore it is that the opinion, that '(my) nature (*sing*) is in itself without body,' has been now employed to bring to its completion the Shastra of one Shloka.'

"All kinds of action (or existence), such as body, nature, 'act' (doctrine), thing, matter, existence' (yeu), are different in name, but the same in meaning. Whichever of these we speak of, the only difference between them is in the word *yeu*, 'to be.'

"This word *yeu* is, in the original language, *subhava*.[3] It is translated in several ways, as 'the substance which gives substance to itself' (*tsï-t'i-t'i*), or as 'without action and with action' (*wu-fa-yeu-fa*), or as 'the nature which has no nature of its own' (*wu-tsï-sing-sing*)." *Analysis and Remarks.*—The author begins with stating, in a rhythmical form, the principles he is about to establish. My substance or body, *i.e.*, my whole nature, material and intellectual, is a passing, changing thing, and is, consequently, not a real substance at all. It is, therefore, only right to say of it that it is empty and not permanent.

This principle agrees with the description given of the Buddhists by Colebrooke, who observes that they are called by their adversaries the orthodox Hindoos, *Sarvavaináscicas*, or "Those who argue total perishableness." They deny the permanent existence of atoms, and only allow that images of things are formed which immediately pass away.

The author then gives his reasons for composing the treatise, and the *Gâtha* or rhythmical statement with which it commences. He wrote it for the sake of such persons as cannot read through the very long and tedious works found in the Buddhist library. He also wished to place in a short compass the argument for the transitory, unreal nature of all existing things, for the use of advanced students; lest they should be influenced by those arguments, self-suggested or presented by others, which go to prove that the world is real and that the information given by the senses is trustworthy.

The composition of Buddhist works is varied by the frequent introduction of passages in a rhythmical form, not indeed with rhymes or any fixed succession of long and short syllables, but with lines constantly of the same length. In the Nepaul originals, there is also a difference in dialect between the prosaic and rhythmical parts, the Sanscrit and Pracrit being interchanged. There is no such transition of dialects in the Chinese translations. The rhythmical parts are called "*Gâtha*," *Kië*; in the old Chinese pronunciation, *Gat*.

The author lays down as his order of procedure, that he will first unfold his meaning, then attack the upholders of opposite views, and afterwards support his own opinions.

He holds that all kinds of action are transitory and not lasting, that the actor or observer is himself nothing real, and that these two things are connected. Hence the doctrine of non-permanence.

The Buddhas and their disciples, he says, had in the belief of the principle of nothingness obtained "liberation" (*móksha*) from the bonds which restrain the soul. The opposite doctrine, which holds that things are permanent, or break off, has never had such an exemplification of its truth.

Colebrooke says that the followers of Kanáde maintained that things are partly perishable and transitory, but in part also unchangeable. His followers are called Vaiséshikas.

The disciples of Buddha here alluded to, *Yuen-kioh* and *Sheng-wen*, occupy the third and fourth rank in the Buddhist scale of being. Their position will be understood by the following scheme copied from a Buddhist work:—

Four degrees in "holiness" (*sheng*).	Buddha.	Intelligence.
	Bodhisattwa.	Knowledge and mercy.
	Yuen-kio.	Perception gained by the study of causes.
	Sheng-wen.	"Listeners," *Shravakas*.
Six states of "ignorance" (*fan*).	Devas.	"Gods," *T'ien*.
	Asuras.	Monsters, demons.
	Men.	
	Pretas.	Hungry ghosts.
	Animals.	
	Naraka.	Hell.

Four lines in the form of *Gâtha* are here introduced, representing the doctrines of opponents. Two views are given—that which regards the universe as permanent, and that which describes it as liable to cessation. Both are considered as erroneous by the champion of Buddhism. Safety is only to be found in the doctrine of nihility.

In again appealing to the testimony of the Buddhas and their disciples, he mentions the Arhans. These form the last in a series of four grades of discipleship. The attainment of a certain amount of enlightenment in the Buddhist doctrine is represented as "fruit." These four grades of discipleship, or "fruits," are called, *Su-da-wan*, *Si-da-gam*, *A-na-gam*, and *A-la-han*. In Sanscrit these names are read "Srôtâpanna," "Sagardagam," "Anagamin," and "Arhan." They are also called the four paths to the Nirvâna.

Lung-shu proceeds to controvert by argument, the opinions of two classes of reasoners, and first of those who hold the doctrine of non-permanence in an incorrect manner. It ought not to be held so as to deny the reality of action, or so as to confound action and inaction. These terms in Chinese, *yeu-wei*, *wu-wei*, may perhaps be translated "actuality" and "non-reality." Their meaning will be seen by the illustrations used. An earthenware bottle is adduced as an example of an "actual thing" (*yeu-wei*), while the Nirvâna belongs to the "non-actual" or *wu-wei* class.

These instances are brought forward to show that things of the two classes of objects must not be confounded. For if actuality be identified with non-reality, a bottle, it is said, would become a non-actual thing, and it would be wrong to say that it was destructible. So if non-actual things were identified with what is actual, the Nirvâna would cease to be indestructible. The distinction, then, between the actual and the non-actual must be preserved.

The Sutras are again appealed to in proof of this doctrine. These works are thus seen to be, in the view of the Buddhist, the standard of truth. They contain the very words of Buddha, which are held to be necessarily true. Several hundreds of these books, thus shown to constitute the *scriptures* of this religion, have been translated into the language of China, and of the other countries where Buddhism prevails. These treatises are not said to be divine, or to be inspired, for the Buddhist has neither God nor inspiration in his creed. He only knows Buddha, the self-elevated human intellect, as the most exalted being; and he looks on his teaching to be the purest truth and the highest wisdom. Throughout the Shastra, which is now presented to the reader, Lung-shu supports his opinions by the authority of the Sutras which Buddha has left for the use of his disciples as the repository of his doctrine.

He goes on to overthrow the notion that the past, the present, and the future are self-produced, and do not come from the action of causes. He observes that the present and the future are as to their nature similar, and controlled by the same laws; but the present results from causes, and therefore the future must also originate in the same manner. If the past, present, and future do not come from causes, he argues that they can be nothing real. at all. The holder of such views would thus fall into the error of Kapila and other heretical teachers.

Kapila, here referred to, was a remarkable personage, perhaps the most noted of the Indian philosophers. He founded the Sankhya school. "This system," says Cousin, in his *History of Modern Philosophy*,[4] "is at once a system of physics, psychology, dialectics, and metaphysics. It is a universal system, a complete philosophy." Cousin says of Kapila that he advocated sensualism, and that "one of the ideas which are most opposed to sensualism being that of cause, Kapila made an effort to destroy it. The argumentation of Kapila is, in the history of philosophy, the antecedent of that of Ænesidemus and that of Hume. According to Kapila, there is no proper notion of cause, and that which we call a cause is only an effect in its relation to the cause which precedes it, which is also an effect for the same reason, and continually thus, so that the whole is a necessary concatenation of effects, without veritable and independent cause."

Professor Wilson, in his learned comment on the *Sankhya Karika*, criticises this statement of the French philosopher, and denies that Kapila asserts the non-existence of cause. He admits, however, that "he may so far agree with the philosophers referred to, in recognising no difference between *material cause and material effects;*" and adds that "his doctrine is that of Brown in his lectures on power, cause, and effect."

There being such a difference of opinion on the views of this Hindoo philosopher, it is interesting to notice in the treatise of Lung-shu, that Kapila is incidentally condemned for denying the existence of cause. Our Chinese evidence goes to uphold the statement of the French philosopher, where he is called in question by his English critic.

Colebrooke questions whether Kapila be not altogether a mythological personage. With this distinct allusion to him in our little work, dating indubitably from near the beginning of the Christian era, we may perhaps infer his historical reality, and we also obtain an approximation to the period in which he lived.

Lung-shu proceeds to say that he did not write for the purpose of confuting such philosophers as Kapila and Uluka, [5] but for the sake of correcting and confirming the views of the disciples of Buddhism.

The philosopher, Uluka, I have not found mentioned by Colebrooke or other writers on the metaphysical systems of India.

It appears to me that Lung-shu is not explicit enough in his argument for the production of events from causes, where he asserts that the present proceeds from causes, and therefore the future does also, being in all respects similar to the present in its nature. He does not first make plain that the present proceeds from cause. [6] As already remarked, Lung-shu appeals repeatedly to the authority of the Sutras. So the advocates of the Sankhya philosophy appeal to the Sutras of Kapila, which are, however, brief aphorisms, and not, like those of Buddha, long treatises. Yet Lung-shu has besides this another test of the validity of doctrines, namely, their reasonableness or unreasonableness. To this second test he here brings the doctrines he opposes and condemns them.

In explaining the introductory stanza, Lung-shu first discusses the origin of the phrase "my body." He observes that it consists of the body and its actions; *i.e.*, it means *myself*. In the region of mental and physical actions, we come to the consciousness of *myself*. In this region the inferior classes of Buddha's disciples continue to wander partially enlightened.

Advancing from this incomplete view, we speak ordinarily of men and things, in the singular, dual, and plural numbers, as separate beings existing independently of each other, thus increasing the first error. The four elements, earth, water, fire, and wind, differ in their nature, as being hard, moist, hot, and moving, and so each man and thing is looked at as having its characteristic differences from others. Hence the common but erroneous expression *my body, my self*.

Lung-shu complains that some persons maintain birth, duration, and destruction to be the same thing. He then proceeds to state that the body in its nature is not permanent, that its being called *body* has arisen from the distinctions which men in their ignorance have made, and that the correct doctrine of the body being non-permanent is inseparably connected with the various physical and mental operations which spring from the body; because, he adds, man is in his entire form non-permanent.

Buddha, in the instructions he gave to the Bikshus his disciples, always held the doctrine that actions are nonpermanent. This must ever be kept in mind in making the statement that the body is non-permanent. Bikshu is one of the names given to the followers of Buddha generally. They are also called *Shamen* and *Ho-shang*.

The author then undertakes to prove the second sentence of his theme, namely, "Thus, then, my body is not a body." The doctrine of non-permanence has been introduced to aid in proving this. The non-permanent is necessarily unsubstantial. The things we see are liable to perish. Therefore they are not real things. We must speak of things as they really are. Hence the words "my body is not body," are correct and appropriate.

The third sentence, when it says, "My body in its nature is not body," asserts that, apart from the unsubstantial and the vanishing, no body exists; and that therefore it is right to say of my own body, that it does not exist.

Cousin, in his lectures already referred to, speaks of the psychology of Buddhism as being contained in two propositions, extracted by Burnouf from Buddhist books.

1st, Thought or spirit—for the faculty is not distinguished from the subject—appears only with sensation, and does not survive it.

2d, The spirit cannot itself lay hold of itself; and in directing its attention to itself, it draws from it only the conviction of its powerlessness to see itself otherwise than as successive and transitory.

Burnouf adds, these theses are radically opposed to Brahmanism, whose first article of faith is the perpetuity of the thinking subject.

We see that the non-permanence of things, which is so important a principle with our author, also pervades the books of Nepaul which Burnouf studied, and constitutes a watchword of Buddhism.

Lung-shu proceeds to observe that some persons hold false views on this subject. One opinion is that independently of the unsubstantial there is substance, but this is contrary to the Sutras. Others say the unsubstantial is my body, but this is wrong (although it is correct to say that my body is unsubstantial), because it is not found in the Sutras. Such are not the words of Buddha, nor are they met with in the great holy Sutras, and they must not be believed.

The last sentence, "I therefore say that it is empty and not permanent," is illustrated by appealing to the teaching of Buddha in one of the Sutras. He takes the eye as an example. There is no eye that does not move, that is not destroyed, that does not change. It is therefore empty and non-permanent. So it is with the other sensorial organs. The nature of them all is to change and decay.

The Buddhists in enumerating the organs of sense, after mentioning the eye, ear, nose, tongue, and body, add the mind. Lung-shu does so in this passage. The mind, as the organ of consciousness, is viewed as a sense. We limit the term sensorial organs to those which are material, but the Buddhist, not believing in the reality of material things, calls every organ by which impressions are communicated a sense.

Buddha having thus expressed his opinion in the Sutras, it is added, we know that all acts are empty, non-permanent, and therefore without body. Thus we arrive at the doctrine that body does not exist.

It should be remembered that the Buddhists regard the acts of the thinking being as one with his substance. They do not distinguish between the agent and the act, but deny the reality and permanence of both in their unity. Thus they will say, as in this case, "all acts" (*yih-ts'iè-fa*) are without body, instead of predicating this of the actor.

Hence also he proceeds to say, that human nature is without body, resting his doctrine on the authority of the Sutras, and adding that it is the object of this entire treatise, "The Shastra of one Shloka," to illustrate it.

The same confusion of the agent with his acts presents itself in the closing sentences of the treatise, where it is asserted that all kinds of action, including body, nature, acts, thing, being, are but different names for the same thing.

All these varieties in phraseology, he adds, are but differences in the term *yeu*, "being." The original word, adds the translator into Chinese, is *subhava*, which is variously explained "the substance which gives substance to itself," "without action and with action," and "the nature which has no nature of its own."

Bhawo, says Gogerly in his *Essay on Buddhism*,[7] is twofold, consisting of moral causative acts and the state of being. Of these, he adds, *kamma-bhawo*, or "moral causative acts," are merit, demerit, and all those actions which lead to existence. The various worlds of the Buddhist universe are designated by the term *bhawo*. "Worlds of sensual pleasure and pain" are *kama-bhawo*. The "Brahma worlds" are *rúpa-bhawo*. The "incorporeal worlds" are *arúpa-bhawo*, and so on. Here the term *bhava* means "states of being."

The numerous modifications of meaning belonging to this word help to account for the three translations of the related word *subhava*, which close the treatise.

I may observe here, that it is common with the modern Chinese Buddhists, to defend the doctrine of the non-reality of material things, by appealing to their liability to destruction. A priest will contend that a wooden table, on the application of fire, passing into smoke and ashes, there is necessarily nothing real in it.

The truth is, that reality and changeableness are both rightly affirmed of a table, or any other material thing. The Buddhist asserts with perfect correctness, that the objects of sense are non-permanent, but he is wrong when he argues that therefore they are unreal. Christianity, modern science, and all sound philosophy agree in ascribing reality and changeableness to the objects of sense. Lung-shu erred in not seeing that these two things can be reconciled.

Footnotes

1. Read before the Shanghai Literary and Scientific Society, 17th November 1857.
2. The "human operations are five," wu-yin—namely, *shè*, "vision;" *sheu*, "reception;" *siang*, "thinking; *hing*, "doing;" *shï*, "perception."
3. This word is a compound of *su*, "good," and *bháva*, one of the twelve causes "being." By Colebrooke and Professor Wilson it is variously translated, "dispositions," "sentiments," "conditions of being." *Abháva* is "privation" or "negation." *Prágabháva* is "present negation of what will be." *Anubháva* is "notion."
4. Translated by O. W. Wight, vol. 1.
5. *Kiai-pi-lo;* in the old pronunciation, *Ka-pi-la. Yeu-leu-kia* (*U-lu-ka*).
6. A friend has, however, suggested to me, that he may regard this as obvious, being what consciousness is ever teaching us.
7. Quoted in Hardy's *Eastern Monachism*.

CHAPTER XX.

EFFECT OF BUDDHISM ON THE PHILOSOPHY OF THE SUNG DYNASTY.

The Sung philosophers differ from Confucius—Five periods of Chinese intellectual development—The Sung writers changed the old cosmogony—The Han writers had already done so—Diagram of the Great Extreme—Other pictorial illustrations—Avoidance of the doctrine of a personal God—Materialistic philosophy of nature—New view of divination.

THE Sung philosophers were separated about fifteen hundred years from Confucius. During this long period differences might well spring up, which accordingly we find.

In reverence for antiquity and the inculcation of the five constant virtues, in teaching the principles of perpetual and universal morality, and in drawing the attention of their countrymen to the ancient models of wisdom and virtue, they agreed with Confucius.

In their cosmogony, their philosophy of nature, their attitude in regard to the ancient practice of divination, and in their explanation of the sovereign power in the world as an abstraction, they differed widely from Confucius.

Four great stages of literary and national development may be pointed to as intervening between the great sage and the age called that of the *Sung ju*. Each of them embraced the course of three or four centuries.

The first is that of Mencius, Siün King, Meh Ti, and Küh Yuen. Orthodox philosophers, heretic philosophers, and a highly popular poet indicated the medley of unfixed thought in which, at that time, the public mind was involved. It was a time of struggle for Confucian and orthodox doctrine, against various speculators in morals and politics who wished to advance some one principle to the detriment of others. But Tauist doctrine was growing yearly in strength.

The second is the Han period. A cloud of critical expounders of orthodoxy, fine historians, editors of the classics, astronomers, astrologers, alchemists, and Tauist philosophers marked this age. Though the authority of Confucius was upheld, and the classics maintained in profound veneration, the tone of speculation was predominantly Tauist. The air was rife with legendary lore. Tauist magic, the hermit life, the medicine of immortality were fervently believed in, and magicians were honoured with popular veneration. The fault of the age was its superstition. Its redeeming feature was its ardent and successful efforts for promoting the restoration of the ancient books and their use in the education of youth.

The third age was Buddhist. It was that of the six dynasties. The riches of the country were lavished on Buddhist structures. In all parts of the empire the people adopted this Indian religion. Hindoo astronomy and mythology, the knowledge of the alphabet and of tones, and the introduction of Buddhist metaphysics date from this time. The Buddhists became a power in literature, and founded a native school of Indian philosophy.

The fourth age was that of the T'ang dynasty. It was a time of luxury and poetry. Han Wen-kung and the poets divided the admiration of the literati of the time between them. The books made in the department of criticism were tonic dictionaries based on the new Indian spelling; no sages appeared, no philosophers of name excepting Han Wen-kung. Such an age of mental inaction and enervating prosperity must be succeeded by a period of mental energy.

Such a period ensued. It was that of the *Sung ju*, the philosophers who now undertook the restoration of the weakened Confucianism, which, while retaining its position, had lost its influence over men's minds. When they appeared on the scene, it had become impossible to retain the system of the ancient sages in its pure and simple form. The religion, the politics, the customs, and superstitions of the people had all changed. But much might, thought they, be done, and the review of their efforts and achievements is a most curious section in the history of humanity, and fraught with salutary warning. They proceeded under the combined influence of Buddhism and Tauism, to extend and reconstruct the ancient system of cosmogony.

As we read the *Yi-king*, the very essence of ancient thought, and the combined work of the most venerated sages, we fail to recognise a distinct cosmogony. Confucius speaks of the Great Extreme as the commencement "of changes. It produced the two figures. These produced the four images, and these again the eight divining symbols." This statement looks ambiguous and uncertain in its meaning. The eight symbols are eight arrangements of strokes. We think, then, of primary arithmetic. Is there much in it besides twice one is two, twice two is four, twice four is eight? Confucius, before and after this passage, is talking of divination. He continues to say: "The eight symbols determine good and ill fortune, and these lead to great deeds. There are no imitable images greater than heaven and earth. There are no changes greater than the four seasons. There are no suspended images brighter than the sun and moon. In preparing things for use, there is none greater than the sage. In determining good and ill luck, there is nothing greater than the divining straws and the tortoise."

Evidently the chief thought of Confucius is upon divination, which was the imitation of natural phenomena succeeding each other in a certain order. If we understand the eight divining symbols to be eight departments of nature, as heaven, earth, fire, water, &c., then we may construct a cosmogony out of the formula above cited. But the aim of the writer was rather to describe the world as the object of the wise man's inquiries, and to point out that he must imitate the laws of phenomenal change which he observes in heaven and earth, and that he may obtain the most valuable results by divination. While the sage looks at his straws, one becomes two, two become four, and four become eight, as the effect of certain transformations. One of the *kwa*, or "symbolic sets of lines," is made up of three or six. Take the former. We find there, say the Chinese, heaven, earth, and man in miniature. So, say I, we may find there anything we like. When the cosmogonical idea enters then, it is indirectly, and it was not the primary sense. In the *Shu-king* there is a passage which speaks of the *Hwang-ki*, the "Emperor's extreme" of perfection. The sense in which *ki* was here used was of course moral. In *Chwang-tsï* we meet with the words, "To be earlier than the Great Extreme, and yet not to be high." The commentator says that the phrase "Great Extreme" here means "heaven, earth, and man, included but not yet separated." *Hwai-nan-tsï*, a Tauist of the Han, says, "To lead out his class to a position higher than the Great Extreme." Here is the budding of that cosmogony which fructified in the Sung philosophers. The Tauists did what the early Confucianists failed to do. They commenced a cosmogony. We find it still more developed in the *Ts'an-t'ung-ki*, a work written by the noted Wei Pe-yang of the Han. Here appears the first map of the Chinese cosmogony, and it wants the "Great Extreme." Bent into three concentric circles are seen the *li-kwa*, representing "fire," and the *k'an-kwa*, representing "water." In the li-kwa, the middle is black and the sides are white. In the *k'an-kwa* the middle is white and the sides are black. They rudely picture a fire giving out flames, and a shining river flowing between two banks. Below this are five small circles, representing the five elements, wood and fire being on the left, metal and water on the right. This diagram was put to a fertile use by the Sung philosophers. They added to it a hollow circle, to represent the "Great Extreme" above, and two hollow circles to represent heaven and earth below. Afterwards Chu fu-tsï made a change. He thought he would improve the diagram by throwing out the elements and introducing in their place the great and little *yin*, and the great and little *yang*. He changed heaven and earth, "the two figures," into *yin* and *yang*.

The Sung philosophers, while they extended the cosmogony by adding the map of the "Great Extreme," added also all the maps printed in the ordinary editions of the *Yi-king*. These maps are not found in any text, nor as prefatory matter are they earlier than the Sung. The Buddhists brought the notion of pictorial illustrations with them from India. Before their time the Chinese made very limited use of illustrated diagrams. Probably the Buddhists took the notion from the Greeks, subsequently to the age of Alexander, when Greeks were in juxtaposition with Hindoos and other Buddhist peoples in Bokharia, Cabul, Afghanistan, and the Punjab.

There were, however, sketches of star groups to the *Sing-king*, "Star classic" (by Kan and Shï) of the Han dynasty, and the strokes of the eight and sixty-four kwa in the *Yi-king, Ts'an-t'ung-ki*, and other works. The arithmetical combinations called *Ho-t'u* and *Lo-shu* were also probably represented by dots or stars. Geometrical diagrams were not known. Though Chen Kung was aware of the property of the right-angled triangle arithmetically, *i.e.*, that the squares of three and four are together equal to the square of five, he never thought of expressing it by a diagram. It needed the Greek genius to initiate the conceptions of geometry.

The later Chinese writers were unconsciously influenced much more by Buddhism, a product of the Indo-European mind, than they ever acknowledged; and they would, under the impressions made on them, imitate the greater effort of the imagination which they there encountered. Thus they tried to complete the thought of the old sages of China, to fill up their outline, and to form into distinctness the shadowy shapes of more ancient ideas. The round line to represent the *T'ai-ki*, the circle half white and half black with the curved diameter which marks light and darkness, or *yin* and *yang*, are new; and the old notion of the four seasons, which was popular in the Han dynasty as explaining the four *siang* or "images," was given up for the great *yin* and the little *yin* and the great *yang* and the little *yang*, phrases new to the Confucian doctrine. We cannot wonder that they gave up the four seasons, for how could the eight *kwa* come out of the seasons? Others said that the four *siang*, or "images," were the animals that pass through metamorphoses, such as the tortoise, the dragon, and the dragon-horse that bore on his back the arithmetical scheme or magic square offered to Yü the Great. But why follow out these ideas? They were unknown to Confucius. They extended the cosmogony without introducing the idea of a personal Creator. This was due to the influence of Buddhism, and the fact that the ancient books had not the doctrine. The peculiar form of their cosmogony was due to Buddhist influence, which inculcates faith in a creating and destroying Fate, blindly impartial, entirely impersonal, and incessantly efficient. If Buddhism had been truly a religion adapted to draw man back to God, his Sovereign and Judge, the true doctrine of creation would have been taught in the Indian Shastras, and the Chinese writers of the Sung dynasty would probably have adopted the idea. But the perversity of Hindoo philosophy was better pleased with irresistible Fate as a substitute for the Divine Ruler.

In taking example from the Buddhists in this particular, the Sung philosophers were the more willing, inasmuch as the teachers of Tauism had preferred the doctrine of spontaneous growth, to represent the origin of the world. The tendency of their speculations was to shut out God from the world, so far as His being in any sense an active Creator.

This remark brings me, by a natural transition, to speak of the difference between Confucius and the Sung philosophers in regard to their philosophy of nature. In ancient China, the notion of five elements was already in existence, but it was not till the Tauists of the Han developed the doctrine that it assumed its modern form. It is remarkable that, after so great an interval, no gleam of a true science of nature should have entered into the intellects of the Sung philosophers. They were too much devoted to antiquity, and too lacking in independence, to shake off the yoke of a materialistic nomenclature.

The minds of Confucius and Mencius were warmed by moral considerations. Political and social questions were to them deeply interesting. They accepted the divination of the "Book of Changes" because Wen Wang and Cheu Kung were the saviours of the state and the advocates of benevolence and integrity. If divination by straws had been introduced, subsequently to the epoch of those sages, by men not taking the rank of sages, the moral instinct both of Confucius and Mencius would have absolutely refused all countenance to it.

Like credit cannot be claimed for the Sung philosophers. Wei Peyang, the Tauist of the Han dynasty, and others from whom they drew ideas, were not the representatives of a system which made morality its centre, but of alchemy and a doctrine of self-cultivation which inculcated physical aids instead of the simple teaching of genuine morality.

The extension of a physical philosophy weakens moral and religious sentiment. The alchemy and astrology of the Han made the Chinese nation less disposed to religious reverence. The occupation of the mind with materialistic ideas and aims obscures the spiritual vision and appetite. It was in this way, to no small extent, that the Chinese nation was prepared to receive Buddhism, partly from religious indifference, and in part also from a desire for fervency in ritual and the acquisition of new spiritual objects on which to fix the soul's gaze. A thousand years more and Buddhism had had its trial, and been found wanting. What, then, should have been the course to be steadfastly pursued by the Confucianists of the Sung period? Undoubtedly, if they desired to follow the example of the sage, they should have opposed tooth and nail the Tauists and Buddhists. Both these religions are defective in the moral element, and that is the very soul of the Confucian system. They would have then done for the superstitious and heresies of their time what Confucius and Mencius did fifteen centuries before. When Luther, in Europe, made a stand for pure doctrine and against asceticism, he did what might to some small extent have been done by the Sung philosophers. Instead of this, they bowed their heads to superstition, allowed idolatry to increase in the land of Confucius, and raised no voice against it.

The most melancholy example of decay in moral and religious instinct is in the denial of a sovereign moral ruler in the universe, and the identification of God with reason and with primeval vapour. This is practically done by Chu fu-tsï, and he is on this account sharply condemned by writers of the present dynasty. The ancient Chinese understood by *T'ien* either the personal Ruler of the world, or the physical firmament. Chu fu-tsï said *T'ien* is nothing but *li*, "reason;" and elsewhere he identifies *li* with *k'i*, "vapour." Such was the unhappy result of the spread of the Tauist physical system and the Buddhist atheism in China.

The last thing I shall mention is the different attitude of Confucius and the Sung philosophers in regard to divination.

When Confucius lived, the ancient magic was still in existence, and, if we take for granted the statements of the *Kia-yü*, he practised it himself. However this may be, he praised it to the skies in the *Yi-king*. Nothing was to be compared with the straws and the tortoise for solving difficulties in politics, and for unravelling the enigmas of nature. He believed in divination because of its antiquity and the great names connected with it. The whole of it was swept away about the time of Ts'in Shïh-wang, B.C. 220, not by that emperor himself, for he highly venerated it, but from want of faith on the part of the people. It is said that the reason was that the books were lost which taught the rules. If so, it was not by order of Ts'in Shïh-wang. Want of faith is the more likely reason. The Sung philosophers certainly did not believe in the benefits attending the use of the straws and tortoise in divining, or they would have recommended to the reigning emperor that the old divination should be restored. The Sung writers do not in so many words deny the efficacy of divination. Their object is plain. They wish to veil the weaknesses of the ancient sages. It is necessary to do this in order to maintain the reverence accorded to the sages. They would not like to acknowledge the superstition of these much-admired men. But if driven closely in argument, the modern

Confucianist admits the uselessness of divination, and that he himself is without faith in it.

If we are to believe the modern literati, the faults of the Sung ju are numberless. I have chosen a few of their novelties and heresies for the consideration of the student of Buddhism and the other religions of China.

CHAPTER XXI.

FENG-SHUI; OR, THE WIND AND WATER SUPERSTITION OF THE CHINESE.

An obstacle to civilisation—Meaning of Feng, "Wind"—Of Shui, "Water"—Use of cyclic characters—Meaning of Lung, "Dragon"—Names of the geomancers—Hindoo nomenclature—Sha-ch'i "Destructive vapour"—Dark arrow—Chen-wu, or "Protecting shield"—Feng-shui professedly based on the "Book of Changes"—Modern Feng-shui is based on the Han-lung-king—Buddhist element in Feng-shui—The four elements of the Greeks—The Hindoo "Air and water" is Feng-shui—Earth, water, fire, and air are creative forces, existing in successive kalpas, and forming successive worlds—Resemblance to the theories of the Ionian philosophers—Geomancy in the T'ang dynasty—Rahu and Ketu—The Feng-shui system grew out of Buddhism—Native element in Feng-shui—Nine fancied stars—Causes of the contour of hills and plains—Stars of the six houses—Feng-shui inconsistent with genuine Confucianism.

EVERYTHING can be made plainer by investigation. Everything can be understood better by the bringing together of facts. The *Feng-shui* of the Chinese deserves to be examined, for it is one of the great obstacles to the progress of civilisation.

It interferes with commercial enterprise. It checks the efforts of missionary zeal. It interrupts the free thought of the people, and keeps them wrapped in the mummy folds of ancient prejudices.

Within the last thirty years this peculiar system of native Geomancy [1] has been made the ground for refusing the establishment of the electric telegraph at Shanghai, of railways, of a road from Tientsin to the Chai-tang coalmines, and of I do not know how many more manifest and desirable improvements, all which would be of the greatest advantage to the people of the district. I begin with the explanation of terms. *Feng*, "Wind," is the first which occurs. It may be illustrated in this way.

A grave should not have a hollow near it. The wind will blow into the grave from that hollow and gradually disturb the bones and the coffin. In ten years they will be half turned over. In twenty years or so they may be entirely turned over. In that case the posterity of the dead will suffer by a kind of material necessity. Such a wind is called a *wa-feng*, from *wa*, "hollow." An outer wind must not be allowed to invade the chamber of the dead, for fear the family fortunes should be disturbed. Thus the filial piety which takes care of the tombs of parents has a material reward, and may be nothing beyond a coarse selfishness; on the other hand, the want of it is visited by a natural retribution, involving sickness, poverty, loss of descendants, and degradation in the social scale.

The aim of the geomancer is to find a spot where the *feng*, "cold air which issues from the earth," is hidden. This they call *ts'ang-feng*. Where there are no hollows it is safe to dig the grave, for here there is no outlet by which this pernicious wind may disturb the dead.

The second term to be explained is *Shui*, "Water." The grave must be carefully chosen. The configuration of the earth is caused by the dragon, whose shape is seen in the mountain boundary cast upon the evening sky. The dragon may be traced to its source. It is observable in the flow of the mountain stream, or in the contour of the earth. The hollow river bed and the variety of hill and valley are caused by the dragon. Trace the water of a valley to its source; that is the point from which commences the influence that controls human destiny. Water is the element in which the dragon delights. Its winding shape as it meanders through a plain gives evidence of this, for the dragon prefers crooked paths. Since then the dragon gives prosperity, elevates the king and the sage, and is the symbol of all exaltation, social, political, or moral, it is all important to consider the position of water when selecting the site of the grave. In the valley of the Ming tombs the water flows from the north-west, passes under a bridge in front of the grave of the emperor Yung-lo, and then pursues its way down towards the plain of Peking on the south-east. Hills in horse-shoe form embrace the valley. The *feng-shui* is good.

If the water flows past a certain point of the geomancer's compass, it causes prosperity; at another, it brings misfortune. If, for instance, to be more particular in detail, the branching point of water be at the north-east, north-west, south-east, or south-west points of the compass, it is possible that there may be prosperity. If it be at the east-north-east, west-south-west, south-south-east, or north-north-west, the elder sons and brothers of the deceased will become scattered and poor. Water at the east by north, west by south, south by east, or north by west points, will ensure happiness to his children, they not being the eldest or youngest. The same children will suffer misfortune if water flow past the north by east and west points.

The chief use of the geomancer's compass is to determine, in regard to the water, the direction of flow, the primary source, the points of junction, and the points from which it starts afresh at a new angle. The grave must be chosen so that the presaged fate, as fixed by the manual of geomancy, may be of the most favourable kind.

The cutting of a new road would alter the course of water, and in various ways affect the calculation of the geomancer; and, as the graves of the past generation are found everywhere, there is no spot where the minds of the people will not be disturbed by projects involving the construction of roads. If the mistake in the selection of a grave site leads to poverty, sudden death, and other calamities, may not a railway cutting, or any disturbance in the course of streams, be equally deleterious? The faith in *feng-shui* must be first eradicated before the Chinese can be induced to look with favour on railways or any description of new roads. If the government should consent to such improvements, their action ought to be accompanied by edicts and publications authoritatively condemning the superstition, and showing what solid reasons there are for disbelieving the whole system of the geomancers. This would aid greatly in soothing the minds of the hostile and calming the fears of the ignorant.

But to proceed: the water before a tomb must be running water. Riches and rank flow like water capriciously from one point to another. Hence riches and rank are supposed to depend on the undisturbed flow of the stream which passes under the bridge in front of the tomb. Man inhabits the tomb, and his destiny is affected by the surrounding circumstances. Riches and rank are attached to flowing water, and, if due care is taken by the geomancer and by the posterity of the dead, a perpetual stream of worldly honour and wealth may be expected to flow into the possession of the family.

It may be instructive to dwell for a moment on this superstition, proving, as it does, that quite as dense a cloud of ignorance rests on China as upon Europe before it was illumined by the sun of Christianity and of modern knowledge. On the geomancer's compass the twelve cyclic characters, *tsu ch'eu, yin*, &c., are inscribed at equal distances interspersed with other cycles. The first, *tsu*, begins at the north point, and is at the back of the tomb, which faces the south. The order of the words is from east to west, according to the diurnal motion of the sun and stars. Let the observer imagine himself standing at the back of one of those common tombs, which are protected on the north side [2] by a long curved bank overgrown with grass. Behind him on the horizon is *tsu*, next on the left is *ch'eu*, and so on to the south point, *wu*. If there is a bend in the course of the water, or a junction of two streams on the north at *tsu*, the posterity of the occupant of the grave will be thieves if poor, and robbed if rich. If on the northeast they will die young, and be left as widows, and men without children. At the third division, they will be greatly subject to diseases. If the geomancer notices that the bend is in the east point of the horizon, he will be bound to foretell that the posterity of the dead will be vagabonds. At the next two stations the special evils indicated are disobedience and rebellion at the one, and at the other the consequence will be that a snake will grow of itself in the tomb. This is a very bad sign, and presages restlessness for the bones of the dead and the fortunes of the living. It brings the evil wind of unhappy destiny with special force upon the occupier of the tomb. The south indicates that the descendants of the dead will lead licentious lives. Here I stop; but the geomancer does not rest till he has boxed the compass with a variety of evils supposed to befall the possessor of an ill-chosen site for his grave. Such a system is well adapted to increase the authority of the *feng-shui sien-sheng*, or "geomancer." He must be well skilled in all the indications which the traditions and books of his profession single out as of importance.

These deceivers of their fellow-men who make their living by practising on the superstitious tendencies of t their patrons, are sometimes wanting in care for their reputation. They often carry the thing too far. They are held up to ridicule not uncommonly by the people, and especially because the word *feng*, "wind," is also identical in sound with *feng*, "lunatic." The country people ridicule them as they stand on the grave site to make observations, or creep on the ground, or sit on their thighs, or superintend the erection of a mound of grass clods, or come out at evening with a lanthorn to set on the mount, as an assistance to them in considering at a distance the desirable or unfavourable features of the site in question.

Very like is all this to the astrology of the Chaldeans, that system of magic and fortune-telling against which Christianity had to fight in the days of Hippolytus and Origen. The one applied the cycles of astronomy to divination with the object of making gain by telling fortunes. The other makes use of the same cycles in geomancy to obtain money by forefending evil and coaxing a good destiny upon him who pays the conjuror. He will become the most popular and best esteemed geomancer who makes the most cunning observations on the contour of the country and the arrangement of the streams of water at the spot where the grave is, or where it is intended to be made.

It is often the case that the care bestowed by the Chinese on the graves of their ancestors may be less from respect for the deceased than from fear of ill consequences to themselves and their descendants. Large sums are spent by the rich in the hope of obtaining the best possible *feng-shui* for their ancestral tombs. Thus the stream of prosperity will always flow continuously onwards in the history of their families, securing them freedom from poverty, misery, sickness, and obscurity. The filial piety of China is less sincere than is by many supposed. It is more selfish than generous, more calculating than spontaneous. The moral sense is deadened in this country by the prevailing desire for riches and rank; and the moral retribution which attends the acts of individuals and nations, is too much hidden from view by a superstitious belief in an unintelligent physical retribution, [3] such as is taught by the Buddhists. When God as governor is banished from the world, atheistic philosophers substitute an impersonal Fate, whose decrees sometimes are in harmony with the moral sense in man, but are perhaps much oftener influenced by low motives, such as are believed by the superstitious to control the acts of the fetish. In this sense it may be said that the Chinese have retrograded in proportion as the *feng-shui* and similar superstitions have extended among them. In the days of Confucius the moral sense was probably brighter than it is now, and there was less of superstition. He lived nearer to the early times of the Old Testament monotheism. Even in his age, if we compare the knowledge of God then possessed by the Chinese with that found in the older classics, we are compelled to admit that there was deterioration. He felt less than the emperors T'ang and Wen Wang, the influence of the personal idea of God as the actual moral governor of the world. As the faith in a personal God grew dim, the moral sense also lost its keenness, and the physical heaven came to be regarded as an object of worship.

The third word I shall explain is *Lung*, "Dragon." The word means that which rises and is lofty in location. It is used of mountains and of national or individual prosperity. The fabulous dragon of China is a monster with scales like a crocodile, and having five-clawed feet. He has no wings, and when he rises in the air, it is by a power he is supposed to possess of transforming himself at pleasure. He can make himself large or little, and rise or fall, just as he chooses. The Chinese dragon, which is a flying saurian, is not like the Greek dragon, which belonged to the serpent family, but seems to be an original Chinese creation, or is connected in some ancient and unknown way with the West. For our present purpose it is sufficient to regard it as purely native, and the most probable cause I can name of the attributes of the dragon is similarity of sound with words meaning "high" and "ascend." Among the words with which it may be identified by etymology, through the mutations of letters, are *shang*, "to ascend;" *cheng*, "the upward motion of steam;" *teng*, "to go up;" *sheng*, also "to go up;" *lung*," high;" and *lung*, "hill." The geomancer calls all high land *lung*, and all low land *shui*. The dragon rules the high land, and water the low land. The chains of hills which almost encircle Peking are the protecting dragon, which is believed to ensure its prosperity. The hills which surround in a similar way the Ming tombs are the dragon, which for three centuries protected that dynasty. The mountain chains which bound the province of Chi-li are connected with the Manchurian mountains which cradled the imperial family in the days of its comparative obscurity. As the seat of empire is in Peking, and it is there the reigning family resides, it is of the highest importance not to disturb its protecting dragon. On plains the Chinese make a long mound behind a tomb. This is also the protecting dragon of that tomb and of the family it represents. It is called the hill, and its office is to keep off the north wind. When high land is wanting, trees make an excellent shield against bad influence. [4]

The geomancer's books say that the dragon follows the course of the water. He originates his influence where the water takes its beginning, and remains permanently where two streams meet. They mean here the influence which produces happiness and misery by a capricious retribution mixed with a coarse natural philosophy. Divine Providence is here kept out of view, and is by implication denied. The elements—fire, air, earth, and water—dominate. It is by their combinations and activities that human fate is determined. The geomancer's dragon causes men's elevation, longevity, and riches; and his influence varies according as he has more of water, or of earth, or of any other element. The course of the dragon must be in each instance examined, and it is decided by the direction of the water. But the contour of the ground, whether rising or falling, high or low, must also be considered. Such investigations were made, for example, in regard to the site of the grave of the emperor Yung-lo, and hence the selection of that beautiful valley where the Ming emperors are buried. The Manchu emperors afterwards despoiled the tombs of that dynasty. Much of the teak timber and marble was brought away to use in the new edifices of Yuen-ming-yuen and the other pleasure grounds of the imperial family. Then they began to fear the consequences on themselves and their descendants. The influence from the Ming tombs on the north might have a disastrous effect upon them while enjoying their summer retirement. They therefore erected those geomantic walls which are seen on the hill sides facing north-north-east on the way to Hei-lung-t'an from Peking. These walls, it was supposed, would check the pernicious influences which might otherwise strike them from the invisible retributive power, which was still supposed to watch over the last resting-place of the once mighty dynasty of the Ming.

It is plain that the geomancer's capricious retribution, if believed in by a nation, must have most injurious consequences in its manifest interference with the doctrine of moral retribution. It is of a piece with the luck of the Chinese calendar, the belief in the efficacy of red colour and favourite moral sentences in keeping off demons, the choice of days for marriages and funerals, and the remainder of the endless list of native superstitions still believed in in this country.

In describing the effect of the dragon, the geomancers say he can remove the "spirit of death," the *sha-ch'i*, and preserve life. The *sha* is a malicious principle, the shed of the Hebrew and Arabic languages, and the *ch'itgur* of the Mongols. When this principle invades the body, man dies. They believe, however, that this enemy who kills and injures men is not invincible. The dragon has the power of checking it. It is curious to notice that here we have to do with impersonal yet living principles. The *sha* does not receive a proper name. In a Western country these superstitions would have been clothed in the language of a graceful mythology. The Chinese, belonging altogether to a more primitive and prosaic type than the Greek race, are content with simply calling them good and evil principles.

I shall now say a few words on the professional names assumed by the geomancers. They call themselves professors of *ti-li*, "the doctrine or description of the earth," "geography." This name is in contrast with *tien-wen*, "astronomy," which means the description of heaven astronomically and astrologically, as *ti-li* geographically and geomantically is of earth.

What astrology is when compared with astronomy, such is geomancy when compared with geography. The astrological section in the geomancer's books is bulky. They tell us that the stars shining down (or coming down, for they suppose them movable) give the mountains their form. Some adopt the Hindoo nomenclature, and make the Sumeru mountain the centre of the mountain and river system of the world. Others, who object to offer so great a concession to the foreign doctrine of Buddhist books, prefer to assign this honour to Kwun-lun, the old Chinese name of the mountains dividing Thibet from Tartary. On the north side of these mountains, the Chinese probably resided for a time before proceeding to take possession of their present home, and the same chain has always taken a prominent place in their notions of geography. It is the backbone from which the other mountain chains proceed, and they form together a kind of terrestrial skeleton. The rivers form the veins and arteries, and the mountains the bones, of a living earth. The whole is imagined to be so like the heavens, that certain stars correspond to certain terrestrial spaces, and exercise rule over them. Kwun-lun rules the hills, as the Pole star rules the stars. When the geomancer takes his position to inspect a site for a grave, house, or city, he fixes upon a spot which is called *hiue*, a name that may be translated into English by, what are indeed possibly, its etymological equivalents, "hole" or "hollow." The windings of the surface in its neighbourhood, whether stone, sand, or loam, extending all round until the view is bounded by hills or the horizon, constitute the constellations which encircle it as the stars do the pole. As in heaven, the twenty-eight zodiacal groups represent the Blue dragon in the east, the Red bird in the south, the White tiger in the west, and the Black warrior in the north, so it is supposed to be in the limited horizon of which the centre is the required site. It is in accordance with this system, half astrological and half geomantic, that the professor of *ti-li* proceeds in searching for what he calls the "true dragon" in each case.

The expression *k'an-yü* is also used. This is a favourite name on the signboards of Peking geomancers. The best explanation of this phrase seems to be that which represents *k'an* as "heaven," *yü* as "earth." *K'an* is the covering let down over an idol, as in the phrase *Fo-k'an*, "A shrine for Buddha," and it here represents the sky as a canopy stretched over the world. *Yü* is the "chariot" in which man is borne. It is not so well known as it should be, that in China in the Han dynasty a gleam of true light shone on the minds of some of the literati in regard to the system of the world. They accepted the noble idea, probably propagated from the West through Central Asia, that the earth moves, while the heavens are at rest. Pythagoras, if this be true, had disciples even so far away as China. It is possible that the phrase *k'an-yü* may hint at this idea. Hence the application of the *yü*, "chariot," to geography and the earth.

Another term requiring explanation is *sha-ch'i*. It is this which is feared when a *ying-pei*, or "shield wall," is erected before a house door. The dangerous vapour known as *sha-ch'i*, causing various calamities, might enter by an unprotected door. Every house entrance in Peking has its devices for preventing straight access. The path must wind, and many methods are employed to save the house from the unwelcome intrusion. But there may be some confusion here; for the idea of a winding entrance to a house arises from the desire to keep men at a distance, as well as demons, and to make a limit between what is public and what is private.

The "secret arrow," *an-tsien*, is a name given to evil influences coming by a small lane in front of a door, or the lane itself is so called. To oppose the bad influences travelling along a lane towards an open door, a stone lion on a pillar, carved with characters indicating the capability of resistance, is placed opposite the entrance, and it is thought to be so useful that nearly every lane in Peking is thus defended. This and similar "protecting shields" are termed *chen-wu*. Some Buddhist structures are built to act as *chen-wu*. Such are pagodas and temples. In the same way operate inscriptions and tigers cut in paper. It is usual to carve stone pillars employed as *chen-wu* with the words *Tai-shah-shï-kan-tang*, because T'ai-shan is the most honourable of mountains, and mountains are a protecting shield to buildings and graves. The carving of the above sentence (meaning, "This stone from T'ai-shan dares to resist") is supposed to constitute a sufficient barrier.

Among other things that should not be opposite to a house door are a well, a grindstone, the corner of a wall, a temple, two streets crossing, and the entrance to a lane.

Among things that protect a house and its inmates is a little image of Kwan-ti, god of war, erected on the roof. A stone arrow is also employed for a similar purpose. It is believed to be a defence against the "dark arrow" of the malignant demon.

Among inscriptions over a door of great efficacy is one in honour of Kiang T'ai-kung, a hero of the Chen dynasty—"Kiang T'ai-kung is here; there is then no fear," *Kiang-t'ai-kung-tsai-tsï-pe-wu-king-kü*.

To have a temple behind a house is a most favourable sign. To be on the east side is also lucky. But to be on the west is bad, and on the north worse. *Yang-chai, yin-chai*, the "light house and dark house," each has its *feng-shui*. In regard to the origin and history of *feng-shui*, a few notes here appended may be found useful in the absence of minute information on an obscure subject.

It professes to be based on the *Yi-king*, where a rude system of nature is traced by means of a cycle of eight elements, including heaven, earth, mountains, lakes, thunder, &c. On this are founded methods for seeking good fortune and avoiding ill. On account of its classical authority and repute, every fortune-teller naturally claims that his rules find their origin here.

The real *feng-shui* of the present generation is, however, to be found rather in the *Han-lung-king* and such works which are of modern date. The name of this treatise means the "Book for shaking the Dragon." It is of the last century.

It is a system which has been in course of formation since the Han dynasty, and has in it Buddhist, Tauist, and Confucian elements, or, as it should rather be stated, Buddhist and native.

Let us begin with the Buddhist. The very name *feng-shui* has in it a tinge of Hindoo notions. The Buddhist Hindoos in China taught the Indian natural philosophy. Their elements were four, namely:—*ti*, "earth;" *shui*, "water;" *hwo*, "fire;" *feng*, "air." As these agree with the Greek doctrine of physics, we may perhaps ascribe its origin to Greece or rather to Babylon, that great centre of ancient civilisation which deserved still more than Egypt to be called "Mother of the sciences."

Writers on India tell us that the natives of that country, when they speak of climate, always call it "air and water." [5] Since then the Chinese word *feng*, "wind," was used by them for air, one of the four elements, it is highly probable that the Hindoo physics have something to do with the origin of the name by which the Chinese geomantic doctrine is known.

To illustrate the way in which the old Hindoo philosophers discoursed on the elements, I shall here mention [6] that they speak of white clouds as having in them more of the element of earth, of black clouds as having more of water, of red as having more of fire, and of yellow as having more of air.

Thunder they believe to be caused by the meeting in the clouds of the wind area with the water area, of the wind area with the earth area, and of the wind area with the fire area.

Calamities caused by wind, fire, and water have local limits in the Buddhist universe. Thus fire works destruction no higher than to the paradise called *Kwang-yin t'ien*, "The heaven of brightness and sound." [7] So also with the other elements, each has its sphere and its period of efficiency. The *kalpas* are terminated by one or other of these powerful elemental forces. By their interaction the world is formed, changed, destroyed, and renewed. It was under the influence of such a philosophy that Milton said (for in his time the Greek doctrine of the elements was still undisturbed in Europe)—

>"Air, and ye elements the eldest birth
>Of nature's womb, that in quaternion run,
>Perpetual circle multiform, and mix
>And nourish all things, let your ceaseless change
>Vary to your great Maker still new praise."

The heaven of Brahma is said to have been formed by wind blowing on water, in which grew up of itself a vast mass of moist matter. On this again the wind blew, and out of it formed the palace of Brahma, which exhibited in abundance the most beautiful combinations of the precious metals and stones of every kind known to man.

The sea is said to have been formed by the mighty winds of heaven blowing upon the earth till they dug in it a vast hollow. In this was placed an immense collection of water, which settled itself in its bed and became the ocean.

Here the wind is seen as a great creating agency. *An impersonal actor* is the aspect in which each of the four elements is regarded by the Hindoo philosophy of nature. This accords well with the superficial view of natural phenomena taken by the Eastern Asiatic mind. The Semite and the believer in the Bible view the events of creation and of universal nature as caused by God. Science comes into the field of nature, and finds out what are the second causes operating to produce observed phenomena. The Christian believer, when convinced of their truth, accepts the results of science as safe and genuine additions to our knowledge, and as harmonising with the teachings of religion. With the Eastern Asiatics it is different. The elemental philosophy of the ancient Hindoos could not be scientific, nor could it base its system of nature on a series of patient observations. It was not in the capacity of the Hindoo to undertake such inquiries. He was content, then, to imagine where he could not discover. He therefore willingly adopted that view of nature—probably in its origin Greek, and ultimately Babylonian—which made of the four elements as many active powers controlled in their working, not by a conscious will, but by a blind yet retributive necessity.

It is interesting to note the resemblances between the Hindoo physical system of the world and that of the Ionian philosophers. Thales of Miletus, who lived B.C. 600, held that water is the origin of things. Out of water everything is derived, and to it everything ultimately returns. Heraclitus of Ephesus believed the one principle which underlies all phenomena to be fire. The world is formed, he taught, by evolution from fire; not made by God or by man. This fire is a rational intelligence controlling the universe. It also is the human soul. Anaximenes said that the physical principle which originates nature is air, and all the elements may be resolved into this. Air made dense gave birth to the earth, and from the earth were formed the heavenly bodies. The air acts by motion impressed on it from eternity, causing in it alternate rarefaction and compression. This air he thought to be eternal. Anaximander of Miletus was a friend of Thales. He held the elements of the world to be simple and unchangeable, and taught that they formed all things by concurrence with homogeneous particles already existing. [8]

Let it be observed that all these philosophers regarded matter as the cause of all things. They lived two centuries before Anaxagoras, Socrates, Plato, and Aristotle, who extended their inquiries into the world of mind, and taught a system in which either mind in the abstract, or God, was regarded as the source of the world.

No more do they resemble Pythagoras, who, living early enough to be the contemporary of some of them, formed a system of his own based on numbers. The secret soul of the world which causes its various phenomena is a principle of harmony.

Zeno, founder of the Stoics, coming after Socrates and Plato, went back to that principle of the Ionian philosophy which finds the origin of the universe in physical elements. The universe, he said, comes into being when the primary substance passes from the state of fire into that of air, then takes the form of water, and finally throws off both its thick portions to become earth, and its rarer parts to become air, afterwards fire. He also held with Heraclitus and with the Hindoos, that the world passes through successive periods of decay and reformation, that is to say, the Indian *kalpas*.

There does not seem much danger, then, in ascribing the Hindoo philosophy of the elements to the Ionian school for its germ. The effect of Alexander's conquest was felt in India in new views communicated on mathematics, astronomy, architecture, and physics. Hence we learn why the doctrine of the four elements was so extensively taught by the Buddhists in Chinese literature of that religion.

According to this view, the *feng-shui* of the Chinese may be traced to the early Greek philosophy as one of its causes. During the three centuries before the birth of Christ the region of the Punjab was ruled for a long period by Greek kings, and it was here that many of the Buddhist books were written. Some of the most prolific writers of this religion resided in the Punjab and its neighbourhood during the Greek domination over Persia, Parthia, Bactria, and a part of North-western India. What wonder if they proceeded to supplement their system by the materialistic philosophy of the Ionians? They were pleased with a cosmogony which had no recourse to the doctrine of a Creator.

The following account of what took place in the eighth century will illustrate the influence of Buddhism on the geomancy of that time. Sü Kien, an official of high rank, when about to bury his wife, inquired of a friend how he should construct the grave with regard to its mound and limits. His friend told him of a Buddhist priest of the city of Hwang-cheu, who knew how to connect the affairs of men with those of demons and spirits. The grave should be deep and narrow; deep for darkness, and narrow for security. Below the surface twelve feet is the limit of earth, and eleven feet lower is the commencement of water. The earth and water regions have each a dragon to take care of them. The dragon reveals himself in the one case in six years, in the other case in twelve. If a trench be of ordinary limits, the spirit's path is not tranquil. The grave should therefore be twenty-four feet deep. Instead of lime-plaster, use starch. Do not place earthenware pitchers in the tomb, because they are allied to the element of fire. Do not place gold in the tomb, lest it should become an elf. Do not place orpiment or arsenic in the tomb, because they are hot by nature. Let the grass and trees on the tomb be withered and not fresh. Melt iron into the shape of cows and pigs; they will keep the two dragons in subjection. Smooth and clean jade-stone has the power to harmonise the hundred spirits of nature. Place it in the tomb to illuminate the path of the spirits.

As a further proof of Hindoo influence on the Chinese mind in the formation of the circle of ideas known as the *feng-shui, t'ien-wen*, and *ti-li*, may be mentioned the names Rahu [9] and Ketu, to denote the genius of the ascending and descending nodes of the moon's orbit. Also the use of the triangle, connecting three points of the horizon a hundred and twenty degrees apart, in casting the horoscope is common to China and India. Then also from the mention in books of geomancy of the Sumeru mountain as the centre of the world, it is evident that they have borrowed from India.

It was for such portions of Buddhist teaching that the Chinese mind had a special affinity. The Chinese are fond of materialism. As Shakyamuni taught Buddhism, it was an ascetic morality. His followers soon gave it a decidedly metaphysical cast. Then followed the materialistic phase, when magic, astrology, and geomancy were developed. The Hindoo Buddhists who taught in China brought with them the whole educational system of their time. In it was included much belonging to the three branches of superstition just mentioned.

In accordance with this view *feng-shui* as now believed is a very modern thing, and subsequent to the spread in the country of Hindoo thought. The mixing of Indian with Chinese ideas produced both the Sung philosophy [10] and the modern *feng-shui*, which has been chiefly developed in the present dynasty.

I now proceed to the native element in the *feng-shui*. This may be made, so far as it is physical, to include astrology and the doctrine of starry influences and the elements as taught in the native Chinese literature. The nine fancied stars which move about in the air, and are either lucky or malignant according to circumstances, must here be referred to. They form an extensive portion of the geomancer's system of follies. All this may be described as the Tauist part of the *feng-shui*.

After this a few words must be added respecting the moral or Confucian element in the *feng-shui*, and the effect of the example of distinguished Confucianists in encouraging popular superstition on this subject.

After a brief allusion to the north star and the chief northern constellations, the writer of the work called *Han-lung-king* goes on to describe minutely the influence of the nine stars, or influences, which move through the atmosphere and cause prosperity and adversity to men.

The first is *Tan-lang*, "Covetous wolf." It has twelve characteristics. Of these five are lucky and seven unlucky. The lucky are pointed, round, flat, straight, and small. The unlucky are not in the middle, crooked, one-sided, precipitous, turned over, broken, and empty. The pointed is shaped like a bamboo sprout. The round is complete on all sides. The flat is perfectly level like a lying silkworm. The straight indicates absence of one-sidedness. The other characteristics are the appearance of being ready to fall over, the presentation of a precipitous cliff, of the breaking off of a watercourse, hollowing into caves, and so on.

Diagrams in accordance with these indications are given of neighbouring hills which are supposed to exert a corresponding influence on a grave according to their shape. The writer adds in the rough poetry of books such as this, "Men say the covetous wolf is good, not knowing that pure and chaste desires are still more important. With all the advantages derivable from the covetous wolf, without pureness and honour, no person, even if he acquired rank, would attain to the three highest, anciently known as the San-kung." The prevailing element is wood.

Looking at the diagram only, the reader sees a conical hill or elevation, a mushroom shaped outline, and a series of four or five conical hills presented in half profile. These appearances all prove the presence of the "covetous wolf."

The second moving star is *Chü-men*," Great door." The form loved by this spirit is flat at the top and square on the sides. When a hill presents the appearance of a square or trapezium with the upper line horizontal, the phenomenon is caused by the presence of this influence. Wood is the prevailing element.

The third star is *Lu-tsun*, "Rank preserved." Nine shapes in hills mark its presence. Its favourite shape has a flat top, a cylindrical body like a drum, and at the bottom it spreads into five branches like the toes of the human feet. Properly it should be a malignant star, because its shape partakes of a spotted and mixed nature. But it is able to adapt itself to conditions which secure good luck. It causes men to attain the lower ranks of promotion, such as the chief magistracy of cities of the second and third ranks, and, in certain circumstances, gives the control of troops or of literary examinations. The five-toed appearance is represented in the map as sometimes three or four toed. There are also other modifications. Earth is the ruling element.

The fourth star, Wen-chü, "Literary windings," belongs to the element of water. It loves the shape of the snake when seen moving with three or four bends of the body. The "Men of the Dragon," *Lung-kia*, as the geomancers call themselves, can detect the presence of this influence in the contour of hills. It has, like the other stars, a normal and several occasional shapes. When thin, it is the snake proper; if thicker, it is a caterpillar; if still wider, it becomes a cast net. The geomancers profess to attend to the points of bending in the snake, because these indicate the line of water-flow and of the dragon's influence.

The fifth star is *Lien-cheng*, "Purity and uprightness." Its element is fire. The ancients highly valued it, says the manual, and called it Red flag and "Brilliant vapour," *Yau-k'i*. It likes a lofty position, rugged heights, umbrella folds, and the shape of a flattened ball. One form it assumes is that of the "Dragon tower," *Lung-leu*, which is a conical elevation, overtopping all beside it. Another is that of the "Palace of precious things," *Pau-tien*, in forming which several cones of equal height are seen in parallel rows. The imaginations of the geomancers lead them also to fancy the appearance in rocky outline of the tortoise and the serpent guarding some little mountain gorge. This is considered to be an indication of the best kind of dragon influence, for here passes some water channel.

The sixth star is *Wu-chü*, "Military windings." Its element is metal. It is round at the top and broad at the bottom, like a bell or an inverted cooking-pan. In judging of the hill shapes that belong to this star, it is easy to mistake the demon for the dragon. This is specially the case when the shape observed is that of an inverted spoon, the spoon being like the tail of the Great Bear, or rather the "Seven stars," usually called *Pe-teu*, in their entireness. The demon and the dragon are both in the habit of assuming the shape of an inverted "dust-pan" (*ki*), an inverted "spoon" (*sho*), and an inverted "palm," *chang* (palm of the hand). The skill of the geomancer is displayed in distinguishing the appearances. The demon may affect any one of the nine stars; and, as there is the fourfold form, square, round, crooked, and straight, there may be thirty-six shapes to be considered. Generally speaking the locality of the demon is behind the "grave site" (*hiue*), and the corresponding genius in front of it is called *kwan*, "officer." If the demon and the genius of office look at the tomb site, it is a lucky sign. If they turn their backs to it, the dragon of prosperity will not take up his place there. The seventh star, *Po-kiun*, "Breaker of the phalanx," is referred to metal. It has one normal and four peculiar shapes. The normal shape is that of three round-headed cones, seen one rising above another like the folds of a flag when carried by a person walking. Below it has ugly-looking points like spear points. Persons seeing these conclude too hastily that this star is malignant and unlucky. It is so, but in certain circumstances it may become highly serviceable for acquiring riches and rank. Consider what stars it corresponds to in the sky. Its power is formed by the descending influence of the "Three terraces," *San-t'ai*, three pairs of stars in our Great Bear. Upon high hills the celestial essence of these stars collects, and becomes formed into six terrestrial or atmospheric stars, called *Lu-fu*, the "Six palaces." They are all mingled with the influences of the five elements.

STARS OF THE SIX HOUSES.

	Shape.	Element.	Name.
1.	Round	Metal	*T'ai-yang*, "Great light"
2.	Oblong, round	Metal	*T'ai-yin*, "Lesser light."
3.	Round head, long body	Wood	*Tsï-k'i*, "Purple vapour."

4. Alive, crooked,
   moving   Water   *Yue-pu*, "Moon disturber."
5. Square   Earth   *Ki*, "Plan."
6. Conical   Fire   *Lo*, "Net."

The eighth star, *Tso-fu*, "Left assistant," is under the influence of the element of metal. Its normal shape is that of a head with a napkin wrapped round it, in front high, behind low. This star is a servant to the great dragon, who gives shape to the constellations of astronomy. *Fu* (the eighth) and *Pi* are two stars seen near α in Hercules, called by the Chinese *Ti-tso*, "Emperor's throne," and by European astronomers, *Ras Algethi*. On account of their proximity to the throne, it is assumed that these stars confer honour on men by their influence if happily directed.

The ninth star, *Yeu-pi*, "Right assistant," has no fixed shape. Its element is water. Flatness is its favourite characteristic. Where hills break off and give place to the plain, it loves to be. It rules even surfaces. It is therefore called *Yin-yau*, "Hidden glory." It is also fond of narrow threads and dim vestiges of things. The snake creeping through grass, the fish leaping on sand, the spider's thread, the traces of horses' hoofs, and the strings of the lyre are presided over by this star. It likes that which is half real and half unreal, and which is scarcely visible to the eye. The aid of this star is said to be particularly valuable in cases of doubtful *feng-shui*. The unskilled geomancer will say, "This is a level plain, I can make nothing of it; I need some elevation to guide me in the diagnosis of the neighbourhood." He forgets that water flows not only down a hill but even on a plain, and that there is a difference of level there. One inch is enough for the true "discerner of the dragon." Or the tyro in the mysteries of the *feng-shui* folly may say, "This ground is wet. The fault is fatal. You must not bury your dead here." Fool that he is, he perceives not that to decide so hastily is most unwise. Does not the wetness come from an unusual flow of water? When the water disappears, this place will be soon as dry as those which are higher. The Right assistant loves this state of doubt, and hence the differences in opinion between geomancers respecting the characteristics of the same spot or region.

It may be said generally in regard to the nine stellar influences that, when seeking for a lucky hollow, you find, for example, here the appearance of a breast, there of a swallow's nest, here a ploughshare, there a comb, here the turned-up hand, there the spear or lance, and there a hanging lanthorn; these effects of starry influence point out the true nature of the desired "hollow" (*hiue*). The dragon makes the hollow, and in seeking it the correct indications of the dragon's action must be followed.

It would be of little use to follow the Chinese geomancers further into the lucky and unlucky effects of these stars, their division of hills into "male" (*hiung*) and "female" (*ts'ï*), into "patriarch" (*tsu*) and "small hills" (*siau-feng*), and into "branches" (*chi*) and "stems" (*kan*). Enough has been said.

This whole doctrine of starry influences may be readily traced back to the system of the Tauists in the Han period. Hwai An-tsï, Wei Pe-yang, Pau Po-tsï, and others, taught just such a philosophy of nature as might give origin to the more modern views of the geomancers. Astrology and alchemy were then in their glory. The former of these influenced geomancy and encouraged popular belief in moving starry influences. From whence came that astrology? The answer should be from Western Asia and India, but full data on this point are wanting. Not only the imaginary stars of the geomancers must be traced to the Han period, but all those star genii and demons of the imperial calendar which are popularly believed to be in perpetual movement in people's houses, in streets, and in the air, may be assigned to the same origin. It was then that the habit began in China of regarding the stars as movable beings regulating the affairs of kingdoms, cities, and individuals. Though the names of the nine stars are new, they are identified by the geomancers with the seven stars of the Great Bear and two neighbouring stars. They move up and down in the ether of space, and are either visible as individual stars, or, if invisible, traverse the world each with an elemental force of its own, to give form, character, and vigour to those parts of nature to which they attach themselves.

The remaining element in *feng-shui* which now comes to be considered is moral. The choice of a grave is to be made in accordance with the rules of geomancy, because filial piety requires it, and it is sanctioned, it is said, by the example of the sages.

To prove, however, that Confucius himself believed at all in any of the nonsense connected with geomancy is very difficult. It is said in the biography of the sage by Sï-ma Chien that, not knowing where his father's grave was, he inquired of the mother of a friend. Learning from her the locality, he buried his mother there. In the *Li-ki* it is said of Confucius that he was at first unwilling to make a mound over the grave, because the ancients did not. At last he consented to carry out the suggestion, but the person left in charge of this duty soon came to the sage to announce in an agitated manner that rain had fallen and reduced the mound to a level. Confucius regretted that he had allowed himself to depart from primitive simplicity. These little incidents seem to show that he had no notion of geomancy, and that he loved simplicity.

In early times it was enough for emperors to be buried on high mountains under a large mound, while feudatory princes were content with hillocks, and the common people found their last resting-place in the plain. There was no thought then of the course of water flowing past the tomb.

An ancient said, "I have been of no benefit to mankind while living. Let me not injure them when I am dead. Choose my burying place where the earth yields no food for man." Others have said, "If a man dies on the hills, let him be buried on the hills. If he dies in the lowlands, let him be buried in the lowlands." This was said with a view to economy. It would be a useless expense to convey the body to a distance. For the same reason another noted person of the Han period ordered his son to bury him without a coffin in a grave dug in the ground. In the T'ang dynasty a high officer gave directions that he should be buried in a plain manner, without monument or stone of any kind, and over his grave the villagers were to be allowed to plough and sow as of old.

Such dying instructions as these have been carefully preserved by the Chinese literati, who felt that they were more in accordance with true wisdom than the follies which afterwards grew into vogue. They show the proper standpoint of the genuine Confucianist. With him everything must give way to moral considerations.

In arguing against *feng-shui* and the other superstitions of the Chinese, we ought to find on this ground a fast friend in the true follower of Confucius. The freedom of Confucius from superstition is one of the best proofs of the greatness of his mind, and a main cause of his ascendancy over the literary class. His utterances on the danger of excessive reverence to the *kwei-shen* have been a barrier against Buddhism, and prevented the extension of its soporific influence over the whole nation. The literati have thus been kept in an independent and self-sustained position, and have not become quite overwhelmed by this intrusive foreign element. Hence, the scions of scholarly families and students who have read extensively are trained in a school of ideas antagonistic to superstition. These men, therefore, may be appealed to in aid of our opposition to the *feng-shui*. They are ashamed of it. They disown it if brought in argument to close quarters. They only comply with it from an unwillingness to act contrary to custom. The great minds among them avoid even the appearance of compliance, but these are not many.

Considering that the enlightened Chinese are thus disposed, there could be no harm done by a studied attack on the whole system of geomancy in a book prepared for the purpose. It would not be offensive to the true Confucianist, and it would afford opportunity to teach much good philosophy and truer views of nature than those to which they have been accustomed. But perhaps the whole structure is so flimsy that it will fall of itself, without laying siege to it or directing the ordnance of argument against it. The shining of true science may pale its ineffectual fire, and cause it to disappear as a thing of darkness, without special effort to bring about its extinction.

Footnotes

1. Geomancy is properly divination by means of lines or points drawn on the earth. The Chinese *feng-shui* may be called "geomancy," because it divines by means of lines noticed in the shape of streams and hills.
2. In Southern China this bank is carried around the north, east, and west sides.
3. This is the *karma*, which is essential to the Buddhist metempsychosis.
4. See Essay by Rev. Dr. Yates.
5. See Sir James Martin's *Influence of Tropical Climates on Europeans*.
6. *Fa-yuen-chu-lin*, chap. iv. This work is a Buddhist cyclopædia of the T'ang dynasty.
7. *Fa-yuen-chu-lin*, chap. i.
8. Smith's *Dictionary of Greek and Roman biography and Mythology*.
9. In Chinese, *Lo-heu* for *La-hu*. The twenty-eight constellations of the Chinese zodiac were identified with the Hindoo *Nakshatras* in the Han dynasty.
10. It would be interesting to trace the effect of Greek and Indian materialistic philosophy on the formation of the modern Chinese cosmogony. It is not uncommon for doctrines to be attributed to the Chinese as a nation which only belong to a particular modern sect of the literati. While some writers attack the Chinese for beliefs which they do not hold, such an examination of the modern native philosophy might prove useful.

CHAPTER XXII.

BUDDHIST PHRASEOLOGY IN RELATION TO CHRISTIAN TEACHING. [1]

Use of Buddhist terms in the Nestorian inscription, A.D. 781—Mo, "demon;" in Sanscrit, mara—Ti-yü, "hell," is naraka—Ten judges of hell—Among them Pau Cheng, the famous judge of the Sung dynasty—The Sung philosophers encouraged the popular belief in future retribution—This prepares for Christianity—T'ien-t'ang, "heaven"—Defects of this term—Ming-kung, &c., as names for "heaven"—Buddhist paradises possibly borrowed from Western Asia or some other country farther west—Redemption—Ti-tsang and Kwan-yin—Pity—Instruction—Effect of sin—Decreed forgiveness to penitents—Secret merit—Happiness and merit confounded—Sin and misery confounded—Illustration from the narrative of a Christian convert.

WE teach the Chinese the Christian religion by means of their own language, and in their vocabulary of religious terms many words and phrases of Buddhist origin have come into common use.

The Syrian inscription, A.D. 781, shows that no scruple was felt by the first Christian missionaries in China in adopting many Buddhist terms.

We find there *mo*, "devil." This is the common word used in *mo-kwei*. Both name and being are of Hindoo origin; the "delusions of the devil" are called *mo-wang*. Hell is called "palace of darkness," *an-fu*. The "ship of mercy" conveys the faithful disciples across the sea to heaven. The ship is *ts'ï-hang;* "heaven" is *ming-kung;* Christian "monks" were called *seng,* from the Sanscrit *sanga,* "assembly;" a "monastery" is called *sï*, as by the Chinese Buddhists; a "monk's robe" is called *kia-sha,* which is the Sanscrit word for "gown," *kashaya.*

Buddhism throve in the T'ang dynasty. It was the era when Hiuen-tsang went to India. His journey was an instance of the depth of religious faith which characterised the Chinese followers of Gautama in his age, and it also secured an immense increase of popularity to the ideas of his sect. Buddhism was very powerful in the court, and profoundly influenced the literature. Translations from Sanscrit were made with extreme care, and received from the literati a high literary finish. The influence of Buddhism is distinctly seen in the dictionaries of the time, in the syllabic spelling, in the discovery of the four tones, and the settlement of the laws of poetry consequent on that discovery. The poets and critics of the T'ang dynasty were conscious of great obligations to Buddhism, and made scarcely any decisive and persistent effort to check the spread of popular faith in that religion, and the general adoption of Hindoo phrases and terms in the language. Han Yü, in his *Fo-ku-piau,* was an exception.

The Syrian Christians extended their missions in China at a time when Buddhism was in the ascendant, and adopted terms from the professors of that religion which indicate a more extensive principle of imitation than either the Roman Catholics or the Protestants have in later times thought of adopting. The reason is found in the popularity of Buddhism in the capital of China in the time of the Nestorian missionaries. That religion was much favoured at court, and was the chief agent in teaching the future state and the superiority of the monastic life as a means of subduing the passions. Both Buddhism and Christianity came from the West; and it would be for the Nestorians difficult to maintain the mutual independence of the two religions, agreeing as they did in a belief in a world of happiness and of misery for mankind after the present life. The fact that the Nestorian monks called themselves *seng,* as the Buddhists do, has some light thrown on it by an incident in the life of Matthew Ricci. He adopted a Buddhist priest's dress and shaved his head. But after making trial for a time of this costume he changed it for that of the Confucianists, as it was worn in the Ming dynasty. Perhaps the Nestorian priests adopted and retained the Buddhist costume in ordinary life, and reserved their own ceremonial robes for special occasions, as the Roman Catholics do now with the Confucianist.

The word *seng,* for "priest," they probably took to be an exact equivalent of their *cohen.* So in colloquial English, we call the Buddhist monks Buddhist priests. We have given up the word *bonzes,* the Japanese term introduced by Portuguese and other Romish missionaries, into European accounts of the religion of this part of the world. To call them priests at all is, however, somewhat negligent English. The Roman Catholics have done better to call their "monks" *sieu-shi*, and their "nuns" *sieu-nü,* rather than to style them *seng* or *ho-shang,* and *ni-ku* or *ni-seng. Sieu* is "cultivate moral virtues;" *shi*, "scholar," "person;" *nü* is "woman."

Times have changed. The Buddhists are not now wafted to a proud position by the gales of popular applause; and still less in the present dynasty, than in the Ming dynasty, would the Jesuit gain any advantage by following the example of Ricci while he was in South China, in adopting the Buddhist garb.

In discussing Buddhist phrases capable of being applied in Christian teaching, I will begin with *mo,* the "devil." This is in Sanscrit *mara.* The *maras* are, in Buddhist phraseology, a class of demons. They are not known to the Brahmans. The word is formed from the root *mar,* "death," and is an Aryan personification of death. By the Buddhists the *maras* are regarded as a king with a host of followers. They wage war against Buddhism, and when Shakyamuni was living he had successful contests with them. In Buddhist books all temptations are demons. A demon is hidden in everything that can cause evil to man. The demon of anger prompts to sin in every case of sinful anger. So of lust, of drunkenness, of theft, and each form of sin.

The use of *mo* has become so extended that in our translations of the Bible it is freely used for the Greek διαβολος, *diabolus* in the literary and colloquial versions. To Christian converts it gradually assumes a Christian sense in proportion as they are instructed in the Biblical representations of the power, agency, and character of Satan. But if not instructed, the views of the convert are Buddhistic. These views are brought into connection with "possession," as seen in an intoxicated man, an importunate beggar who cannot be got rid of, an opium smoker who is under the dominion of his habit, or a scholar who cannot cease from study. Such persons are possessed by a demon who is called *kwei*, but in the poetry of the Tang and the Sung dynasties he might be called *mo*. A writer is free from the *mo-chang*, "demoniacal film or hindrance," when his thoughts and language flow freely and beautifully.

The main idea is often that of causing trouble by possession. *Ju-mo*, "a demon entering," is a phrase which is quite commonly used to express the idea. To "become deluded," "to be deadened to," are also thus described. *Nan-mo* or *nan-kwei* are common examples of the way in which "demons causing trouble" is expressed.

Evidently it is necessary in using *mo* for the Christian sense, to distinguish accurately the peculiar meaning of the word in the heathen religions. The Christian *mo-kwei* is more intensely wicked than the Buddhist *mo-kwei*. But both in Europe and in Asia, in ancient or modern times. we nowhere find the demon world dissociated from the phenomenon of possession in popular language. It is one of the primitive identities, permanently retained in the phraseology of all religions. Another common Buddhist expression is, *ti-yü*, "earth's prison." The Sanscrit *naraka*, "the abodes of demons," places of punishment underneath the world of men, are so designated.

The advantage of the employment of this term is that it is ready for use, that it agrees with our word "hell" in being a place of punishment; and, further, that the visible universe being to the Chinese consciousness in two parts, viz., heaven and earth, it must always be convenient to the

Christian teacher to speak of "hell" as belonging to earth. The objections to its use are great. It misplaces the locality. No modern Christian books place hell underground. It is plural as much as singular, while our word for the place of punishment is always singular. Further, it gives the Confucianist occasion to say that we have borrowed from the Buddhists, and that we must share in the same condemnation which the adherents of that religion have had to endure.

The authors who have reasoned against Christianity on the ground of the identity of the doctrine of hell being much the same in the two religions, and that we have borrowed from the Buddhists, are Sü Ki-yü in *Ying-hwan-chï-lio*, Wei Yuen in *Hai-kwo-t'u-chï*, and the king of Corea in his edict against Christianity, taken away from the hill fort at the mouth of the Corean river, by the United States naval force which captured the fort eleven years ago.

The words used for "hell" in our translations of the Bible are *yin-fu* (the hidden palace), *yin-kien* (the dark world). The natives also use *yin-sï*, the (place of hidden judgment). *Ti-yü* is never used in our translations, at least the recent ones; but all missionaries use it colloquially, and it finds its place in our catechisms. These phrases, *yin-fu*, *yin-kien*, *yin-sï*, are very modern. They are subsequent to the teaching of the metempsychosis in China. The term used for hell in the Syrian inscription A.D. 781 is *an-fu*, "palace of darkness," a phrase borrowed from the Buddhism of the time, and meaning the same as *yin-fu*.

Since the Sung dynasty, the popular notion of hell in China has been formed chiefly by the prevalent representations of the ten tribunals seen in temples and in the *Yü-li* (probably A.D. 1068) and other works. Punishments are here depicted in the most frightful forms. The incendiary is bound by a chain to a hot cylinder, which he clasps with his arms and legs; flames are being poured forth from the top and sides of the cylinder. Those who guard written characters from desecration enjoy honours and wealth. Those who waste grains of rice and millet are seen changed into horses, sheep, and oxen. The retribution corresponds with the sin and the merit in all cases.

In the consent of the governing class to those popular representations of hell which we see painted with charcoal on the white walls of temples, or formed with moulded and painted figures of clay, or taking the form of prints in popular Tauist literature, we see an important concession. While the literary class do not believe in heaven or in hell, they see the advantage that may be derived from them in the inculcation of virtue. In the hands of the moral teacher, future retribution is a powerful engine for good. This is recognised by the governing class so far, that they encourage the people to have in temples the horribly grotesque and alarming models in clay of future punishment which we see there. The celebrated judge Pau Cheng, of the Sung dynasty, who died A.D. 1062, is the fifth of the ten judges. The rest are all Chinese, as we know by their surnames, and probably actual judges of about the same period.

The late Dr. Medhurst, when visiting T'ien-mu shan, in the vicinity of Hang-cheu, was hospitably entertained by the magistrate of the *hien* city of Hiau-feng. In the course of conversation he asked his host what he expected would be his lot in the future state. He replied that he supposed he would become a *C'heng-hwang-ye*. This little circumstance shows how the Sung dynasty practice of canonising good magistrates has taken hold upon the country, and made the people think a magistracy in the invisible world quite as attainable as a like post of honour in the present state of existence. Often, however, they will, in using phrases of this kind, speak jokingly. Sung dynasty emperors were the first to practise, so far as I know, the appointment of local magistrates for the invisible world, with jurisdiction over particular cities. None of the Sung philosophers lifted up a voice against it. They allowed the up-growth of the religious usages and arrangements connected with the Tung-yo miau, the Ch'eng-hwang miau, and the T'u-ti miau. All of these temples are erected to divinities who are supposed to deal with mankind in the future state in the way of just retribution for their crimes.

These and other judicial divinities were elevated to their posts with the assistance of the literary class, who are, however, ashamed to recognise them in their writings. They kneel before them as officers on duty, encourage the people to believe in the reality of their jurisdiction, and avoid protesting against them in their writings. What the literati believe in their hearts to be a monstrous fiction, is to be allowed on account of its moral and political benefits.

What shall the Christian missionary in these circumstances do with the native doctrine of retribution? He will assure the people that there is revealed in the Christian Scriptures a retribution just, comprehensive, and inevitable. He may allude to the modern origin of the Ten judges, and condemn the Sung philosophers for their insincerity in allowing, if not inventing, this mythological creation. He may proceed to condemn the Buddhist also for teaching that Yama is judge in the invisible world, when, according to their own metaphysics, Yama is nothing; and for urging the Chinese to accept a doctrine of hell punishments which they teach, not as what they really believe, but as a means to an end. In this they set an example of false teaching which the Confucianists were only too ready to accept and imitate. The Christian retribution will come before the Chinese mind on quite a different footing, as resting on the instruction of a divine Saviour.

But let us be candid in acknowledging the aid we receive from Buddhists in previously spreading far and wide among the people the idea of a moral retribution; for this helps us to bring over more quickly to the understanding of the Christian faith on this point, any of the population who are familiar with the Buddhist teaching.

This is the case even with sects like the *Sin-siu* in Japan. That sect professes to believe in absorption into the absolute. Many Buddhists profess to take the Western heaven as the goal of their hopes. But these beliefs or aspirations are capable of being reconciled with beliefs in the heavens and hells of the metempsychosis, and they are actually taught along with them. Even the most metaphysical Buddhists, and those who have the most abstruse notion possible of the Nirvâna, still teach as exoteric doctrine the metempsychosis as known in India.

That I am not wrong in imputing to the literati who belonged to the later Sung dynasty, and especially Chu Hi, a principal part in the encouragement of the popular belief in future retribution, may be shown by the chronology. The author of the *Yü-li*, a Tauist named Tan Chi, who was the first to give currency to the legend of the Ten royal judges, lived more than a century before Chu Chï. The two brothers, Ch'eng Ming-tau and Cheng Yi-chwen, lived a little before Tan Chï, in the early part of the eleventh century. The elder died the year before the Yü-li was made; the younger lived for nearly twenty years after. Then came the time of Hwei-tsung, who is said to have deified Chang Yi with the title Yü-hwang to-ti, and who was carried with his son into Tartary a prisoner under the Nü-chih dynasty. This was the period of the founding of this new Tauist school of a future state, with ten judicial courts, and with Yü-hwang to-ti enthroned as a judge of human actions. Then was the time also that Tsï-hwang shang-ti and Feng-tu to-ti were made divine judges, each with his special court for the determination of the happiness or misery in the future state of each individual man.

Chu fu-tsï witnessed all this and did not protest against it. He saw also rising round him the novelty of the Ch'eng-hwang miau, with its judicial apparatus, its magistrate for trying cases in Hades, and its array of clay servitors, with arrangements for periodical processions through the region over which he had jurisdiction, for the sake of knowing the good and bad conduct of individuals. He saw these things and made no struggle against the extension of superstition. The worst he said of Buddhism was, that the doctrine of Yang and Mih was better. The reaction against Buddhism, so far from beginning with him, began rather, as I think, with the expulsion of the images of Confucius, which had in the Sung dynasty found their way into the temples of Confucius in cities. This expulsion took place in the Ming dynasty, and in the present dynasty the reaction against Buddhism has been stronger among the literati. But the pictures of the ten hells have come to be more and more used.

It is important to note that Chu fu-tsï lived in an age when the Tauist images, and the mythology connected with them received a great development, against which he made no protest. Chu Hi ought not to be put forward as the authoritative representative of Chinese thought; and some foreign scholars appear to me to have erred in regarding his views as final, and as the accepted expression of Chinese thought, ancient and modern. In fact, there is scarcely any one who has been by later writers more heavily condemned. His influence has been great, and it continued long, and some of his works are still authorised school-books; but his authority as a thinker and a scholar, is in the present dynasty challenged and criticised severely by all independent writers, without an exception.

It is possible that Chu Hi may have felt that the doctrine of future retribution is likely to be true. He was certainly rather fond of reading Buddhist books. He may not have cared to contradict what was to *some extent* perhaps true. Let it be borne in mind that in the "Book of Odes" he approves of the rendering in a certain well-known passage, "The soul of Wen Wang moves up and down in the presence of the Eternal." Scholars not in favour of the continued existence of the soul after death usually explain this away.

The term *t'ien-t'ang*, for "heaven," seems to be founded on the use of *t'ang* as a "hall" for holding a court. Heaven is present to the native mind as a vast hall where the Deity sits in celestial state with subordinate divinities as his assessors. The phrase is not Hindoo, but the idea is Hindoo. In other words, the Chinese have made a phrase of their own, to fit the Buddhist notion of a paradise or palace of the gods. The reason is not far to seek. The Buddhist translators, when rendering the word "god" used *t'ien* invariably. The Sanscrit *deva*, the Latin *deus*, and the Bengali *debta*, have no other equivalent in Chinese than *t'ien*, "heaven." At the same time *devaloka*, the "heaven of a deva," is also translated by *t'ien*, thus causing some confusion. This mixture of two senses has led to the addition of *t'ang*, in ordinary colloquial use, for heaven as a paradise. This phrase *t'ien-t'ang*, "heavenly hall," is of course modern and subsequent to the spread of Buddhism.

The narrow limitation of the word to the sense "hall" is an objection, but Christians all feel that the chief and prevailing sense is in the word *t'ien*. The Christian usage omits *t'ang* as often as it admits it, even in colloquial intercourse and in preaching. In the various translations of the Bible, *t'ien-t'ang* is never used. *T'ien-kung*, "palace of heaven," is not inappropriate for the throne-scene in the fourth chapter of the Book of the Revelation; but it is not used in the Chinese versions of the Scriptures. Like *ti-yü* for "hell," it is limited to colloquial use in Christian literature. In Buddhist books, tien-tang is not used for "heaven," but *t'ien-kung*, "palace of the gods," which is so used, is a good deal like it, and resembles *ming-kung*, "bright palace," which is found in the Syrian inscription for "heaven," and in late Christian literature occasionally. *Ming-kung* and *t'ien-t'ang* are both of them phrases formed on the Hindoo notion of heaven.

"Heaven" and "hell" are both embraced in *yin-kien*. The invisible world includes states of happiness as well as misery. This reminds us of Homer, where, in the eleventh Book of the *Odyssey*, he describes the interviews of Ulysses with many of the shades of the dead, including his own mother. The palace of Pluto and the abodes of the dead were regarded by Homer and his contemporaries as underground. Was not the notion of *ti-yü*, "earth's prison," taken to India from countries farther west? Egypt may have been the parent of the idea of a subterraneous prison of the dead. We find the notion in Egypt, in Greece, in Babylon, and in India; but it is not in the Vedas. It was either originated in India after the Vedic age, or it was then introduced from elsewhere. I prefer somewhat the hypothesis of Western origin, on account of the similarity of the view held of the future state as given in Buddhist books, with those found in the religious books of Western races.

We are beginning to find out how fruitful was the Greek mind, not only in inventing, but in communicating the knowledge of inventions. The traces of Greek influence are found in Hindoo architecture, in Hindoo astronomy, in Hindoo arithmetic, and in Hindoo philosophy. The Sanscrit writing is now admitted to be of Semitic origin. The Hindoo hells which are first found in the "Laws of Manu," of uncertain date, somewhere between B.C. 800 and B.C. 500, and then in the Buddhist books, and which are intimately connected with the metempsychosis, may have come from Western countries, and subsequently have been elaborated into the Hindoo shape, when the universe based on the metempsychosis was in course of construction by the Hindoo mind; at any rate when Chinese critics charge Christianity with borrowing "heaven and hell" from the Buddhists, we are right in pointing out that the Olympus of the Greek gods, and the Hades of Pluto (Poseidon), in Homer, are more ancient conceptions than the Buddhist hells and paradises; and that, whether it was from Egypt, from Babylon, or from some other source, the borrowing is on the whole more likely to have been the other way. Otherwise, why do the oldest Hindoo books say nothing of the "earth prisons" and the "palaces of the gods"?

Redemption.—Each Buddha and Bodhisattwa is a redeemer. I notice here *Ti-tsang-wang p'u-sa*. He is called *Yeu-ming-kiau-chu*, "Teacher of the unseen world." Full of benevolence and grace towards mankind, he opens a path for self-reformation and pardon of sins.

The phrases here used are such as we employ in describing the Christian redemption. The Buddhist redemption is moral; for it includes repentance, and rescue from the net of the delusions of Maya, partly moral and partly mental (*Maya-saus*, "a juggler," "idealism," "delusion"). It brings the idea of grace before the people. That grace is pity in the heart of Buddha, or some Bodhisattwa such as Kwan-yin, prompting them to teach true doctrine to those who have gone astray. In the Buddhist books the Bodhisattwa expresses a wish and proceeds to accomplish it. In the Tauist books, however, the utterance of the wish is attributed to *Ti-tsang* or *Kwan-yin*, but the issue of the decree of salvation is ascribed to *Yü-hwang ta-ti* or *Tsï-hwang shang-ti*. The love of Buddha is self-prompted, and is the result of a determination entered on millions of years before in an earlier life. It may be doubted whether this self-originating love can logically be claimed by the Buddhists; for they also believe in an impersonal fate which compels the succession of events just as they happen. But it is better wherever we find a moral love like that of Buddhism, being at once the enemy of vice and the friend of virtue, to recognise its existence and assign due credit to it.

This being so, it seems proper to say, further, that the resemblances with Christianity are most striking. (1.) There is the self-prompted pity of P'u-sa for mankind. (2.) P'u-sa saves men by instruction, from the punishments in which they will certainly be involved in the hundred and thirty-eight hells. (3.) The cause of future punishment is sin committed in the "present life," *yang-kien*. (4.) The god of the Tauists is represented as promulgating a gracious decree, to remit the punishment of hell for those who repent.

Such is the way in which redemption is represented in modern Tauist works, where a Buddhist element is freely intermingled. A mixed mythology and scheme for a fictitious salvation had grown up in the Sung dynasty, and continued to prevail till the present time in works like the *Yü-li*. In it we see a sort of preparation for Christianity, in the way of familiarising the minds of the people with phraseology which may be used in describing the Christian redemption in several particulars.

The purely Buddhist notion of the Western heaven, and the disciples of the Tauist sect leading the soul to that abode of happiness, are also introduced without scruple in these Tauist representations. I have often thought that the religious pilgrims, pictured with banners in their hands inscribed with the sentence *tsie-yin-si-fang*, "we will lead you to the Western heaven," a Tauist priest in front, pencil in hand, ready to write on the head of new disciples met upon the way the sign of initiation to the religious life, might be very effectively used as an illustration to describe the zeal which Christians ought to show in holding aloft their banner in the path of their pilgrimage, and in the readiness which they should exhibit to look out on the way for the victims of sin and error, and induce them to join in the march to the heavenly city.

Secret merit.—Any virtuous actions are meritorious, and form a stock which may be heaped up like grain in a barn, and constitute a man's treasure of benefits to come. No good action, says the Buddhist, is lost. The spirits unseen will be sure to take note of it. If you do good, there is an absolute certainty that you will receive benefits by way of recompense. Hence the phrase *tsi-yin-kung*, "accumulation of secret merit."

A curious confusion takes place here, through that mental tendency which sometimes mixes the cause of an act with the event. Merit produces happiness. Therefore the name happiness is given to merit. In Mongolian Buddhism *boyin* is both "happiness" and "merit." Etymologically, it is the Chinese *fu*, "happiness;" doctrinally, it is any good action. In the ordinary language of social life, it is either happiness or religious merit. In Chinese Buddhism, *tsui-fu* means either "misery" and "happiness," or "sin" and "virtue." You may translate them either way; *tsui* is "misery," but it is also "sin;" *fu* is "happiness," but it is also "merit." In the ordinary use of *sheu-tsui* in Chinese, "bear suffering" is the idea. The conception of "sin" is lost. This is the effect of Buddhist teaching.

The following passages occur:—*T'iau-t'o-tsui fu-chï-kwan*, "leap out of and escape the gate of misery and happiness;" *sien-t'sung-tsui-fu-yin-kwo-i-jan-sing-wu*, "first wake up with a shock from (the delusive dream of) causes and effects, of misery and happiness."

The effect of Buddhist doctrine on heaven and hell may be judged of partially by a statement in No. 480 [2] of the *Wan-kwo-kung pau*. An account is there given by a convert of the Basel mission, in the district of Sin-an, near Canton, of his personal experience, first as a heathen and afterwards as a Christian. After leading a dissolute life for some years, he began at the age of twenty-seven to read such books as *Pau-ying-lu*, *Yin-chï-wen*, and *Kan-ying-p'ien*. These teach future retribution in the most appalling language when describing the torments of the wicked, and they make use of the most inviting pictures of the happiness of the virtuous.

He then read also *Yü-li-ch'au-chwen*. He says regarding it, that it speaks of "heaven," *t'ien-t'ang*, as a place of incomparable glory, and of "hell" or "earth's prison," *ti-yü*, as the abode of misery indescribable. He continues: "At this time I was so affected by what these books said, that I felt my very hair and bones grow stiff with fear at the thought of the character of my past life. Coming to myself I looked up to heaven and said, 'How shall I escape the punishment of earth's prison?' My conscience condemned me. Waking and sleeping I could get no rest. I continued to read books exhorting to virtue, and meditated deeply on them. I kept on saying to myself, 'Do nothing wrong, but practice every good deed;' or else I thought in my innermost mind about the words, 'Lust is the most deadly of all sins, and filial piety the chief of all virtues.' Of these words I made a warning and a rule. Sometimes I presented a written petition to Wen-ch'ang ti-kiün, declaring my determination to live virtuously. At other times I made it a daily habit to go morning and evening to the image of Kwan-yin and burn incense before it, at the same time reading the 'Book (*King*) of Kwan-yin,' and praying to that divinity to rescue me from my miseries. I also prayed to High Heaven, making use of four sentences:—'I strike my head and worship the blue heaven;' 'My ruined life has been marked by thousands and tens of thousands of sins;' 'I pray thee to have pity on me;' 'I beg forgiveness for all past sins.' I was so full of alarm, that I was anxious to perform some meritorious act to free me from all my sins. "Occasionally also on returning home, I presented incense, and read a prayer to the kitchen god, and was accustomed to take the manual for the worship of the god, and recite passages to various members of the family, exhorting them to compliance with the direction to be very reverential to the kitchen god. I also urged my parents to avoid eating beef and dog's flesh, for the preservation of their good fortune.

"My desire to be virtuous grew greater as I observed the cheats and craft of the world, and the selfishness and greed of many persons. I was at that time bent on becoming a good man, and superior to others, and so acquiring a variety of high rewards."

He then proceeds to show that all this time he was himself deluded in a multitude of ways, and firmly bound in the snares of ignorance, till, by the help of his grandmother, an old lady of eighty-seven years, who had been for years an excellent Christian, he was brought to the exercise of faith in Christ and His Gospel.

Undoubtedly this is an example extremely interesting and instructive, as showing how the Buddhist doctrine of heaven and hell prepares for the Christian. I proceed to detail the steps of this man's conversion. The old lady had five sons, all of whom, except our convert's father and the eldest, followed their mother in adopting Christianity. The opposition of these two sons to Christianity continued for years, and the writer of the account was brought up an unbeliever. The grandmother, coming one day to chapel, slipped her foot, and sustained a severe injury. A Christian helped our convert in taking care of her, and in applying his medical skill to cure her. While he was doing this, he plied our convert with exhortations to accept the new doctrine. As he spoke of the coming judgment, and of heaven and hell, our convert felt himself deeply moved. It just suited his mode of fear and of longing. It helped him to make up his mind and give his will a fixed direction, so that he yielded himself to the influence of the new religion and became a secret believer. When his grandmother reiterated her earnest appeals to him to adopt the true faith, he consented. He still felt, however, afraid of calumny and reproach, and confined his praying to the schoolroom where he taught. At last, he says, he felt stronger faith, went to join in worship at the chapel, met the missionary, and was afterwards soundly chastised by his parents. He was subsequently baptized, and entered the training institution of the Basel Mission.

Let attention be given here to the circumstance, that this man, a genuine convert to Christianity, had made an unsuccessful attempt at a moral self-reformation in connection with the Buddhist doctrine of heaven and hell, and the moral teaching inculcated in the universally-known Tauist publications, the names of which he mentions in his account.

The retribution proclaimed by Buddhism led him to an outward reformation, consisting in the abandonment of a vicious life. At this time he had a glimmering of certain truths, found imbedded in heathen beliefs. He had the moral intention leading him to forsake some sins, but he did not achieve a satisfactory escape from doubt and temptation. This could only be the gift of Christianity; yet, in Buddhism, he had the guidance of a certain light which led him to become a seeker for truth. Christianity found him not altogether cold and dull, but in an inquiring and unsatisfied attitude. He was looking for more light than that of Buddhism—for stronger love than that of Buddhism—for a brighter hope than that of Buddhism. These he found in the Gospel.

Not only had the moral teaching of Tauist books and the Buddhist doctrine of heaven and hell a distinctly perceptible effect in inclining him strongly to self-reformation, but the habit of Buddhist devotion, in the form of reciting passages from liturgical books, and prayers for aid to escape from misery, helped him in commencing a quasi-religious life. The petition to Wen-ch'ang ti-kiun, a star god, is a written prayer burnt in the incense flame. The prayer to Kwan-yin is an appeal to the powerful divinity, who promises to exercise her delivering power as a P'u-sa to every supplicant. The habit of prayer was already formed, when he was induced by faithful Christian friends and relatives to pray to the God revealed in the Bible. When he did so, he begged the recovery of his grandmother, in order, he adds, that she might lead him and his family with her to the hall of worship. His grandmother recovered, and he felt that his prayer was answered. This led him to great earnestness in prayer and strength of faith; for she was confident that the cure took place by the immediate exercise of God's power, and in answer to prayer. His habit of heathen devotion was transmuted into Christian devotion. Christianity takes man as it finds him, and makes him, by teaching and training, a servant of God.

I do not in any way doubt that Buddhist doctrines have been, for the Christian teacher, most important preparation for Christianity; and that, through the spread of these doctrines, the Chinese people look upon Christianity with much less strangeness, and accept its doctrines with much less difficulty, than otherwise they would have been able to do.

On the other hand, it may be said that Buddhist priests do not easily become converts; that Polynesians, Negroes, un-Mohammedanised Malays, and the mountain tribes in Birmah and India, become converts more readily than the Chinese. This, perhaps, has been so hitherto, but I doubt if it will be so in the future. There have been causes which have operated to check the progress of Christianity in China. They have been chiefly originated by the Confucianists. When opposition from the literati is removed, it is surprising with what ease Christianity can be propagated. One reason of this is, that the minds of the people are impregnated with Buddhist ideas and the language with Buddhist expressions.

Footnotes

1. This paper was read in the spring of 1878, before an association of missionaries resident in Peking.
2. Published at Shanghai, March 16th, 1878.

CHAPTER XXIII.

NOTICE OF THE WU-WEI-KIAU, A REFORMED BUDDHIST SECT.

Originated two hundred and seventy years ago by a native of Shan-tang—No showy ceremonial—No images—Sacred books six in number—Interview of the founder with the emperor of the period Chena te—Discussion with opponents—Victory—One of their leaders was crucified.

INTERSPERSED through the village population of the eastern provinces of China are to be found the adherents of a religion called the *Wu-wei-kiau*. They are little known, usually belong to the lower ranks of life, and have few books. Their principles, however, render them remarkable. They are a kind of reformed Buddhists. Their system is more like Buddhism than any other religion, but they are opposed to idolatry. They appear to be strongly and sincerely convinced of the goodness of their opinions, and they hold with tenacity the uselessness of image worship. This circumstance has often attracted the attention of missionaries at Shanghai and Ningpo, and I have thought that a notice of the sect would not be without interest.

This sect has existed in China for about two hundred and seventy years. Its originator was Lo Hwei-neng, a native of Shan-tung. In imitation of the Buddhist title *tsu*, he is called *Lo-tsu*, "the patriarch Lo." His opinions have spread with considerable rapidity through the adjoin-provinces—

Kiang-nan, Che-kiang, and An-hwei, and may advance farther. The name of the sect is *Wu-wei-kiau*, which, translated literally, means the "Do-nothing sect." The idea intended by it is, that religion consists, not in ceremonies and outward show, but in stillness, in a quiet, meditative life, and in an inward reverence for the all-pervading Buddha. Buddha is believed in, but he is not worshipped. There are temples, if they may be so called, but they are plain structures, destitute of images, and having in them only the common Chinese tablet to heaven, earth, king, parents, and teacher, as an object of reverence.

The phrase wu-wei, to "do nothing," occurs in the writings of the early Tauists, long before Buddhism appeared in China. In the "Book of Reason and Virtue" (*Tau-te-king*), it is said by Lau-kiün: "The highest virtue is not (intentionally) virtuous, and on this account it is (deserving of the name) virtue. The lower sort of virtue is (anxious) not (to be) wanting in virtue, and therefore it is not (true) virtue. The highest virtue *does nothing*, and consequently does not trust to (or rest on) any action. Virtue of an inferior kind (anxiously) acts and trusts to action."

This is the controversy that has been so often raised between the contemplative and the active man. In China Confucius and his school are the advocates of activity, and Lau-tsi and his followers of contemplation. These philosophers both discussed the art of government, the one with the aid of idealism, the other under the guidance of (something like) materialism. The phrase *wu-wei* is one of the watchwords of idealistic and mystical schools in China; while *yeu-wei*, "action," a phrase of opposite signification, is the cry of systems which favour materialism.

I give another quotation. It is from the second of the great Tauist authors, *Chwang-tsï*. "The way of heaven," he says, "is 'not to act' (*wu-wei*), and therein and thereby to be the most honoured of all things. The way of men is to act' (*yeu-wei*), and to be involved in trouble." When Buddhism entered China, a system much more purely idealistic than Tauism, this phrase *wu-wei* was soon recognised as the equivalent to the phrase *hü-wu-tsi-mie*, "vacancy, stillness, and destruction" of that foreign religion.

The resemblance in principle between Buddhism and Tauism was in this respect too evident not to be remarked. The similarity became still closer when the esoteric branch of Buddhism, established by Bodhidharma, and developed by the Chinese Buddhists who succeeded him, extended itself so much as quite to overshadow the older exoteric branch. External Buddhism seeks after the Nirvâna, encourages the worship of images, appoints prayers for the dead, and makes use of much outward show to win the multitude. This is *yeu-wei*, or "reliance on action." The mystic Buddhists resist such a method of attaining the ends of religion. They recommend "inaction," or *wu-wei*. It is from them that the Wu-wei sect has sprung. The name is a favourite Tauist expression, but the source of the religion is Buddhism.

Lo-tsu, the founder of this religion, was a native of Lai-cheu fu, in Shan-tung. He was introduced, say the books of the sect, to the emperor of the Ming dynasty of the period Cheng-te. The following account is given of the interview, in the work *Lo-tsu-ch'u-shï-t'ui-fan-ping-pau-kiuen*. A hundred thousand foreign soldiers had invaded China, and an army of ten times that number had been sent out to repel them. The army failed in its enterprise, and Lo-tsu offered to the commander to drive back the invaders. He shot an arrow into the air, when a lotus-flower descended with a loud noise, and the enemy seeing it became terrified and immediately fled. The emperor was informed of this, and Lo-tsu was called to his presence. The emperor thanked him for his success, and asked him how he came to possess this miraculous power. Lo-tsu denied having any supernatural power, and attributed the deliverance of the state to the protection of the dragons and the gods. The emperor then directed him to shoot arrows into the air, when a shower of lotus-flowers appeared. The emperor was enraged, and ordered him to be imprisoned and starved to death as a sorcerer. While he lay in captivity, mourning over his fate and reciting prayers to Buddha, a revelation seemed to dart into his mind. He said to his jailer, "I have five books to make known to men." The jailer called in Chang Kung-kung to confer with him, who encouraged him to commit his books to writing. He therefore sent for two of his disciples, Fuh-hi and Fuh-pau, to come from the Wu-t'ai mountain, where they resided, to act as his amanuenses. Two other persons, noted in the history of his religion, namely, Wei Kwo-kung and T'ang Shang-shu, were witnesses of the correctness of the transcript.

The five works whose origin is thus described constitute the sacred books of the religion. They comprehend the following six subjects:—

1. *Hing-kio-kiuen* (which describes painful efforts after emancipation, resulting in perception of the excellence of this religion), "Chapter of the movement of the feet."
2. *T'an-shï-kiuen*, "Lament over the world."
3. *P'o-sie-kiuen*, "Overthrow of false doctrine."
4. *Cheng-sin-kiuen*, "Inclination of the mind to the right doctrine."
5. *T'ai-shan-kiuen*, "Becoming like the mountain T'ai-shan" (confirmation chapter).
6. *Ts'ing-tsing-kiuen*, "The mind and nature purified and quieted."

These works were presented, continues the story, to the emperor, who recalled the author to his presence and received him more favourably than before. The three friends abovementioned, being officers high in rank, interceded for him, and became sureties for his good conduct.

At this juncture seven foreign Buddhists arrived at court, bringing a brass Buddha as a present. Lo-tsu was appointed to hold a discussion with them. He was introduced as the *Wu-wei-tau-jen*, "Religious man who maintains the principle of non-action." The foreign priests asked him why he assumed this name. "By means of it," he replied, "I shall be able to overturn your brass Buddha of three thousand pounds weight today. Men do not know this principle, and therefore they seek for false doctrine. My method is clear and perfect; it is suited for the whole world." To this it was replied by the foreign priest, "Do not use boastful words; I can make a gourd sink to the bottom of the sea and iron tongs swim on the surface. Can you do so?" The foreign priest expects that our hero will not be able to explain his riddle, but he is mistaken. A ready reply is given, "Man's nature is like the full moon, which, when it emerges from the horizon, shines to the bottom of the sea, across the surface, and everywhere. To sink and to swim, then, become the same. When my 'nature' (*sing*), like the moon, shines bright and clear, my life returns to the bottom of the sea. In the view of my spiritual nature, born directly from heaven, iron may swim and the gourd may sink."

The foreign priest then asked him why he did not chant books of prayers. He answered "That the great doctrine is spontaneous, man's nature is the same with heaven. The true unwritten book is always rotating. [1] All heaven and earth are repeating words of truth. The true book is not outside of man's self. But the deceived are ignorant of this, and they therefore chant books of prayers. The law that is invisible manifests itself spontaneously, and needs no book. The flowing of water, the rushing of the winds, constitute a great chant. Why, then, recite prayers from books?"

The founder of the Wu-wei religion was again asked why he did not worship images of Buddha. He answered, "A brazen Buddha melts, and a wooden Buddha burns, when exposed to the fire. An earthen Buddha cannot save itself from water. It cannot save itself; then how can it save me? In every particle of dust there is a kingdom ruled by Buddha. In every temple the king of the law resides. The mountains, the rivers, and the great earth form Buddha's image. Why, then, carve or mould an image?"

I remark here, in passing, that at this point we must consider Buddha as God in the view of these religionists. He is to them that Being whose glory and whose acts are seen in every object of nature. But, then, this Buddha is not a personal being, the ruler and father of the world. He cannot be prayed to. He cannot love me, or be the object of my love. When religionists of this class say they see Buddha everywhere, it is only the reflection of the thoughts and emotions of their own minds that they refer to.

Again he is asked why he does not burn incense? He replies, "That ignorant men do not know that every one has incense in himself. What is true incense? It is self-government, wisdom, patience, mercy, freedom from doubts, and knowledge. The pure doctrine of the Wu-wei is true incense, pervading all heaven and earth. Incense is everywhere ascending. That incense which is made by man, the smoke of fragrant woods, does not reach heaven. The winds, clouds, and dew are true incense, always shedding itself forth through the successive seasons of the year."

He was asked once more, "Why do you not light candles?" He answered "That the world is a candlestick. Water is the oil. The sky is an encircling shade. The sun and moon are the flame lighting up the universe. If there is light within me, it illumines all heaven and earth. If my own nature be always bright, heaven will never become dark. It will then be perceived that the king of the law is limitless."

It should be noticed that the king of the law is a personification of the doctrine believed. The mind reflects on the doctrine till imagination pictures it to the intellectual eye as a glorious image. This is the king of the law.

When the discussion was over, the seven priests all confessed themselves worsted, and begged Lo-tsu to become their instructor. The book adds that the emperor was highly pleased, and ordered the books of Lo-tsu to be engraved. They were published, continues the record, in the thirteenth year of Cheng-te from the imperial press, A.D. 1518.

I met recently with a former adherent of this religion who is now a Christian. He was baptized recently by the late Bishop Russell of Ningpo, of the Church Missionary Society. He gave me much information respecting the sect to which he had previously belonged. He still thinks its principles are good. It enjoins virtue, and its tendencies are, he considers, of an excellent kind, but it does not show *how* goodness is to be *attained*. He therefore left it and became a Christian.

On asking him the meaning of the discussion before the emperor, and if it was not fictitious, he said that the army of foreign invaders means the sensorial organs, the six thieves, as they are called by the Buddhists. The arrow shot in the air is the heart. The foreign priests who oppose the true doctrine are *mo-kwei*, "demons."

This use of fiction to recommend religious dogmas is in keeping with the usual character of the Buddhist books. Unlimited license is taken by the authors in inventing a suitable tableau of characters and scenery, in which the doctrines to be taught may be prominently represented.

Two other persons—*Ying-tsu* and *Yau-tsu*—have, at different periods, taken the lead in this sect. Ying-tsu is said to have discoursed on *fa* (dharma) "the law," as Lo-tsu did on *king* the "books."

There is another personage beside Buddha spoken of by these religionists, the *Kin-mu*, "Golden mother." She dwells in a heaven called *Yau* (to shake) *chu* (to dwell) *kung* (palace). My informant considered that she represents God, in the idea of this religion, more nearly than Buddha does, because she is an object of worship. On my inquiring why this divinity should be female, he said that *Kin-mu* was the mother of the soul, as the female parent was of the body. *Yan chu kung* may be Jasper pearl palace. She is said to protect from various calamities, and is prayed to for deliverance from sickness, and to save the deceased from miseries in the unseen world.

The origin of her name is found in the Chinese theory of the elements, among which *kin*, "gold," "metal generally," stands first in order. This and many other Tauist notions are blended with Buddhist principles in the system maintained by the followers of the *Wu-wei-kiau*.

They have four principal festivals, of which two are to celebrate the day of the birth and death of Lo-tsu. The others are the new year and the middle of the eighth month. On these occasions, three cups of tea and nine small loaves of bread are placed on the table by appointment of Lo-tsu. The number nine refers to the strokes of the *pa-kwa*, or "eight diagrams," in which nine is the most fortunate number. The bread is called *k'ien-k'wan*, "heaven and earth," also in imitation of the names of the eight diagrams of the "Book of Changes."

The sect is sometimes called *Ch'a-kiau*, "Tea sect," and *Man-t'eu-kiau*, "Bread sect," in consequence of the usage here mentioned. These appellations are, however, nothing but popular nicknames.

They have in their chapels, tablets to the emperor and to the five names of honour—heaven, earth, prince, parents, and teacher. They are strict vegetarians, and argue tenaciously for the metempsychosis. They have no ascetic institute like the Buddhists, but allow the family institution to be undisturbed.

They were persecuted in the Ming dynasty. One of their leaders was crucified by nailing on the gate of a city in Shantung. On one occasion, some persons of this sect addressed me in a missionary chapel in Shanghai, with the remark that their religion resembled the Christian in this respect, that one of their leaders was crucified.

They have not since been subjected to persecution, but their religion is still prohibited, and its name is found among those charged with teaching depraved doctrines, in some editions of the "Sacred Edict."

My informant told me, further, that the doctrine of the non-existence of matter is not held by this sect—though it might have been expected from their close adherence to Buddhism that they would have maintained it—but that they simply regard all material things as perishable. When the world comes to its end, the Golden mother will take all her children—*i.e.*, all believers in this religion—home to the *yau-chu* heaven.

The *Wu-wei-kiau* is usually spoken of by the Confucianists as a corrupt sect, with secret political designs; but its adherents appear at present to be entirely innocent of any illegal aims. They are, so far as can be seen, intent on religious objects, and sincerely attached to their system. We may yet see many of them exchanging abstract philosophical dogmas for Christian truth. Their opposition to idolatry is a preparation for Christianity, and they deserve great attention from those who are engaged in teaching the Chinese the religion of the Bible.

They are very determined vegetarians. When they become Christians, they prefer to free themselves from the bondage of the prohibition by eating some small quantity of animal food, as a proof to others of their change of religion. This is entirely voluntary on their part.

In the vicinity of Shanghai, a few years since, this happened in the case of a florist and his wife. The wife was a woman of influence and decision. She signalised her change of religion by inviting friends to a feast and partaking in their presence of a certain portion of animal food.

Footnotes

1. There is an allusion here to the chanting a liturgy, as the revolving common Buddhist description of preaching Buddhist dogma, and of the wheel of the law.

CHAPTER XXIV.

BUDDHISM AND TAUISM IN THEIR POPULAR ASPECTS.

The popularity of Buddhism rests on its doctrine of retribution, and not on its ethics—Magical claims of the Tauists—Kwan-yin, since the twelfth century, usually a female—Powers and claims of Kwan-yin—
Popular Buddhism loves to have prayers said for the dead—Hopes for paradise hereafter—Popular Tauism believes in haunted houses, in charms, and in the efficacy of the wizard in controlling demons—The present head of the Tauists and chief magician—Went from Western China to Kiang-si, where he has ever since resided as hereditary Pope—
The Tauist divinity Yu-hwang shang-ti has incarnations assigned to him—Chang Sien the bowman, a physician—Tail-cutting delusion—
Tauist prayers for the dead—The Buddhist Yen-lo wang, "God of death"—The eight genii—The eighteen Lo-hans—The Tauist delusions dangerous politically—T'ien-tsin massacre—Need of the light of education—The effect of the assault of Christianity on these religions.

BY the popular aspects of these two religions, I mean their aspects at the present time, in as far as they exercise an influence on the popular mind. They were popular formerly in a sense different from that in which they are popular at present. Thus, preaching was common among Buddhists in the early ages of their religion. The principal duty of a shaven monk was to explain the doctrine of Shakyamuni as a deliverance from the misery of life. At present the popularity of Buddhism certainly does not rest on any activity in expounding the doctrines of their faith that we have the opportunity of witnessing. It rests rather on the supposed magical powers of the priests, on the merit believed to attach to gifts presented for the support of monks, monasteries, and liturgical services, and on the wide-spread belief that such merit will be followed by all kinds of happiness. The early books of Buddhism abound in beautiful moral precepts, proceeding from the lips of a man who, through a long life, was animated by a pure and lofty asceticism. They are tinged with a proud scorn of worldly glory, and with a firm consciousness that there is nothing so good for a man as to listen to the teaching of his own better nature, while he shuts his ears closely to the siren voices of all sins and all temptations. Assuredly this is not what makes Buddhism popular now. For these early books are never, or almost never, read in the liturgical services; and as to striving to be good, the Buddhists do not act so as to indicate that this aim is vital and vigorous among them. The sharp eyes of the Confucianists are upon them, and the judgment they pass on them is unfavourable. The Confucianists represent them as drones in the community. They describe them as not like the useful silkworm, which gives to man the material of the textile fabric, but as being like the moth, which destroys that fabric. Then, why is Buddhism still believed by the people? The answer is, that they believe in the magical efficacy of Buddhist prayers, and in moral causation; or, in other words, the law of moral retribution which Buddhism teaches. It is on these accounts that money flows into the Buddhist treasury for the erection and repair of temples and pagodas, and for the support of innumerable priests. If I give money to gild sacred images, the law of causation will give me back happiness—*Yin-kwo pu-mei.*

The history of Tauism has been similar. What has come now of the philosophy of Lau-kiün and Chwang Cheu? It is much too abstruse for the modern Tauist mind. The Tauists of the present day do not occupy their attention with mysterious speculations on the pure and the true.

Nor yet do they give attention to the alchemy of the Han dynasty. They have ceased to experiment on the elixir of life, or the transmutation of all metals into gold. Instead of this, they occupy themselves with writing charms for driving demons out of houses, and with reading prayers for the removal of calamities. When you meet a Tauist of this generation, you do not meet with either an alchemist or a philosopher. The man you see claims, however, to be able to do very great things. He will undertake to drive out a demon from the body of a madman, and from a haunted house, to cure the sick by magic, and to bring rain in time of drought by his prayers. He will protect by his charms the quiet citizen and the adventurous traveller from all sorts of dangers; and, when there is mourning in the house, he will—like the Buddhist monk—hire out his services to read passages from the liturgies of his religion, which shall, by their magic power, quickly transfer the soul of the dead to the land of happiness on high.

A Chinese writer says in a characteristic way: "The three religions differ in their doctrines. Yet as to the aim, to save mankind, they are at one. In Buddhism no personage holds so large a place in saving mankind as Kwan-shï-yin. In Tauism there is no one equal to Lü Chun-yang. In the *Ju-kiau* there is no one to be compared with Confucius and Mencius." In this extract, [1] Kwan-yin is represented as more prominent in saving men than Buddha himself. Such is the modern development of Buddhism, and it is the popular Buddhism of the day. Kwan-yin was introduced into Indian Buddhism not long before the Christian era. In China, Kwan-yin was worshipped probably in the Han dynasty, but was not so popular as afterwards. A modern change has taken place in the image of Kwan-yin. Down to the early part of the twelfth century, Kwan-yin was represented as a man. In a book of drawings of the time of Siuen-ho, [2] and in the works remaining of famous painters of the T'ang and Sung dynasties, Kwan-yin is always a man. In later times it has become the custom to represent Kwan-yin frequently as a woman. This has been the custom for about six hundred years. Kwan-yin is in masculine costume in temples where great attention is paid to precedent, but the popular taste is in favour of a goddess rather than a god. Hence the appellation in English, "Goddess of Mercy," founded on the phrases commonly applied to her, *Ta-ts'ï ta-pei kieu-k'u kieu-nan*, "Great mercy, great pity; salvation from misery, salvation from woe." That one of the many metamorphoses of Kwan-yin should have become a very common—in fact the most common—image of this divinity, may be taken as an indication that, in deifying ideas, the Buddhist mind in China delights to assign feminine attributes to that of mercy. It is easy to understand how the *Sung-tsï Kwan-yin*, or "Kwan-yin, the giver of sons," should become extremely popular.

The salvation of mankind by teaching is a conception very characteristic of Chinese Buddhism. This belongs to all those fancied personages called Fo and P'u-sa. For example, the mission of Kwan-yin is the salvation of men. It is symbolised by her thirty-two metamorphoses. In these shapes she enters various kingdoms as a saviour. Among these representations are seen the eighty-four thousand arms and hands with which she guides the ignorant and the lost. The doctrines taught by Kwan-yin are the non-existence of matter, and the infiniteness of the knowledge and mercy of Buddha. All evils are summed up in ignorance. To acquire knowledge of the emptiness of existing things is to become saved. It is this that is meant by the salvation of men through the agency of the goddess of mercy. In accordance with a vow she assumes some one of her thirty-two shapes, and proceeds to the various kingdoms of the world to convert men, and to the regions where gods, giants, demons, and fairies reside, to protect, instruct, and save all. Kings, governors, and people are renovated by the power of mercy. They are said to lose their fear, to be extricated from the thrall of delusion, to become perfect, and to have the power of aiding themselves or others. Kwan-yin is represented as being able, by uttering charms, to assume numberless shapes for the sake of saving. She saves by mercy, by wisdom, by entering into a state. She obtains the great self-reliant power by which she can ensure that those who pray for sons and those who pray for the state of *samadhi* shall attain it, and those who pray for deliverance from dangers, or for old age, shall also secure them. She is able to give Nirvâna to her petitioners by the same power. This is said to be her great mercy and pity. All the Buddhas and Bodhisattwas have powers analogous to these. But none are so prominent, perhaps, in this respect, as Kwan-yin. Manjusiri (*Wen-shu*), whose seat of worship is Wu-t'ai shan in Shan-si, is, even in North China, where his worship most prevails, much less thought of than Kwan-yin. Probably P'u-hien, the seat of whose worship is Wo-mei shan, in the province of Sï-ch'wen, is even less esteemed than Manjusiri, and *a fortiori* than Kwan-yin. It would seem, then, to be a fact important in modern Buddhist history, that the most popular of the divinities of this religion should be presented first with male and afterwards with female attributes, and that the change of sex in the images should have been accomplished within the last few centuries.

Yet it should not be forgotten that Kwan-yin is, properly speaking, to be regarded as masculine even at the present time. The feminine form is a specially popular metamorphosis. If we wish to go further back and to be still more careful in our analysis, Kwan-yin is but a form of Buddha, coming into the world of suffering mankind in a lower position than Buddha, in order more effectually to instruct and save the ignorant. Thus P'u-hien and Wen-shu are in the same way said to be ancient Buddhas appearing among men as the two helpers of Shakyamuni, who styles one of them chang-tsï, "eldest son," and the other siau-nan, "little boy." Wen-shu is the god of wisdom, and P'u-hien of action. Wen-shu rides a lion, and P'u-hien an elephant. The lion symbolises boldness, bravery, and a fresh, eager, and advancing spirit. The elephant indicates care, caution, gentleness, and a weighty dignity. This is Buddhist symbolism. It is interesting in itself, because it explains the images. The object of the images is partly instruction, and partly the awakening of devout feelings in the minds of worshippers. The image of a Fo or a P'u-sa is intended to combine in its appearance wisdom, benevolence, and victory—the wisdom of a philosopher, the benevolence of a redeemer, and the triumph of a hero. All perfections are collected in the holy image—perfect power, perfect virtue, infinite compassion, infinite boldness, and infinite knowledge. These are intended to be represented in the images. This symbolism is, however, not exactly what excites faith and devotion in the rich supporters of the Buddhist religion. It is rather a belief in the magical power of the Buddhist divinities and priests, and confidence in the doctrine of retribution for the bestowment of liberal gifts.

Priests are invited to perform a liturgical service for the dead. It is called *kung-te*, "merit." Its object is to give the deceased a better position in the next life than he would otherwise enjoy. This is founded on the metempsychosis. Souls may be re-born in a better or worse state of existence. The magical power of Buddha may exalt a man from a birth into hell to a birth into the world once more. Buddha's power may cause a poor man to be born in the next life as a rich man. The choir of priests wield this power. They profess to have the power to *ch'au-tu-ling-hwun*, "save the soul." This means to transfer the soul from an undesirable abode in the next life to a very happy one. The people believe that the priests by beating cymbals and drums, knocking the wooden fish and chanting prayers, can redeem the deceased person from the punishment due to his sins. This is expressed by the phrase, *shu-tsui*, "redeem from guilt."

For a service of one day in the house of the dead person, the name *tso-kung-te* is used. For a service of three days, *pai-ch'an* is often used. The favourite name (much may be learned from favourite names) *O-mi-to Fo* tells of an expected paradise. It speaks of the longing for a happy hereafter. Here Buddhism has abandoned the legitimate Nirvâna of Shakyamuni, and preferred to allow the people's craving for immortality to dominate the philosopher's dogma of a return to the absolute. A favourite title of Omi-to Fo is *Tsie-yin Fo*, "The guiding Buddha." He guides from earth to the Western paradise. The legend of O-mi-to is connected with that of Kwan-yin. The school which teaches it is called that of "The peaceful land." In China and Japan this school has always been a popular one. It is so especially in Japan. I was much struck while in that country with inscriptions on tombs. A large number of the inscriptions in ordinary cemeteries indicate that the person there buried died in hope of being taken to "The peaceful land." It is different in China, where Confucianism has prevented Buddhism from taking a firm hold on the hearts of the people. No such inscriptions occur in Chinese cemeteries. Japan has been more thoroughly penetrated with Buddhism than China. Yet in China the funeral procession for the dead bears many marks of Buddhist influence, though the ordinary cemeteries do not. Thus the *hwun fan*, or "soul's banner," carried before a coffin in such a procession has on the top a lotus-flower, and below three strips of cloth, the middle one of which contains the characters *pan-yi*, which imply faith in the departure of the soul to the Western heaven. The "portrait of the dead," *shen-siang*, is placed beside it in what is called the *tso-ting*. Below the portrait is a tablet to be worshipped. On the right hand is another banner called *ming-tsing*, on which are recorded the titles of the deceased. Now it will be noticed here that the wooden frame like a baldachino holding the picture is Buddhist. It contains the stool on which a Buddhist monk sits crosslegged when living, and on which he is placed sitting in the same attitude when dead. Five Buddhist priests and five Tauists read prayers at the grave of persons who are rich and high in office. The liturgies read are such as the *Sin-king*, "Heart classic," and the *Kwan-yin-king*. In reference to use in funeral processions, these liturgies are called *Chwen-ts'ai-king*, "Liturgy for 'turning' (or guiding) the coffin" on its path to the grave. The Nirvâna is too abstruse for the popular faith. It has been replaced by the Paradise of the Western heaven.

The belief in the existence of hermit heroes, and of various malevolent spirits and demons, is a marked characteristic of popular Tauism. Haunted houses are avoided in all parts of China. The power of expelling demons from haunted houses and localities, is believed to belong chiefly to the hereditary chief of the Tauists, Chang Tien-shï, and subordinately to any Tauist priest. To expel demons he wields the sword that is said to have come down, a priceless heirloom, from his ancestors of the Han dynasty. All demons fear this sword. He who wields it, the great Tauist magician, can catch demons and shut them up in jars. These jars are sealed with a "charm" (*fu*). I have heard that at the home of this chief of wizards on the Dragon and Tiger mountain in the province of Kiang-si, there are many rows of such jars, all of them supposed to hold demons in captivity. The wizard himself is believed to be a power. The charm is a power. The sword he wields is a power. The efficacy of a charm is increased by the supposed magical gifts of the Tauist wizard from whom it is obtained. To secure the services of the great Kiang-si wizard is very expensive. Only the wealthy who can expend a thousand taels of silver without being pinched can afford the luxury of feeling quite sure that, by the agency of this wizard, the demons who trouble them are completely subjugated. The residence of this wizard is called Chên-jên fu. In giving him the title *Chên-jên*, the meaning is that he is regarded as having attained perfect power and virtue. He is the ideal man. Men under the domination of the passions are not called *Chên-jên*. The Tauist discipline gives a man the rule over himself and over nature. He who possesses this is called a "True man." The word *chên*, "true," cannot be fully translated into English in such cases as this without embracing the ideas "real," "perfect," "ideal," and "most elevated." It is higher than *sien*, "immortal," but not so high as *sheng*, "holy."

The present chief wizard is like his predecessors. His wife belongs to a Kiang-si family. Tauism in the persons of its wizards retains marriage. Buddhism introduced the disuse of marriage. Tauism, being anterior to that much more ascetic and self-denying system, knew nothing of celibacy.

It may be asked, from whence came the wizards and their charms, and their supposed power to subdue the bad influences of demons in disturbing neighbourhoods by apparitions and uncanny noises, and in causing sickness and death? It may be answered, that before the introduction of Buddhism, but especially in the Han dynasty, this folly was rife in the popular belief, and has continued so till now. There were wizards in the Shang dynasty, but no details remain of what they did. In the Han dynasty, the wizards stand out in their completeness. They were greatly honoured by prince and people, and have continued to be so in the person of the Chang T'ien-shï till the present day.

This personage assumes a state which mimics the imperial regime. He confers buttons like the emperor. He has about thirty persons constituting his courtiers and high officers. Tauists come to him from various cities and temples to receive promotion. He invests them with certain titles, and gives seals of office to those Tauists who are invested. They have similar powers to his, and can, for example like him, subdue demons by pasting charms on doors, which prevent them from entering. The Chang Tien-shï, in his capacity as a sort of spiritual emperor, addresses memorials to Yü-ti in heaven. His position will be understood from this circumstance. He is chief official on earth of Yü-hwang-ti in heaven, and as such is in the habit of addressing to him "memorials" called *piau*. His duty is defined as the driving away and expulsion of demons by charms, and their destruction by the magic sword.

In all parts of China, the charms seen pasted on the doors of houses testify to the dominant idea of popular Tauism, and to the universal fear of demons, which Tauism encourages. Certainly it is not Confucianism that maintains in rigour this absurd dread of evil spirits wandering through the air, disturbing the public tranquillity, occasioning alarms which sometimes spread like an epidemic from city to city, and leading the uninstructed populace to trace fevers, madness, ague, drowning, accidental death of travellers, suicide, and any sort of unaccountable discomfort, to the imaginary agency of invisible and malevolent beings. To subdue them is the office of the Tauist magician. The person honoured with the credit of having invented the charm is Chang Tau-ling. It was called *fu*, because written on bamboo tallies such as were anciently used by officers of government, and which are made to fit in shape one with another as a security against imposture, in accordance with the meaning of the verb *fu*. They are to be seen pasted on door lintels, the occupants of the house believing that the sight of the magical characters written on the charm will prevent evil spirits from entering.

The magicians were in the Han dynasty called—not without a touch of sarcasm—the "Feathered scholars" (*Yü-shi*), as being able to fly. The legend of Chang Tau-ling, ancestor of the Chang T'ien-shï, head of the Tauist hierarchy at the present time, is sometimes stated as follows:—In the latter part of the second century, this Pope of the Tauists, if he may be so called, was engaged in the province now called Sï-ch'wen in the *Ho-ming shan* (Mountain where the crane *sien-ho* calls), in manipulating the "elixir of the dragon and tiger," *lung-hu-tan*. He met a spirit who said, "In the Pe-sung mountain is a stone house where may be found writings of the three emperors and a liturgical book. By getting these you may ascend to heaven, if you pass through the course of discipline which they enjoin." He dug and found them. By means of them he was able to fly, to hear distant sounds, and to leave his body. Lau-kiün then came down to him on the night of the feast of lanterns, and ordered him to subdue the demons of the "Shu country" (*Sï-ch'wen*), in order to confer blessings on humanity. Lau-kiün gave him a powerful and secret "charm" (*lu*), a "liturgy" (*king*), a "composition in verse or measured prose" (*kiue*), a "sword" (*kien*), and a "seal" (*yin*). After going through a thousand days of discipline, and receiving instructions from a certain goddess called Yü-nü, who taught him to walk about among the stars, he proceeded to fight with the king of the demons, to divide mountains and seas, and to command the wind and thunder to come and go. All the demons fled before him, leaving not a trace behind of their retreating footsteps. On account of the prodigious slaughter of demons by this hero, the wind and thunder were reduced to subjection, and various divinities came with eager haste to acknowledge their faults. In nine years he gained the power to ascend to heaven and prostrate himself before the first in rank of the Three Pure Ones. A temple in Ch'eng-tu is said to have been the place where Lau-kiün discoursed to Chang Tau-ling. He afterwards went eastward, and settled his residence on the mountain *Lung-hu shan*, where his descendants have ever since resided in possession of great honour and emolument, as his hereditary representatives. The present occupant of the patriarchate had to fly at the time of the T'ai-p'ing rebellion, and the temple where he resides was partially destroyed. The repairs of the buildings are now nearly completed.

The popular divinity, Yü-hwang shang-ti, is an ancient magician, exalted to this dignity probably by the Tauist writers of the T'ang dynasty.[3] In the *Pen-hing-king* of the Tauist collection it is said, that a magician of the Chang family was the son of a king in a former *kalpa*, who, instead of succeeding his father, became a hermit, and after eight hundred *kalpas*, and much patient endurance of injuries, attained to the rank of the "Golden immortals" (*Kin-sien*), and at the same time a Buddha with a special title, *Tsing-tsing-tsï-jan-chio-ju-lai*, "The pure, calm, and spontaneously perceiving Ju-lai." After a million more *kalpas* he became Yü-ti, or *Yü-hwang ta-ti*, "Emperor of all the immortals." In the same way, *Tsï-wei ta-ti*, "God of the stars round the north pole," is the emperor who rules over the presiding gods of all the stars, according to the one account. The magician Chang and the magician Liu mounted dragons and rode up through the sky towards heaven, and Chang gained in the race.

In the Tsin dynasty, A.D. 300, Cheu Hing is reported to have died and risen again. He is said to have related what he saw when dead. He saw *T'ien-ti*, the "Heavenly emperor," enter the chief hall of his palace. Clouds, purple in colour, dense and dark, obstructed the view above him. His face was a square foot in size. Cheu Hing was told by those on his right and left, "This is the heavenly emperor Chang." His palace is the Yü-ts'ing kung, which is represented in temples by a building beneath the abode of the Three Pure Ones. It is the heaven to which the soul flies when Tauist prayers are supposed to help the dead to reach the Tauist heaven. The expressions are—*Hwun fei ch'ung-siau*, "The soul flies to the high firmament;" *Ling-t'eng t'ien-kung*, "The soul ascends to the heavenly palace." These passages are the earliest I have yet found giving the family name Chang to Yü-ti. This magician or god Chang is to be distinguished from Chang Tau-ling as already described, ancestor of the present Chang T'ien-shï, and from the medical divinity Chang Sien, who was, in fact, a distinguished physician of the Sung dynasty. The personage called Chang Sien, in common Chinese paintings, with bow and arrow shooting at the moon, is this physician who lived about seven hundred years ago.

In the tail-cutting delusion, which died out in 1879, after spreading over the country like an epidemic, we see an example of Tauist ideas. The fairy that cuts off hair is checked and prevented by a charm. A written charm curled up in the plaited queue at the back of the head is a protective shield against all the assaults of witchcraft. Tauism attempts to soothe the fears of the people by this artifice. In Peking lately I myself heard that a writer of charms hired men to go along the streets shouting to people that for safety they should place charms in their hair, and detailing cases of the loss of queues in the night, or while men were sleeping in the daytime. These hired men brought to the writers of charms a great increase of custom. Every one wished to buy one. There must be something in it, for every one talked of it. We must, they said to themselves, buy a charm. The charm used in Peking against the danger of waking without a queue, consists of four mysterious characters, which are all found in Kang-hi's dictionary. They were, we are there told, used against a similar delusion in the Ming dynasty.

The Tauism of today meets us with this special characteristic. Yet it is but one part of the popular Tauism, which in great part consists of a monastic institute for reading liturgical books after the Buddhist fashion.

Dr. Yates says, in his lecture on Ancestral Worship and Fung-shui, that Buddhism borrowed from Tauism. But, in fact, it is rather the other way in the main. Buddhism indeed borrowed from Tauism the worship of Kwan-ti, as it has borrowed from Confucianism the use of ancestral tablets for the worship of the priests of a monastery. But there is no room for doubt, that the general programme of the arrangements of a

Tauist monastery, with the occupations of the inmates, is Buddhistic. The whole scheme of prayers for the dead is so. As to prayers for rain, they are essential in China in every religion. For popular and for state reasons it is necessary to have them, the reason being the same in all Buddhist countries. When therefore the Hindoos and other Buddhists came to China, and found prayers for rain already existing in the Confucian, the imperial, and the popular worship, they would in offering prayers for the same object, be only doing what they were accustomed to do in their own country. They can scarcely be said to be borrowed by any religion. The popular character of the prayers of the Tauists for the dead is different in some respects from the Buddhist, but in the chief features it is evidently imitated. The old classical word *ts'iau*, for example, is not used in describing the services of the Tauists for the dead. The phrase *pai-ch'an* is used. One is called *Ch'au-t'ien-ch'an*, or "Prayer of looking toward heaven;" another is *Yü-hwang-ch'an*, "Prayer of Yü-hwang." This word *ch'an* is Buddhist. The object of reciting these books is to save the souls of the dead by affording them a speedy ascent to the palace of Yü-hwang. The hell of the Buddhists is repeated by the Tauists in their descriptions of the future state. The variety of torments and punishments to be inflicted on criminals in the next world may be seen with all the harrowing details in the temples of *Tung-yo to-ti*, "The god of *T'ai-shan*," a mountain god who is supposed to rule the under world. He corresponds in attributes somewhat to *Ti-tsang-wang p'u-sa*, the Buddhist deliverer from hell. Like this Buddhist god, he rules only as a saviour and shares his authority with a large group of inferior divinities, whose offices as ministers of punishment to those who deserve chastisement, are illustrated on the walls by rough paintings, or by clay images, moulded and painted in the Chinese method, in the temples of *Tung-yo to-ti*. Among statements which I made years ago and have now to correct as imperfect or erroneous is this, that the Tauists have no hell, but only a heaven. In fact they have both, for the rough wall drawings and clay mouldings found in the east and west buildings of the temples of *Tung-yo* prove it. These are not, however, many centuries old, and they form a part of the mass of legend and myth which they have unscrupulously borrowed from the Buddhists. *Yama*, "God of Death" in India, the *Yen-lo-wang* of China, with the ten courts of judgment which rule over the guilty, sentences them to punishment and has it administered after death. This forms the basis of the Tauist hell.

Modern Chinese art is very much pervaded with Tauist ideas. The eight genii meet us everywhere. The manufacturers of porcelain, bronze, and carved bamboo ornaments are never weary of representing these eight personages. They belong to the class of hermits. The love of external nature was very much developed in the T'ang dynasty. Poetry was the favourite occupation of the literati. They gave attention to no severe studies. Every beautiful spot among lakes, waterfalls, and mountains was selected for a hermitage or a monastery. Buddhism and Tauism received a wonderful expansion. It was just the era for the legends of the eight genii to spring into existence. It was an age of sentimental feeling. The great national poets flourished in the same dynasty as the eight Tauist hermits. Li T'ai-pe and Tu Fu gained their fame at the same time that the sixteen, and afterwards eighteen, Lo-hans became popular. These Lo-hans are the Buddhist equivalents of the fairies and hermits of Tauism. The sixteen were Hindoos, while the two added names were those of Chinese Buddhists. All the eight genii were Tauists of the T'ang dynasty.

We see the effect of Buddhist and Tauist teaching in the present race of Chinese. The Tauist religion especially is responsible for those superstitions which have a dangerous character. The epidemic of the fairy powder was fatal to the peace of communities. The absurd charges brought against the martyred Sisters of Mercy in Tientsin were based on ideas which, although usually represented as popular, and as the native growth of the Chinese mind, are in fact correctly placed to the account of Tauism. It is dangerous to the state that religious teachings should be encouraged which tend to foster and originate popular delusions entailing such frightful results. Every man, whether a Christian or not, ought on moral grounds, and on the greatest happiness principle itself, if he thinks that is a safer basis, to desire the extinction of a religious system which encourages dangerous and lying delusions. Then there is the tail-cutting. The Tauists accept and endorse the whole system of popular delusion which originated the tail-cutting. They believe in the existence of just such fairies as are said to cut off men's queues. They make money by selling the charms which are represented to be a protection against such demons. Popular Tauism then is worthy of decided condemnation, from every Christian and every enlightened lover of mankind, whatever be his belief. There are beliefs in the Tauist religion which not only need to be attacked by books written from the Christian standpoint of thought, but which may very properly be condemned in the proclamations of magistrates, on account of their tendency to produce dangerous tumults and lamentable breaches of the peace. What a field is here presented for the teaching of science, and the spread of a practical system of improved education in China! Dense intellectual darkness clouds the people's minds. There is pressing need for the extension of a system of education which should strike at the root of superstition and enable the rising youth of the country to avoid falling into the thrall of those delusive imaginations which have grown up under the fostering care of the Tauists during the last two hundred years.

It is a great misfortune for a nation to have an extensive sacerdotal caste, whose interest it is to continue, generation after generation, the belief in deceptive fancies which check the free growth of true ideas and all healthy habits of thought. Their livelihood depends on the people continuing to believe in demons, fairies, and charms. The missionary and the schoolmaster, the magazine and the newspaper, are all needed to check these bad influences, and replace dangerous and injurious popular notions, by healthy and useful knowledge, to he gathered from God's two books, that of Nature and that of Revelation. Then as to the effects of Buddhism, it may be said to have been good in some respects. It bears a consistent testimony to the vanity of the world, and the essential and immense superiority of soul purity to earthly grandeur. But in founding on this a monastic institute, it has followed a wrong plan, and failed to attain the purity desired. It teaches the need of a personal redeemer to rescue from the moral evils attendant on our present existence. But this redeemer is a Buddha or a Bodhisattwa, a man or being possessing none of the powers attributed to him. Among the prominent and most pernicious evils for which the popular Buddhism of the present day is responsible is idolatry. It is an enormous evil that Buddhism has placed the Buddhas and Bodhisattwas in the position in the reverence of the people, that ought to be held only by the Creator and Father of the world. Idolatry puts fiction in the stead of truth, and, as we every day see in China, renders the mind indifferent to truth. This, too, is a vast evil. Confucianism makes everything of morality; and the worship of Buddhist images, when it is complied with, becomes a moral duty on the part of the emperor or the magistrate, only because it is *li* (ceremonial duty), not because the Buddhist religion itself can have any just claim to it. But Buddhism, by putting forward the image, debases and misleads the national mind, by drawing it away from the proper object of human worship. Our great contest as Christian missionaries is with Confucianism. There is found the intellect, the thought, the literature, the heart of the nation. But we have also a preliminary struggle with Buddhism and Tauism. These constitute three mighty fortresses, erected by human skill and effort, to impede the progress of Christianity. Confucianism is the citadel of the enemy raising its battlements high into the clouds, and manned by multitudes who are animated by a belief in their superiority and their invincible strength. The taking of this fortress is the conclusion of the war. But Buddhism and Tauism each represents a fortress which must also be captured and destroyed. So far as argument and intellect are concerned, these fortresses are weakly manned. But think of the numbers, the millions on millions, who are deceived by these superstitions, and held fast by chains of spiritual darkness. Let the Christian host of soldiers press on, and detail its battalions, first to overthrow these strongholds of rebellion against God; and when they are destroyed, let another earnest effort be made to destroy the last and strongest of the towers of the enemy. Then, when all these three fortresses are overthrown, and China becomes a subject kingdom under the Messiah's peaceful reign, it will be the greatest triumph ever achieved for Christianity since the time when the emperor Constantine became a Christian, and the Roman religion and power, and the Greek philosophy were dragged as captives behind the car of the victorious Redeemer.

Footnotes

1. From *Ping-shu-pi-t'an*.
2. From A.D. 1119 to 1126.
3. The title Yü-ti occurs in Tauist books earlier than the T'ang dynasty, but not the full title with four characters. This belongs evidently to the T'ang dynasty, the age of Buddhist influence, and to the belief in metamorphoses, and a former life, borrowed from India. I asked the Tauist patriarch when in Shanghai, how long it was since Chang T'ien-ti first received his title. He only replied, "From the beginning of the universe."

CHAPTER XXV.

ON THE USE OF SANSCRIT BY THE CHINESE BUDDHISTS.

Changes in Chinese sounds since the time of the Buddhist transliteration of Indian words—Examples of Sanscrit words in old and new Chinese—The importance of translations made in A.D. 60 to A.D. 76 for reading the Four Books—The Hindoo translators did not speak pure Sanscrit—Sanscrit was the language of the books—No Pali books in China—The translators spoke Pracrit—The term po-li, "glass"—Use of Sanscrit words in magic—Dharani—Inscription in six languages at Kü-yung kwan.

THE Chinese characters have been written in the same form and with the same sort of pencils since the time of Wang Hi-chi, A.D. 350.

During these fifteen centuries, while the writing taught in all schools has been unchanged, the sounds attached to the characters have been in a state of slow and constant flux.

Thus, the translator Kumarajiva wrote his name with four Chinese characters then called *Ku-ma-la-zhip*. They are now *Kieu-*(or *Chieu*) *mo-lo-shï*.

All sonant initials, such as *g, d, b, z, zh, j*, have changed in the interval to surds, viz., *k, t, p, s, sh, ch*. In words pronounced with the tone called *hia-ping*, the aspirates *k', t', p', ch'* come in place of *k, t, p, ch*, which occur in words pronounced with the tones *hia-ping, hia-ch'ü,* and *hia-ju*.

Final *m* has changed to final *n*. Finals *k*, *t*, *p* have been dropped; also the vowels have all changed their values, *a* to *o*, *ya* to *e*, *u* to *yeu*, &c.

The compilers of Kang-hi's dictionary have provided tables of the old sounds, with characters chosen to represent the pronunciation as it formerly was. They are to be read with the powers of the letters of the Sanscrit alphabet. Natives not knowing the Sanscrit letters cannot escape from the confusion in which they are involved by the difference between the old and new pronunciations. The foreign student will find that the principle here laid down is a key to unlock the difficulties of the subject.

The following examples will help to familiarise the learner with the method:—

Sanscrit.	Old Chinese.	New Chinese.
Buddha	*But*	Fo
Amogha Vajra	*A-mo-ga bad-ja-ra*	O-mo-k'ia po-che-lo
Upâsaka	*U-pa-sa-ka*	Yeu-po-so-kia
Viharapala	*Bi-ha-la-pa-la*	Pi-ho-lo-po-lo
Bodhiruchi	*Bo-di-lu-chi*	P'u-t'i-lieu-chï
Paramiti	*Pat-la-mit-ti* [1]	Po-le-mi-ti
Mahêshwara	*Ma-hi-shu-la*	Mo-hi-sheu-lo
Shanaishchara	*Sha-nai-shat-chat-la*	She-na-yi-shï-che-lo
Prasenajit	*Pat-la-si-na-ji-ta*	Po-lo-sï-na-shï-to
Mahapadma	*Ma-ha-pa-de-ma* [2]	Mo-ho-po-t'e-mo
Udyâna	*U-dyung-na*	U-chang-na
Sangadeva	*Seng-ga-de-ba*	Seng-k'ia-t'i-p'o
Achârya	*A-cha-li-ya*	O-che-li-ye
Shakradeva Indra	*Shak-ka-la-de-ba n-da-la*	Shï-kia-lo-t'i-p'o Yin-t'o-lo
Dhârani	*Da-la-ni*	To-lo-ni

The admission of the principle that the Chinese pronunciation has changed, and that the recognised Mandarin orthography is nothing more than that of a modern dialect, will be found to throw a light much needed on the use of Sanscrit by the Chinese Buddhists.

It is also necessary to recognise the principle, that the Hindoo Buddhists in China were men who spoke the dialects of Central India, Northern India, &c. M. Stanislas Julien's *Méthode pour Déchifrer et Transcrire les noms Sanscrits* makes no allusion to these subjects. The consequence is that all his immense industry has failed to make a window that would have illuminated this dark room. Yet that does not hinder his work from being indispensable to the student on this subject. It gives the Sanscrit words. It gives the modern Chinese pronunciation. These two factors are tabulated alphabetically. The student can with this help proceed rapidly. But if he wish to understand why such and such Chinese characters were chosen, and not prosecute his researches mechanically, he must allow for the influence of dialects and the incessant change of language on both sides of the Himalayas.

It is necessary to take the finals of the Southern Chinese dialects, and the initials of the dialects spoken in Central China at the present time, as our sign-posts, pointing out to us what was the pronunciation of the T'ang dynasty and of the previous age; and this must be done with the addition of aid from the Japanese and Corean transliteration of Chinese sounds, through the spread of Buddhism many centuries ago.

It was about three hundred and forty years after the death of Mencius, and five hundred and fifty after the death of Confucius, that the translations from Sanscrit were made. By learning the powers of the Chinese syllabary with the help of the transliterations then made, we can come quite near to the classical age of Chinese literature, and approximate to the actual pronunciation of the great Chinese sages. For the method and proofs, I may here refer the reader to my *Introduction to the Study of the Chinese Characters*.

Particularly is the "Sutra of Forty-two Sections" worthy of attention, on account of its being the translation of Kashiapmadanga and his friend Chu-fa-lan. It is highly important for fixing the pronunciation of the Chinese, at the time when they taught Buddhism at Lo-yang, in the reign of Ming-ti, A.D. 58 to A.D. 76. From their use of characters it is clear, that at that time the modern *Fo* was *But; O-lo-han* was *A-la-han; ch'an,* "contemplation," was *dian* or *dan; Nie-p'an,* "Nirvâna," was *Nit-ban* or *Nir-ban; Kia-she,* the name of "Kashiapa" Buddha, was *Ka-shap* or *Ka-shiap; P'u-t'i,* the word *Bodhi,* "knowledge," was *Bo-di. Sha-men,* the "Shramana," was *Sha-men,* having about the same sound as now. *Pi-k'ieu* or *Pi-ch'ieu,* the "Bikshu," was *Bi-k'u. Ch'iau-ch'en-ju,* for "Godinia," was *Go-din-nia. O-na-han,* a certain grade in discipleship, was *A-na-gam,* agreeing with the Sanscrit "Anagama." *Pi-chï,* for the Sanscrit "Pratyeka," was *P'ak-tie,* the Pali being *Patiekan.* So it was probably not Pali that Kashiapmadanga spoke, though he was a native of Central India. *Sü-t'o-hwan,* for "Srotapanna," another grade of discipleship, was *So-da-ban* or *Su-da-wan.* The last of these is the more likely, for the character is the same as that used in writing "Nirvâna." The Pali is *Sotapan;* so that the translator did not speak Pali.

The greatest initiator of change in the choice of characters was Hiuen-tsang, about A.D. 645. He altered the characters according to his opinion of what the selected symbols ought to be. His selection of characters is a gauge of the pronunciation of his time. His translations, however, have not become popular. The older usage of words has kept its place.

The language in which the Buddhist sacred writings were first compiled may have been Pali; but that from which they were translated into Chinese was Sanscrit. The Pali books were a separate set of originals. The Sanscrit originals alone are known to the Chinese. The manuscripts, the inscriptions, the charms cut on copper mirrors, the lucky sentences under eaves and over doors in monasteries, are in Sanscrit; and in polyglot books printed at Peking, Sanscrit is the language employed.

Koeppen, page 186, in saying that the Chinese also have a number of Pali texts, has been misled by Gutzlaff. This missionary had lived in Siam, where Pali is the sacred language, and was there accustomed to the idea that Pali was the original language of Buddhism. This view he brought with him to China, and when he saw Sanscrit inscriptions in the island of P'u-to, he took them to be Pali. From him the opinion spread, but it is an error. The Buddhists of Birmah, Siam, and Ceylon have never spread their religion in China or Japan, or introduced their sacred books into those countries.

The Nepaul Buddhists preserve the sacred books in Sanscrit, and not in Pali. But Burnouf also found certain portions of the Nepaulese books written in Pracrit. The groundwork was Sanscrit. The language occasionally used was Pracrit. The language known by the Chinese as the *Fan* language was shown to be undoubtedly Sanscrit, by Julien's version of the works of Hiuen-tsang, the traveller who visited India, and who has described the Sanscrit language in his autobiography. It is the language of "Brahma" (*Fan;* old sound, *Bam*).

Brahmanical ideas form a strong element in Buddhism. Sanscrit words and Sanscrit writing are peculiarly sacred in the view of the Brahmans. This idea has been borrowed by the Buddhists. They preferred to use the words and writing which were most sacred. With this Shakyamuni would naturally have nothing to do. His instructions were oral. He was a great moral teacher and metaphysical logician. It was his disciples in the centuries that followed him that introduced Sanscrit writing, as the chief medium of recording his instructions. It is they that are responsible also for the charms, and for the faith in magic which stimulated their use.

So many Brahmans announced themselves believers in Shakyamuni's doctrines, that Sanscrit became at once a favourite medium for the embodiment of his teaching by writing, even though Shakyamuni himself spoke Pali or Pracrit, as he probably did.

In the same way it may be said that Pali was then so extensively spoken, that it was inevitable that it should, in the region watered by the Lower Ganges, become also a medium for the preservation of the sacred books.

This double form of the sacred books had much to do with the separation that sprang up between the Northern and Southern schools of Buddhism. The peculiarities of the Chinese transcription deserve to be considered.

The Pracrit of the early Chinese translators was, for example, nearer to Sanscrit than to Pali in the sound of *prajna*, "wisdom." The characters adopted are directed to be pronounced *pat-nia*. The Pali is *paññya*.

There was also in the Pracrit of the early Chinese translators a very clear pronunciation of *b* for the Sanscrit and Pali *v*. This is shown by the constant selection of Chinese characters sounded with *b* or *p*, according to the old pronunciation. For example, the city "Vaishali," near the modern Patna, is spelt *Bai-sha-li*. The Pali sound is *Vesali*. Dr. E. J. Eitel, in his *Hand-book of Chinese Buddhism*, page 27, has said, that "Chinese texts consider Pali as the ancient and Sanskrit as the modern form even as regards the system of sounds." If he will direct his attention to these facts, he will perhaps admit that not the Pali, but a certain Pracrit form or forms of the Hindoo language, prevalent at the time in Central and Northern India, was or were at the basis of the Chinese old texts, The Hindoo translators in China would have Sanscrit texts chiefly before them, and Pracrit texts occasionally. Their pronunciation was not pure Sanscrit, but was modified by Pracrit peculiarities.

In the flourishing period of Buddhism, in the region watered by the Ganges, at the time of the Greek invasion, and afterwards, the art of writing lately introduced was put to extensive use in the Buddhist monasteries. Those institutions fostered education, which was then very much in Buddhist hands. While the people spoke Pali and Pracrit, Sanscrit was the language of education, and hence the fondness shown for it by the Buddhists. Burnouf held that there was a double text, a Pracrit text for the laity and a Sanscrit for the literati.

King Kanishka in Cashmere called a council, the fourth; and in the writings edited by this assembly, Sanscrit was the language.

The language of Magadha in the time of the emperor Ashôka was a Pracrit. This was probably much used by the Hindoo Buddhists who came to China.

An argument against Pali is to be found in the careful selection of Chinese words commencing with *sh*, to represent the Sanscrit *sh;* but *sh* is not a letter known to the Pali, just as it was wanting in the ancient Greek and Latin. The original text of the early Chinese translations before the days of Hiuen-tsang must have had *sh* fully developed. It probably dropped *ra* in *sharira*, "a relic," and *sti* in *Shravasti*, name of the capital of an ancient kingdom called Kosala, and lying near Kapilavastu.

I place here some remarks on *po-li*, "glass," a favourite word. In Buddhist glossaries, the Chinese *po-li* is derived from the Sanscrit word *spatika*, "crystal." Many of the Hindoo Buddhists who came to China—perhaps all—spoke dialects of Sanscrit, but not the Sanscrit itself. The *s* was dropped, and the final *ka*. The *t* in *ti* became *l*, as in the Turkish *belur*.

The rock crystal of China comes from Turkestan, and would bring its own name with it from that country. Buddhist makers of glossaries would prefer to derive the word from Sanscrit, as the mother of all knowledge. They have passed over without remark the possibility that the Chinese word may come from the Turkish.

The word *po-li* for "glass," formerly pronounced *pa-li*, has been in common use in China since the T'ang dynasty. It came in with Buddhism and the international trade with Turkestan.

I believe that the initial *s* in *spatika* might be an accretion and not original, just as most probably *smelt* is later than *melt*, and *sneeze* than *nose*, and *stannum* than *tin*. Curiously we find in the Mongol vocabulary *bolor*, "crystal," "glass;" *bolor daboso*, "rock salt;" *bolo ch'ilagon*, "a polishing stone," a rolling stone used in smoothing the clods of a ploughed field. Compare Turkish *bileghi*, "whetstone." Let it be noticed that glass-dust is used by polishers and grinders.

425

Whether the *bôli* or *bali* is of Turanian origin and has originated the Sanscrit *spatika*, it would be interesting to know. *Ballur* is Arabic for "crystal;" *spashta* is Sanscrit for "clear;" *berrak* is Turkish for "clear," "limpid." Probably here is the root; but who shall decide?

In Buddhist magic there has been extensive use of the Sanscrit characters. The doctrine of magic has been developed by the Buddhists very systematically, and to an almost unexampled extent. It arose from the same tendency in the Hindoo mind, which produced those vast fictions in the description of the universe, and in the narrative of the past, that distinguish the native literature of that country. The love of the wonderful led the Hindoo authors to forsake, at the same time, the fair bounds of history and the sober reality of nature. Here it is easy to perceive a similarity to the Arabians. There is, in their fictions, the same fondness for splendid scenes and striking supernatural effects. This would be poetry were it not very much overdone. The same circumstances of gaudy magnificence are again and again repeated, and the reader is wearied with the unending recital of marvellous events, invented after one model, and whose one object is to excite an undistinguishing admiration of the power displayed.

By magic is here meant the supernatural power attributed to the Buddhas and Bodhisattwas, or claimed by the ordinary priests, and which is exercised by charms, mystic formulæ, incantations, finger-postures, and such-like means.

It is not the power of God acting through nature that is here intended, but the power of the priest, through his charms, virtues, and superior knowledge. The magical result is effected by the never-erring retributive fate which is the cause of everything that occurs, and which is responsive in the most complete manner to Buddhist wisdom and goodness.

The use of the Devanagari writing for the purposes of magic is an instructive instance of the power of superstition to delude the human mind. The words used by the magician for the most part have no meaning. They are senseless clatter. The sounds are Sanscrit, but the words usually not so. These absurd compositions of unmeaning sounds are of various lengths. They occur frequently in the books of the Great Development. They are engraved on stone monuments on the way side, on imperial roads, and at places of resort for Buddhist pilgrims. They also form a chief part of the liturgies in use in the monasteries and at funerals.

Om-mani-padme-hum is one of the most common. *Padme* is "lotus;" *mani* is a "precious stone;" *om* is a sacred "Hindoo symbol." It is written in Sanscrit characters under the eaves of all the lama temples in Peking. In these temples it meets the eye everywhere.

The Thibetan character is based on the Sanscrit. It is also found cut on monuments, both for charms and for intelligible inscriptions. It is the chief language for liturgical use among the Thibetans and Mongol lamas in Peking, except in two instances. In the Mahakala *miau*, the Mongol sacred books are read. In a temple, Fa-hai sï, near the hunting park, the Manchu is read. The Chinese lamas in Peking read Thibetan prayers, while the Chinese priests of the old Chinese Buddhism read, of course, in Chinese.

In all these forms, the syllables of the charms are the same. They are written in Sanscrit, or in the other languages mentioned.

At the pass called Kü-yung kwan, near Peking, there is a stone monument containing a charm in six languages, viz., Sanscrit, Chinese, Thibetan, Nü-chih, Ouighour, and Mongol. It was cut in the time of the Mongol emperors. It contains the same charm written with the characters employed for all these languages. It was intended as a protection to the emperor in going to and coming from the summer palace, at that time beyond Tu-shï k'eu, and also to all travellers on this much frequented road between China and Mongolia.

There are also some monuments inscribed with Sanscrit charms in Peking at the present time, which date from about seven hundred years ago. They are stone octagonal pillars. One is at the monastery called Hwa-yen sï, near the park of the Altar of Heaven and the city gate known as Kiang-cha men. These octagonal pillars are called *shï-chwang*, and they are placed in the courts of temples. There is one kept on the premises of the London Missionary Society in Peking.

Sanscrit inscriptions are supposed, like pagodas and monasteries, to have a lucky effect on the neighbourhood where they are found, and on those who erect them by their benefactions and goodwill.

A muttered charm is called "dharani," or, in Chinese, *cheu*.

Footnotes

1. S. Julien is wrong in making the first of these four characters end in *n*. It is *pat* in old Chinese; but *pat* was often *par*. See p. 201 of my *Introduction to the Study of the Chinese Characters*. Thus the famous word *karma*, "cause," "fate," was transliterated *kat-ma*, the *t* being heard as *r*.
2. The character *de* should be transliterated *dek*. That the *k* was then lost is shown by its use in this case. The loss of *k* final was beginning.

CHAPTER XXVI.

BOOKS AND PAPERS THAT MAY BE CONSULTED FOR THE STUDY OF CHINESE BUDDHISM.

Foĕ kouĕ ki, by Remusat—Works of Julien—Interesting passage from Fa-hien—Translations by Beal—Schott, Über den Buddhaismus in Hoch Asien und in China—Writings of Palladius—Eitel's Hand-book for the Student of Chinese Buddhism—Watters' account of Chinese Buddhism—Eitel's Three Lectures, and article on Nirvâna.

AMONG these works may be mentioned the translation of *Foĕ kouĕ ki*, or "Relation of the Buddhist Kingdoms," by Abel Remusat [1]. This work is very fully annotated by Remusat, Klaproth, and Landresse.

The same interesting book of Chinese travels has been rendered into English by the Rev. S. Beal, [2] and also by Mr. H. A. Giles. [3] These two translations have not the advantage of abundant annotations.

The works of Professor Stanislas Julien on Chinese Buddhism are— (1) *Histoire de la Vie de Hiouen-thsang et de ses Voyages dans l'Inde, depuis l'an* 629 *jusqu'en* 645; (2) *Mémoires sur les Contrées Occidentales, Traduits du Sanscrit en Chinois, en l'an* 648, *par Hiouen-thsang, et du Chinois en Français par S. Julien*, 2 vols., royal 8vo; (3) *Les Avadanas, Contes, et Apologues Indiens*, &c.

These works are characterised by the thorough and exact scholarship of the author. They form a most valuable addition to our knowledge of India and other Asiatic countries in the seventh century, and in the Sung period before that time, during which Buddhism had still the vigour of its youth.

Both Fa-hien and Hiuen-tsang will be admitted by every candid reader to deserve the reputation for patience in observation, perseverance in travel, and earnestness in religious faith which they have gained by the journals and translations they left behind them.

Fa-hien says, near the end of his narrative, that he sailed from Java in a ship on board of which were about two hundred men. They had provisions for fifty days, and were bound for Canton. After a month, a tempest and violent rain almost overwhelmed them. The passengers were all in alarm. Fa-hien prayed to Kwan-yin, and all the believers in China, to implore of the gods to give them aid and quell the storm. When it became calm, the Brahmans on board said that this Samanean, meaning Fa-hien, ought to be put ashore on an island, because it was he that had brought on them this hurricane. "Why should we all be exposed to danger for the sake of one man?"

A friend of Fa-hien said, "If you put this Samanean on shore, put me ashore also, or else kill me. If you put this Samanean ashore, on arriving at the land of Han I will denounce you to the king. The king of the land of Han is very much attached to the doctrine of Buddha and honours the monks."

The merchants were in doubt what to do, and did not venture on severe measures. The sky continued thickly overcast, and the embarrassment of the mariners increased.

They were seventy days on the voyage. Provisions and water began to fail. The cooks took sea water to use in cooking food, the good water they kept for drinking. Two pints were assigned to each. As the water came near its end, the merchants consulted together, and said that the voyage to Canton ought not to have been more than fifty days. They were long past this time, and ought now to change their course to the north-west, and make for the coast.

In twelve days and nights they reached Lau-shan,[4] on the south shore of the Shan-tung promontory, and found there good water and beans. After so dangerous a voyage, with such fatigues and so many fears, they arrived at last at this unknown shore. On seeing a plant called *Li-ho-ts'ai*, they were convinced that they were indeed in China. This plant was a proof of it, although they met no men nor any traces of men. Some thought they were all near Canton. Others thought Canton was long passed. No one knew what part of the coast they had reached.

Going ashore in a boat they met two hunters, and Fa-hien was employed to interpret. From them they found that they were in Ts'ing-cheu in the province now known as Shan-tung, and on the north side of the promontory in the Gulf of Pe-chi-li. From this point the merchants found their way to Yang-cheu, and Fa-hien to the capital, Ch'ang-an. This was in the year A.D. 414.

The student has also at his command—*A Catena of Buddhist Scriptures front the Chinese*, by Samuel Beal; and *The Romantic Legend of Sâkya Buddha*, by the same.

The work of Schott, *Über den Buddhaismus in Hoch Asien und in China*, contains much valuable information on the contents of Chinese Buddhist books. Written in 1846, it was anterior to the clear drawing of the boundary between Northern and Southern Buddhism by Burnouf, and also preceded by several years the publication of Spence Hardy's works on Singhalese Buddhism, viz., *Eastern Monachism* (1840), and *Manual of Buddhism* (1843).

He says of Nirvâna that it is the emptiness which every intellectual object will include in itself when liberated. In so far the Nirvâna is like the original being, before each creative act; but it differs from the original essence in this, that all forms of life and matter come out of the original essence, but cannot come from the Nirvâna; because nothing can come from it, and it is incapable of having in it any individuality, mental or material.

To the genuine disciple of the Buddhist teaching, to put himself under the mystic and heaven-sent guide to the Nirvâna, is the *alpha* and *omega* of his efforts. Just so to the genuine follower of Confucius, to hold office, to serve the emperor, and become a cabinet minister or censor, constitute his great earthly aim.

Our author points out, with great correctness, the relation of Tauism to Buddhism. Buddhism has borrowed nothing from Tauism, while Tauism has borrowed much from Buddhism.

After his description of Chinese Buddhism, Schott has added a translation of a work of the school of the *Tsing-tu* or "Peaceful land." This work is also illustrated fully with notes by the translator. It is a well-selected example of current Buddhist teaching in China.

The reader of the *Tsing-tu-wen* (that is the name of the book translated) is informed by the native author, that he is not to expect advantage only in the future life from his study of the books of the school of the Peaceful land. They are adapted to benefit him in the present life by transforming him into what the book represents as a good Buddhist.

The late learned archimandrite Palladius, resident for many years in Peking as a member of the Russian Ecclesiastical Mission, was a profound student of Chinese Buddhism. The result of his very extensive reading was embodied in two papers printed in the "Researches of the Members of the Russian Mission in Peking." One is a "Life of Buddha;" the other describes the subsequent philosophical development of Buddhism. These "Researches" have been translated into German. The *Hand-book for the Student of Chinese Buddhism*, by Dr. E. J. Eitel,[5] is a dictionary of proper names, dogmas, and Buddhist terms generally, arranged alphabetically. The student of Buddhism obtains in this work an important help to his studies. The author has devoted great attention to this subject, and has, in addition to his own investigations, here placed within reach of his readers, many contributions from the immense learning in this department, of Julien, Burnouf, and Koeppen.

Buddhism is not so powerful in China as to cause alarm to the Christian missionary, in view of the coming struggle which he anticipates. But the history of its introduction, and the nature and extent of the influence it has produced on the Chinese mind and literature, are extremely interesting subjects. The Hindoo missionaries tried hard to bring the Chinese to accept the mythology and religious doctrines of their country at the time when it was Buddhist. Their translations abound in Sanscrit words, which it was hoped the Chinese would learn, but this they failed to do. Names of things as well as names of persons, words expressive of doctrines, abstract names, classes of mythological beings, adjectives, arithmetical and astronomical expressions, and many long compound terms are imported in full into the Chinese text. To explain them glossaries were prepared. But they expected more zeal and perseverance in their Chinese neophytes than they have shown, and the consequence is that the glossaries are not looked at, and the Sanscrit names are passed over by the reader of the Chinese texts as an abracadabra which he is glad to miss.

Buddha's heart is, for example, spoken of as *Anuttara samyak sambôdhi*, pronounced in the era of the Hindoo translations, *A-no-ta-la sam-mo sam-bo-di*. *An* is the negative, *uttara* is "superior;" *sam* means "perfect," "good," "same;" *samyak* is given in the Sanscrit dictionary, "all," "wholly," "fitly." *Bôdhi* is "intelligence," "the intellect," "the holy fig-tree," "knowledge of God," and as an adjective, "wise;" etymologically it is "that which distinguishes;" that is, "the intellect," and hence "that which is distinguished," "doctrine," "the object of the highest study." From this has come the title Buddha the "perceiver," "the sage."

Whoever will study Buddhism, must know what these and other such words mean; and Dr. Eitel's object has been to provide a handbook in which a mass of information has been collected, adapted to aid the inquirer. In this instance he must look under the words *Anuttara* and *Bôdhi*. If he is reading a Chinese Buddhist production, he must first consult the Chinese index at the end of the volume. This mode of using the *Sanscrit-Chinese Dictionary* is a little cumbrous, but perhaps it is preferable to the perpetuation in a work of this kind of the Mandarin pronunciation, as given in Morrison, Wade, and other authors. Sanscrit books having been translated fourteen centuries ago, the powers of the Chinese characters which represented Hindoo words have changed in the meantime. As Dr. Eitel justly remarks: "To the language then spoken in China no modern Chinese dialect comes nearer in sound than the very Sanskrit or Pali forms themselves."

The difficulty might be met, if we had a dictionary of Chinese words with the ancient and modern pronunciations arranged in succession, as in K'ang-hi, but in a more complete form than in that work. For example, if in Morrison's *Syllabic Dictionary*, under the syllable *Fuh*, between the character and the meanings were inserted "old sound, *But;* Amoy, *Put;* Nanking, *Fuh;* Peking, *Fo;*" every one would thus be in a position to know what the old sounds of the characters are. It would then be feasible to compile a Chinese-Sanscrit, instead of a Sanscrit-Chinese, dictionary.

But as the student of Chinese must also learn to consult works arranged according to the radicals, like Kang-hi itself, Dr. Eitel's arrangement of the dictionary forms no bar to its usefulness.

Among the longer and more valuable articles in this work are those on *Kwan-yin* or "Avalakitês'vara," *Buddha* or "S'âkyamuni," "Samâdhi," "Sanskrita," "Nâga," "Mañdjus'rî," "Amitâbha," "Dhyâna," "Nâgârdjuna," "Naraka," "Triratna," "Nirvâna," and "Trikâya." The spelling here given is that of an author who, somewhat oddly, has followed the French orthography in writing the Sanscrit sounds *ch*, *sh*, and *j*.

The best key to the understanding of Buddhism is to be found in the study of the life of its founder. In Shakyamuni himself humanity is first seen, then divinity. A young prince, handsome, strong, heroic, surrounded by pleasures, and tempted by the most brilliant worldly prospects, is deeply affected by observing the miseries of human life. He becomes a changed man, forsakes his father's palace for a hermit's cell, practises and then teaches a rigid asceticism, and dies at eighty, after a long career occupied partly with the instruction of a numerous band of disciples, and partly with extatic contemplation. He is deified at the moment of death; that is, his disciples elevate him to the summit of humanity, honour him as the best of teachers, and announce that he is for ever rescued from the revolutions of life and death. He has entered the Nirvâna, and when his body has been burned, the *sharira*, or small reddish residuum, is honoured as a sacred relic possessing marvellous powers, and over it a pagoda must be erected.

Such a phenomenon—a great and disinterested mind, founding the monastic institute, and teaching multitudes of both sexes and every caste the escape from sorrow to the eternal rest of the Nirvâna—was sufficient in the condition of Hindoo society, as it was two centuries before the expedition of Alexander, to account for the early history of Buddhism. In his account of *Kwan-yin* (Avalôkitêsh'vara) our author has gone too far, when he supposes there was a Chinese divinity of this name before the introduction of the Mahayana into China. Nothing is easier than to attach to the imaginary former lives of the great Bodhisattwas, any incidents of old biography in any age or country, of a marvellous kind, and adapted to be, in the Buddhist sense, edifying. Such incidents were ascribed by the Chinese Buddhists to the presence of Kwan-yin, nearly as in the Earl of Beaconsfield's *Lothair* the opportune arrival of a Roman shopkeeper's wife, who shows a benevolent interest in the welfare of that hero, is believed by the pope and his cardinal to be an appearance of the Virgin Mary. Hence the author of that romance sarcastically describes Lothair as being for a time, in the opinion of every one in Rome, high and low, "the most favoured man in this century;" yet the net failed to entrap him through his want of faith.

Kwan-yin "looks on" (*kwan*) "the region" (*shi*) of sufferers whose "voices" (*yin*) of many tones, all acknowledging misery and asking salvation, touch the heart or the pitiful Bodhisattwa. She looks with a thousand eyes that she may see them all, and stretches out a thousand arms that she may save them all.

Kumarajiva himself adopted the name *Kwan-shï-yin*. The translators of the T'ang period, two centuries later, brought to view the true etymology as given by our author, but they did not succeed in changing the course of the legend or the name of the divinity. Kumarajiva preferred the more popular and edifying designation. The two meanings, Kwan-tsï-tsai and Kwan-shi-yin, doubtless existed together in Kumarajiva's country, Cashmere, just as afterwards in China. The Mahayana doctrine had prevailed there already for nearly two hundred years, from the time of Nagarjuna, given in the *Hand-book*, A.D. 194

The remarkable extension of the Mahayana literature (*Hwa-yen-king*, *Fa-hwa-king*, &c.) in Cashmere, Kashgar, Balkh, and what is now Cabul, aided by the conversion to Buddhism of the Indian Getæ, the *Yue-ti* of Chinese history, renders the dialects there spoken early in the Christian era important for the determination of the language employed by the first Hindoo missionaries in China.

Our author says the Pali was first used, and afterwards the Sanscrit. It would be more correct to say that the Magadha dialect was first used, then the dialect of Northern India, such as was spoken in Cashmere, and afterwards the Sanscrit. In the Han dynasty, under Ming-ti, Kashiapmadanga, who came from Magadha, the modern Bahar, used the dialect of that country, which differed from the Pali among other things in retaining from Sanscrit the letter *sh*. [6] If Kashiapmadanga, the most ancient of the translators, had chosen Chinese words whose initial was *s* to write the Sanscrit *Shramana* and *Kashiapa*, it might be said that he used the Pali. [7] In the "Sutra of Forty-two Sections" he used *Sha-men*, and thus originated that name, to be used ever after as the designation of the members of the Buddhist community in China. For Kashiapa he wrote *Ka-shiap*.

The second era of translators, A.D. 400, was that of Kumarajiva of Cashmere. There can be no doubt that he made use of *sh* and *s* as separate letters, for he never confounds them in his choice of Chinese characters. The Chinese words already introduced by his predecessors he did not alter, and in introducing new terms required in the translation of the *Mahayana* literature (*Ta-ch'eng*), or "Greater Development," he uses *sh* for *sh*, and usually *b* for *v*. Thus the city "Shravasti" was in Pali *Savatthi*, and in Chinese *Sha-ba-ti*. Probably Kumarajiva himself, speaking in the Cashmere dialect of Sanscrit, called it *Shabati*.

Two centuries later, the fashion of close adherence to Sanscrit came into use under the leadership of Hiuen-tsang. For example, instead of *Bi-k'u*, which is like the Pali Bhikkhu (probably also found in the Magadha language), *Bit-ch'u*, was written, evidently with the intention of restoring the Sanscrit *sh*. Our author gives a different reason.

The great value of such a guide as this *Hand-book* in the study of Chinese Buddhism will be understood by the student, when he finds that almost all the important words in doctrine and biography are here traced to their Sanscrit originals, and explained with the aid of recent European criticism. Thus *Ho-shang*, the most popular term for "Priest," is *Upadhyâya*, the president of an "assembly," or *sangha*. The "Three Precious Ones" are *Buddha*, the personal teacher; *Dharma*, the Law or body of doctrine; and *Sangha*, the Priesthood. The term *sam-mei* is explained as the "samâdhi" of the original Sanscrit. "Samâdhi signifies the highest pitch of abstract ecstatic meditation, a state of absolute indifference to all influences from within or without, a state of torpor of both the material and spiritual forces of vitality, a sort of terrestrial Nirvâna consistently culminating in total destruction of life. 'He consumed his body by Agni (the fire of) Samâdhi' is a common phrase."

The expression *Tau-pi-an*, "Arrival at that shore," is explained as the Chinese equivalent of *Paramita*, embracing the six means of passing to the Nirvâna. These are—1. "Charity" (or giving), *Dâna;* 2. "Morality," *Shîla* (good conduct); 3. "Patience," *Kshânti;* 4. "Energy," *Virya;* 5. "Contemplation," *Dhyâna;* 6. "Wisdom," *Prajna*.

In the account of Nirvâna, Dr. Eitel touches on a subject of great interest, namely, the expectation of immortality asserting itself in Buddhism, in spite of the overwhelming influence of a metaphysical system adverse alike to the belief in God and to that in immortality. Shakyamuni said in his last moments, "The spiritual body is immortal." But he said just before, "All you Bikshus, do not be sad. If I lived in the world for a *kalpa*, on arriving at the time I must still be annihilated. Not to leave you when the hour has arrived is impossible. In gaining benefit one's-self, others are benefited. The system of doctrine is already perfect. Should I live longer, it would be of no benefit to you. All that were to be saved, whether in the paradises of the Devas, or in the world of mankind, have already been saved. As to those who have not been saved, the causes which will ultimately lead to their salvation have already been put in operation. From this time forward I exhort you, my disciples, to expand, explain, and propagate my doctrine, and thus" (here follows our author's quotation) "the 'spiritual body' (*fa-shen*) of Ju-lai will be constantly present, and will not be annihilated at all."

Much cannot be built on this passage from the "Sutra of the dying instructions of Buddha," but Dr. Eitel is quite right in arguing the continued existence of the Buddhas from their occasional reappearance after death for the salvation of living beings, and also from the dogma of the "Western Paradise."

Why, in his article on Dhyâna, the author has omitted any reference to the *Ch'an-men* does not appear. He has, however, given an account of the twenty-eight patriarchs, the last of whom, Bodhidharma, introduced into China the Buddhist sect called the *Ch'an-men*, which has played in some respects the same part in China that the *Jainas* did in India. It has almost supplanted the original Buddhism, and has always made much of the esoteric deposit of doctrine and its transmission along with the robe and rice bowl from patriarch to patriarch. The meaning of the names, however, differs. *Jaina* means "the conqueror," while *dhyâna*, the Indian prototype of the Chinese *dan*, later *ch'an*, signifies "meditation."

In the notice of the *nagas* there are some interesting references to "serpent" worship, that very widespread and ancient superstition, which seems to have originated in the first ages, and to have spread from the

Babylonian region to the most widely separated countries. The stones of Avebury in Wiltshire, not far from Stonehenge, retain the serpentine shape in which the Druids, or the predecessors of the Druids, arranged them. The Hebrew *nahash*, Gaelic *narar*, and English "snake," are word-forms which preserve the old idea; and the account of the temptation in Genesis furnishes us with a probable origin for the traditions of serpent worship among various nations.

In Eastern Asia the *nagas* were looked on as well disposed. Hence the Birmese confound them with the *devans*, while the Chinese regard them as good and powerful and call them *lung*, the Greek *drakôn*, and the German *schlange*.

On the six paths of transmigration the reader will find information under the heads *Gâti, Prêtas, Asura, Amôgha,* &c.

But it is time to stop. Buddhism is a subject which easily ramifies into so many directions, that it is necessary to limit these remarks.

Mr. Watters' papers on *Chinese Buddhism* have been already referred to, in the sketch of the history of Chinese Buddhism in an early part of this volume. They contain a historical summary of Chinese Buddhism, an account of the Buddhas, and a sketch of the Confucianist opposition.

Dr. Eitel's valuable *Three Lectures on Buddhism*, and an article by him on the "Nirvâna of Chinese Buddhism," in the *Chinese Recorder*, June 1870, should be consulted by the student.

In "Buddhism in China," by Rev. S. Beal, the reader will find much to interest. Mr. Beal believed in the Persian influence which produced the legend of Amitabha, and in the Sabean origin of Sukhavati (Socotra), the island of the blessed. In this he is right.

The works of Sir Monier Williams and Dr. Rhys Davids on Buddhism generally are the productions of writers of great erudition and long experience. They naturally throw valuable light on Chinese Buddhism from the Indian side. Sir Edwin Arnold's "Light of Asia" is a charming poem, which has made Buddhist thought familiar to many readers who knew nothing of it before. Some works from Pali have been translated in the "Sacred Books of the East." Such is the number of new publications on the subject of Buddhism, that it is evident the reader has it in his power to obtain a thorough knowledge of this religion. He can test for himself how far it softens manners and teaches kindness, encourages faith in the supernatural, and testifies to the vanity of the world; at the same time he will learn that for the revelation of moral evil and its remedy, of God and of immortality, Buddhism makes no effort that can for a moment compare with the work which Christianity has done for mankind.

Footnotes

1. *Foĕ kouĕ ki, ou Relation des Royaumes Bouddhiques; par Chy Fa-hian.*
2. *Travels of Fa-hian and Sung-yun, Buddhist Pilgrims, from China to India.*
3. *Records of Buddhistic Kingdoms.*
4. Lau-shan is near Kiau-cheu, latitude 36°, east longitude 5° 25´. The port of Kiau-cheu exports felt hats, umbrellas, fruit, and cabbages to Shanghai.
5. This account of Dr. Eitel's book is reprinted from the Chinese Recorder, where it appeared in 1871 as a review.
6. See Burnouf and Lassen's *Essai sur le Pali.*
7. The Pali forms are *Samana, Kassapa.*

BIBLIOBAZAAR

The essential book market!

Did you know that you can get any of our titles in large print?

Did you know that we have an ever-growing collection of books in many languages?

Order online:
www.bibliobazaar.com

Find all of your favorite classic books!

Stay up to date with the latest government reports!

At BiblioBazaar, we aim to make knowledge more accessible by making thousands of titles available to you- *quickly and affordably*.

Contact us:
BiblioBazaar
PO Box 21206
Charleston, SC 29413